Alexis de Tocqueville

Democracy in America

Alexis de Tocqueville

Democracy in America

Abridged, with Introduction, by
SANFORD KESSLER

Translated and Annotated by
STEPHEN D. GRANT

Hackett Publishing Company, Inc.
Indianapolis/Cambridge

Copyright © 2000 by Hackett Publishing Company, Inc.

16 15 14 13 12   3 4 5 6 7 8

For further information, please address
  Hackett Publishing Company, Inc.
  P. O. Box 44937
  Indianapolis, Indiana 46244–0937
  www.hackettpublishing.com

Cover design by Brian Rak and John Pershing
Interior design by Meera Dash

Library of Congress Cataloging-in-Publication Data
Tocqueville, Alexis de, 1805-1859.
  [De la démocratie en Amérique. English]
  Democracy in America / Alexis de Tocqueville ; abridged, with
introduction, by Sanford Kessler ; translated and annotated by
Stephen D. Grant.
      p.   cm.
  Includes bibliographical references (p.) and index.
  ISBN 0-87220-495-2 (cloth)—ISBN 0-87220-494-4 (pbk.)
    1. United States—Politics and government. 2. United States—Social
conditions. 3. Democracy—United States. I. Grant, Stephen D., 1948-
II. Title.
JK216 .T6513   2000
320.473—dc21   99-089940

ISBN-13: 978-0-87220-495-9 (cloth)
ISBN-13: 978-0-87220-494-2 (pbk.)

CONTENTS

CONTENTS OF THE UNABRIDGED
DEMOCRACY IN AMERICA

The chapters and sections included in this abridgment appear in **bold-face** type followed by the page number of this translation.

PART TWO

PART TWO
INFLUENCE OF DEMOCRACY ON THE
SENTIMENTS OF THE AMERICANS

DEMOCRACY IN AMERICA:
AN INTRODUCTION

Alexis de Tocqueville wrote *Democracy in America* to help early 19th-century France preserve its liberty while making a bumpy and politically painful transition from aristocracy to democracy. Although his concern with America was secondary, he treats our democracy comprehensively, relating it to our unique history, to enduring features of our national life, and to our prospects for remaining free. Despite the passage of time, *Democracy in America* remains an invaluable political resource for all people who love liberty and arguably contains the best single account of the United States ever written.[1]

Tocqueville begins this account by offering a fresh perspective on the origins of American liberty and the factors that sustain it. Most Americans consider the Declaration of Independence the chief source of our free principles and the U.S. Constitution their chief safeguard. Tocqueville, however, deems our national character more vital to our liberty than the Constitution and entirely ignores the Declaration of Independence. He also credits the New England Puritans with shaping our national character, thus making them more America's true founders than the authors of these venerable documents.

In analyzing the state of American liberty in the 1830s, Tocqueville addresses certain questions regarding our national life that still trouble and divide us. These pertain to the role of religion in public affairs, race relations, the condition of women and the family, the health of our civil society, and the influence of wealth on politics, among others. Tocqueville's answers to these questions cannot fully satisfy us, partly because the United States is far more diverse and historically mature than the country he knew. Nor need we accept the principles and premises that inform his views. Yet Tocqueville's thoughts on our present-day concerns are always illuminating and richly reward careful study.

---

1. All references to *Democracy in America* in this Introduction are to Gallimard page numbers (listed in the margins of this translation). Volume One of *Democracy in America* was published in 1835; Volume Two in 1840. Tocqueville considered both volumes complementary parts of a single work, and I shall do the same (II, 7). Seymour Drescher argues, however, that the two volumes should be considered as "substantially independent works." See Seymour Drescher, "More than America: Comparison and Synthesis in *Democracy in America*" in *Reconsidering Tocqueville's Democracy in America*, ed. Abraham S. Eisenstadt (New Brunswick and London: Rutgers University Press, 1988), pp. 79, 77–93.

The fate of American liberty also looms large in Tocqueville's work, eliciting from him warnings that clearly merit attention. Most relate to a fear that future Americans would fail to achieve a proper balance between liberty and equality. Although we generally consider these two principles harmonious, Tocqueville thought them capable of clashing under certain circumstances. Unchecked economic liberty could lead to oligarchy, for example, while excessive equality could extinguish political liberty. Democracies, in his view, are especially prone to this latter danger because equality charms their citizens while concealing its harmful qualities. Tocqueville designed a "new political science" in *Democracy in America* to check these evils and, more broadly, to chart a new course for democratic statesmanship.

To America and Beyond

Alexis de Tocqueville was born in Paris on July 29, 1805, to a distinguished aristocratic French family that had been decimated by the French Revolution. The events surrounding this trauma cast a pall over his childhood that left him somewhat melancholic for life. His intellectual journey to America began one night in 1821 when an encounter with skeptical Enlightenment writings in his father's library forever shattered his youthful Catholic faith. This encounter helped transform the budding lawyer and magistrate into a political philosopher and statesman who never flinched when his well-considered views conflicted with his feelings, interests, or the spirit of his age. His political reflections during the late 1820s led him to embrace liberalism, the freedom-oriented politics forged by the Enlightenment and tempered somewhat in post-Napoleonic France by disgust with revolutionary excess.[2]

After breaking ranks with most of his conservative intimates by halfheartedly endorsing the liberal July Revolution of 1830, Tocqueville and his friend Gustave de Beaumont requested and received permission from the new government to study American prison reforms. Tocqueville went to America ostensibly for this purpose, but with the deeper aim of "carefully scrutinizing" all elements of American life.[3]

The two Frenchmen arrived in the United States in May 1831, and embarked on an arduous and at times dangerous nine-month cross-

---

2. André Jardin, *Tocqueville: A Biography*, trans. Lydia Davis with Robert Hemenway (New York: Farrar Straus and Giroux, 1989), pp. 1–12, 56–87, esp. 61–62 [hereafter cited as Jardin, *Tocqueville*].

3. Jardin, *Tocqueville*, pp. 88–92.

country journey of discovery. America was then in the heyday of Jacksonian democracy, a tumultuous period in our nation's history that saw the rise of abolitionism and machine politics, attempts to nullify national laws, a rebirth of religious revivalism, the massive displacement of Native Americans, and a great brouhaha over the second Bank of the United States.[4]

Tocqueville and Beaumont saw all this and more on their trek, which took them from the semisophisticated cities of the Northeast to the raw edge of the Western frontier, from French Quebec to French New Orleans, and from dismal prison chambers to the White House. While traveling, they interviewed diverse Americans including Charles Carroll, the oldest signer of the Declaration of Independence; a displaced Choctaw Indian en route to exile; the somewhat disreputable Sam Houston of later Texas fame; and President Andrew Jackson, a man Tocqueville considered violent and mediocre.[5]

After returning to France in February 1832, Tocqueville spent several years on a "second" or mental visit to America, during which he used travel journals and correspondence; American writings, both historical and political; the constructive criticism of friends and relatives; and, above all, political philosophy to reflect on his experiences. These diverse sources enabled him to ground his empirical observations of our country in a rich theoretical framework.[6]

In 1835, Tocqueville married Mary Mottley, a middle-class Englishwoman several years his senior. The publication of Volume One of *Democracy in America* during that year quickly established Tocqueville as a luminary of his age. In 1839, he used his burgeoning fame to launch a political career, serving first as a legislator in the constitutional monarchy of Louis-Philippe and then briefly as foreign minister in the short-lived Second Republic established by the Revolution of 1848.

---

4. Two valuable histories of the Jacksonian era in the United States are Edward Pessen, *Jacksonian America: Society, Personality, and Politics* (Homewood, IL: Dorsey Press, 1978) and Charles Sellers, *The Market Revolution: Jacksonian America, 1815–1846* (New York and Oxford: Oxford University Press, 1991). The best account of Jacksonian political life remains Marvin Meyers, *The Jacksonian Persuasion: Politics and Belief* (New York: Vintage Books, 1960).

5. George Wilson Pierson, *Tocqueville and Beaumont in America* (Baltimore and London: Johns Hopkins University Press, 1996), pp. 319 ff., 619 ff., 428, 664, 506–7, 597–8, 610 ff. Pierson's classic work, originally published in 1938, is an indispensable source for understanding Tocqueville's American experiences.

6. James T. Schleifer, *The Making of Tocqueville's Democracy in America* (Chapel Hill: University of North Carolina Press, 1980), pp. xxi, 3–34 [hereafter cited as Schleifer, *Making*]; Jardin, Tocqueville, pp. 48–53.

He critically assessed this event and its aftermath in his autobiographical *Recollections*, which he wrote in 1850–1851.[7]

Tocqueville left politics in disgust after Louis Napoleon's coup d'etat in 1852 dashed his slim republican hopes, and he spent the rest of his life writing *The Old Regime and the Revolution*, his great political history of France. He published Volume One of this work to critical acclaim in 1856 and died of tuberculosis in Cannes on April 16, 1859, while completing Volume Two.[8]

A Character-Oriented Statecraft

Tocqueville considered the French Revolution and the July Revolution of 1830 parts of an irreversible, worldwide democratic revolution that had changed and would continue to change the course of human affairs forever. This democratic revolution, as he describes it, carried something new in its wake: an "equality of conditions" that institutes popular sovereignty, levels class distinctions, and sanctifies the idea of equality itself [I, 1].

France, on becoming more democratic, tottered helplessly between languor and chaos, as faction and excess partisanship enfeebled civil society, divided natural political allies, and undermined respect for legitimate authority and rights. Squabbling French politicians and theorists seemed bent on destroying their country despite their professed intentions to save it. Liberals attacked all remnants of the Old Regime, arguing that France required a broad-based, secular constitutional democracy with strong protections for liberty, while conservatives argued for a virtue-oriented politics that would strengthen the Catholic Church and the French nobility at liberty's expense.

Tocqueville sought to mediate this dispute in *Democracy in America* by assessing the relative merits of aristocracy and democracy, of faith and reason in building character, and of character and institutions in promoting political health. His judicious treatment of these matters served to remind partisans in France and elsewhere that partisans see only partial truths.

Tocqueville was a liberal because he cherished liberty, and a democrat for compelling if somewhat more complicated reasons.[9] First, he considered democracy the rock-bottom foundation of modern political life. No

---

7. See, in general, Jardin, *Tocqueville*, chap. 16–24.

8. See, in general, Jardin, *Tocqueville*, chap. 25–28.

9. See Jean-Claude Lamberti, *Tocqueville and the Two Democracies*, trans. Arthur Goldhammer (Cambridge, Mass.: Harvard University Press, 1989), pp. 42, 53–63 [hereafter cited as Lamberti, *Two Democracies*].

legislator, however wise or powerful, he asserts, could secure liberty without making equality his "first principle and credo" [II, 328]. Yet, after bowing somewhat sadly to this necessity, Tocqueville pronounced in favor of democracy for giving equal rights to all. Aristocracy, a regime based on force and birth-linked privilege, was, in his view, so "repugnant to natural equity" that no fair-minded person could prefer it [I, 417].

Yet Tocqueville also warned his fellow democrats of the dangers associated with their impending triumph. Democracy comports with liberty ideally and up to a point, he believed, but threatens liberty when pushed beyond its just and natural limits. All of France knew, of course, that the passion for equality could endanger liberty in revolutionary times, especially when combined with unbridled popular sovereignty. Such was the chief lesson of the Reign of Terror. Thus, Tocqueville wholeheartedly joined prominent French liberals such as Benjamin Constant (1767–1830) in supporting institutions that check tyranny whatever its source.[10]

Unlike these liberals, however, Tocqueville loved liberty more for the virtues it enabled than for its own sake.[11] Only a virtuous people, he believed, could lead worthy lives and defend their liberty in times of crisis. He also thought that democracy can corrupt people in normal times and as a matter of course. Democrats tend toward individualism, a phenomenon that causes people to turn inward and to neglect their public responsibilities. They also become overly materialistic, slavishly devoted to public opinion, and envious of any superiority, no matter how natural or worthy. These tendencies weaken human attachments, unbend the springs of virtue, and ultimately debase political life.

Thus, Tocqueville thought that constitutional government cannot secure liberty by itself, especially if its free principles are devoid of purpose. Accordingly, he sided with French conservatives in wanting to use politics to promote virtue, albeit indirectly and for liberal ends. Healthy mores can support liberty without good laws, he argued, but no laws, no matter how well designed, can sustain liberty among a debased people [I, 322–23].

Tocqueville also joined these conservatives in tapping aristocratic wisdom for his project of democratic character building. Aristocracy, as he understood it, honors reason and virtue in principle despite its tendency to oppress. At its best, it produces farsighted statesmen and philosophers, tightens social ties, promotes altruism, and nourishes an instinctive love for liberty, at least among the few. In these respects, it

---

10. See Lamberti, *Two Democracies*, pp. 71–74, 79 ff., for a discussion of the differences between Constant's and Tocqueville's liberalism.

11. Lamberti, *Two Democracies*, pp. 42, 62.

serves human nature better than democracy and supports a healthier form of political life. Tocqueville sought to create these goods on a democratic basis, an endeavor that made him, as he put it, a "liberal of a new kind."[12]

First among the resources needed for this project was religion, which Tocqueville considered the "most precious heritage" from aristocratic times [II, 151]. Democracy needs religion, he believed, to give freedom spiritual depth, moral content, and the limits needed to render it secure. Despotism can "do without faith," he claimed, "but not liberty. . . . what can be done with a people that is master of itself, if it is not subject to God?" [I, 308].

Some scholars conclude on the basis of such remarks that Tocqueville's overall argument in *Democracy in America* is religiously based, or at least supports the truth of Christianity. His account of the democratic revolution as divinely inspired seems to support this view, as do his favorable references to the Bible, his frequent jabs at materialism, and his assertions that human greatness requires a belief in the soul's immortality.[13]

Yet the bulk of the evidence suggests that Tocqueville was a rationalist. In *Democracy in America*, he discusses Christianity's usefulness to freedom at length but never affirms its truth. He also never refers to the Bible as divinely inspired, never elevates otherworldly above thisworldly concerns, and never locates his political thought within a Christian theological tradition. Finally, while Tocqueville professed Catholicism [I, 309], his correspondence indicates that he wanted to believe in the faith but could not.[14]

Tocqueville's eclecticism as a thinker and his unwillingness to acknowledge his intellectual debts make it singularly difficult to identify the philosophical roots of his politics.[15] Most scholars consider Tocqueville's

---

12. See Pierre Manent, *Tocqueville and the Nature of Democracy*, trans. John Waggoner (Lanham, Md.: Rowman and Littlefield, 1996), chap. 2 and 7. Alexis de Tocqueville. *Oeuvres Complètes*, ed. Gustave de Beaumont, 9 vols. (Paris: Michael Levy, 1860–1866), 5:431 (my translation).

13. See, for example, Joshua Mitchell, *The Fragility of Freedom: Tocqueville on Religion, Democracy, and the American Future* (Chicago and London: University of Chicago Press, 1995), pp. 99–101, 162–63. I discuss this and other issues pertaining to Tocqueville's religious-political thought at length in *Tocqueville's Civil Religion: American Christianity and the Prospects for Freedom* (Albany, N.Y.: State University of New York Press, 1994). Parts of this Introduction are loosely drawn from material developed more fully in this book.

14. Tocqueville wrote in a letter to his protégé Artur de Gobineau, October 2, 1843: *Je ne suis pas croyant* ("I am not a believer"). See Alexis de Tocqueville, *Oeuvres Complètes*, ed. J.-P. Mayer (Paris: Gallimard, 18?), vol. 9, p. 57; see also Jardin, *Tocqueville*, pp. 528–33.

15. Lamberti, *Two Democracies*, p. 72.

analysis of democracy original, while disagreeing about the source for his understanding of liberty's requirements. Some point to Baron de Montesquieu (1689–1755), others to Jean-Jacques Rousseau (1712–1778), others to Blaise Pascal (1623–1662), and still others to Aristotle (384–322 B.C.) as his master. No one, however, makes anything close to an airtight case. It may be that Tocqueville follows Montesquieu in arguing for limited sovereignty, Rousseau in asserting that character is indispensable to liberty, Pascal in anguishing over reason's limitations, and Aristotle in advising statesmen to strive for what is best politically in relation to existing circumstances.[16]

America's Puritan Heritage: Democracy, Religion, and Liberty

Tocqueville saw in America the "image of democracy itself"—uniquely configured by circumstances to be sure, but mature enough to show its generic potential for good and evil [I, 12]. While warning against facile attempts to copy American laws and mores, he thought that France and other newly emerging democracies could learn much from our long democratic experience. In his mind, America showed the world then and for all time that ordinary people can, if guided by wise leaders, govern themselves, prosper, and even contribute to national greatness—and all without endangering liberty.

According to Tocqueville, as we have seen, America's first wise leaders were pious Puritan statesmen rather than enlightened constitution makers. He did not, of course, mean to disparage the Framers by subordinating their founding role to that of the Puritans. Indeed, he deemed them a remarkable group of lawgivers and valued the Constitution highly for its terse, intricate wisdom. But he credited the Puritans with enabling Americans to aspire to free government, to accept it when offered, and to sustain it over time.

The Puritans accomplished this feat by balancing two seemingly

---

16. See, for example, Lamberti, *Two Democracies* (Montesquieu); John C. Koritansky, *Alexis de Tocqueville and the New Science of Politics* (Durham, N.C.: Carolina Academic Press, 1986) (Rousseau); Peter A. Lawler, *The Restless Mind: Alexis de Tocqueville on the Origin and Perpetuation of Human Liberty* (Lanham, Md.: Rowman and Littlefield, 1993) (Pascal); Stephen G. Salkever, *Finding the Mean: Theory and Practice in Aristotelian Political Philosophy* (Princeton: Princeton University Press, 1990) (Aristotle).

Also compare Montesquieu, *The Spirit of the Laws* XI, 3–4 with Tocqueville, *Democracy*, I, 261–64; Rousseau, *Social Contract*, book 2, chap. 12 with Tocqueville, *Democracy*, I, 308, 319–23; Pascal, *Pensées*, Fr. 20 with Tocqueville, *Democracy*, II, 16–17; and Aristotle, *Politics*, book 4, chap. 1 with Tocqueville, *Democracy*, II, 150–51.

irreconcilable elements: a democratic "spirit of liberty" and an aristocratic "spirit of religion" [I, 42]. The "spirit of liberty" was Christian in origin but came to America via a philosophical method, or democratic way
of thinking, that empowered private, rational judgment. The Puritans
used this method to create a form of popular sovereignty based on the
idea that the majority is enlightened enough to govern society by right.
This idea, which alone sufficed to make people free, eventually spread
from New England to the far corners of the American world [I, 258].

At the same time, the "spirit of religion" made the Puritans passionate God seekers, willing to sacrifice comfort, sustenance, and life itself
to attain salvation. Keenly aware of human sinfulness, they chose to live
by a stern notion of political virtue, or an "idea of rights" as Tocqueville
put it, that firmly embedded their freedom in Old Testament orthodoxy
and moral law. John Winthrop's definition of liberty as being only for
"all that is just and good" perfectly captures the aristocratic flavor of
their religious ethos [I, 41, 248].

The Puritans' idea of rights required them to care for their less fortunate brethren as well as to control their own behavior. Considering wealth
instrumental to piety, they freely taxed themselves to address a multitude
of social needs that European countries at the time generally ignored.
These included relief for the poor, public works, and an extensive system
of public education [I, 44–45]. Although the Puritans tolerated and even
sought material prosperity, they considered selfishness of any sort to be a
perverse form of idolatry, the "enemy of truth and peace" [I, 41].

Tocqueville suggests in *Democracy in America* that democracy gradually transformed America's small cluster of Puritan communities over
time into a grand Christian commonwealth of small, sovereign states
and enlightened, free citizens [I, 57, 258, 304; II, 209]. The U.S. Constitution protected the country as a whole from tyranny through institutional devices such as federalism and the separation of national powers. In
the states, where most political activity took place, lawgivers abolished
primogeniture and established equal voting and property rights for white
males. Such changes nationwide ensured that neither powerful individuals nor social barriers could thwart the people's will and transformed
erstwhile aristocrats and potential revolutionaries into a prosperous, pa-
triotic, law-abiding, as well as pious, middle class.

This powerful middle class shaped American mores in the 1830s.[17]
Without hereditary wealth, most of its members were forced to work

---

17. Historian Edward Pessen challenges Tocqueville's description of Jacksonian
America as an egalitarian, middle-class society, claiming that "not equality but general inequality among the people was the 'central feature' of American life during
the Jacksonian era." Pessen, *Jacksonian America*, chap. 5, esp. p. 86.

hard to acquire and maintain the necessities and comforts of life. Indeed, the love of wealth and the fear of losing it gave America its distinctive idea of honor which determined the kinds of activities public opinion praised and blamed. All considered it honorable to engage in profitable labor, to acquire a practical education, to marry and raise a stable family, and, it appears, to lead a genuine Christian life [II, 234, 243–44, 158–59].

Tocqueville shows the careful reader, though, that democracy actually secularized America's national character as it expanded, making its true Christian moment in history relatively brief. Equality fosters skepticism as well as the love of wealth, he believed, and makes democrats reject religious authority and obligation [II, 11–12]. In a key rhetorical statement regarding America's national character in the 1830s, Tocqueville explains why this democratic drive for independence rendered the biblical concept of rights obsolete.

> Do you not see that the religions are becoming weaker and that the divine notion of rights is disappearing? Do you not see that morals are being corrupted and that with them the moral notion of rights is fading?
>
> Do you not see that on all sides belief is giving way to argument, and sentiments to calculations? If, in the midst of this universal tremor, you do not succeed in linking the idea of rights to personal interest, which presents itself as the sole fixed point in the human heart, what then will you be left with for governing the world, except fear? [I, 249]

Eighteenth-century American statesmen accommodated this drive for independence by extending the "spirit of liberty" deep into the theological realm. The Puritans cherished religious liberty for their communities but required individuals to subscribe to established orthodoxies and harsh moral codes. Their more secular descendents, in contrast, separated church and state, established the rights of conscience for individuals, and made reason rather than Revelation the ultimate arbiter of religious truth [I, 415].

Tocqueville attributed the strength of American Christianity in the 1830s largely to these changes. By "diminishing the apparent strength of religion," he remarked, Americans have "succeeded in increasing its real power" [I, 310]. Yet he also showed careful readers that the overall level of piety in America during this time was lower than it seemed. Many Americans were skeptics and tended to feign belief or to reject those elements of religion that conflicted with their selfish, rational view of the world [I, 304, 314; II, 12].

According to Tocqueville, American churchmen coped with this new state of affairs by liberalizing Christianity itself. To this end, they

stressed behavior over doctrines, downplayed miracles and the supernatural, and promoted religious toleration. They also emphasized the tangible benefits of piety and trimmed Christianity's moral teachings, making
an especially pretty peace with the love of wealth. These changes transformed most American orthodoxies into reasonable religions cleansed,
for the most part, of their supernatural and altruistic elements. While ex-
ternally strong in the 1830s, American Christianity no longer had inner
vitality and independent moral force.[18] Most Americans loved their religion, but more for its political utility than for its truth [I, 306; II, 33–34,
132–33].

By the 1830s, American moralists had also accommodated the
democratic drive for independence by replacing our virtue-oriented idea
of rights with an interest-oriented one. The lessons American children
learned about property rights reflected this shift. The biblically oriented
Puritans taught that property was a gift from God to be used for His purposes. In Tocqueville's America, however, children learned that wealth
was labor's just reward and that property ownership entailed no social
obligations [II, 158–59].[19]

This new idea of rights also transformed American family life. Early-
19th-century Americans no longer viewed marriage vows in sacred terms,
as the Puritans had, but as secular contracts that obliged both spouses
because each understood and freely accepted their conditions. Also,
women received an Enlightenment education that prepared them to think,
speak, and act for themselves. This freedom enabled them to explore their
social environment, safeguard their own virtue, and marry according to

---

18. Historian Nathan O. Hatch presents strong evidence to support Tocqueville's
observations here. He argues that American Christianity experienced rapid and dra-
matic democratization from 1780 to 1830, the years of the early republic. In his
view, the fundamental changes that took place during this time include: (1) a widespread rejection of learned theologians and traditional orthodoxies, (2) a breakdown
in the distinction between clergy and laymen, (3) a generalized assertion of the pri-
macy of individual conscience, or the right of individuals to think and act for themselves, and (4) a corresponding elevation of public opinion as a primary religious
authority. See Nathan O. Hatch, *The Democratization of American Christianity*
(New Haven: Yale University Press, 1989), pp. 3–6, 9, 14, 35, 77, 81, 162, 182.

Other historians claim, however, that Tocqueville failed to grasp the nature and
significance of evangelicalism, a phenomenon they consider central to any account
of early-19th-century religion. See, for example, Doris Goldstein, *Trial by Faith: Religion and Politics in Tocqueville's Thought* (Amsterdam: Elsevier Scientific Publishing, 1975), pp. 19, 25–26.

19. See also John Winthrop, "A Model of Christian Charity," in *The American Puritans: Their Prose and Poetry*, ed. Perry Miller (Garden City, N.Y.: Doubleday, 1956),
pp. 78–84.

their own best judgment and inclinations [II, 213–14, 206–8].

Finally, the new idea of rights changed America's conception of politics. For the Puritans, self-government was a necessary means to fulfill their covenantal obligations to God. Tocqueville's Americans also valued self-government, but more for secular than for religious reasons. In fact, most engaged in political activity for the sake of acquiring wealth. Their political parties, as Tocqueville describes them, were little more than glorified interest groups with hazy claims to justice, and public service, in their eyes, was more a career than a religious calling [I, 178–83, 229–30, 245–47; II, 109–12].

Fearing that an interest-oriented idea of rights would unduly magnify selfishness, American moralists designed a new secular strategy for promoting virtue that sought to prevent their countrymen from behaving in coarse and destructive ways. The centerpiece of this strategy was a doctrine Tocqueville called "interest rightly understood" [II, 127–30]. This doctrine, which stressed the links between virtue and private advantage, further strengthened the spirit of liberty at religion's expense by giving individuals a right to make moral judgments that was as absolute as their right to determine religious truth.

Under the aegis of "interest rightly understood," most Americans in the 1830s were virtuous, albeit largely for selfish reasons. Children learned that honesty is the best policy, politicians served their constituents to further their careers, and women were chaste and submitted to conjugal authority for the sake of social acceptance and respect.

Most Americans also learned to further their interests by combining with others, an associational skill that Tocqueville considered the "mother science" of democracy [I, 117]. Armed with this knowledge, they created a vital civil society made up of diverse social, political, economic, moral, and religious associations. These associations fostered self-confidence and social responsibility while substituting for the various secondary bodies that checked the abuse of power in aristocracies [II, 113–26].

Tocqueville found much to admire in American democracy of the 1830s: strong families, a vibrant civil society, and a working constitutional system governed by a prosperous, politically active middle-class majority. He also liked America's new ethical and religious-political arrangements, which retained the link the Puritans established between the "spirit of liberty" and the "spirit of religion," but elevated the former above the latter in important respects. This shift, in his view, properly accommodated the widespread American desire for religious and moral autonomy. Yet it also enabled a modified Christianity to remain the "first" of America's political institutions and as such to play a pivotal role in keeping our country moral and free [I, 306].

America's Long-Range Problems

Tocqueville worried more about the future of American liberty than his generally bright account of Jacksonian democracy suggests. He feared that America's new ethical system would fail to protect minority rights in difficult cases, when virtue required sacrifices that neither selfishness nor a weakened Christianity could justify. Such was already the case in America's dealings with Native and African Americans. The existence of these discrete minorities, set apart by "visible and imperishable signs," occasioned heinous abuses of majority power [I, 358]. Tocqueville also thought that American majorities might someday lose their freedom either at the hands of an industrial aristocracy, or, more likely, at the hands of democratic despotism, a novel form of tyranny that thrives on atheism, ignorance, and selfishness.

Race

The slow, relentless destruction of North America's native population by Europeans is described in some detail by Tocqueville, but he did not consider this particular form of tyranny a danger to the United States as a whole. In his view, however, slavery and its attendant evils posed the gravest of threats to America's future [I, 340].

Tocqueville deemed the physical treatment of slaves in the 1830s brutal but did not dwell on it, choosing instead to focus on the unprecedented crimes against their spirit [I, 332, 377; II, 175]. He also noted that free African Americans enjoyed few of freedom's fruits. Northern laws discriminated severely against them, and what the laws did allow, public opinion forbade. Thus, with none but phantom rights, they could not vote, sit on juries, benefit from the due process of law, or make social contact with whites. All in all, the free states seemed to compete with each other to see which could make the lives of their black inhabitants most miserable [I, 358–59].

Tocqueville believed that the sharp cultural differences that existed between Northern and Southern whites as a result of slavery could destroy the Union [I, 391–93]. His worst fear, though, and one that haunted all thoughtful Americans, was that a bloody civil war between the two races would break out, ultimately annihilating one of the two. The outcome of such a war, he predicted, would depend on whether or not the Union survived. If it did, Tocqueville thought the whites' numerical superiority would make them victorious. If the Union dissolved, Southern blacks with numbers and desperation on their side would overpower Southern whites, despite the latter's economic and political superiority [I, 376].

In Tocqueville's view, there were only two ways to avoid race war in America: blacks and whites had to either separate completely or mingle completely. Separation would require the emancipation and expatriation of the slaves, a plan supported by prominent American statesmen such as Thomas Jefferson (1743–1826) and later Abraham Lincoln (1809–1865). Tocqueville liked this plan but considered it highly impractical. Blacks constituted more than one-fifth of all Americans in the 1830s, and not even massive colonization could halt their population growth. These demographics led Tocqueville to conclude that African Americans would remain in America unless they were entirely destroyed [I, 372].

Tocqueville also assessed the prospects for a free, interracial society after slavery was abolished. A large mulatto population in certain parts of the United States testified to this possibility, although most mulattoes were conceived under coercive conditions. While intermarriage was compatible with Christian, democratic principles, and was even allowed in some Northern states, most whites recoiled from the practice. Furthermore, Tocqueville warned that racial justice would have to be achieved immediately after emancipation to forestall strife. Once free, he feared, blacks would quickly resort to violence if denied their rights [I, 378–79].

American slavery would end, Tocqueville predicted, because the forces of modernity opposed it, Christianity considered it unjust, and the country's long-term economic interests required its abolition. He believed, however, that intransigent prejudice would prevent America from ever becoming a free, interracial society. By the 1830s, most Americans held that God's moral laws served their self-interest. This was the unmistakable lesson of the doctrine of interest rightly understood. But interest, at least as Americans of the time understood it, did not require that free blacks be treated fairly or charitably. Only religion could demand such things, but, as Tocqueville put it, the golden age of Christian morality was already long past [II, 130].

Industrialization

Economic inequality does not loom large in Tocqueville's portrait of America, in part because most Americans who dotted his landscape were middle class rather than rich or poor. Indeed, one critic considers his relative silence on this issue partially due to a "failure of imagination" in a work that professed to see America's future writ large.[20] Yet Tocqueville does devote one brilliant chapter of *Democracy in America* to the dangers of oligarchy, which he feared would result from industrialization.

---

20. Jack Lively, *The Social and Political Thought of Alexis de Tocqueville* (Oxford: Clarendon Press, 1962), p. 217.

The keys to the rapid development of industry—the principles and techniques of mass production—were already quite well known in the 1830s and were quickly becoming commonplace. Indeed, America had already begun to industrialize in Tocqueville's day although capital was then scarce and great fortunes rare [I, 255; II, 164–67].

Tocqueville predicted that future American industrialists would constitute a "manufacturing aristocracy"—that is, a powerful new class with the will and the means to exploit the masses [II, 167]. He imagined, strangely enough, that strong American majorities would create this monster class themselves by unjustly and unwisely excluding the wealthy from public life. Might not this group, with no appropriate outlet for its natural political ambitions, someday use its wealth to corrupt or even overturn America's democratic institutions? "If the permanent inequality of conditions and aristocracy ever enter the world once again," Tocqueville warned, "one may predict that they will come in through this door" [II, 167].

Yet Tocqueville discounts this danger shortly after describing it. Modern, as opposed to traditional, aristocrats, he concluded, would lack the corporate spirit, the political support, and the legal privileges needed to govern legitimately. Nor, given their economic dependence on vast middle-class markets, would they have the heart for usurpation. Most Americans, in turn, would tolerate these industrial giants, both because they admire wealth and because they love the cheap consumer goods that mass production brings. Indeed, the "secret threads" of interest connecting the middle to the new upper class would be so numerous, Tocqueville notes, that the former could "hardly strike" the latter "without harming itself" [II, 259].

Tocqueville was not sanguine, however, about the fate of the work force that industrial capitalism would consign to the assembly line. He knew quite well that mass production was by its very nature intellectually stunting and morally degrading. "What ought one to expect," he asks, "of a man who has employed twenty years of his life in the making of pinheads?" [II, 164]. He also knew that the moral ties that once bound master to man were gone forever. Interest alone governed the cold, hard world of the marketplace and would not, even if enlightened, dictate fair treatment or respect for workers' rights unless it was profitable. Under these circumstances, factory workers would be ignorant, impoverished, dependent, and wholly unfit for citizenship.

Democratic Despotism
Tocqueville also questioned whether Americans in general could ever become sufficiently enlightened to pursue even their own long-term interests

intelligently. Virtually no one, he thought, could acquire adequate knowledge of his or her own good, enlightenment claims notwithstanding. All need some principle of authority to navigate through life. Thus, the relevant question for him when assessing popular mores was not whether individuals defer to an authority when making important life choices, but rather to what authority they defer [II, 16–19].

Tocqueville feared that having rejected the authority of religion, Americans would blindly come to accept, and therefore become enslaved to, the power of majority opinion. This tyranny of the majority over thought, as he calls it, rests squarely on an unblinking faith in intellectual equality. If all can equally discover the truth, as democrats suppose, then truth must coincide with the beliefs of the greatest number. As the truth's arbiter, the majority tends to shape what democrats think, feel, and honor. Resistance to its dictates, at least in Tocqueville's day, required enormous courage. In democracy, he notes, it is "very difficult to believe what the mass rejects, and to profess what it condemns" [I, 258; II, 268].

As we have seen, American public opinion in the 1830s supported a relatively weak form of Christian morality and an interest-oriented idea of civic virtue. Yet it also issued two interrelated commands to all Americans that tended to undermine this support. The first, which was quite strident, was to acquire wealth at all costs. The second, more muted command was to abandon otherworldly hopes. In obeying these orders, Tocqueville's Americans became restless, rootless wanderers ready to change their plans, their friends, their jobs, and their homes for an elusive secular paradise. Such strivings made them somewhat lonely, somewhat anxious, and quite unable to enjoy life despite their prosperity. "One cannot work more laboriously" than Americans "to be happy," Tocqueville laconically remarked [I, 253; II, 142–45].

Despite all of this, American majorities were openly hostile to criticism even from friends such as Tocqueville and were ill-equipped to choose leaders who could serve their true, as opposed to their apparent, interests. These defects, in Tocqueville's view, accounted for the dismal quality of American statesmanship in the early 19th, as opposed to the late 18th, century. "The most remarkable men are rarely called to public office," he lamented, and "the race of American statesmen has gotten much smaller. . . ." [I, 203, 268–70].

Tocqueville feared that chronic sadness, selfishness, and self-deception would eventually make American majorities passive and would weaken, rather than strengthen, their disposition to govern. As strong, independent minds vanished from the scene, less hardy souls could stop thinking altogether and forfeit the essence of political liberty while keeping its outward form. Finally, democracies naturally centralize political power by undermining the secondary bodies that defend private rights and particular interests. Unchecked, these dangers could lead to "administrative" or "democratic" despotism, a nanny state that subjects willing people to its benign, but soul-destroying, power [II, 295–303].

Tocqueville's description of democratic despotism is one of the most haunting parts of the *Democracy*. The people in this regime vote but generally refrain from all other types of political activity. Considering the government their own, they allow it to extend its power indefinitely as long as it treats them equally and promotes their economic well-being. The more dependent the people become on government, the more willing they are to sacrifice their rights to its political designs. The rulers, in turn, guide and instruct them in the various incidents of life. Eventually, the people lose the faculties of thinking, feeling, and acting for themselves and come to resemble a herd of "timid and industrious" animals [II, 324–25].

Democracy, Religion, and Liberty Today

Tocqueville linked our future prospects to our distant past—that is, to the unique combination of democracy, religion, and liberty bequeathed to us by the Puritans. Democracy would always drive this triad, he predicted, further strengthening the passion for equality that by the 1830s had made most white Americans alike. This passion would also continue to secularize America's national character, he believed, thereby making us more skeptical and selfish than our ancestors and more vulnerable to tyranny. How accurate are these predictions with regard to early-21st-century America?

History seems to have confirmed Tocqueville's prediction that Americans would become more homogeneous over time. Democratic leavening now blurs all indigenous social distinctions and softens the rough cultural edges that immigrants bring to the national melting pot. Small things are revealing in this respect, such as our hatred of snobbery, our passion for inclusiveness, our tendency to cloak authority relations in the garb of equality, and our difficulty in preserving ethnicity amid the pressures for assimilation. Almost all Americans, whatever their background, are now motivated by a love for wealth. Money talks especially loudly in democracies, as Tocqueville showed, where self-reliant equals must generally pay for the help they need rather than being able to get assistance from an interdependent social network [II, 237].[21]

---

21. John A. Hall and Charles Lindholm, *Is America Breaking Apart?* (Princeton: Princeton University Press, 1999), pp. 99–100, 131–32.

America's passion for equality has also sundered social and political barriers that Tocqueville once considered impregnable. His assessment of slavery and racial prejudice in the 1830s led him to assert, for example, that blacks and whites would never live together peacefully, much less on equal terms. Indeed, the continued existence of racial prejudice and of a poor, powerless African American underclass suggests that he may have been correct. But Tocqueville's prognosis for the future of race relations was too bleak. Our achievements in race relations, while insufficient, are clearly greater than Tocqueville thought possible.

Tocqueville erred regarding black-white relations because he underestimated the range of moral resources available to Americans fighting slavery and its legacy. These include the principle of equality in the Declaration of Independence, the nascent Christian abolitionist movement of the 1830s, the moral strengths of the slaves themselves, and the almost religious reverence with which large segments of American public opinion regarded the Union as an instrument of freedom.[22] Although Tocqueville observed that great crises could produce great democratic statesmen [I, 206], he never imagined that a man such as Abraham Lincoln could fundamentally alter the course of American history by artfully using these resources against slavery and national disintegration. Nor could he foresee that a century later a black religious leader, Martin Luther King, Jr., would draw on some of the same resources to turn public opinion against the most blatant forms of racial prejudice.

America's industrial workers also fared better than Tocqueville expected, generally escaping the degrading poverty and dependence he consigned them to. Most proved more mobile, more versatile, and more powerful than Tocqueville thought possible, and eventually developed the skills necessary to become effective democratic citizens. Labor unions and government intervention, of course, contributed significantly to their success. Although the regulated market now dictates terms of employment, American industrialists benefit more often than not from treating their workers well. The bottom line still holds, however, and corporate selfishness in the new global economy clearly threatens this harmony of interests, much to the workers' disadvantage.[23]

---

22. See, for example, Sean Wilentz, "Many Democracies: On Tocqueville and Jacksonian America" in *Reconsidering Tocqueville's Democracy in America*, ed. Abraham S. Eisenstadt (New Brunswick and London: Rutgers University Press, 1988), pp. 210–11, 273; Thomas G. West, "Misunderstanding the American Founding" in *Interpreting Tocqueville's Democracy in America*, ed. Ken Masugi (Savage, Md.: Rowman and Littlefield, 1991), p. 166.

23. See Benjamin R. Barber, *Jihad vs. McWorld: How Globalism and Tribalism Are Reshaping the World* (New York: Ballantine Books, 1996), pp. 23–32.

Finally, Tocqueville clearly missed how much America's passion for equality would transform the relations between the sexes. Tocqueville's Americans considered men and women morally and intellectually equal but denied women social and political rights on the grounds that nature intended them for domestic life. Tocqueville approved of these arrangements and apparently considered them permanent. "You do not see American women . . . manage a business, . . . enter the political sphere," he asserted, or consider "conjugal authority as a . . . usurpation of their rights" [II, 219–20].[24] Since he wrote, however, women have achieved considerable equality in virtually all areas of public life. Most married Americans now also share decision-making and deny Tocqueville's claim that nature made one sex fit to rule and the other to obey.

Some scholars also question whether the United States has become less religious. For these, the facts that most Americans pray, attend religious services, and claim to believe in God show that religious authority still governs popular morality.[25] Yet other signs indicate that the secularizing forces Tocqueville observed in the 1830s have indeed become stronger.

Consider, for example, the current status of religious liberty. Most Americans now link this principle to their feelings rather than to reason or Revelation, thus virtually detaching it from the concept of objective religious truth. This new, more subjective approach to faith has increased "religious individualism," or the tendency to define one's own relationship to God, using Bible, church, and clergy perhaps as resources but not as authoritative guides. Thus, despite our high level of religious observance, we generally feel no obligation to subscribe to orthodoxy or to follow the difficult moral precepts of our faiths. While the recent growth of Protestant evangelicalism, traditional Catholicism, and orthodox Judaism has checked the erosion of religious authority somewhat, religious individualism continues to undermine traditional moral restraints on private and public behavior.[26]

Many thoughtful Americans favor this development, either because they believe institutional arrangements are sufficient to solve knotty

24. Sarah and Angelina Grimké provide evidence that at least some American women were actively striving for equal social, political, and marital rights in the 1830s. See *The Feminist Papers from Adams to de Beauvoir*, ed. Alice Rossi (New York: Bantam Books, 1974), pp. 306–22.

25. Alan Wolfe, *One Nation After All* (New York: Penguin Putnam, 1998), pp. 44–49 [hereafter cited as Wolfe, *One Nation*].

26. Wolfe, *One Nation*, pp. 55, 61, 70–71, 81–82, 87, 98, 298; see also James Davison Hunter, *Evangelicalism: The Coming Generation* (Chicago and London: University of Chicago Press, 1987).

political problems or because they think greater liberty will foster healthier mores.[27] Tocqueville, on the other hand, would probably view these changes with alarm. As we have seen, he distrusted the political efficacy of institutions alone, and doubted that an increase in freedom leads to moral progress. Indeed, he believed that public opinion would shape the morals of most Americans and consequently wanted its religious component to remain as strong as possible.

Assessing whether Tocqueville's concerns are justified is, of course, a complicated matter. In general, Americans today are a hard-working, creative, and self-reliant people whose achievements stand tall in the annals of world history. We are also decent, compassionate, and honest albeit mostly in local settings and for selfish reasons.[28] Our Constitution, while creaky in spots, continues to work reasonably well to protect individual freedom. Finally, our moderate and stable politics, our economic prosperity, and our broad religious tolerance have enabled us, for the most part, to avoid the grosser types of conflict and depravity that still afflict so much of the world.

Nonetheless, Tocqueville's concerns for the future of American liberty must be taken seriously, if only because so many of his warnings remain prescient. Tocqueville thought that a harsh, powerful industrial aristocracy could one day overturn America's popular government, although he discounted this possibility, as we have seen. Yet some critics claim that industrialists actually have snatched political power from the people and now serve themselves under the facade of constitutionality.[29]

Did such a takeover occur? Tocqueville would probably argue no, holding that these critics confuse political inequality with economic inequality, a condition quite compatible with majority rule as long as wealth is fluid. He also believed, as we have seen, that America would tolerate an aristocracy of sorts if its middle class continued to prosper and its proletariat remained small. Indeed, Tocqueville thought that America's middle class would stabilize its politics, and his famous prediction that revolution will not happen here has surely trumped Karl Marx's dire warnings regarding the inevitability of class conflict under capitalism [I, 249; II, 258–69].

Yet Tocqueville's optimism regarding America's ability to contain

---

27. Wolfe, *One Nation*, p. 282; Christopher Wolfe and John Hittinger, eds. *Liberalism at the Crossroads: An Introduction to Contemporary Liberal Political Theory and Its Critics* (Lanham, Md.: Rowman and Littlefield, 1994), pp. xii–xiii.

28. Wolfe, *One Nation*, pp. 289–93.

29. See, for example, William Greider, *Who Will Tell the People: The Betrayal of American Democracy* (New York: Simon and Schuster, 1993).

wealth within politically acceptable boundaries was perhaps not fully justified. Tocqueville knew that American office holders were bribable in the 1830s but thought that enlightened self-interest would always prevent them from exercising anti-majoritarian power. He also noted favorably at the time that money could not buy democratic elections. In today's America, however, wealth often shapes public policy, and attaining office requires access to great sums of money. At the same time, the Constitution is now more democratic than ever, and politicians are as preoccupied with public opinion polls as with fundraising. Under these circumstances, it is difficult to determine who truly rules America or to gauge the extent to which wealth has corrupted the political process.

Tocqueville also feared that the same factors that made most Americans self-absorbed moneymakers in the 1830s could, in the future, foster a widespread and politically dangerous form of egoism. Unfortunately, this type of egoism now does indeed cast a long shadow over our generally bright political horizon. Its manifestations include excessive violence, a preoccupation with comfort and convenience, fragmented families, a coarse popular culture, and a disinclination to engage in politics.

Although most Americans seem happy, at least according to public opinion polls, a high incidence of crime, substance abuse, mental illness, and mindless escapism indicate that we are, at least on some level, as restless and anxious as our early-19th-century ancestors.[30] These evils are at least partially due to a weakening of the social ties and spiritual goods that, in Tocqueville's view, give depth and dignity to life.

Tocqueville feared that America would succumb to democratic despotism if its moral resources became seriously depleted. This form of tyranny comes about, we recall, when a people freely cedes political power to a strong bureaucratic state that promotes equality and material well-being at the expense of genuine liberty. Tocqueville recognized, of course, that a large United States needs an "active and powerful" national government if only to provide for various needs that exceed the capacities of state governments. Indeed, he advocated strengthening national power at the expense of state power in the 1830s. Yet the size of today's national government would probably alarm Tocqueville, as would its long administrative reach into the affairs of daily life.

The Tasks of Statesmanship

Tocqueville considered democracies able to secure liberty, but only with the help of wise statesmen. Such leaders must endeavor to strengthen

---

30. Wolfe, *One Nation*, p. 287.

those elements of their nations that bolster liberty and weaken those elements that undermine it. Tocqueville knew, of course, that the tasks of
statesmanship change with circumstances and that there is no set formula for successful democratic governance. Thus, in his "new political
science," he provides broad guidelines for future leaders rather than
attempting to micromanage their efforts [II, 150].

One such guideline requires those who govern to utilize their country's native resources. Perhaps, therefore, Tocqueville would advise
American statesmen today to strengthen the spirits of religion and liberty in light of current conditions. At their best, these spirits nourished
freedom by fostering respect for individual rights, for social responsibility, and for spiritual aspirations.

American statesmen can bolster a sagging "spirit of religion," Tocqueville suggests, by stressing the long-term advantages of personal self-re-
straint and farsighted public-spiritedness. Over time, he hoped, such
future-oriented behavior would imperceptibly predispose skeptics toward
faith. Despite his strong preference for Christianity, Tocqueville would
also have statesmen support all religions in America in ways that respect
the separation between church and state. "What is most important" for a
free society, he reminds us, "is not so much that all citizens profess the
true religion, but that they profess some religion" [I, 304; II, 155–57].

Perhaps because he recognized the ultimate fragility of modern faith,
Tocqueville's final recommendations in *Democracy in America* stress
the means for strengthening the "spirit of liberty." Thus, he praises a
host of institutional safeguards for liberty that promote respect for rights
while affording them concrete protection. In America, these include trial
by jury, due process of law, judicial independence, and, most important,
a free press. Voluntary associations are also essential to this mix, as is
political participation, which Tocqueville considered the best antidote
for soul-destroying individualism [II, 328–32, 109–12].

As we have seen, Tocqueville's political science relies rather heavily
on the principle of "interest rightly understood," which he considered
the only firm foundation for democratic virtue. Yet Tocqueville thought
that this principle, if practiced habitually, could foster a genuine love of
liberty, of truth, and of other aristocratic elements in human nature that
equality threatens, but can never fully extinguish [II, 112, 157].

In *Democracy in America*, Tocqueville summons our love of truth by
asking us to transcend the barriers that democracy poses to independent
thought. These include an unwarranted faith in our own goodness and in
public opinion, the always powerful and often invisible arbiter of democratic behavior. Only critical thinkers, he believed, could profit from a

book that asks its readers to address their own shortcomings for the sake of liberty.

Tocqueville was cautiously optimistic about America's prospects, in part because he thought that democrats could learn to think critically and even to attain a fair portion of self-knowledge [II, 26, 50–51]. Such beliefs led him to write *Democracy in America* rather than to lament "in secret over the fate of [his] fellow men" [II, 335]. This book, which you are about to read, invites us all to face the future as Tocqueville did— with courage, hope, and a strong resolve to strive for the best democracy can offer.

SANFORD KESSLER

EDITOR'S NOTE

This is an abridged edition of Tocqueville's *Democracy in America* designed for classroom use and for the general reader. No abridgment, of course, can do justice to this masterpiece, which should be read in its entirety whenever possible. I have included the table of contents from the unabridged work to indicate the full range of subjects it treats while highlighting the chapters contained herein. These chapters constitute almost half the entire work and, I hope, the bulk of material that is central to Tocqueville's thought. Most are uncut and appear as Tocqueville wrote them. The necessary omissions are indicated by dots. Finally, I have included a short bibliography, which includes easily available editions of Tocqueville's other writings and a sampling of the best Tocqueville scholarship published in recent years.

I am happy to acknowledge those who assisted me in this work. I would first like to thank Stephen D. Grant for the superb translation of Tocqueville's work that graces this book. I would also like to thank Mark Yellin for suggesting this project to me and Elias Baumgarten, Ruth W. Grant, Stephen D. Grant, Jack Jacobs, Marvin Meyers, and Sheva Zucker for reading and commenting on earlier drafts of my Introduction. I, of course, absolve them of responsibility for its shortcomings. Special thanks also go to editors Brian Rak and Meera Dash of Hackett Publishing Company and Christopher Kelly, Hackett's reader, for supporting this project and gently, but firmly, prodding me to make it better.

S. K.

TRANSLATOR'S NOTE

The text of Tocqueville's *De La Démocratie en Amérique* followed in this translation accords with that in *Oeuvres Complètes, Tome 1, Volumes 1 & 2*, ed. J.-P. Mayer, Éditions Gallimard, Paris 1961 (1966).

The translation adheres as closely as possible to the precise sense of Tocqueville's French within the limits of the need to translate it into comprehensible English. I have tried to translate important terms like *moeurs* and *lumières* consistently. Footnotes for each of these terms acquaint the reader with something of their history and meaning. I have also made use of footnotes at some points to describe nuances or ambiguities in the French that have been lost in the need to choose one, intelligible and not hopelessly awkward, English equivalent.

Some modification has been made to Tocqueville's punctuation in the interest of readability, and with a bow toward modern usage. In particular, he used the semicolon where we might sometimes have used a comma, period, or colon; and he used it generously, on occasion producing long, single-sentence paragraphs whose clauses are linked together only by a series of semicolons. Some, but not all, of these sentences have been broken up, and then not entirely; the aim was to make only the minimum necessary changes. Tocqueville's paragraphing remains unchanged throughout.

For help with the translation, I want to thank Christopher Kelly and Jennifer Terni; and for help with the English text and footnotes, Sanford Kessler and Ruth Grant. Thanks to Jennifer Horney of the National Humanities Center for bringing to our attention the James Goodwyn Clonney painting on the cover. Finally, working with Hackett's editors, from Brian Rak and Meera Dash to the anonymous and exceptional copyeditor, has been an unmixed pleasure.

S.D.G.

DEMOCRACY IN AMERICA

VOLUME ONE[*] [1]

INTRODUCTION

Among the new objects that attracted my attention during my stay in the United States, none struck me with greater force than the equality of conditions. I easily perceived the enormous influence that this primary fact exercises on the workings of the society. It gives a particular direction to the public mind, a particular turn to the laws, new maxims to those who govern, and particular habits to the governed.

I soon recognized that this same fact extends its influence far beyond political mores[†] and laws, and that its empire extends over civil society as well as government: it creates opinions, gives rise to sentiments, inspires customs, and modifies everything that it does not produce.

In this way, then, as I studied American society, I saw more and more, in the equality of conditions, the generative fact from which each particular fact seemed to flow, and I kept finding that fact before me again and

---

* Pages in brackets [ ] refer to the Gallimard edition of *Democracy in America*. (For full bibliographic information, see the Translator's Note.)
   Numbered footnotes are Tocqueville's. Footnotes marked by an asterisk are the translator's.

† The French word translated as "mores" is *moeurs,* and derives from the Latin *mores.* Tocqueville explicitly says in the first volume of *Democracy in America* that he uses *moeurs* in the way the ancients used *mores:* "I apply it not only to moral habits properly so-called [*moeurs proprement dites*], which one might call the habits of the heart [*les habitudes du coeur*], but to the different notions men have, to the different opinions which have currency among them, and to the whole body of ideas from which the habits of the mind [*les habitudes de l'esprit*] are formed" (Vol. 1, Part 2, Chap. 9 [300]). However, Part Three of the second volume is entitled "Influence of Democracy on *moeurs* [moral habits] Properly So-Called."
   No single word can capture the complexity of Tocqueville's use of *moeurs. Moeurs,* moreover, has a long and by no means seamless history of uses in French, including: (1) moral habits (good or bad); (2) morals (often in the sense of good morals: in this usage, one may possess or lack *moeurs* simply); (3) the habitual ways of an individual, a people, or a society (in this sense, *moeurs* may be translated as "ways" or "way of life," "manners," "customs" or "usages," or "mores"); and (4) the habitual behavior or ways of animals, which is the subject of ethology. Depending on the context, *moeurs* will be translated as moral habits, morals, or mores. *Moeurs* will never be translated as "customs" or "usages," in order not to produce confusion with *coutumes* and *usages,* which are narrower in meaning than *moeurs,* and appropriately translated as "customs" or "usages."

again as a central point to which all of my observations were leading.

Then I cast my thoughts back toward our hemisphere, and it seemed to me that I could make out there something analogous to the spectacle that the New World was offering me. I saw the equality of conditions which, without having attained its extreme limits, as it has in the United States, was approaching those limits more each day; and this same democracy, which was reigning over the American societies, appeared to me to be advancing rapidly toward power in Europe.

From that moment, I conceived the idea for this book.

A great democratic revolution is occurring among us; everyone sees it, but everyone does not judge it in the same way. Some think of it as something new, and taking it to be an accident, they hope to be able still to arrest it; whereas others judge it to be irresistible, because it seems to them to be the most unremitting, the most ancient, and the most permanent fact that we know of in history.

Let me turn for a moment to France as it was seven hundred years ago: I find it divided up among a small number of families who possess [2] the earth and govern the inhabitants; the right of command thus descends from generation to generation with their patrimonies; men have only a single means of acting upon one another, force; one finds only a single origin of power, property in land.

But then the political power of the clergy succeeds in establishing a base for itself and soon extends its reach. The clergy opens its ranks to all, to the poor and to the rich, to the commoner and to the lord. Equality begins to penetrate to the heart of the government by way of the Church, and he who had vegetated as a serf in an eternal servitude places himself as a priest in the midst of the nobles, and will often take a seat above the kings.

As the society becomes over time more civilized and more stable, the different relations between men become more complicated and more numerous. The need for civil laws makes itself strongly felt. Then the jurists make their appearance; they leave the obscure precincts of the courts and the dusty nooks of the clerks' offices, and they will sit in the court of the prince, alongside the feudal barons covered in ermine and armor.

The kings ruin themselves in great enterprises; the nobles exhaust themselves in private wars; the commoners enrich themselves in commerce. The influence of money begins to make itself felt on the affairs of State. Trade is a new source that opens the way to power, and the financiers become a political power that is despised and flattered.

Little by little, enlightenment* spreads; the taste for literature and the arts is awakened; the mind then becomes an element of success; knowl-

---

* The term translated as "enlightenment" is *les lumières*. *Les lumières,* the plural form of the French word for "light," can mean natural intellectual capacity, or it can mean

edge is a means of government, intelligence a social force; the learned come to take part in public affairs.

To the extent, however, that new routes for arriving at power are discovered, the value of birth is lowered. In the 11th century, nobility had an inestimable value; by the 13th century, it is purchased. The first act of ennoblement takes place in 1270, and in the end equality is introduced into the government by the aristocracy itself.

During the seven hundred years that have just passed, it sometimes happened that in order to struggle against the royal authority or in order to take power away from their rivals, the nobles gave political power to the people.

Still more often, the kings caused the inferior classes of the State to participate in the government in order to pull down the aristocracy.

In France, the kings showed themselves to be the most active and the most unremitting of levelers. When they were ambitious and strong, they worked to raise the people to the level of the nobles; and when they were modest and weak, they allowed the people to place itself above [3] themselves. The former helped democracy by their talents, the latter by their vices. Louis XI and Louis XIV took care to make everyone equal below the throne, and finally Louis XV himself descended with his court into the dust.

As soon as the citizenry began to possess the earth in ways that did not follow feudal tenure, and personal property, having become widespread, was able in its turn to create influence and give power, discoveries were no longer made in the arts, improvements were no longer introduced into commerce and industry, without creating just so many new elements of equality among men. From this moment, all the techniques that are discovered, all the needs that come into being, all the desires that demand to be satisfied, are advances toward universal leveling. The taste for luxury, the love of war, the empire of fashion, the most superficial passions of the human heart as well as the most profound, seem to work in concert to impoverish the rich and enrich the poor.

From the time that the works of the intellect became sources of power and of riches, each development of science, each new piece of knowledge, each new idea, had to be considered as a source of power placed within the reach of the people. Poetry, eloquence, memory, the charms of the intellect, the fires of the imagination, depth of thought, all these gifts that the heavens distribute haphazardly, were to the benefit of

acquired knowledge or learning. One translation of *les lumières* is "enlightenment," as in the Enlightenment; *Le Siècle des Lumières* is "the Century of Enlightenment." *Une lumière* is a person of great intelligence or worth; we would say, a "leading light."

democracy, and even when they were in the possession of its adversaries, they still served its cause by highlighting the natural greatness of man. These conquests therefore spread with those of civilization and enlightenment, and literature was an arsenal open to all, where the weak and the poor came each day to look for arms.

When one searches through the pages of our history, one comes across almost no great events during the last seven hundred years that did not turn to the profit of equality.

The Crusades and the wars of the English decimate the nobles and divide their lands; the institution of free municipalities* introduces democratic liberty into the bosom of feudal monarchy; the invention of firearms equalizes the commoner and the noble on the field of battle; the

---

* The French word translated as "free municipalities" is *communes*.

Under feudalism, the *communes* were the free towns whose inhabitants—those who lived in the town or *bourg* and therefore were called *bourgeois*—were granted a charter to govern themselves. In post-revolutionary France, the *commune* was the smallest administrative district of the country, but the word was also used to refer to the inhabitants of the *commune* as a collectivity. *Municipalité* could refer to the administration of the *commune* (the mayor, his deputies, and the municipal council) or to the *commune* itself.

"Municipality" derives from the Latin *municipium:* during the Roman empire, a *municipium* was a city whose inhabitants were allowed to continue to govern themselves according to their own laws and through their own officials. English usage followed Roman usage: historically, an English "municipality" was a town, city, or district that was granted the privilege of self-government.

The single word *commune*—together with the adjective *communal*—runs like a thread through Tocqueville's text. It is a complex thread, because *commune* has several different senses in Tocqueville's usage. He uses it (1) for the primordial *local political community* that Tocqueville supposes to arise naturally whenever men are brought together, and which therefore lacks a recorded founding, i.e., does not depend constitutionally on a royal or seigneurial grant: this usage echoes some 19th-century English writers' use of "township" (Oxford English Dictionary) and also the claim that the "liberties" of many French *communes* were not granted by royal charter but were "immemorial" (*Dictionnaire de Littré*); (2) for the free, self-governing municipalities of Europe; (3) for the less free, "administered" municipalities of Europe, in particular those of France; and (4) for the American township, especially Tocqueville's model of municipal liberty (*liberté communale*), the New England township. See Vol. 1, Part 1, Chap. 2 [28, 39–40]; 4 [55]; 5 [58–67, 79–81, 92–94].

Translating *commune* as "local community" does not sufficiently convey the sense that it is above all and first of all a *political* entity; neither does "town." "Local political community" is more precise but too informal. It does not sufficiently reflect either the fact that the *communes* were constituted or sanctified by law, or Tocqueville's point that liberty sanctified in law is a necessary condition of effective liberty. Translating *commune* literally as "commune" would conserve the important sense of *commune* as *la commune*, meaning the bourgeoisie or the people—the "commons"—as opposed to the nobility. This sense of *commune* is very important to Tocqueville's argument, as sense (1) above suggests. However, "commune" carries, in

printing house offers equal resources to their intelligence; the post office puts knowledge on the threshold of the poor man's hut as well as at the door of the palace; Protestantism maintains that all men are equally able to find the way to heaven. America, which is discovered, presents a thousand new ways to wealth and delivers riches and power to the obscure adventurer.

If, beginning in the 11th century, you examine what is happening in [4] France every fifty years, at the end of each of these periods you will not fail to notice that a double revolution has been occurring in the state of the society. The noble will have gone down in the social scale, the commoner will have risen; the one descends, the other climbs. Each half century brings them nearer to each other, and soon they will be touching.

And this is not just particular to France. In whatever direction we cast our glance, we perceive the same revolution to be continuing throughout the entire Christian world.

Everywhere, one saw the various incidents in the life of peoples turn to the profit of democracy. All men helped it by their efforts: those who were looking to contribute to its successes and those who had no thought to serve it; those who fought for it and those who declared themselves its enemy; all were pushed pell-mell in the same direction, and all worked in concert, some in spite of themselves and the others unwittingly, blind instruments in the hands of God.

The gradual development of the equality of conditions is thus a providential fact, whose principal characteristics it possesses: it is universal, it is durable, and each day it escapes human power. All events, as all men, serve its development.

Would it be wise to believe that a social movement that comes from such a distance can be suspended by the efforts of a generation? Do you

English usage, too much historical baggage (one must eventually relate Tocqueville's concept to Utopian Socialists, Parisian *communards*, and even hippies, but only after first understanding Tocqueville's own sense of *commune*). And translating *communal* as "communal" is misleading: *communal* in French is whatever pertains to the *commune* or municipality; the English word "communal" would be rendered in French as *commun*. However, "municipality" is sanctioned by English historical usage and retains the sense of *commune* as a political entity—a political entity, moreover, whose center is at least somewhat urban rather than purely rural.

In order to preserve the thread of Tocqueville's usage, *commune* will everywhere be translated as "municipality" or "free municipality," and *communal* as "municipal," with one exception. Where Tocqueville uses *commune* to refer specifically to its American form, *commune* is more properly translated as "township." This choice of words will also serve to highlight the distinctiveness of the American form of *commune*, as Tocqueville himself does for his French readers when he writes of "*la commune de la Nouvelle-Angleterre (Township)*" and "*la réunion communale (town-meeting)*." Vol. 1, Part 1, Chap. 5 [60, 61].

think that after having destroyed feudalism and vanquished the kings, democracy will retreat before the bourgeois and the rich? Will it stop now that it has become so strong and its adversaries have become so weak?

Where, then, are we heading? None can say, for to begin with we lack the terms of comparison: among Christians in our time, conditions are more equal than they have ever been at any time or in any country in the world; thus the magnitude of what has already occurred prevents us from envisaging what more may occur.

The entire book you are going to read was written under the impression of a sort of religious terror produced in the soul of the author by the sight of this irresistible revolution that has advanced for so many centuries through all obstacles and that one still sees advancing today in the midst of the ruins it has made.

It is not necessary for God himself to speak in order for us to perceive the certain signs of His will; it suffices to examine the ordinary course of nature and the constant tendency of events. I know, without the Creator [5] raising His voice, that the heavenly bodies follow in space the arcs that His finger has traced.

If long observation and sincere meditation work to lead the men of our time to recognize that the gradual and progressive development of equality is at the same time the past and the future of their history, this single discovery would give to this development the sacred character of the will of the sovereign master. To want to stop democracy would then appear to be to struggle against God himself, and it would only remain for the nations to accommodate themselves to the social state that Providence is imposing on them.

The Christian peoples appear to me to offer in our day a fearsome sight. The movement that is sweeping them onward is already so strong that one cannot suspend it, and it is not yet so strong that one despairs of directing it: their fate is in their hands, but soon it will escape them.

To instruct democracy, to reinvigorate if possible its beliefs, to purify its morals, to regulate its movements, to substitute little by little the science of public affairs for its inexperience, the knowledge of its true interests for its blind instincts; to adapt its government to times and places; to modify it according to circumstances and men: such is the first of the duties imposed in our time upon those who direct society.

A new political science is necessary for a wholly new world.

But this is hardly what we are thinking of: placed in the middle of a rapidly flowing current, we fix our eyes obstinately on some remnants that are still visible on the bank, while the current drags and pushes us backward toward the abysses.

There are no peoples in Europe among whom the great social revolution that I have just described has made as rapid progress as among us, but it has always moved forward haphazardly here.

Never have the chiefs of State given any thought to preparing for it in advance; it occurred in spite of them or without their being aware of it. The most powerful, the most intelligent, and the most moral classes of the nation did not seek to seize hold of it in order to direct it. Democracy was thus abandoned to its untamed instincts; it grew like those children, deprived of paternal care, who raise themselves in the streets of our cities and whose only knowledge of society is of its vices and its miseries. We seemed still to be unaware of its existence when it seized power without warning. Then each individual yielded servilely to its slightest desires; it was worshipped as the image of strength. Later, when it was weakened by its own excesses, the legislators conceived the imprudent project of destroying it instead of seeking to instruct and correct it, and without wanting to teach it to govern, they thought only of driving it out [6] of government.

The result of this has been that the democratic revolution has occurred in the matter of the society without the change that was necessary to make this revolution useful occurring in the laws, the ideas, the habits, and the mores. Thus we have democracy, minus that which ought to moderate its vices and emphasize its natural advantages; and seeing already the ills that it causes, we are still unaware of the good it can yield.

When royal power, leaning for support upon the aristocracy, peacefully governed the peoples of Europe, society, in the midst of its miseries, enjoyed several kinds of happiness that are difficult to comprehend and appreciate in our time.

The power of a few subjects raised insurmountable barriers to the tyranny of the prince; and the kings, feeling themselves moreover clothed, in the eyes of the crowd, in an almost divine character, drew, from the very respect that they fostered, the will to not abuse their power.

Placed at an immense distance from the people, the nobles nevertheless took the kind of benevolent and calm interest in the fate of the people that the pastor accords to his flock; and, without viewing the poor man as their equal, they watched over his destiny as over a trust placed in their hands by Providence.

Not having conceived of the idea of any social state other than its own, nor imagining that it could ever be equal to its leaders, the people received their favors and did not debate their rights. The people loved its leaders when they were mild and just and submitted ungrudgingly and without servility to their rigors, as to unavoidable ills sent to it by the arm of God. Custom and mores had in any case erected boundaries to tyranny and set up a kind of right in the very midst of force.

The noble not having any thought that anyone wanted to take from him the privileges that he believed to be legitimate, and, the serf regarding his inferiority as an effect of the immutable order of nature, it is understandable that a kind of reciprocal benevolence could be set up between these two classes whose lots were divided so differently. One saw, then, inequality and misery in society, but men's souls were not degraded by it.

It is not the exercise of power or the habit of obedience that depraves men, it is the exercise of a power that they regard as illegitimate and the obedience to a power that they regard as usurped and oppressive.

[7] On the one side was property, force, leisure, and with them the pursuit of luxury, the refinements of taste, the pleasures of the intellect, the cultivation of the arts; on the other, work, coarseness, and ignorance.

But in the heart of this ignorant and coarse mass, one came across energetic passions, generous sentiments, profound beliefs, and savage virtues.

The social body organized in this way was able to have stability, strength, and above all, glory.

But here the ranks of society are mixed up* with one another; the barriers erected between men are lowered; the great domains are divided, power is split up and shared out, enlightenment is spread, intelligence is equalized; the social state becomes democratic, and the empire of democracy in the end establishes itself peacefully in institutions and in mores.

I conceive, in consequence, a society where all, regarding the law as their own work, would love it and would submit to it without difficulty; where, the authority of the government being respected as necessary and not as divine, the love that one would bear toward the head of the State would be not a passion but a reasoned and calm sentiment. Each one having rights and being assured of conserving these rights, there would be established between all the classes a virile confidence and a sort of reciprocal condescension,† as far removed from pride as from servility.

---

* The verb translated as "mixed up" is *se confondent*. The verb *confondre* can mean to mix, unite, or merge two or more things so that they form a whole in which they are no longer distinguishable as separate entities. In this way, it can also mean "to be confused with one another," as in the expression "to be confounded with."

† The words translated as "a sort of reciprocal condescension" are *une sorte de condescendance réciproque. Condescendance* means to "consent with disdain." It is a kind of prideful complaisance on the part of superiors toward their inferiors; its opposite is deference. Strictly speaking, *reciprocal* condescension is an oxymoron, if one tries to visualize two people each of whom looks down upon the other. The "sort" that befits democrats might have to strip condescension of pride, or at any rate of the pride which disdains or looks down.

Taught its true interests, the people would understand that in order to profit from society's goods, one must submit to the costs it imposes. The free association of the citizens would be able then to replace the individual power of the nobles, and the State would be protected from tyranny and from licentiousness.

I understand that in a democratic State constituted in this manner, the society will not be immobile; but the movements of the social body will be able to be regulated and progressive. If one encounters less brilliance there than in the bosom of an aristocracy, one also finds less misery; pleasures will be less extreme and well-being more general; the sciences less grand and ignorance rarer; feelings less energetic and habits milder; one will notice there more vices and fewer crimes.

Lacking the enthusiasm and ardor of belief, enlightenment and experience will sometimes obtain great sacrifices from the citizenry. Each man, being equally weak, will feel an equal need of his fellows; and knowing that he cannot obtain their support except on the condition that he lend them his help, he will perceive without difficulty that for him particular interest is mixed up with the general interest.

The nation, taken as a whole, will be less brilliant, less glorious, perhaps less powerful, but the majority of the citizens in it will enjoy a more [8] prosperous lot, and the people in it will prove to be peaceful, not because they despair of doing better, but because they know they are doing well.

If all in such an order of things were not good and useful, society at least would have appropriated to itself all that it could of the useful and good, and men, abandoning forever the social advantages that aristocracy can provide, would have taken from democracy all the good things that the latter is able to offer them.

But we, by quitting the social state of our forebears, by throwing pell-mell behind us their institutions, their ideas, and their mores, what have we taken up in their stead?

The prestige of the royal power has vanished without being replaced by the majesty of the laws; in our day, the people has contempt for authority, but it fears it, and this fear extracts from the people more than was formerly given by respect and love.

I perceive that we have destroyed the individual existences that were separately able to fight against tyranny. But I see the government which inherits alone all the prerogatives wrested from some families, corporate bodies, or men: the sometimes oppressive but often conserving power of a small number of citizens has been succeeded by the weakness of all.

The division of fortunes has diminished the distance that separated the poor from the rich; but in coming closer, they seem to have found new reasons to hate each other, and casting glances full of terror and envy at each other, they push each other mutually away from power. For the one as for the other, the idea of rights does not exist, and force appears to both of them to be the only reason in the present, and the only guarantee of the future.

The poor man has kept most of the prejudices of his fathers without their beliefs, their ignorance without their virtues; he has accepted the doctrine of interest in order to regulate his actions, without knowing the science of it, and his egoism is as deprived of enlightenment as was his devotion in former times.

Society is calm, not because it is conscious of its strength and its well-being, but on the contrary because it believes itself to be weak and infirm. It fears that if it makes an effort it will die: each one senses the malady, but no one has the courage and the energy necessary to seek something better; one has desires, regrets, sorrows, and joys that produce nothing visible or durable, much like the passions of old men that end only in impotence.

Thus we have abandoned the good things that the old state of affairs could offer without acquiring the useful things the current state of affairs [9] could offer; we have destroyed an aristocratic society and, stopping complacently in the midst of the ruins of the old structure, we seem to wish to stay there forever.

What has occurred in the intellectual world is no less deplorable.

Hindered in its march or abandoned without support to its disordered passions, democracy in France has upset everything that it came across during its passage, shaking whatever it did not destroy. It has not taken hold of the society little by little, in order to peacefully establish its empire there; it has not ceased to march forward in the midst of the disorders and agitation of battle. Driven by the heat of battle, pushed beyond the natural limits of his opinion by the opinions and excesses of his adversaries, each man loses sight of the very object of his pursuits and uses a language that corresponds badly to his true sentiments and his secret instincts.

From this arises the strange confusion we are constrained to witness.

I search my memory in vain, and I find nothing that merits greater sadness or pity than that which passes beneath our eyes. It seems that in our day the natural connection that unites opinions with tastes and actions with beliefs has been broken; the sympathy that has always been visible between the sentiments and ideas of men appears to be destroyed, and it is as if all the laws of moral analogy were abolished.

Christians full of zeal are still found among us, whose religious souls love to nourish themselves with the truths of the other life; these will be animated without doubt in favor of human liberty, the source of all moral grandeur. Christianity, which made all men equal before God, will not begrudge seeing all men equal before the law. But through a confluence of strange events, religion finds itself momentarily bound to the powers that democracy is toppling, and it often happens that it rejects the equality that democracy loves and curses liberty as an adversary, whereas by taking it by the hand, it would be able to sanctify its efforts.

Besides these religious men, I find others whose gaze is turned toward earth rather than toward heaven. Partisans of liberty, not only because they see in it the origin of the most noble virtues, but above all because they consider it as the source of the greatest goods, they desire sincerely to secure its empire and to give men a taste of its benefits: I know that they will hasten to call religion to their aid because they must know that the reign of liberty cannot be established without that of morals, nor can a foundation be given to morals without beliefs. But they [10] have noticed religion in the ranks of their adversaries, and that is enough for them: some of them attack it, and the others do not dare to defend it.

The past centuries have seen base and venal souls advocate servitude, while independent spirits and generous hearts struggled without hope to save human liberty. But in our day one often comes across naturally noble and proud men whose opinions are in direct opposition to their tastes and who extol the servility and baseness that they have never accepted for themselves. There are others, to the contrary, who speak about liberty as if they were able to sense what is sacred and grand in it and who noisily demand on behalf of humanity the rights that they have always depreciated.

I see virtuous and peaceable men whose pure morals, calm habits, affluence, and enlightenment place them naturally at the head of the populations that surround them. Full of a sincere love for the fatherland, they are ready to make great sacrifices for it: however, civilization often finds them to be its adversaries; they confuse its abuses with its benefits, and in their minds the idea of evil is indissolubly joined to the idea of what is new.

Nearby I see others who, in the name of progress and endeavoring to treat man as having only a material nature, want to discover what is useful without being concerned with what is just, science far removed from beliefs, and well-being separated from virtue: these call themselves the champions of modern civilization, and they place themselves insolently at its head, usurping a position that is abandoned to them and for which they are unworthy.

Where are we then?

Religious men fight against liberty, and friends of liberty attack religions; noble and generous spirits praise servitude, and base and servile souls extol independence; honest and enlightened citizens are enemies of all progress, while men without patriotism and without morals make themselves apostles of civilization and enlightenment!

Have all the centuries thus resembled our own? Has man always had before his eyes, as in our day, a world where nothing is connected, where virtue is without genius, and genius without honor; where the love of order is mixed up with the taste for tyrants, and the sacred cult of liberty with contempt for the laws; where conscience throws only a dubious clarity on human actions; where nothing anymore seems either forbidden, or permitted, or decent, or shameful, or true, or false?

[11]   Will I think that the Creator made man in order to leave him to wrestle with himself endlessly in the midst of the intellectual miseries that surround us? I cannot believe it: God is preparing for European societies a more stable and calmer future; I am ignorant of His designs, but I will not cease to believe in them because I cannot penetrate them, and I will prefer to doubt my own lights* rather than his justice.

There is a country in the world where the great social revolution I am speaking of seems to have almost reached its natural limits; there, it has taken place in a simple and easy manner, or rather one may say that this country is witness to the results of the democratic revolution that is taking place among us, without having had the revolution itself.

The emigrants who came to settle in America at the beginning of the 17th century disengaged in a certain fashion the principle of democracy from all those against which it struggled in the bosom of the old societies of Europe, and they transplanted it alone on the shores of the New World. There, it was able to grow in liberty and, marching forward with the mores, to develop peacefully within the laws.

It appears to me beyond doubt that sooner or later we will arrive, like the Americans, at the nearly complete equality of conditions. I do not conclude from this that we might be called upon one day to necessarily draw, from a similar social state, the political consequences that the Americans have drawn from it. I am very far from believing that they have found the only form of government that democracy can give to itself; but it suffices that in the two countries the generative cause of the laws and the mores be the same in order for us to have an immense interest in knowing what it has produced in each of them.

It is therefore not only in order to satisfy a curiosity, in any case legitimate, that I have examined America; I wanted to find lessons there from which we might profit. It would be a strange mistake to think that I wanted to write a panegyric; whoever reads this book will be quite well convinced that such was not my design. Nor was my goal to extol such a form of government in general, because I am among those who believe

---

* The word translated as "lights" is *lumières*. See the note on *lumières*, Vol. 1, Part 1, Introduction [2].

that there is almost never absolute goodness in the laws. I have never even claimed to judge whether the social revolution, whose course seems to me irresistible, was advantageous or disastrous for humanity. I accepted this revolution as an accomplished or nearly accomplished fact, and among the peoples who have seen it occur in their midst, I have sought out the one in which it attained the most complete and peaceful development, in order to discern clearly its natural consequences and to perceive, if possible, the means of making it profitable to men. I admit [12] that in America I saw more than America: I looked there for an image of democracy itself, its inclinations, its character, its prejudices, and its passions. I wanted to get to know it, if only to know at least what we must hope or fear from it.

In the first part of this work, I have therefore tried to show the direction that democracy, given over in America to its inclinations and abandoned almost without constraint to its instincts, naturally gave to the laws, the direction that it imparted to the government, and in general the power that it obtained over public affairs. I wanted to know what were the good and bad things produced by it. I looked at which precautionary measures the Americans had made use of in order to direct it and which others they had omitted, and I tried to distinguish the causes that allowed it to govern society.

My aim was to depict in a second part the influence that the equality of conditions and the government of democracy exercise in America over civil society, over habits, ideas, and mores, but I am beginning to feel less enthusiasm for the accomplishment of this plan. Before I could thus accomplish the task that I had proposed to myself, my work will have become nearly useless. Someone else will soon show to the reader the principal traits of the American character and, concealing under a light veil the gravity of the scene, lend to the truth charms with which I would not have been able to adorn it.[1]

---

1. At the time I published the first edition of this work, M. Gustave de Beaumont, my traveling companion during my voyage to America, was still working on his book entitled *Marie, or Slavery in the United States*, which has since appeared in print. The principal aim of M. de Beaumont was to highlight and make known the situation of the Negroes in the midst of the Anglo-American society. His work will throw a sharp and new light on the question of slavery, a vital question for the united republics. I do not know if I am mistaken, but it seems to me that M. de Beaumont's book, after having powerfully interested those who will want to be moved by it and look for vividly depicted scenes in it, ought to obtain an even more solid and durable success among those readers who, before everything else, want true observations and profound truths.

I do not know if I have succeeded in making understood what I saw in America, but I am certain of having sincerely desired to do so and to have never knowingly given in to the desire to fit the facts to ideas, instead of submitting the ideas to the facts.

When a point could be established with the aid of written documents,
[13] I have taken care to recur to the original texts and the most authentic and highly regarded works.[1] I have indicated my sources in notes, and anyone can verify them. When it was a matter of opinions, political customs, or observations of mores, I sought to consult the most enlightened men. If it happened that the matter was important or doubtful, I was not content with a single witness, but only made up my mind on the basis of the entire body of the evidence.

Here the reader must of necessity take me at my word. Often I could have cited, in support of what I say, the authority of names that are known to him or who at least are worthy of being known to him, but I have kept myself from doing so. The stranger often learns, beside the hearth of his host, important truths that the latter would perhaps keep from his friends; with him, the host unburdens himself of a silence to which he is obligated; he does not fear his indiscretion, because the stranger is just passing through. Each of these confidences was written down by me the moment I received it, but they will never leave my notebook; I prefer to damage the success of my accounts than to add my name to the list of travelers who give back grief and embarrassment in return for the generous hospitality that they have received.

I know that, despite the care I have taken, nothing will be easier than to criticize this book, if anyone ever thinks of criticizing it.

Those who want to look at it closely will find, I think, in the entire work, a mother thought[*] that links, so to speak, all its parts. But the diversity of objects that I have had to treat is very great, and he who

---

1. Legislative and administrative documents were given to me with an obligingness whose memory will always arouse my gratitude. Among the American officials who aided my research in this way, I will mention above all M. Edward Livingston, then Secretary of State (now Minister Plenipotentiary to Paris). During my stay at the seat of Congress, M. Livingston was happy to send me the majority of the documents that I possess relating to the federal government. M. Livingston is one of those rare men that one takes a liking to upon reading their writings, that one admires and honors before even having made their acquaintance, and to whom one is happy to owe a debt of gratitude.

* The words translated as "a mother thought" are *une pensée mère:* the thought that is the progenitor or "mother" of all other thoughts. Tocqueville in Volume 2 of *Democracy in America* speaks of a "mother-passion" (Part 1, Chap. 5 [33]), "mother science" (Part 2, Chap. 8 [117] and [124]), "mother ideas" (Part 1, Chap. 10 [49]), and "mother thought" (Part 2, Chap. 1 [102]).

undertakes to oppose an isolated fact to the body of facts that I cite, or a detached idea to the body of ideas, will succeed without difficulty. I would therefore like him to do me the favor of reading me in the same spirit that governed my work, and that this book be judged by the general impression it leaves, as I myself came to decide things, not on the basis of such or such a reason, but on the basis of the bulk of reasons.

Nor must it be forgotten that the author who wishes to make himself understood is obliged to push each of his ideas to all their theoretical consequences and often up to the limit of the false and the impracticable, because if it is sometimes necessary to depart from the rules of logic when one acts, one cannot do the same when one discourses, and it is al- [14] most as hard for a man to be inconsistent in his arguments as it is to be consistent in his actions.

I conclude by pointing out myself what a great number of readers will consider as the capital defect of the work. This book does not exactly follow anyone; in writing it, I have intended neither to serve nor to oppose any party; I have undertaken to see not other than, but further than the parties; and while they occupy themselves with the next day, I wanted to ponder the future.

. . .

VOLUME ONE, PART ONE   [26]

CHAPTER 2

THE POINT OF DEPARTURE AND ITS IMPORTANCE
FOR THE FUTURE OF THE ANGLO-AMERICANS

The usefulness of knowing the point of departure of peoples in order to understand their social state and their laws.—America is the only country where one can see clearly the point of departure of a great people.—In what respect all the men who came to populate English America resemble each other.—In what respect they differ.—An observation applicable to all the Europeans who came to establish themselves on the shores of the New World.— Colonization of Virginia.—Colonization of New England.— Original character of the first inhabitants of New England.— Their arrival.—Their first laws.—Social contract.—Penal code borrowed from the legislation of Moses.—Religious ardor.— Republican spirit.—Intimate union of the spirit of religion and the spirit of liberty.

A man comes into the world; his first years are passed obscurely among the pleasures and work of infancy. He grows; he begins to mature into manhood; the world's doors finally open to receive him; he enters into contact with his fellow men. We study him then for the first time, and we believe we see taking form in him the germ of the vices and virtues of his mature age.

That, if I am not mistaken, is a great error.

Go back in time: examine the infant in his mother's arms; see the outside world reflected for the first time in the still obscure mirror of his intelligence; contemplate the first examples that strike his eyes; listen to the first words that awaken in him the dormant capacities of thought; finally, witness the first struggles that he must sustain; and only then will you understand the origin of the prejudices, habits, and passions that will dominate his life. Man is almost entirely whole in the swaddling blankets of his cradle.

Something analogous to this occurs in the life of nations. Peoples continue to feel the effects of their origins forever. The circumstances that have accompanied their birth and aided their development influence the entire course of their history.

[27]   If it were possible for us to go back to the first elements of societies and examine the first movements of their history, I do not doubt that we would discover there the first cause of the prejudices, the habits, the dominant passions, everything that in the end composes what we call national character. There we would come upon the explanation for customs that today appear contrary to the reigning mores, laws that seem to be in opposition to accepted principles, and opinions without coherence that one comes upon here and there in society, like those fragments of broken supports that one sometimes sees hanging from the vaults of an old edifice and which no longer support anything. In this way, we would explain the fate of certain peoples whom an unknown force seems to draw toward a goal of which they themselves are unaware. But up to now the facts were lacking for such a study; the spirit of analysis came to nations only when they grew older, and when they finally thought to contemplate their beginnings, time had already enveloped them in a cloud, and ignorance and pride had surrounded them with fables, behind which the truth was hidden.

America is the only country where one could witness the natural and calm development of a society, and where it was possible to describe precisely the influence exercised by the point of departure on the future of States.

At the time when the European peoples descended upon the shores of the New World, the traits of their national characters were already well fixed; each of them had a distinct physiognomy; and since they had already arrived at that degree of civilization that leads men to study themselves, they transmitted to us a faithful picture of their opinions, their mores, and their laws. The men of the 15th century are almost as well known to us as those of our own. America thus shows us in broad daylight what the ignorance or barbarism of the first ages hid from our eyes.

Close enough to the epoch when the American societies were founded to be able to know in detail their first elements, but far enough removed from this time to be able to judge what these seeds have produced, the men of our day seem destined to see further into human events than their predecessors. Providence has placed in our hands a light that our fathers lacked and has allowed us to discern, in the fate of nations, the first causes that the obscurity of the past hid from them.

When, after having studied attentively the history of America, its political and social state is examined with care, one feels profoundly convinced of this truth: that there is not an opinion, not a habit, not a law, I might say not an occurrence, that the point of departure does not ex- [28] plain without difficulty. Those who read this book will thus find in the present chapter the germ of what follows and the key to almost the whole work.

The emigrants who came, at different periods, to occupy the territory that today covers the American Union, differed from each other in many respects; their goals were not the same, and they governed themselves according to different principles.

These men, however, had between them some common traits, and they all found themselves in a similar situation.

The tie of language is perhaps the strongest and most durable that can unite men. All the emigrants spoke the same language; they were all children of a single people. Born in a country agitated for centuries by party conflict, and where the factions had been obliged, each in their turn, to place themselves under the protection of the laws, their political education occurred in this rough school, and one saw spread among them more notions of rights and more principles of true liberty than among most of the peoples of Europe. At the time of the first emigrations, municipal government, that fertile germ of free institutions, had already penetrated deeply into English habits, and with it the dogma of the sovereignty of the people had been introduced into the very heart of Tudor monarchy.

At that time, Europe was in the midst of the religious conflicts that shook the Christian world. England had rushed with a sort of fury into this new course. The character of the inhabitants, which had always been solemn and thoughtful, had become austere and argumentative.

Education had increased greatly during these intellectual conflicts; in them, the mind had received a more profound culture. While the nation had been busy talking about religion, morals had become purer. All of these general traits of the nation reappeared, more or less, in the physiognomy of those of its sons who had come to search for a new future on the opposite shore of the ocean.

One additional observation, to which we will have occasion to return later, is not only applicable to the English, but also to the French, the Spanish, and all the Europeans who came to settle successively on the shores of the New World. All the new European colonies contained, if not the development, at least the germ of a complete democracy. Two causes led to this result: one can say that, in general, on departing the mother country, the emigrants had no idea of any superiority whatsoever of some of them over the others. It was scarcely the fortunate and powerful who emigrated, and poverty as well as misfortune are the best guarantees of equality that we know of among men. On several occasions, however, it happened that some great lords went to America as a result of political or religious conflicts. They made laws there in order to establish the hierarchy of ranks, but it was soon evident that American soil absolutely rejected territorial aristocracy. It was obvious that in order to clear this wild terrain, nothing less was needed than the constant and involved efforts of the proprietor himself. After the ground was prepared, it was found that its products were in no way great enough to enrich at the same time a master and a tenant farmer. Thus the terrain was broken up naturally into small domains that the proprietor cultivated alone. Now, it is the land which interests aristocracy; it is the soil to which it is attached and on which it leans for support. It is not privileges alone that establish it, it is not birth which constitutes it, but property in land transmitted by inheritance. A nation may present immense fortunes and great misery; but if the fortunes are not based on land, although poor and rich are to be seen in it, there is not, in truth, aristocracy.

[29]

All the English colonies therefore shared, at the time of their birth, a great family resemblance. All, from their beginnings, seemed destined to offer the spectacle of the development of liberty: not the aristocratic liberty of their mother country, but the bourgeois and democratic liberty of which the history of the world had not yet revealed a complete model.

In the midst of this general resemblance, however, some very strong shades of difference were visible, which it is necessary to point out.

In the great Anglo-American family two principal branches can be distinguished that, up to the present, have spread without merging entirely, one in the South, the other in the North.

Virginia received the first English colony. Emigrants arrived there in 1607. Europe, at this time, was still singularly preoccupied with the idea that gold and silver mines consituted the riches of peoples: a disastrous idea that has done more to impoverish the European nations that have abandoned themselves to it, and destroyed more men in America, than war and all bad laws together. It was thus gold seekers who were sent to Virginia,[1] men without resources and manners, whose restless and turbulent spirit troubled the infancy of the colony[2] and made its progress uncertain. Then manufacturers and farmers arrived, a more moral and [30] calmer race, but in almost no respect did it stand higher than the inferior classes of England.[3] No noble thought, no spiritual system governed the founding of the new establishments. Scarcely had the colony been created when slavery was introduced;[4] this was the crucial fact that would exercise an immense influence on the character, the laws, and the whole future of the South.

Slavery, as we will explain later, dishonors work; it introduces idleness into the society, and with it ignorance and pride, poverty and luxury. It enervates the powers of intelligence and weakens human activity. The influence of slavery, combined with the English character, explains the mores and the social state of the South.

On this same English background, the North manifested completely opposite characteristics. Here, I will be permitted some details.

---

1. The charter granted by the English crown in 1609 contained among other clauses one according to which the colonists would pay the crown one-fifth of the product of the gold and silver mines. See *The Life of Washington,* by Marshall, vol. 1, pp. 18–66.

2. A large portion of the new colonists, says Stith (*History of Virginia*), were disordered young men from good families, whom their parents had had shipped out in order to protect them from an ignominious fate. Former domestics, men who had committed fraud in the process of going bankrupt, debauched persons, and others of this ilk, who were more fit to pillage and destroy than consolidate the establishment of the colony, made up the rest. Seditious leaders easily carried this troop off into all sorts of extravagances and excesses. See, relative to the history of Virginia, the works that follow:

History of Virginia from the first Settlements to the year 1624, by Smith.

History of Virginia, by William Stith.

History of Virginia from the earliest period by Beverly, translated into French in 1807.

3. It was only later that a certain number of rich English landowners came to settle in the colony.

4. Slavery was introduced around the year 1620 by a Dutch vessel that disembarked 20 Negroes upon the banks of the James river. See Chalmer.

It is in the English colonies of the North, better known as the New England States,[5] that the two or three principal ideas were combined which today form the bases of the social theory of the United States.

The principles of New England first spread into the neighboring States; they then gradually spread to the States farthest away, and they ended, if I can thus express myself, by *penetrating* the entire confederation. They now exert their influence beyond its limits, over the whole American world. The civilization of New England was like those fires set on high slopes that, after having spread heat around themselves, still tint the outer limits of the horizon with their light.

[31]   The founding of New England offered a new spectacle; everything there was singular and original.

The first inhabitants of almost all the colonies were men without education and resources, whom poverty and misconduct had forced out of the countries in which they were born, or greedy speculators and entrepreneurs of industry. There are some colonies that cannot even claim this kind of origin: Santo Domingo was founded by pirates, and the courts of justice in England have assumed responsibility for populating Australia.

The emigrants who came to establish themselves on the shores of New England all belonged to the prosperous classes[*] of the mother country. Their being brought together on American soil presented, from the outset, the singular phenomenon of a society without either great lords or a lower class, and without, so to speak, poor or rich. There was proportionately more enlightenment spread among these men than in any other European nation of our day. All, perhaps without a single exception, had received a fairly advanced education, and several of them had become known in Europe for their talents and their learning. The other colonies had been founded by adventurers without families. The New England emigrants brought with them admirable elements of order and morality; they went into the wilderness with their wives and their children. But what distinguished them above all from all of the others was the very aim of their enterprise. It was not necessity which forced them to abandon their country: they left behind there a social position whose loss they might have regretted and assured means of living. Nor did they go into the New World in order to improve their

---

5. The New England States are those situated east of the Hudson: today they number six:

1° Connecticut, 2° Rhode-Island, 3° Massachusetts, 4° Vermont, 5° New-Hampshire, 6° Maine.

* The words translated as "prosperous classes" are *les classes aisées,* which are the classes that are prosperous or comfortably well-off without being rich.

situation or increase their riches: they tore themselves away from the sweet pleasures of the fatherland in order to obey a purely intellectual need; in exposing themselves to the inevitable miseries of exile, they wanted to bring about the triumph of *an idea.*

The emigrants, or as they so well called themselves, the *pilgrims,* belonged to that sect in England, the austerity of whose principles had caused it to be given the name of Puritan. Puritanism was not only a religious doctrine; it also merged at several points with the most absolute democratic and republican theories. From this it acquired its most dangerous adversaries. Persecuted by the government of the mother country, the rigor of their principles offended by the daily course of the society in whose midst they were living, the Puritans sought a land so barbaric and so deserted that they could live there in their own way, and there pray to God in liberty.

Some quotations will make better understood the spirit of these pious adventurers than anything that we might add ourselves.   [32]

Nathaniel Morton, the historian of the first years of New England, introduces the subject in this way:[6] "I have always believed," he says, "that it was a sacred duty for us, whose fathers received such numerous and memorable proofs of divine goodness in the establishing of this colony, to perpetuate its memory in writing. What we have seen and what was told to us by our fathers, we must make known to our children, so that the generations to come will learn to praise the Lord; so that the line of Abraham His servant and the sons of Jacob His chosen always keep the memory of the miraculous works of God (*Psalm* CV, 5, 6). They must know how the Lord brought His vine into the desert; how He planted it and drove the heathens away from it; how He prepared a place for it, sunk its roots deeply and then let it spread and cover the land far and wide (*Psalm* LXXX, 13, 15); and not only that, but also how He guided His people toward His holy tabernacle, and established it on the mountain of His heritage (*Exodus,* XV, 13). These facts must be known, so that God may obtain from them the honor that is due to Him, and so that some rays of His glory may fall on the venerable names of the saints who served as His instruments."

It is impossible to read this beginning without being penetrated despite oneself by a religious and solemn impression; one seems to inhale there an antique air and a kind of biblical fragrance.

The conviction that animates the writer elevates his language. To our eyes, as to his, this is no longer a small troop of adventurers going to

---

6. *New England's Memorial* (Boston, 1826), p. 14. See also the *History* of Hutchinson, vol. II, p. 440.

seek their fortune beyond the seas; it is the seed of a great people whom God comes to put down with His own hands onto a predestined land.

The author continues and depicts the departure of the first emigrants in this way:[7]

"It is thus," he says, "they left this city (Delft Haven) which had been for them a resting-place; however they were calm; they knew that they were pilgrims and strangers here below; they were not attached to earthly things, but raised their eyes toward heaven, their dear fatherland, where God had prepared for them His holy city. They arrived finally at the port where the vessel awaited them. A great number of friends who could not depart with them had wanted to follow them at least up to that point. The night passed without sleep; it was passed in outpourings of

[33] friendship, in pious discourse, in expressions full of a true Christian tenderness. The next day they went on board; their friends still wished to go with them there; it was then that profound sighs were heard, that tears were seen to flow from all eyes, that long hugging and kissing and ardent prayers were heard that made strangers themselves feel moved. The signal to depart being given, they fell on their knees, and their pastor, raising to heaven eyes filled with tears, commended them to the mercy of the Lord. Finally they took leave of one another, and said a goodbye which, for many of them, would be their last."

The emigrants were around one hundred fifty in number, including women and children as well as men. Their aim was to found a colony on the banks of the Hudson, but, after having wandered for a long time on the ocean, they were finally forced to land on the barren coasts of New England, at the spot where the city of Plymouth now stands. The rock upon which the pilgrims descended is still pointed out.[8]

"But before going further," says the historian whom I have just quoted, "let us consider for a moment the immediate condition of this poor people, and admire the goodness of God who saved them."[9]

"They had now crossed the vast Ocean, they arrived at the end of their voyage, but they saw no friends to welcome them, no habitation to

---

7. *New England's Memorial*, p. 22.

8. This rock has become an object of veneration in the United States. I have seen fragments of it carefully conserved in several cities of the Union. Does this not show very clearly that the power and greatness of man is entirely in his soul? Here is a stone that the feet of some wretched people touched for an instant, and this stone becomes celebrated; it attracts the gaze of a great people; its debris is venerated, its dust shared out far and wide. What has become of the thresholds of as many palaces? Who cares about them?

9. *New England's Memorial*, p. 35.

offer them shelter; it was the middle of winter; and those who know our climate know how rough are the winters, and what furious storms then ravage our coasts. During this season, it is difficult to traverse familiar terrains, and even more to establish oneself on new shores. About them appeared only a hideous and desolate wilderness, full of animals and savage men, of whose ferocity and number they were ignorant. The earth was frozen; the soil was covered with forests and bush. The whole had a barbaric aspect. Behind them, they saw only the immense Ocean which separated them from the civilized world. In order to find a bit of peace and hope, they could only turn their gaze to heaven."

One must not believe that the piety of the Puritans was only specula- [34] tive, nor that it had nothing to do with the course of human affairs. Puritanism, as I said above, was almost as much a political theory as a religious doctrine. Scarcely disembarked upon this inhospitable shore, which Nathaniel Morton just described, the emigrants' first concern is thus to organize themselves into a society. They pass immediately an act which holds:[10]

"We, whose names follow, who, for the glory of God, the development of the Christian faith and the honor of our fatherland, have undertaken to establish the first colony on these distant shores, we agree by this present act, by mutual and solemn consent, and before God, to form ourselves into the body of a political society, with the aim of governing ourselves and of working to accomplish our goals; and by virtue of this contract, we agree to promulgate laws, acts, ordinances, and to choose, as needed, magistrates to whom we promise submission and obedience."

This occurred in 1620. From that time on, emigration continued without letup. The religious and political passions that tore apart the English Empire during the whole reign of Charles the First each year pushed new swarms of sectarians onto the shores of America. In England, the focal point of Puritanism continued to be found among the middle classes; most of the emigrants came from the heart of the middle classes. The population of New England grew rapidly, and while the hierarchy of ranks still dictatorially classified men in the mother country, the colony presented more and more the new spectacle of a society homogeneous in all its parts. Democracy, such as antiquity had not dared

---

10. The emigrants who created the state of Rhode Island in 1638, those who established themselves at New Haven in 1637, the first inhabitants of Connecticut in 1639, and the founders of Providence in 1640, all began by drawing up a social contract that was submitted to the approval of all the interested parties. *Pitkin's History*, p. 42 and 47.

to dream of, broke away from the midst of the old feudal society completely grown and fully armed.

Happy to rid itself of the seeds of troubles and the elements of new revolutions, the English government observed this huge emigration without concern. It even furthered it with all its power and seemed scarcely concerned with the destiny of those who came to American soil to seek a refuge from the harshness of the government's laws. It seemed that [the English government] regarded New England as a region given over to dreams of the imagination and one that should be abandoned to the free experiments of innovators.

[35]   The English colonies, and this was one of the principal causes of their prosperity, always enjoyed more internal liberty and more political independence than the colonies of other peoples, but nowhere was this principle of liberty more completely applied than in the States of New England.

It was then generally admitted that the lands of the New World belonged to the European nation that had first discovered them.

In this way, almost the whole coast of North America became an English possession toward the end of the 16th century. The means employed by the English government to populate the new lands were diverse: in certain cases, the King put a portion of the New World under a governor of his choice, charged with administering the country in [the King's] name and under his immediate orders;[11] this was the colonial system adopted by the rest of Europe. Other times, he granted to a man or to a company the ownership of certain portions of country.[12] All the civil and political powers were thus concentrated in the hands of one or several individuals who, under the supervision and control of the crown, sold the lands and governed the inhabitants. Finally, a third system consisted of giving to a certain number of emigrants the right to form themselves into a political society, under the patronage of the mother country, and to govern themselves in all that was not contrary to [the latter's] laws.

This mode of colonization, so favorable to liberty, was put into practice only in New England.[13]

---

11. This was the case in the state of New York.

12. Maryland, the Carolinas, Pennsylvania, New Jersey were of this type. See *Pitkin's History*, vol. 1, pp. 11–31.

13. See in the work entitled: *Historical collection of state papers and other authentic documents intended as materials for an history of the United States of America, by Ebenezer Hasard, printed at Philadelphia MDCCXCII*, a great number of documents precious for their content and their authenticity, relating to the first period of the colonies, including the different charters that were granted

In 1628,[14] a charter of this nature was given by Charles the First to [36] some emigrants who came to found the colony of Massachusetts.

But in general, charters were not granted to the colonies of New England until a long time after their existence had become a *fait accompli*.* Plymouth, Providence, New Haven, the State of Connecticut, and that of Rhode Island[15] were founded without the aid and in a sense without the knowledge of the mother country. The new inhabitants, without denying the supremacy of the mother country, did not go and draw from it the source of their powers; they made constitutions for themselves, and it was only thirty or forty years afterward, under Charles the Second, that a royal charter made their existence legal.

It is therefore often difficult, when one scans the first historical and legislative works of New England, to perceive the link which attaches the emigrants to the country of their ancestors. One sees them at each moment performing an act of sovereignty: they appoint their magistrates, make peace and war, make regulations to enforce public order, give themselves laws as if they came under the jurisdiction of God alone.[16]

There is nothing at once more remarkable and more instructive than the legislation of this period; it is there above all that one finds the key to the great social enigma that the United States presents to the world of our day.

Among these works, we will single out particularly, as one of the

---

to them by the crown of England, as well as the first acts of their governments.

See equally the analysis of all these charters done by M. Story, Justice of the Supreme Court of the United States, in the introduction to his *Commentaries on the Constitution of the United States.*

It emerges from all these documents that the principles of representative government and the external forms of political liberty were introduced into all the colonies almost from their birth. These principles had received greater development in the North than in the South, but they existed everywhere.

14. See Pitkin's History, p. 35, t. I. See The History of the colony of Massachusetts, by Hutchinson, vol. 1, p. 9.

* The French expression *fait accompli* ("an accomplished fact") retains its French meaning in English usage: a fact or deed that has been accomplished and cannot be revoked; an act accomplished without prior consultation.

15. See id., pp. 42–47.

16. The inhabitants of Massachusetts, in establishing the criminal and civil laws and the procedures and courts of justice, departed from the practices followed in England: in 1650, the name of the king no longer appeared at the head of judicial warrants. See Hutchinson, vol. 1, p. 452.

most characteristic, the code of laws that the small state of Connecticut
gave itself in 1650.[17]

The legislators of Connecticut[18] dealt first with the penal laws, and to
compose them, they conceived the strange idea of drawing from the sacred texts:

"Whosoever worships a God other than the Lord," they begin by saying, "will be put to death."

Ten or twelve measures follow of the same nature, borrowed textual-
ly from *Deuteronomy, Exodus,* and *Leviticus.*

[37]   Blasphemy, witchcraft, adultery,[19] and rape are punished with death;
the same penalty is applied to an affront by a son against his parents.
The legislation of a coarse and half-civilized people was thus transport-
ed into the midst of a society of enlightened minds and mild mores; in
consequence, the penalty of death has never been more prevalent in the
laws or applied to fewer guilty persons.

The legislators, in this body of penal laws, are concerned above all
with the care to maintain moral order and good morals in the society;
thus they are constantly invading the domain of the conscience; there are
almost no sins that they do not end up subjecting to the censure of the
magistrate. The reader has seen with what severity these laws punished
adultery and rape. Simply keeping company, between those who were
unmarried, was severely punished. The judge was left the discretion to
impose upon the guilty parties one of three penalties: a fine, whipping,
or marriage;[20] and, if we are to believe the records of the old tribunals of

---

17. Code of 1650 (Hartford, 1830), p. 28.

18. See equally in the *History* of Hutchinson, vol. 1, pp. 435–56, the analysis of
the penal code adopted in 1648 by the colony of Massachusetts; this code was
drawn up on principles analogous to those of Connecticut.

19. Adultery was likewise punished by death in the law of Massachusetts, and
Hutchinson (vol. 1, p. 441) says that several persons in fact suffered death for
this crime; he cites in this regard a curious anecdote from the year 1663. A married woman had had amorous relations with a young man; she was widowed,
and she married him; several years passed: the public finally having come to
suspect the intimacy which had hitherto prevailed between them, they were subject to a criminal prosecution; they were put into prison, and both of them just
escaped being condemned to death.

20. Code of 1650, p. 48.

It happened, as it appears, that sometimes the judges pronounced these several penalties cumulatively, as one sees in a judgment rendered in 1643 (*New
Haven Antiquities,* p. 114), which holds that Marguerite Bedfort, convicted of
having committed reprehensible acts, will suffer the penalty of being whipped
and that she will be enjoined to marry with Nicolas Jemmings, her accomplice.

New Haven, proceedings of this sort were not rare; one finds, on May 1st, 1660, a judgment bearing a fine and a reprimand against a young woman accused of having uttered some indiscreet words and of having allowed herself to be kissed.[21] The Code of 1650 abounds with preventive measures. Indolence and drunkenness are severely punished in it.[22] Innkeepers may not give more than a certain quantity of wine to each consumer; a fine or whipping punishes a simple lie when it has the potential to harm.[23] In other places, the legislator, completely forgetting the grand principles of religious liberty which he himself claimed in Europe, coerces, by threat of a fine, attendance at religious services,[24] and he goes so far as to punish with severe penalties,[25] and often with death, [38] Christians who want to worship God in a different way than his own.[26] Finally, sometimes the passion to regulate that possesses him leads him to occupy himself with concerns that are most unworthy of him. It is thus that one finds in the same code a law prohibiting the use of tobacco.[27] One must not, furthermore, lose sight of the fact that these bizarre or tyrannical laws were not imposed, they were passed by means of the free, active participation of all of the interested parties themselves, and that the morals were even more austere and puritan than the laws. In 1649, one sees a solemn association form in Boston with the aim of preventing the worldly luxury of long hair.[28]

Such deviations shame the human spirit; they attest to the inferiority

---

21. *New Haven Antiquities*, p. 104. See also, in the *History* of Hutchinson, vol. 1, p. 435, several judgments as extraordinary as that one.

22. *Id.,* 1650, p. 50, 57.

23. *Id.,* p. 64.

24. *Id.,* p. 44.

25. This was not peculiar to Connecticut. See among others the law passed on September 13, 1644, in Massachusetts, which condemned the Anabaptists to banishment. *Historical Collection of State Papers*, vol. 1, p. 538. See also the law published October 14, 1656, against the Quakers: "Whereas," says the law, "that an accursed sect of heretics called Quakers has just arisen . . ." Measures follow which punish with a very heavy fine the captains of vessels which bring Quakers into the country. The Quakers who succeed in entering are whipped and shut up in a prison in order to labor there. Those who defend their opinions are first given a fine, then condemned to prison and driven out of the province. Same collection, vol. 1, p. 630.

26. In the penal law of Massachusetts, the Catholic priest who sets foot in the colony after having been driven out of it is punished with death.

27. Code of 1650, p. 96.

28. *New England's Memorial*, p. 316.

of our nature which, incapable of firmly grasping the true and the just, is reduced most often to choosing only between two excesses.

Alongside this penal legislation, so strongly marked by the narrow spirit of the sect and by all the religious passions that persecution had stirred up and that were still in ferment at the bottom of souls, is found situated, and in a way linked together with them, a body of political laws which, written two hundred years ago, still seems very far in advance of the spirit of liberty of our age.

The general principles upon which modern constitutions rest, those principles which most Europeans of the 17th century barely comprehended and which were then only incompletely triumphant in Great Britain, are all recognized and defined by the laws of New England: the intervention of the people in public affairs, the free voting on taxes, the accountability of the agents of power, individual liberty, and judgment by a jury are all established there without argument and in fact.

[39]   These generative principles receive there an application and development that no nation of Europe has yet dared to give to them.

In Connecticut, the electoral body was composed, from the beginning, of all the citizens, which is easy to understand.[29] Among this nascent people there then prevailed an almost perfect equality of wealth and, to an even greater degree, of knowledge.[30]

In Connecticut, at this time, all of the agents of executive power were elected, up to and including the governor of the state.[31]

Citizens above sixteen years of age were obliged to bear arms; they formed a national militia that elected its own officers and had to be ready at any time to come to the defense of the country.[32]

It is in the laws of Connecticut, as in all those of New England, that one sees come into being and develop the municipal independence which still today constitutes the principle and the life of American liberty.

In most of the European nations, political life began in the regions superior to the society and was communicated, little by little and always in an incomplete manner, to the different parts of the social body.

In America, on the contrary, one can say that the township was orga-

---

29. Constitution of 1638, p. 17.

30. From 1641, the General Assembly of Rhode Island unanimously declared that the government of the State was a democracy and that power rested upon the body of free men, who alone had the right to make laws and to exercise oversight of their execution. Code of 1650, p. 70.

31. *Pitkin's History*, p. 47.

32. Constitution of 1638, p. 12.

nized before the county, the county before the State, the State before the Union.

In New England, by 1650, the township is completely and definitively constituted. Interests, passions, duties, and rights group themselves around the individual township and attach themselves strongly to it. In the heart of the township one sees a political life reign that is real, active, entirely democratic, and republican. The colonies still recognize the supremacy of the mother country; it is monarchy which is the law of the State, but already republicanism is living fully within the township.

The township selects magistrates of every kind; it taxes itself; it allocates and collects these taxes itself.[33] In the township of New England, the law of representation is not accepted. It is in public and in the general [40] assembly of citizens that one deals, as at Athens, with the affairs that touch the interest of all.

When one studies attentively the laws which were promulgated during this first age of the American republics, one is struck by the legislator's knowledge of government and the theories advanced by him.

It is obvious that he forms an idea of the obligations of the society toward its members that is more elevated and more complete than that of the European legislators of that time and that he imposes upon society obligations from which it is still exempt elsewhere. In the States of New England, from the beginning, the condition of the poor is provided for;[34] strict measures are taken for the maintenance of the roads, and officials are appointed to oversee them;[35] the townships have public registers where the result of general deliberations, deaths, marriages, and the births of citizens are written down;[36] clerks are assigned to maintain these registers;[37] officers are charged with the administration of successions lacking claimants, and others with oversight of the boundaries of inherited property; several have for their principal functions the maintenance of public tranquility in the township.[38]

The law enters into a thousand different details in order to anticipate and satisfy a host of social needs, about which we have still today only a confused idea in France.

But it is in the prescriptions relating to public education that, from its

---

33. Code of 1650, p. 80.

34. Code of 1650, p. 78.

35. *Id.,* p. 49.

36. See the *History* of Hutchinson, vol. 1, p. 455.

37. Code of 1650, p. 86.

38. *Id.,* p. 40.

first principle, one sees revealed in its full light the original character of American civilization.

"Whereas," the law says, "Satan, the enemy of human kind, finds his most powerful weapons in the ignorance of men, and it is important that the enlightenment given by our forefathers not remain buried in their tomb;—whereas the education of children is one of the first interests of the State, with the help of the Lord . . ."[39] Measures follow which create schools in all the townships, and force the inhabitants, on pain of heavy fines, to obligate themselves to support them. Advanced schools are founded in the same manner in the most populous districts. The municipal magistrates must see to it that the parents send their children to school; they have the right to impose fines upon those who refuse; and if [41] resistance continues, the society, which then puts itself in the place of the family, takes hold of the child and removes from the fathers the rights which nature had given them, but which they have exercised so badly.[40] The reader will have no doubt noticed the preamble to these ordinances: in America, it is religion which leads the way to enlightenment; it is the observance of divine laws which leads man to liberty.

When, after having thus glanced rapidly at the American society of 1650, one examines the state of Europe and particularly that of the continent around this same time, one feels penetrated by profound amazement: everywhere on the continent of Europe, at the beginning of the 17th century, absolute monarchy stood triumphant over the debris of the oligarchic and feudal liberty of the Middle Ages. In the heart of this brilliant and literary Europe, the idea of rights had never perhaps been more completely unrecognized; the peoples had never had less experience of political life; the notions of true liberty had never been less on men's minds; and it was then that these same principles, unknown to the European nations or despised by them, were proclaimed in the wilderness of the New World and became the future symbol of a great people. In this society, so modest in appearance, the most daring theories of the human mind, with which no statesman of that time had deigned to concern himself, were put into practice; left to the originality of his nature, the imagination of man improvised there a set of laws without precedent. In the heart of this obscure democracy which had not yet given birth either to generals or philosophers or great writers, a man could stand up in the presence of a free people and give, to the acclamation of all, this beautiful definition of liberty:

39. Code of 1650, p. 90.
40. Code of 1650, p. 83.

"Let us make no mistake about what we must mean by our indepen-dence. There is in fact a sort of corrupt liberty, common to animals as well as to man, which consists in doing whatever one pleases. This liber-ty is the enemy of all authority; it suffers all rules impatiently; with it, we become inferior to ourselves; it is the enemy of truth and peace; and God believed He had to combat it! But there is a civil and moral liberty which finds its strength in union, and which it is the mission of power it-self to protect: this is the liberty to do without fear all that is just and good. We must defend this sacred liberty against all hazards, and if nec-essary risk our lives for it."[41]

I have already said enough to place the character of Anglo-American [42] civilization in its true light. It is the product (and this point of departure must always be present in our thought) of two elements which are per-fectly distinct, which are in addition often at war with one other, but which, in America, have been in some way successfully incorporated in one another, and wonderfully combined. I mean to speak of *the spirit of religion* and *the spirit of liberty*.

The founders of New England were at one and the same time fierce sectarians and passionate innovators. Held within the narrowest bonds of certain religious beliefs, they were free of all political prejudices.

From this came two different but not contrary tendencies whose traces are easy to find everywhere, in mores as well as in laws.

Some men sacrifice their friends, their family, and their country to a religious opinion; one might think them absorbed in the pursuit of this intellectual good that they have come to purchase at so high a price. However, one sees them seek material wealth and moral pleasure with almost equal fervor; heaven in the other world, and material well-being and liberty in this one.

In their hands, political principles, laws, and human institutions seem malleable things which can be bent and combined at will.

Before them the barriers fall which imprisoned the society in the bo-som of which they were born; the old opinions which for centuries gov-erned the world vanish. A course almost without limits, a field without a horizon, open up before them: the human mind rushes forward into them; it searches through them in all directions; but, arriving at the lim-its of the political world, it stops of itself; trembling, it puts away the use

---

41. Mather's *Magnalia Christi Americana*, vol. II, p. 13.

  This speech was made by Winthrop; he was accused of having committed arbitrary acts as a magistrate; after having made the speech of which I have just quoted a portion, he was acquitted with applause, and from then on he was al-ways reelected governor of the State. See Marshall, vol. 1, p. 166.

of its most formidable faculties; it abjures doubt; it renounces the need
to innovate; it abstains even from lifting the veil from the sanctuary; it
bows with respect before truths which it accepts without discussion.

Thus, in the moral world, everything is classified, coordinated, anticipated, decided in advance. In the political world, everything is agitated,
contested, uncertain; in the one, passive obedience, although voluntary;
in the other, independence, contempt for experience, and jealousy of all
authority.

Far from damaging each other, these two tendencies, so opposite in
appearance, work together in harmony and seem to lend mutual support
to one another.

[43]   Religion sees in civil liberty a noble exercise of the faculties of man;
it sees in the political world a field freed up by the Creator for the efforts
of the intellect. Free and powerful in its sphere, satisfied with the place
that is reserved for it, it knows that its empire is established all the better
because it reigns only by its own strength and dominates the hearts of
men without help.

Liberty sees in religion the companion of its struggles and its triumphs, the cradle of its infancy, the divine source of its rights. It considers religion as the safeguard of mores, and mores as the guarantee of the
laws and of its own durability.

The Reasons for Some Peculiarities Presented by
the Laws and the Customs of the Anglo-Americans

*Some residues of aristocratic institutions in the midst of the most
complete democracy.—Why?—One must distinguish with care
what is Puritan in origin and what is English in origin.*

The reader must not draw conclusions that are too general and too absolute from the foregoing. The social condition, the religion, and the mores
of the first emigrants exercised without doubt an immense influence on
the fate of their new country. However, it was not in their power to found
a society whose point of departure was located only within themselves;
no one can disengage himself entirely from the past; and it happened
that, sometimes intentionally, sometimes unwittingly, they mixed together with ideas and practices that were their own, other ideas that they held
because of their education or the national traditions of their country.

When one wants to understand and judge the Anglo-Americans of
our day, one must therefore distinguish with care what is Puritan in origin or English in origin.

One often comes across laws or customs in the United States that contrast with all that surrounds them. These laws seem drawn up in a spirit opposite to the dominant spirit of American legislation; those mores seem contrary to the whole of the social state. If the English colonies had been founded in an obscure century, or if their origin were already lost in the dark night of time, the problem would be insoluble.

I will cite a single example to make my thought understood.

The civil and criminal legislation of the Americans knows only two means of action: *imprisonment* or *bail*. The first act of a legal process [44] consists of obtaining bail from the defendant, or, if he refuses, imprisoning him; afterward one debates the validity of the warrant or the gravity of the charges.

It is obvious that such legislation is directed against the poor and favors only the rich.

The poor man cannot always make bail, even in a civil matter, and, if he is constrained to go and await justice in prison, his forced inaction soon reduces him to destitution.

The rich man, on the contrary, always succeeds in escaping imprisonment in civil matters; even more, if he commits a crime, he easily evades the punishment which ought to be his: after giving bail, he disappears. One can thus say that for him all the penalties that the law inflicts are reduced to fines.[42] What is more aristocratic than such legislation?

In America, however, it is the poor who make the law, and they habitually reserve for themselves the greatest benefits of the society.

It is in England that one must look for the explanation of this phenomenon: the laws I am talking about are English.[43] The Americans did not change them, although they are repugnant to the body of their legislation and to the bulk of their ideas.

The thing a people changes least, after its customary practices, is its civil legislation. The civil laws are only familiar to the lawyers, that is to say, to those who have a direct interest in maintaining them just as they are, good or bad, because they know them. The great body of the nation is scarcely acquainted with them; it sees them in action only in particular cases, understands their tendency only with difficulty, and submits to them unthinkingly.

I have cited one example, but I could have pointed out many others.

The picture presented by American society is, if I can express myself in this way, covered with a democratic layer, under which one sees show through from time to time the ancient colors of aristocracy.

---

42. There are without doubt some crimes for which there is no bail, but they are very few in number.

43. See Blackstone and Delolme, book 1, chap. x.

CHAPTER 3

THE SOCIAL STATE OF THE ANGLO-AMERICANS

The social state is ordinarily the product of a fact, sometimes of laws,
most often of these two causes combined; but once it exists, one may
consider it as itself the first cause of most of the laws, customs, and
ideas which govern the conduct of nations; what it does not produce, it
modifies.

In order to understand the legislation and the mores of a people, it is
therefore necessary to begin by studying its social state.

That the Outstanding Feature of the Social State of the Anglo-Americans Is to Be Essentially Democratic

First emigrants to New England.—Equal among themselves.—
Aristocratic laws introduced in the South. Period of the
Revolution.—Change in the laws of inheritance.—Effects
produced by this change.—Equality pushed to its ultimate
limits in the new States of the West.—Equality of intellect.

One could make several important remarks about the social state of the
Anglo-Americans, but there is one of them that dominates all of the
others.

The social state of the Americans is eminently democratic. It has had
this character since the birth of the colonies; it has it still more in our day.

I said in the preceding chapter that a very great equality prevailed
among the emigrants who came to establish themselves on the shores
of New England. Even the germ of aristocracy was never planted in
[46] this part of the Union. All that could ever be established there were intellectual influences. The people acquired the habit of revering certain
names as symbols of enlightenment and virtue. The voice of some citizens acquired a power over the people that could reasonably have been
called aristocratic, if it could have been transmitted invariably from father to son.

This happened east of the Hudson; to the southwest of this river, and
descending all the way to Florida, it was different.

In most of the States located to the southwest of the Hudson, great
English landowners had come to settle. Aristocratic principles, and with
them English laws of inheritance, had been imported there. I have described the causes which prevented a powerful aristocracy in America
from ever being established. These causes, while they did exist to the

southwest of the Hudson, had, however, less power there than they did
to the east of this river. In the South, one man alone could, with the help
of slaves, cultivate a great extent of land. There were thus rich landowners in this part of the continent; but their influence was not precisely
aristocratic, as it is understood in Europe, since they possessed no privileges, and since cultivation by slaves gave them no tenant farmers, and
consequently no patronage. Nevertheless, the great landowners, south
of the Hudson, formed a superior class, with its own ideas and tastes,
and in general concentrating political activity within itself. This was a
sort of aristocracy little different from the mass of the people whose
passions and interests it easily embraced, and exciting neither love nor
hate; in sum, weak and not very durable. It was this class which, in the
South, placed itself at the head of the insurrection: the American Revolution owes it its greatest men.

At this time, the society in its entirety was shaken: the people, in
whose name one had fought, the people, having become a power, conceived the desire to act itself; its democratic instincts were awakened; by
breaking the yoke of the mother country, one acquired a taste for every
kind of independence: individual influences ceased little by little to
make themselves felt; habits as well as laws began to march in concert
toward the same goal.

But it was the law of inheritance which caused equality to take its ultimate step.

I am astonished that the public law experts, ancient and modern, have
not attributed to the laws of inheritance[1] a greater influence in the course [47]
of human affairs. These laws, it is true, are civil in nature, but they ought
to be placed at the head of all the political institutions because they have
an incredible influence on the social state of peoples, of which the political laws are only the expression. They have, in addition, a certain and
uniform manner of operating on the society; in a way, they take hold of
generations before their birth. Through them, man is armed with an almost divine power over the future of his fellow men. The legislator establishes, once, a rule for the citizens' inheritances, and he rests for

1. I mean by the laws of inheritance all the laws whose principal goal is to settle the disposition of property after the death of the owner.

The law of entail is one of these; it also has the result, it is true, of preventing the proprietor from disposing of his property before his death; but it imposes
on him the obligation to conserve his property only with a view to passing it on
intact to his heir. The principal goal of the law of entail is therefore to settle the
disposition of property after the death of the proprietor. The rest is the means
that it employs.

centuries: once movement is imparted to his work, he can withdraw his hand from it; the machine acts through its own forces and heads as if by itself toward a goal indicated in advance. Constituted in a certain manner, it combines, it concentrates, it groups around some head, property, and soon afterwards power; in a way, it causes landed aristocracy to spring forth from the soil. Governed by other principles, and launched in another direction, its action is still more rapid; it divides, it shares out, it scatters property and power. It then sometimes happens that people take fright at the rapidity of its march: despairing of stopping its movement, they try at least to put difficulties and obstacles in front of it; they want to counterbalance its action by contrary efforts. Futile efforts! It grinds up or explodes everything that is encountered in its passage; it rises and falls unceasingly on the ground, until nothing is any longer visible except a shifting and impalpable dust, upon which sits democracy.

When the law of inheritance permits, and even more when it orders the equal division of the property of the father among all the children, its effects are of two sorts; it is important to distinguish them, although they tend to the same end.

By virtue of the law of inheritance, the death of each proprietor brings a revolution in property; not only does property change owners, but it changes, so to speak, in nature; it is unceasingly divided up into smaller portions.

That is the direct, and in a way material, effect of the law. In the countries where the law establishes the equality of distributions, property, and particularly landed wealth, must therefore have a permanent tendency to shrink. Nevertheless, the effects of this legislation would only make themselves felt in the long term, if the law were left to its own [48] forces, because if the family is not composed of more than two children (and the average for families in a country peopled like France is only, say, three), these children, in dividing up the fortune of their father and their mother, will not be poorer than each of the latter individually.

But the law of equal distribution does not only exercise its influence on the fate of property; it acts upon the very soul of the owners and summons their passions to its aid. It is its indirect effects which rapidly destroy great fortunes and, above all, great estates.

Among the peoples where the law of inheritance is founded upon the right of primogeniture, landed estates pass most often from generation to generation without being divided. It results from this that the spirit of family is in a way made material in the earth. The family represents the earth, and the earth represents the family; it perpetuates its name, its origin, its glory, its power, its virtues. It is an imperishable testimony to the past and a precious guarantee of future life.

When the law of inheritance establishes the equal division of inheritances, it destroys the intimate link which existed between the spirit of family and the conservation of the earth: the earth ceases to represent the family, because, as it cannot avoid being broken up after one or two generations, it is obvious that it must unceasingly diminish and end up disappearing entirely. The sons of a great landowner, if they are few in number, or if chance is favorable to them, may indeed maintain the hope of not being less rich than their founder, but not of possessing the same property as he; their riches will necessarily be composed of other elements than his.

Now, from the moment when you take away from landowners a great interest of sentiment, of memories, of pride, of ambition in conserving the earth, you can be assured that sooner or later they will sell it, because they will have a great pecuniary interest in selling it, since personal assets[*] produce a higher return than real assets, and lend themselves much more easily to the satisfaction of the passions of the moment.[†]

Once divided, great estates are no longer reconstructed: for the small proprietor obtains more revenue from his field,[2] proportionately, than the great landowner from his; he therefore sells it for much more than the latter. In this way the economic calculations which brought the rich man to sell vast properties, hinder him even more from buying up small [49] properties in order to recompose great ones.

What one calls the spirit of family is often founded on an illusion of individual egoism. One seeks to perpetuate oneself and to immortalize oneself in a way through one's posterity. Where the spirit of the family ends, individual egoism returns to its true inclinations. As the family no longer presents itself to the mind as anything more than a vague, indeterminate, uncertain thing, each one concentrates on the convenience of the present; one thinks of establishing the following generation, and nothing more.

---

[*] *capitaux mobiliers:* literally, "movable capital or assets." Real assets or capital like the landed estates Tocqueville discusses are *immobliers*, "immovable."

[†] In this paragraph Tocqueville plays on the double meaning—moral and economic—of the word *intérêt*, "interest." The law of inheritance once supported "a great interest" (*un grand intérêt*) in the conservation of great estates; its dismantling brings to the fore the "pecuniary interest" (*intérêt pécuniaire*) in selling them. Not only does personal property yield a higher return (*plus d'intérêts:* "more interests") than real property, but great estates, Tocqueville will say in the next paragraph, yield proportionately less return than small estates. Tocqueville constantly discusses how men become interested in one thing or another. In view of the importance of "interest rightly understood"—*intérêt bien entendu*—in Tocqueville's thought, his every use of the word *intérêt* merits attention.

2. I do not mean that the small proprietor farms better, but that he farms with more passion and more care, and makes up by work what he lacks in art.

One therefore does not seek to perpetuate his family, or at least one seeks to perpetuate it by other means than landed property.

Thus, not only does the law of inheritance make it difficult for families to conserve intact the same estates, but it takes away from them the desire to attempt to do so, and it draws them, in a way, to cooperate with it in their own ruination.

The law of equal division acts in two ways: in acting on the thing, it acts on the man; and in acting on the man, it arrives at the thing.

In both ways it succeeds in profoundly attacking landed property and in making families as well as fortunes disappear rapidly.[3]

It is not for us, Frenchmen of the 19th century, who witness daily the political and social changes brought about by the law of inheritance, to doubt its power. Each day we see it pass and pass again over our soil, knocking over the walls of our dwellings in its way, and destroying the fencing around our fields. But if the law of inheritance has already accomplished much among us, much still remains for it to do. Our memories, our opinions, and our habits pose powerful obstacles to it.

[50]   In the United States, its work of destruction is almost finished. It is there that one can study its principal results.

English legislation respecting the transfer of property was abolished in almost all the States at the time of the Revolution.

The law of entail was modified in such a way as to hinder only in an imperceptible manner the free circulation of property.

The first generation passed away; the earth began to be divided. The movement became more and more rapid as time passed. Today, when scarcely sixty years have passed, the aspect of society is already unrecognizable; almost all the families of the great landowners have sunk into the common mass. In the State of New York, where there were a great number

---

3. The earth being the most solid form of property, one encounters from time to time rich men who are disposed to make great sacrifices in order to acquire it and who are willing to lose a considerable portion of their revenue in order to secure the rest. But these are accidents. The love of property in land is no longer normally found except in the case of the poor person. The small landed proprietor, who has less enlightenment, less imagination, and less passion than the great, is in general preoccupied only with the desire to increase his property, and it often happens that inheritance, marriage, or commercial luck furnish him little by little with the means to do so.

Alongside the disposition which leads men to divide the earth, there therefore exists another which leads them to aggregate it. This disposition, which is sufficient for preventing properties from being infinitely divided, is not strong enough for creating great landed wealth nor above all for maintaining it in the same families.

of them, two of them barely linger on above the abyss that is ready to seize them. The sons of these opulent citizens are today merchants, lawyers, or doctors. Most of them have fallen into the most profound obscurity. The last trace of ranks and of hereditary distinctions is destroyed; the law of inheritance has everywhere completely accomplished its task.

It is not that in the United States, as elsewhere, there are no rich; I do not even know of a country where the love of money occupies a larger place in the human heart, and where a more profound contempt is professed for the theory of the permanent equality of property. But wealth circulates there with an incredible rapidity, and experience teaches that it is rare to see two generations receive its favors.

This picture, however colored one supposes it to be, still gives only an incomplete idea of what occurs in the new States of the West and the Southwest.

At the end of the last century, daring adventurers began to penetrate the valleys of the Mississippi. This was like a new discovery of America: soon the majority of emigrants went there; one then saw unknown societies emerge all of a sudden from the wilderness. States whose very name did not exist a few years earlier took their place within the American Union. It is in the West that one can observe democracy having reached its ultimate limit. In these States, improvised in a way by chance, the inhabitants arrived yesterday on the soil that they occupy. They barely know each other, and each is ignorant of his nearest neighbor's past history. In this part of the American continent, the population therefore escapes not only the influence of great names and great riches, but that natural aristocracy which flows from enlightenment and virtue. None there exercise that respectable power which men grant to the memory of a life entirely occupied in doing good before their eyes. The new States [51] of the West already have inhabitants, but society does not yet exist there.

But it is not only fortunes that are equal in America; equality extends up to a certain point to the intellects themselves.

I do not think that there is a country in the world where, in proportion to the population, there are as few ignorant persons, and fewer learned men, than in America.

Primary education there is within the reach of everyone; higher education there is within the reach of almost nobody.

This is easy to understand, and is as it were the necessary result of what we have suggested above.

Almost all Americans are prosperous;* therefore they are able easily to get the first elements of human knowledge.

---

* The words translated as "are prosperous" are *ont de l'aisance*. *Aisance* is a level of wealth that is not rich but allows for a commodious life, a life of ease (*aise*).

In America, there are few rich men; almost all Americans must therefore practice a profession. Now, every profession requires an apprenticeship. The Americans are therefore only able to devote the first years of life to the general cultivation of the intellect: at fifteen years, they enter upon a career; their education thus most often ends at the moment when ours begins. If it is pursued beyond that point, it is not directed toward more than a special and profitable subject; one studies a science as one takes up a trade; and one takes from it only the applications whose present utility is recognized.

In America, most rich men began as poor men; almost all men of leisure were, in their youth, busy men. The result of this is that when one might have the taste for study, one does not have the time to devote oneself to it, and, when one has acquired the time to devote oneself to it, one no longer has the taste for it.

There is therefore no class in America in which the taste for intellectual pleasures is passed on with inherited prosperity and leisure, and which honors the work of the intellect.

In consequence, the will as well as the ability to devote oneself to this work is lacking.

In America, a certain common level of human knowledge has been established. All minds approach it, some by rising, others by falling.

One thus encounters an immense multitude of individuals who have approximately the same number of notions in regard to religion, history, the sciences, political economy, legislation, and government.

Intellectual inequality comes directly from God, and man cannot prevent it from always recurring.

[52]   But it happens, at least from what we have just said, that the intellects, while remaining unequal, just as the Creator wished, find equal means at their disposal.

In this way therefore, in our day, in America, the aristocratic element, always weak from its birth, is if not destroyed, at least weakened, in such a way that it is difficult to assign to it any influence whatsoever in the course of human affairs.

Time, events, and laws have, on the contrary, made the democratic element there not only preponderant, but almost unique. One cannot perceive there any influence of family or group; often one cannot even discover there any individual influence that is at all durable.

America therefore presents, in its social state, the most strange phenomenon. Men there prove to be more equal by their fortune and by their intellect, or, in other terms, more equally strong than they are in any country in the world, and than they have been in any century within historical memory.

Political Consequences of the Social State of the Anglo-Americans

The political consequences of such a social state are easy to deduce.

It is impossible to think that equality will not end up penetrating the political world just as it has penetrated elsewhere. One cannot conceive of men eternally unequal among themselves with respect to a single point and equal with respect to the others; they will therefore, after a time, arrive at being equal in all.

Now, I know of only two ways of making equality prevail in the political world: one must give rights to every citizen or not give them to anyone.

For the peoples who have reached the same social state as the Anglo-Americans, it is therefore very difficult to perceive a middle term between the sovereignty of all and the absolute power of one alone.

One must not delude oneself that the social state I have just described does not lend itself almost as easily to either of these two consequences.

There is, in fact, a virile and legitimate passion for equality which provokes all men to want to be strong and esteemed. This passion tends to elevate the small to the rank of the great; but there is also in the hu- [53] man heart a depraved taste for equality, which leads the weak to want to draw the strong down to their level, and which reduces men to a preference for equality in servitude over inequality in liberty. It is not that the peoples whose social state is democratic naturally disdain liberty; on the contrary, they have an instinctive taste for it. But liberty is not the principal and constant object of their desire; what they love with an eternal love is equality; they rush forward toward liberty by rapid impulse and by sudden efforts, and, if they miss the goal, they resign themselves to it; but nothing can satisfy them without equality, and they would rather consent to perish than to lose it.

On the other hand, when the citizens are all almost equal, it becomes difficult for them to defend their independence against the assaults of power. None among them then being strong enough to struggle alone with advantage, it is only the combination of the forces of all of them which can guarantee liberty. Now, such a combination does not always exist.

Peoples can therefore draw two great political consequences from the same social state: these consequences differ prodigiously among themselves, but they both result from the same fact.

As the first ones presented with this fearsome alternative that I have just described, the Anglo-Americans have been rather fortunate to avoid absolute power. Their circumstances, their origin, their enlightenment, and above all their mores, have allowed them to found and to maintain the sovereignty of the people.

CHAPTER 4

THE PRINCIPLE OF THE SOVEREIGNTY
OF THE PEOPLE IN AMERICA

It dominates all of American society.—The application of this
principle that the Americans were already making before their
revolution.—The development that was given to it by this
revolution.—The gradual and irresistible lowering of the
property qualification for voting.

When one wishes to speak of the political laws of the United States, one
must always start with the dogma of the sovereignty of the people.

The principle of the sovereignty of the people, which always exists
more or less at the bottom of almost all human institutions, ordinarily
remains, so to speak, buried there. One obeys it without recognizing it,
or if sometimes it happens to appear for a moment in broad daylight,
one soon hastens to plunge it back into the shadows of the sanctuary.

The national will is one of those terms that has been the most widely
abused by intriguers of all times and demagogues of all ages. Some saw
its expression in the votes bought by a few agents of power; others, in
the votes of an interested or fearful minority; there are even some who
have discovered it fully expressed in the silence of peoples, and who
have thought that from the *fact* of obedience issued, for them, the *right*
of command.

In America, the principle of the sovereignty of the people is not hidden or sterile as it is among certain nations: it is recognized by the mores, proclaimed by the laws; it expands with liberty and attains its
ultimate consequences without obstacles.

If there is a single country in the world where one may hope to appreciate on its just merits the dogma of the sovereignty of the people, to
study it in its application to the affairs of society, and to judge its advantages and dangers, that country is assuredly America.

I have said previously that, from the beginning, the principle of the
[55] sovereignty of the people had been the generative principle of the majority of the English colonies in America.

At that time, however, it was far from dominating the government of
the society as it does in our day.

Two obstacles, one internal, the other external, slowed down its inva-
sive march.

It could not show itself openly in the laws since the colonies were still
constrained to obey the mother country; it was thus reduced to concealing

itself in the provincial assemblies and above all in the township. There it spread in secret.

At that time, American society was not yet prepared to adopt it in all of its consequences. Enlightenment in New England, and riches south of the Hudson, exercised for a long time, as I have shown in the preceding chapter, a sort of aristocractic influence which tended to compress into a few hands the exercise of the powers of society. It was still far from being the case that all public officials were elective and all citizens electors. The right to vote was everywhere constrained within certain limits and subordinated to the existence of a property qualification for voting. This property qualification was very weak in the North, more considerable in the South.

The American Revolution broke out. The dogma of the sovereignty of the people emerged from the township and took possession of the government; all classes put themselves at risk for its cause; one fought and triumphed in its name; it became the law of laws.

A change almost as rapid occurred in the interior of the society. The law of inheritance completed the breaking up of local influences.

At the moment when this effect of the laws and of the Revolution began to reveal itself to everyone's eyes, victory had already been irrevocably pronounced in favor of democracy. Power was, by this fact, in democracy's hands. It was no longer even permissible to struggle against it. The upper classes therefore submitted without a murmur and without struggle to an evil that was henceforth inevitable. What ordinarily happens to fallen powers happened to them: individual egoism took hold of their members; since they could no longer tear power from the hands of the people, and because they did not detest the multitude enough to take pleasure in defying it, they no longer thought of anything except winning its goodwill at any price. The most democratic laws were therefore passed in a mutual rivalry by the men whose interests they hurt the most. In this manner, the upper classes did not arouse popular passions against themselves, but they themselves hastened the triumph of the new order. Thus—singular phenomenon!—the democratic impulse was all the more irresistible in the States where aristocracy had the deepest roots.

The state of Maryland, which had been founded by great lords, proclaimed the first universal suffrage[1] and introduced into the whole of its government the most democratic forms. [56]

When a people begins to tamper with the property qualification for voting, one can predict that it will end up, after a more or less long period

---

1. Amendments made to the constitution of Maryland in 1801 and 1809.

of time, making it disappear completely. That is one of the most invariable rules governing societies. As the limitation on electoral rights is reduced, the need to reduce it still more is felt; because, after each new concession, the forces of democracy increase and its demands grow with its new power. The ambition of those who are left below the property qualification is inflamed in proportion to the great number of those who are above it. The exception finally becomes the rule; concessions follow upon one another without respite, and one no longer stops until one has arrived at universal suffrage.

In our day, the principle of the sovereignty of the people has attained in the United States all of the practical developments that the imagination can conceive. It has freed itself from all the fictions with which one took care to surround it elsewhere; one sees it assume every form, according to the necessity of the case. Sometimes the people in a body make the laws as in Athens; sometimes deputies, which universal suffrage has created, represent it and act in its name under its almost immediate surveillance.

There are countries where a power, in a way external to the social body, acts on it and forces it to march in a certain path.

There are others where force is divided, being placed at one and the same time in the society and outside of it. Nothing like this is seen in the United States; there, society acts by itself and on itself. Power exists only within it; one comes across almost nobody who dares to conceive and above all express the idea of seeking it elsewhere. The people take part in composing the laws by choosing the legislators and in their application by electing the agents of the executive power. One can say that the people governs itself, so much is the share left to the administration weak and restricted, so much does the latter feel the influence of its popular origin and obey the power from which it emanates. The people reign over the American political world like God over the the universe. It is the cause and the end of all things; everything emerges from it and everything is absorbed into it.

[57]   CHAPTER 5

THE NECESSITY OF STUDYING WHAT HAPPENS WITHIN
THE PARTICULAR STATES BEFORE DISCUSSING
THE GOVERNMENT OF THE UNION

I propose to examine, in the following chapter, what is, in America, the form of government founded on the principle of the sovereignty of the people; what are its means of action, its problems, its advantages, and its dangers.

A first difficulty presents itself: the United States has a complex con- stitution; one notices there two distinct societies engaged, and, if I may explain myself thus, fitted into one another. One sees two governments completely separate and almost independent: the one, ordinary and without well-defined limits, which answers to the daily needs of the so- ciety, the other, exceptional and circumscribed, which only applies to certain general interests. The former are, in a word, twenty-four small sovereign nations, of which the totality forms the great body of the Union.

To examine the Union before studying the State, is to go down a road littered with obstacles. The form of the Federal government of the Unit- ed States emerged last: it was only a modification of the republic, a sum- mary of political principles widespread in the entire society before its emergence and subsisting there independently of it. In addition, the Fed- eral government, as I have just said, is only an exception; the govern- ment of the States is the common rule. The writer who would like to make the totality of such a picture understood before having pointed out its details would necessarily fall into obscurities or redundancies.

The great political principles which today govern American society were born and developed in the *State*; one can have no doubt of it. It is therefore the State which must be understood in order to have the key to all the rest.

The States which in our day compose the American Union all present, with respect to the exterior aspect of their institutions, the same [58] spectacle. Political and administrative life there is concentrated in three centers of activity that one might compare to the different nervous cen- ters that make the human body move.

On the first rung is the *township*, higher up the *county*, and finally the *State*.

The Municipal System in America

Why the author begins his examination of political institutions with the municipality.—The municipality is found among all peoples.—Difficulty of establishing and conserving municipal liberty.—Its importance.—Why the author chose the municipal organization of New England as the principal object of his examination.

It is not by chance that I examine the municipality first.

The municipality is the only association that is so natural that everywhere men are brought together, a municipality forms by itself.

Municipal society thus exists among all peoples, no matter what their customary practices and their laws; it is man who makes kingdoms and creates republics; the municipality appears to come directly from the hands of God. But if the municipality exists from the moment that there are men, municipal liberty is a rare and fragile thing. A people can always set up great political assemblies, because there is usually found within it a certain number of men whose enlightenment substitutes up to a point for the normal practice of political affairs. The municipality is composed of cruder elements that often resist the action of the legislator. The difficulty of establishing the independence of municipalities, instead of diminishing as nations become enlightened, increases with their enlightenment. A very civilized society tolerates only with difficulty the efforts made by municipal liberty: it is appalled by the sight of its numerous aberrations, and despairs of success before having reached the final result of the experiment.

Among all liberties, that of municipalities, which is so difficult to establish, is also the one most exposed to the invasions of power. Left to themselves, municipal institutions would scarcely be able to struggle against an enterprising and strong government; in order to defend themselves successfully, it is necessary for them to have become fully developed and to have entered into national ideas and habits. Thus, to the extent that municipal liberty has not entered into mores, it is easy to destroy, and [59] it cannot enter into mores until it has subsisted for a long time in the laws.

Municipal liberty thus eludes, so to speak, the effort of man. In consequence, it rarely happens that it is created; it comes into being in a way on its own. It develops almost in secret in the depths of a semibarbaric society. It is the continuous action of laws and mores, circumstances and, above all, time, that succeeds in consolidating it. Of all the nations of the continent of Europe, one can say that there is not a single one of them that understands municipal liberty.

It is, however, in the municipality that the strength of free peoples resides. Municipal institutions are to liberty what primary schools are to knowledge; they place it within reach of the people; they give them the experience of the peaceful exercise of it and habituate them to make use of it. Without municipal institutions a nation may give itself a free government, but it does not have the spirit of liberty. Transient passions, momentary interests, chance circumstances may give it the external forms of independence, but the despotism buried in the interior of the social body reappears sooner or later on the surface.

In order to make the reader understand well the general principles upon which the political organization of the township and the county in the United States rests, I have thought it useful to take one State in particular for a model, to examine in detail what happens there, and then to cast a rapid glance at the rest of the country.

I have chosen one of the States of New England.

The township and the county are not organized in the same manner in all parts of the Union; it is easy to recognize, however, that in all of the Union the same principles, more or less, presided over the formation of both of them.

Now, it appeared to me that in New England these principles received more considerable development and attained results that reached further than anywhere else. They therefore reveal themselves there, as it were, in greater relief and thus yield themselves more easily to the observation of the foreigner.

The municipal institutions of New England form a complete and regular whole; they are ancient; they are strong because of the laws, still more strong because of mores; they exercise a prodigious influence on the entire society.

For all of these reasons they deserve our attention.

The Limits of the Township

The township of New England occupies a middle ground between the canton and the municipality of France. It has, in general, two to three thousand inhabitants;[1] it is therefore not so extensive that all the inhabitants do not have more or less the same interests, and, on the other hand, it is populous enough that one is always sure of finding within it the elements of a good administration.

Powers of the Township in New England   [60]

The people is the origin of all powers in the township, as it is elsewhere.—It takes care of its principal affairs itself.—No municipal council.—The greatest part of municipal authority is concentrated in the hands of the Selectmen.—How the Selectmen *act.—General assembly of the inhabitants of the township* (Town-Meeting).—*List of all the municipal officials.— Obligatory and remunerated offices.*

---

1. The number of townships, in the State of Massachusetts, was, in 1830, 305; the number of inhabitants 610,014; which gives an average of around 2,000 inhabitants per township.

The people is the source of social powers within the township just as it is everywhere else, but nowhere does it exercise its power more immediately. The people, in America, is a master that must be pleased up to the utmost possible limits.

In New England, the majority acts by means of representatives when it is necessary to deal with the general affairs of the State. It was necessary that this be so; but in the township where legislative and governmental action is closer to the governed, the law of representation is not accepted. There is no municipal council; the body of electors, after choosing its magistrates, directs them itself in everything that does not involve the pure and simple execution of the laws of the State.[2]

[61]   This order of things is so contrary to our ideas, and so opposed to our habits, that some examples must be furnished here in order that it be well understood.

Public offices are very numerous and much divided within the township, as we will see below. However, the majority of administrative powers are concentrated in the hands of a small number of individuals who are elected annually and who are called Selectmen.[3]

The general laws of the State impose a certain number of obligations on the Selectmen. In order to fulfill them, they do not need the consent of those who come under their jurisdiction, and they cannot evade those obligations without being held personally responsible. State law charges them, for example, with composing the census of electors in their township; if they fail to do it, they make themselves guilty of an infraction of the law. But in everything that is left to the direction of the municipal power, the Selectmen are the executors of the popular will just as among

---

2. The same rules do not apply to large municipalities. Those have in general a mayor and a municipal body divided into two branches; but that is an exception which must be authorized by a law. See the law of 22 February 1822, regulating the powers of the town of Boston. *Laws of Massachusetts*, Vol. II, p. 588. This applies to the large towns. It also often occurs that small towns are subject to a particular administration. In 1832 in the State of New York there were 104 municipalities administered in this way. (*William's-Register.*)

3. Three of them are elected in the smallest municipalities, and nine in the largest. See *The Town Officer*, p. 186. See also the principal laws of Massachusetts relating to the Selectmen:

Law of 20 February 1786, Vol. 1, p. 219;—of 24 February 1786, Vol. 1, p. 488;—7 March 1801, Vol. II, p. 45;—16 June 1795, Vol. I, p. 475;—12 March 1808, Vol. II, p. 186;—28 February 1787, Vol. I, p. 302;—22 June 1797, Vol. I, p. 539.

us the mayor is the executor of the deliberations of the municipal council. Most of the time they act on their responsibility as individuals and merely see to it that, in practice, the principles previously laid down by the majority are faithfully adhered to. But if they want to introduce any change whatsoever in the established order, if they wish to engage in a new enterprise, they must go back to the source of their power. Assume it is a question of establishing a school; the Selectmen convoke on a certain day, at a place agreed upon in advance, the whole body of electors; there, they explain the need that has made itself felt; they make known the means of satifying it, the money that must be spent, the location it is advisable to choose. The assembly, consulted on all these points, adopts the principle, decides on the location, votes the tax, and hands the execution of its will over to the Selectmen.

Only the Selectmen have the right to convoke the town-meeting, but they may be made to do it. If ten proprietors conceive a new project and wish to present it for the assent of the township, they demand a general [62] convening of the inhabitants; the Selectmen are obligated to go along with it, and conserve only the right to preside over the assembly.[4]

These political mores, these social usages are without doubt far removed from our own. I do not at this time wish to judge them or make known the hidden causes which engender them and give them vitality. I limit myself to laying them out.

The Selectmen are elected annually in the month of April or May. The municipal assembly chooses at the same time a host of other municipal magistrates,[5] who are placed in charge of certain important administrative details. Some, called assessors, have to set taxes; others, called collectors, have to collect them. An officer, called a *constable*, is charged with maintaining public order, watching over public places, and assisting in the physical execution of the laws. Another, called the municipal clerk, records all deliberations; he keeps the record of the proceedings of the registry office. A treasurer keeps the municipal funds. Add to these officers an overseer of the poor, whose duty, very hard to fulfill, is to see that the law relating to indigents is carried out; commissioners of schools, who oversee public education; inspectors of roads, who are responsible for all the details of large and small networks of roads, and you will have the list of the principal officials of the municipal administration. But the division of offices does not stop there:

---

4. See *Laws of Massachusetts*, Vol. I, p. 150; law of 25 March 1786.

5. *Ibid.*

among the municipal officers,[6] there are also parish commissioners, whose duty is to pay the expenses of worship; and inspectors of several sorts, some responsible for directing the citizens' efforts in case of fire; others for overseeing the harvests; some for provisionally resolving difficulties that may arise regarding fencing; others for supervising the measurement of timber, or inspecting weights and measures.

In all, there are nineteen principal offices in the township. Every inhabitant is obliged, on pain of a fine, to accept these duties; but in addition the majority of those offices are subject to a remuneration, so that poor citizens can devote their time to them without suffering a loss from it. Furthermore, the American system does not give a fixed remuneration [63] to officers. In general, each act of their administration has a price, and they are remunerated only in proportion to what they have done.

The Township as an Individual Entity[*]

Each is the best judge of what regards only himself.—Corollary of the principle of the sovereignty of the people.—Application of these doctrines made by the American townships.—The New England township, sovereign in everything that relates only to itself, subject in all the rest.—Obligation of the township toward the State.— In France, the government lends its agents to the municipality.— In America, the township lends its agents to the government.

I have said previously that the principle of the sovereignty of the people hangs over the whole political system of the Anglo-Americans. Each page of this book will make known some new applications of this doctrine.

In nations where the dogma of the sovereignty of the people prevails, each individual forms an equal portion of the sovereign and participates equally in the government of the State.

Each individual is thus assumed to be as enlightened, as virtuous, as strong as any other of his fellow men.

---

6. All these magistrates really exist in practice.

To acquaint oneself with the details of the duties of all these municipal magistrates, see Isaac Goodwin, *Town Officer*, Worcester 1827, and the collection of the general laws of Massachusetts in 3 Volumes, Boston 1823.

* *De l'Existence Communale.* The usual translation of *De l'Existence Communale* would be "Township Existence" or "Township Life." However, Tocqueville's text here is not about the daily life or the physical existence of the township, but about its status as, in Tocqueville's words, "an individual like any other" vis à vis the State. This accords with a less common meaning of the word *existence:* an existing individual or entity.

Why then does he obey the society, and what are the natural limits of this obedience?

He obeys the society, not because he is inferior to those who direct it or less capable of governing himself than another man; he obeys society because union with his fellow men seems useful to him and because he knows that this union cannot exist without a controlling power.

In all that concerns the obligations of citizens to one another, he has thus become a subject. In all that regards only himself, he has remained master: he is free and must account for his actions only to God. From which comes this maxim, that the individual is the best as well as the sole judge of his particular interest and that society only has the right to direct his actions when it feels wronged by his act or when it has need to demand his help.

This doctrine is universally accepted in the United States. Elsewhere I will examine what general influence it exercises on the ordinary actions of life, but right now I am speaking about the townships.

The township, taken as a body and in relation to the central government, is only an individual like any other, to whom the theory which I [64] have just pointed out applies.

In the United States, municipal liberty thus flows from the very dogma of the sovereignty of the people. All the American republics have more or less recognized this independence, but among the peoples of New England, circumstances have particularly favored its development.

In this part of the Union, political life originated in the very bosom of the townships; one might almost say that at its origin each of them was an independent nation. When the kings of England later demanded their portion of sovereignty, they limited themselves to taking the central authority. They left the township in the state where they found it. Now the townships of New England are subjects; but in origin they were not so or were barely so. They therefore did not receive their powers; on the contrary, it was they who seem to have relinquished, in favor of the State, a portion of their independence; an important distinction, and one which must remain present in the mind of the reader.

The townships are in general subject to the State only when it is a question of an interest which I will call *social,* that is to say which they share with others.

For everything that relates only to them alone, the townships have remained independent bodies; and among the inhabitants of New England, there are none, I think, who recognize in the government of the State the right to intervene in the direction of purely municipal interests.

One thus sees the townships of New England sell and buy, bring actions and defend themselves in court, overload their budgets or lower

taxes, without any administrative authority whatsoever thinking of opposing them.[7]

As for social obligations, the townships are obligated to satisfy them.
Thus, if the State needs money, the township is not free to grant or
refuse its contribution.[8] If the State wants to open a road, the township is
not free to close its territory to it. If it makes a regulation for maintaining public order, the township must execute it. If it wants to organize education according to a uniform plan throughout the country, the
township is obligated to create the schools required by the law.[9] We will
see, when we discuss the administration of the United States, how and
[65] by whom the townships, in all these different cases, are constrained to
obedience. Here I only want to establish the existence of the obligation.
This obligation is narrow, but the government of the State, in imposing
it, only enacts a principle; for its execution, the township recovers in
general all its rights as an individual. Thus, the tax, it is true, is voted by
the legislature, but it is the township which allocates and collects it; the
existence of a school is ordered, but it is the township which builds it,
pays for it, and runs it.

In France, the tax inspector of the State collects municipal taxes; in
America, the tax inspector of the township collects the State tax.

Thus, among us, the central government lends its agents to the township; in America, the township lends its officials to the government. That
alone makes clear to what degree the two societies differ.

The Municipal Spirit in New England

*Why the New England township attracts the affections of those
who inhabit it.—The difficulty of creating municipal spirit that one
encounters in Europe.—Municipal rights and duties contributing
in America to the formation of this spirit.—The fatherland has
more physiognomy in the United States than elsewhere.—In what
the municipal spirit manifests itself in New England.—What
happy effects it produces there.*

In America, there are not only municipal institutions, but also a municipal spirit which supports them and invigorates them.

---

7. See *Laws of Massachusetts*, law of 23 March 1786, vol. 1, p. 250.

8. *Ibid.*, law of 20 February 1786, vol. 1, p. 217.

9. See the same collection, law of 25 June 1789, and 8 March 1827, vol. 1, p.
367, and vol. III, p. 179.

The township of New England combines two advantages which, everywhere they exist, keenly excite the interest of men; namely, independence and power. It acts, it is true, within an orbit that it cannot leave, but its movements there are free. This independence alone would already give it a real importance, which its population and its dimensions would not secure for it.

It cannot in the end be denied that the affections of men go in general only in the direction of power. One does not see love of the fatherland prevail for long in a conquered country. The inhabitant of New England is attached to his township, not so much because he was born there as because he sees in this township a free and strong corporate body of which he is a member, and which is worth the trouble one takes to run it.

It often happens, in Europe, that the governors themselves regret the [66] absence of municipal spirit; for everyone agrees that municipal spirit is a great element of public order and tranquility, but they don't know how to produce it. By making the municipality strong and independent, they are afraid of splitting up social authority and exposing the State to anarchy. Now, take away power and independence from the municipality, and all you will ever find there are subjects* and no citizens.

Notice, in addition, an important fact: the New England township is so constituted as to be able to serve as a center of lively affections, and at the same time there is nothing close by it that strongly attracts the ambitious passions of the human heart.

The county officials are not elected, and their authority is limited. The State itself has only a secondary importance; its existence is obscure and quiet. There are few men who, in order to gain the right to administer it, agree to go away from the center of their interests and disrupt their lives.

The Federal government confers power and glory upon those who direct it, but the men to whom it is given to influence its future are very few in number. The Presidency is a high office that one succeeds in reaching almost exclusively later in life; and when one arrives at other Federal offices of a high rank, it is in a way by chance and after one has already become famous by following another career. Ambition cannot take them for the permanent goal of its efforts. It is in the township, at the center of the ordinary relations of life, that are concentrated the desire for esteem, the need born of real interests, the taste for power and

---

*   The word translated as "subjects" is *administrés:* literally, "the administered," persons subject to an administrative authority. See at Vol. 1, Part 1, Chap. 5 [94], the similar formulation: *on y trouve encore des sujets, mais on n'y vois plus de citoyens:* "one still finds subjects there, but one no longer sees citizens."

éclat;* these passions, which so often disturb society, change character when they can be thus exercised close to hearth and home and in a way in the bosom of the family.

See with what art, in the American township, care has been taken, if I can thus express myself, to *disperse* power, in order to interest more people in public things. Independently of the electors called from time to time to act as the government, how many different offices there are, how many different magistrates, all of whom, within the limits of their jurisdictions, represent the powerful corporate body in whose name they act! How many men in this way make use of municipal power to their own benefit and interest themselves in it for their own sakes!

The American system, at the same time that it breaks up municipal power among a great number of citizens, also does not fear to multiply [67] municipal obligations. In the United States it is thought with reason that love of the fatherland is a species of religion to which men attach themselves through practice.

In this manner, municipal life in a way makes itself felt at each moment; it manifests itself each day by the accomplishment of a duty or the exercise of a right. This political life imparts a movement to the society that is continual but at the same time peaceful, that stirs it up without disrupting it.

The Americans are attached to the town for a reason analogous to that which makes the inhabitants of the mountains love their country. Among them the fatherland has marked and characteristic traits; it has more physiognomy than elsewhere.

The New England townships have in general a happy existence. Their government is to their taste as well as of their choice. In the bosom of the profound peace and material prosperity that prevails in America, the storms of municipal life are few in number. The management of municipal interests is easy. Moreover, the political education of the people was accomplished long ago, or rather they arrived completely educated on the soil that they occupy. In New England, the division of ranks does not even exist in memory; there is therefore no part of the township that is tempted to oppress the other, and injustices, which strike only isolated individuals, are lost in the general contentment. If the government exhibits defects, and it is certainly easy to point some out, they do not attract attention, because the government really emanates from the governed and

---

* The word translated as "éclat" is *bruit. Bruit* in this context refers to the brilliance, impact, or notoriety in the world of one's deeds, position, or qualities. Éclat entered English usage from the French, where it is a synonym for *bruit*. To make a *bruit* or an éclat means to cause a sensation, a stir, or even a scandal.

because it is enough that it work more or less well in order for a sort of paternal pride to protect it. Besides, they have nothing else with which to compare it. England formerly reigned over all the colonies, but the people always directed municipal affairs. The sovereignty of the people in the township is therefore not only an ancient state, but a primordial state.

The inhabitant of New England is attached to his township because it is strong and independent; he takes an interest in it because he actively participates in running it; he loves it because he has no reason to complain about his lot in it; he invests in it his ambition and his future; he participates in each of the events of municipal life: in this limited sphere that is within his reach, he tries his hand at governing the society; he habituates himself to the forms without which liberty only progresses by revolutions, is penetrated by their spirit, acquires a taste for order, understands the harmony of the different powers, and, finally, gathers together clear and practical ideas on the nature of his obligations as well as on the extent of his rights.

· · ·

On the Political Effects of Administrative [86]
Decentralization in the United States

Distinction to be established between governmental centralization and administrative centralization.—In the United States, no administrative centralization, but very great governmental centralization.—Some unfortunate effects which result in the United States from extreme administrative decentralization.— Administrative advantages of this order of things.—The force which administers the society is less well ordered, less enlightened, less learned, and much greater than in Europe.— Political advantages of this same order of things.—In the United States, the fatherland makes itself felt everywhere.—Support that the governed lend to the government.—Provincial institutions more necessary to the extent that the social state becomes more democratic.—Why.

Centralization is a word that is repeated incessantly in our day and whose meaning nobody, in general, seeks to state precisely.

There exist, however, two kinds of centralization that are very differ- [87] ent and that it is important to know well.

Certain interests are common to all the parts of the nation, such as the formation of general laws and the relations of the people with foreigners.

Other interests are specific to certain parts of the nation, such as, for example, municipal undertakings.

To concentrate in the same place or in the same hands the power to govern the former is to establish what I will call governmental centralization.

To concentrate in the same manner the power to govern the latter is to establish what I will call administrative centralization.

There are points at which these two kinds of centralization merge with one another. But by taking as a whole the objects that fall most particularly within the domain of each of them, one easily succeeds in distinguishing them.

Governmental centralization understandably acquires an immense force when it is joined to administrative centralization. In this manner it habituates men to make a complete and continual abstraction of their will; to obey, not one time and on one point, but in everything and every day. Then not only does it dominate them by force, but even more, it takes hold of them through their habits; it isolates them and then seizes them one by one in the common mass.

These two kinds of centralization lend each other a mutual help; they are drawn to one another, but I cannot believe that they are inseparable.

Under Louis XIV, France witnessed the greatest governmental centralization that one can conceive, since the same man made general laws and had the power to interpret them, represented France to the outside world, and acted in its name. The State, it is I,* he used to say, and he was right.

However, under Louis XIV, there was much less administrative centralization than in our day.

In our time, we see a power, England, in which governmental centralization is carried to a very high degree: the State seems to move there as a single man; it raises immense masses at will and combines and carries all the force of its power anywhere it wishes.

England, which has accomplished such great things for the last fifty years, does not have administrative centralization.

For my part, I cannot conceive that a nation can live nor above all prosper without strong governmental centralization.

[88]   But I think that administrative centralization is only good for enervating the peoples who submit themselves to it because it tends unceasingly to diminish civic spirit among them. Administrative centralization succeeds, it is true, in combining at a given time, and in a certain place, all the available forces of the nation, but it compromises the continued reproduction of those forces. It makes the nation triumph on the day of combat and diminishes its power in the long run. It can

---

*   *L'Etat, c'est moi.*

therefore contribute admirably to the passing greatness of a man, but not to the lasting prosperity of a people.

. . .

[90]

The partisans of centralization in Europe claim that governmental power administers the local communities better than they can administer themselves: that may be true when the central power is enlightened and the local communities are without enlightenment, when it is active and they are lethargic, when it has the habit of acting and they have the habit of obeying. One even understands that the more centralization increases, the more this double tendency grows and the more the capacity of one part and the incapacity of the other become salient.

But I deny that it is so when the people is enlightened, awakened to its interests, and habituated to think about them as it does in America.

I am persuaded, on the contrary, that in this case the collective strength of the citizens will always be more powerful for producing social well-being than the authority of government.

I admit that it is difficult to indicate with certainty the means of awakening a people that is sleeping in order to give it the passions and enlightenment that it does not have. To persuade men that they must take responsibility for their affairs is, I am not unaware, an arduous undertaking. It would often be less difficult to interest them in the details of the etiquette of a court than in the repair of their common dwelling. [91]

But I also think that when the central administration claims to replace completely the free, active participation of the persons primarily interested, it deceives itself or wishes to deceive you.

A central power, however enlightened, however competent one imagines it to be, cannot embrace within itself alone all the details of the life of a great people. It cannot do it because such a task exceeds human powers. When it wishes, through its own efforts, to create and make function so many diverse forces, it contents itself with a very incomplete result or exhausts itself in futile efforts.

Centralization succeeds easily, it is true, in subjecting the external actions of man to a certain uniformity that one ends up loving for its own sake, independently of the things to which it is applied, like those devout believers who adore the statue, forgetting the divinity that it represents. Centralization succeeds easily in giving a regular look to everyday affairs; in ruling skillfully* over the details of social order; in suppressing

---

* The words translated as "ruling skillfully" are *régenter savamment*. This is sharp irony: *régenter* means to govern with excessive or unjustified authority; and *savamment* means "skillfully" in the sense of "cleverly" or "cunningly."

light disorders and small infractions; in maintaining the society in a *status quo* which is not strictly either decadence or progress; in maintaining in the social body a sort of administrative somnolence that the administrators are accustomed to call good order and public tranquility.[50] It excels, in a word, in preventing, not in doing. When it is a question of profoundly stirring the society or imparting a rapid movement to it, its strength abandons it. If its measures ever have need of the active support of individuals, one is then quite surprised by the weakness of this immense machine; it finds itself suddenly reduced to impotence.

It happens sometimes that centralization tries, in desperation, to call the citizens to its aid, but it says to them: You will act as I wish, as much as I wish, and precisely in the direction that I wish. You will take care of these details without aspiring to direct the whole; you will labor in the shadows, and you will judge my work later by its results. It is not in such [92] conditions that one obtains the active support of the human will. It must have liberty in the way it comports itself and responsibility in its actions. Man is so constructed that he prefers to remain immobile than to march without independence toward a goal of which he knows nothing.

I will not deny that in the United States one often regrets not finding those uniform rules that seem constantly to watch over each of us.

One encounters there from time to time great examples of lack of care and of social negligence. From time to time gross blemishes appear that seem to be in complete conflict with the surrounding civilization.

Useful undertakings that demand continual effort and a rigorous exactness in order to succeed often end up being abandoned because, in America as elsewhere, the people proceeds by short-lived efforts and sudden impulses.

The European, accustomed to finding continually at his hand an official who meddles in nearly everything, has difficulty getting used to the different mechanism of municipal administration. In general, one can say that the small details of social order which make life smooth and commodious are neglected in America, but the guarantees essential to man in society exist there as much as anywhere else. Among the Americans, the force that administers the State is less well ordered, less enlightened, less learned, but a hundred times greater than in Europe. There is no country

---

50. China appears to me to offer the most perfect symbol of the type of social well-being that a very centralized administration can give to the peoples who submit themselves to it. Travelers tell us that the Chinese have tranquility without happiness, industry without progress, stability without force, and material order without public morality. There, society always functions rather well, never very well. I imagine that when China is opened to Europeans, they will find there the most beautiful model of centralized administration that exists in the world.

in the world where men make, in the final analysis, as many efforts in order to create social well-being. I know no people who has succeeded in establishing schools as numerous and as effective; churches that have more rapport with the religious needs of the inhabitants; better maintained municipal roads. One must not therefore seek in the United States uniformity and permanence of views, meticulous care for details, perfection of administrative procedures;[51] what one finds there is the picture of [93] strength, a bit untamed it is true, but full of power; and of life, accompanied by mishaps but also by movements and efforts.

I will admit besides, if one wishes, that the villages and counties of the United States would be more usefully administered by a central authority located far from them, and which would remain foreign to them, than by officials chosen from within them. I will acknowledge, if one demands it, that there would be more security in America, that one would make wiser and more judicious use there of social resources, if the administration of the whole country were concentrated in a single hand. The *political* advantages that the Americans obtain from the system of decentralization would still make me prefer it to the opposite system.

Of what matter is it to me, after all, that there is an authority always active, which sees to it that my pleasures are tranquil, which flies ahead of me to turn aside all dangers, without my even needing to think about

---

51. A writer of talent who, in a comparison between the finances of the United States and those of France, has proved that intelligence cannot always compensate for lack of knowledge of the facts, reproaches the Americans with reason for the sort of confusion that prevails in their municipal budgets, and, after having given the model of a departmental budget in France, he adds: "Thanks to centralization, the admirable creation of a great man, municipal budgets, from one end of the kingdom to the other, those of great cities as well as those of the most humble municipalities, do not present less order and method." There, certainly, is a result I admire; but I see most of these French municipalities, whose accounts are so perfect, plunged into a profound ignorance of their true interests and given up to an apathy so invincible that society there seems rather to vegetate than to live; on the other hand, I perceive in these same American municipalities, whose budgets are not drawn up according to methodical plans nor above all uniform ones, a population enlightened, active, and enterprising; there I look upon a society always at work. This spectacle astonishes me; for in my opinion the principal goal of a good government is to produce the well-being of peoples and not to establish a certain order in the midst of their misery. I wonder therefore if it would not be possible to attribute to the same cause the prosperity of the American municipality and the apparent disorder of its finances, the distress of the municipality in France and the perfecting of its budget. In any case, I distrust a good that I find mixed up with so many evils, and I can easily accept an evil which is compensated by so much good.

it; if this authority, at the same time that it removes the smallest thorns from my path, is the absolute master of my liberty and my life; if it monopolizes movement and life to the point that everything around it must languish when it languishes, that everything sleeps when it sleeps, that everything perishes when it dies?*

There are nations like this in Europe, where the inhabitant considers himself as a kind of tenant farmer indifferent to the fate of the place where he lives. The greatest changes occur in his country without his participation;† he does not even know exactly what has occurred; he suspects; he has heard tell of the event by accident. Much more, the fate of his village, the security of his street, the future of his church and of his presbytery do not touch him at all; he thinks that all these things have nothing to do in any way with him, and that they belong to a powerful stranger called the government. For his part, he enjoys his possessions like a usufructuary,‡ without a spirit of ownership and without any ideas whatsoever of improving them. This indifference to himself goes so far that if his own safety or that of his children is finally endangered, instead of taking the responsibility to remove the danger, he crosses his arms in order to wait for the entire nation to come to his aid. This man, [94] besides, although he has made such a complete sacrifice of his free will, does not like obedience more than the next man. He submits, it is true, to the wishes of a clerk, but he takes pleasure in defying the law like a vanquished enemy as soon as force is withdrawn. Therefore, one sees him oscillate incessantly between servitude and license.

When nations have arrived at this point, they must either modify their laws and mores or perish, because the source of public virtues there has run dry: one still finds subjects there, but one no longer sees citizens.

I say that such nations are ready for conquest. If they do not disappear

---

* This passage would have reminded Tocqueville's French readers of the La Fontaine fable *The Wolf and the Dog:* the wolf, who is free but starving, is momentarily attracted to the life of the dog, who is well fed by his masters, but he runs away as soon as he grasps the meaning of the dog's collar.

† The word translated as "participation" is *concours*. This word must not be translated in a way that implies simply the concurrence or consent of the governed in the actions of government. Tocqueville uses *concours* with great frequency in this section of Chapter 5, and it reflects his argument that liberty requires more than consent. Precisely consent alone, without more, gives the appearance of liberty to the "soft despotism" which makes life thorn-free at the price of real freedom. The latter requires the free, active participation or collaboration—the *concours libre*—of the citizens in their own government. See above all Tocqueville's argument in Vol. 2, Part 4, Chap. 6 [325–6].

‡ A person possessing a *usufruct*, which is a right to use something without any right of ownership.

from the world's stage, it is because they are surrounded by nations similar or inferior to them; it is because there still remains in their bosom a sort of indefinable instinct of patriotism, and who knows what unreflective pride in the name the fatherland bears, what vague memory of past glory, which, without being precisely connected to anything, suffices for imparting to them a conserving impulse if the need arises.

It would be a mistake to reassure oneself with the thought that certain peoples have made prodigious efforts to defend a fatherland in which they lived virtually as foreigners. Pay very close attention to it, and one will see that religion was then almost always their principal motive.

The longevity, the glory, or the prosperity of the nation had become for them sacred dogmas, and in defending their fatherland, they were also defending that holy city in which they were all citizens.

The Turkish people has never taken any part in the direction of the affairs of the society; they have, however, accomplished immense undertakings, as long as they saw the triumph of the religion of Mohammed in the conquests of the sultans. Today the religion is disappearing; despotism alone remains: they are declining.

Montesquieu, by granting to despotism a strength that was its own, did it, I think, an honor that it did not merit. Despotism, by itself alone, cannot sustain anything lasting. When one looks at it from close up, one perceives that it is religion and not fear that has made absolute governments prosper for a long time.

No matter what one does, one will never find genuine power among men except in the free convergence and collaboration of wills. Now, there is nothing in the world except patriotism or religion that can make the whole of the citizenry march toward a single goal over a long period of time.

The laws cannot revive beliefs which are dying out, but the laws can interest men in the destiny of their country. The laws can reawaken and [95] direct that vague instinct of patriotism which never abandons the heart of man, and, by connecting it to the ideas, passions, and habits of his everyday life, make of it a reflective and durable sentiment. And let it not be said that it is too late to try it; nations do not age in the same manner as men. Each generation which is born within them is like a new people which comes to offer itself to the hand of the legislator.

What I admire most in America, are not the *administrative* effects of decentralization but the *political* effects. In the United States, the fatherland makes itself felt everywhere. It is an object of solicitude from the village to the entire Union. The inhabitant is attached to each of the interests of his country as to his very own. He glories in the nation's glory; in the success that it obtains, he believes he recognizes his own work,

62   Volume One

and he is uplifted by it; he rejoices in the general prosperity from which
he profits. He has for his fatherland a sentiment analogous to that which
one feels for one's family, and it is again through a kind of egoism that
he interests himself in the State.

Often the European sees in the public official only force; the American sees, in him, right. One may therefore say that in America, man never obeys man but justice or law.

And so he has conceived an opinion of himself that is often exaggerated but almost always salutary. He trusts without fear in his own powers,
which appear to him sufficient for everything. A private man conceives
the idea of some undertaking or other; were this undertaking to have a direct relation to the well-being of society, the idea never occurs to him to
address the public authority in order to obtain its aid. He makes his plan
known, offers himself to execute it, calls the strength of other individuals
to the aid of his own, and struggles hand to hand against all obstacles.
Often, without doubt, he succeeds less well than the State would in his
place; but in the long run the general result of all the individual undertakings surpasses by far what the government would be able to do.

Since the administrative authority is placed at the side of those who
are subject to it, and in a way represents them through themselves, it
arouses neither jealousy nor hatred. Since its means are limited, each
feels that he cannot rely solely upon it.

When, therefore, the administrative authority intervenes within the
limit of its jurisdiction, it does not find itself abandoned to itself as in
Europe. It is not thought that the duties of private persons have ceased
because the representative of the public arrives to take action. Each, on
the contrary, gives him guidance, helps him, and supports him.

[96]   The action of the individual forces is joined to the action of the social
forces, and from this one often succeeds in doing what would be beyond
the power of the most concentrated and most energetic administration to
accomplish.

· · ·

[99]   CHAPTER 6

                  THE JUDICIAL POWER IN THE UNITED STATES
                  AND ITS INFLUENCE ON POLITICAL SOCIETY

        The Anglo-Americans have retained in the judicial power all
        the characteristics that distinguish it among other peoples.—
        However, they have made it into a great political power.—How.—

*In what the judicial system of the Anglo-Americans differs from
all the others.—Why American judges have the right to declare
laws unconstitutional.—How American judges use this right.—
Precautions taken by the legislator to prevent the abuse of
this right.*

I thought I ought to devote a separate chapter to the judicial power. Its
political importance is so great that it seemed to me that it would diminish it in the eyes of the reader to speak about it in passing.

Confederations have existed elsewhere than in America. Republics
have existed in other places than on the shores of the New World. The
representative system has been adopted in several European states. But I
do not think that, until the present, any nation in the world has constituted the judicial power in the same way as the Americans.

The most difficult thing for a foreigner to understand, in the United
States, is the organization of the judiciary. There is no political affair in
which he does not hear judicial authority invoked, and he naturally concludes from this that in the United States the judge is one of the principal
political powers. When afterward he comes to examine the constitution
of the courts, he sees in them, at first glance, only judicial powers and
usages. As far as he can see, the judge seems never to introduce himself
into public affairs except by accident; but this same accident recurs every day.

When the *Parlement* of Paris remonstrated and refused to register an
edict, when it summoned a corrupt official to its bar, one saw in the open [100]
the political action of the judicial power. But nothing like this is seen in
the United States.

The Americans have retained in the judicial power all the characteristics by which we are accustomed to recognize it. They have contained it
precisely within the sphere in which it is accustomed to move.

The first characteristic of the judicial power, among all peoples, is to
serve as arbiter. For the courts to act, there must be a dispute. For there to
be a judge, there must be a legal proceeding. So long as a law does not
give rise to a dispute, the judicial power has no occasion to be concerned
with it. The judicial power exists, but it does not take notice of the law in
question. When a judge, in a legal proceeding, attacks a law that relates
to this proceeding, he extends the sphere of his powers, but he does not
go outside it, since it was necessary for him, in a sense, to judge the law
in order to come to a judgment in the proceeding. When he pronounces
upon a law, without starting from within a legal proceeding, he goes beyond his sphere completely, and he enters that of the legislative power.

The second characteristic of the judicial power is to pronounce upon

particular cases and not upon general principles. If a judge, in deciding a
particular question, annuls a general principle by virtue of the certainty
that, since each of the consequences of this same principle is struck in
the same manner, the principle becomes sterile, he remains within his
natural sphere of action. But if the judge attacks the general principle directly, and annuls it without having a particular case in view, he goes beyond the sphere in which all peoples agree he is to be confined: he
becomes something more important, more useful perhaps than a judge,
but he ceases to represent the judicial power.

The third characteristic of the judicial power is to be unable to act except when it is called upon or, according to the legal expression, when a
case is brought before it. This characteristic is not encountered as generally as the other two. Nevertheless, I think that, despite the exceptions,
one may consider it as essential. By its nature, the judicial power is inac-
tive; it must be set in motion in order for it to move. A crime is de-
nounced to it, and it punishes the guilty; it is called upon to redress an
injustice, and it redresses it; an act is submitted to it, and it interprets it.
But it does not go pursue criminals, seek out injustice, and examine
facts on its own. The judicial power would in a sense do violence to this
passive nature if it were to take the initiative on its own and set itself up
as a censor of the laws.

The Americans have retained in the judicial power these three distinctive characteristics. The American judge can make pronouncement
[101] only when there is a dispute. He is never concerned with anything except a particular case; and, in order to act, he must always wait for a case
to be brought before him.

The American judge thus resembles perfectly the judges of other nations. Nevertheless he is invested with an immense political power.

Where does this come from? He moves within the same sphere and
uses the same means as the other judges; why does he possess a power
that the others do not have?

The cause of this lies in this single fact: the Americans have acknowledged in their judges the right to base their decisions on the *Constitution*
rather than on the *laws*. In other words, they are permitted to not enforce
the laws that appear to them unconstitutional.

I know that such a right has sometimes been claimed by the courts of
other countries, but it has never been granted to them. In America, it is
acknowledged by all the powers; there is not a single party, nor even a
single man, who disputes it.

The explanation for this must be found in the very principle of the
American constitutions.

In France, the constitution is a construction that is, or is supposed to be, immutable. No power can change anything in it: such is the received theory.

In England, the right to change the constitution is recognized in Parliament. In England, the constitution may thus change constantly, or rather it does not exist. The Parliament, at the same time that it is a legislative body, is also a constituting body.*

In America, the political theories are simpler and more rational.

An American constitution is not assumed to be immutable as in France. It cannot be modified by the ordinary powers of the society, as in England. It forms a separate construction that, in representing the will of the whole people, obligates both legislators and ordinary citizens, but that can be changed by the will of the people following the procedures that have been established and in the cases provided for.

In America, the Constitution may thus change, but, as long as it exists, it is the source of all powers. Dominant power is in it alone.

It is easy to see in what way these differences must affect the position and the rights of the judicial body in the three countries that I have cited.

If, in France, the courts were able to disobey the laws, on the ground that they find them unconstitutional, the constituting power would in reality be in their hands, since they alone would have the right to interpret a constitution whose terms could be changed by no one. They would thus put themselves in the place of the nation and would rule the society, [102] at least to the extent that the weakness inherent in the judicial power allowed them to do it.

I know that by refusing the judges the right to declare laws unconstitutional, we indirectly give to the legislative body the power to change the constitution, since there is no longer any legal barrier to stop it. But it is still better to grant the power to change the people's constitution to men who imperfectly represent the people's will, than to others who represent only themselves.

It would be still more unreasonable to give to English judges the right of resisting the will of the legislative body, since the Parliament, which makes the law, also makes the constitution, and since, consequently, one may not, in any case, call a law unconstitutional when it emanates from all three powers.†

---

* The words translated as "constituting body" are *corps constituant*. *Constituant* may also be translated as "constituent," but this can mean a part or element of a whole, whereas a *corps constituant* is a body having the responsibility or right of "constituting," i.e., of making or altering a constitution.

† Tocqueville is referring to the King, the House of Lords, and the House of Commons.

Neither of these two arguments is applicable to America.

In the United States, the Constitution rules both legislators and ordinary citizens. It is thus the first of laws and cannot be modified by a law. It is therefore just that the courts obey the Constitution in preference to all the laws. This results from the very essence of the judicial power: to choose, from among legal dispositions, those which bind him most strictly is, in a way, the natural right of the judge.

In France, the constitution is also the first of laws, and the judges have an equal right to take it for the basis of their decisions; but, in exercising this right, they could not fail to trample on another one even more sacred than their own: that of the society in whose name they act. Here, ordinary reason must give way before reasons of State.

In America, where the nation can always, by changing its Constitution, reduce the judges to obedience, such a danger is not to be feared. On this point, politics and logic are thus in accord, and the people as well as the judge equally conserve their prerogatives there.

When a law that the judge believes to be contrary to the Constitution is invoked before the courts of the United States, he may thus refuse to enforce it. This power is the only one that is peculiar to the American judge, but a great political influence flows from it.

There are, in fact, very few laws that escape judicial scrutiny for a long time, for there are very few that do not offend some individual interest and that litigants cannot or must not invoke before the courts.

[103]   Now, from the moment the judge refuses to enforce a law in a legal proceeding, it immediately loses a portion of its moral force. Those who have been injured by it are from that moment made aware that there exists a means of escaping the obligation to obey it: court cases multiply, and it falls into a state of impotence. One of the following two things then occurs: the people change the Constitution or the legislature revokes its law.

The Americans have thus entrusted their courts with an immense political power, but by obliging them to attack the laws only with judicial means, they have greatly diminished the dangers of this power.

If the judge were able to attack the laws in a theoretical or general fashion, if he were able to take the initiative and censure the legislature, he would enter upon the political stage in brilliant fashion: by becoming the champion or the adversary of a party, he would incite all the passions that divide the country to take part in the conflict. But when the judge attacks a law in an obscure proceeding and with respect to a particular application, he conceals to an extent the importance of the attack from the eyes of the public. His decision has the aim of striking only some individual interest; the law is wounded only by chance.

Besides, the law censured in this way is not destroyed: its moral force is diminished, but its material effect is not suspended. It is only gradually, and under the repeated blows of judicial decisions, that it finally succumbs.

In addition, it is easy to see that by entrusting individual interest with bringing about the censure of the laws, by intimately linking the trial of the law to the trial of a man, one ensures that legislation will not be attacked lightly. In this system, legislation is no longer exposed to the daily attacks of parties. By pointing out the errors of the legislature, a real need is met: one starts from a positive and appreciable fact, since it is this that must serve as the basis for a legal proceeding.

I do not know if this way of acting by American courts, at the same time that it is the most favorable to public order, is not also the most favorable to liberty.

If the judge were only able to attack the legislature frontally, at some times he would be afraid to do so; at others, the spirit of party would incite him to do so every day. In this way it would come about that the laws would be attacked when the power from which they emanate was weak, and they would be obeyed without a murmur when it was strong; that is to say that often the laws would be attacked when it was most necessary to respect them and respected when it became easy to be oppressive in their name.

But the American judge is led onto the terrain of politics in spite of himself. He judges the law only because he has to judge a lawsuit, and [104] he cannot avoid judging the lawsuit. The political question that he must resolve is attached to the interest of the litigants, and he cannot refuse to decide it without causing a denial of justice. It is by fulfilling the narrow duties imposed by the profession of judge that he acts as a citizen. It is true that, in this way, judicial censure, exercised by the courts upon the law, cannot be extended indiscriminately to all the laws, for there are some that can never give rise to this kind of clearly formulated dispute that is called a lawsuit. And when such a dispute is possible, it is still conceivable that no one would want to bring it before the courts.

The Americans have often been aware of this disadvantage, but they have left the remedy incomplete, for fear of giving it, in all cases, a dangerous effectiveness.

Confined within its limits, the power granted to the American courts to pronounce on the unconstitutionality of the laws still forms one of the most powerful barriers that has ever been raised against the tyranny of political assemblies.

• • •

CHAPTER 8

                          THE FEDERAL CONSTITUTION

                                  • • •

**The Advantages of the Federal System in
                General, and Its Special Utility for America**

> *Happiness and liberty enjoyed by small nations.—Power of
> great nations.—The great empires favor the development of
> civilization.—That strength is often the first element of prosperity
> for nations.—The goal of the federal system is to unite the
> advantages that peoples derive from a great territory with those
> that they derive from a small territory.—Advantages that the
> United States derives from this system.—The law bends itself to
> the needs of the people, and the people do not bend themselves to
> the necessities of the law.—Activity, progress, taste, and habit of
> liberty among the American peoples.—The public spirit of the
> Union is only the* summary *of provincial patriotism.—Things
> and ideas circulate freely in the territory of the United States.—
> The Union is free and happy like a small nation and respected
> like a great one.*

In small nations, society's eye penetrates everywhere; the spirit of improvement descends into the smallest details: the ambition of the people
being much tempered by its weakness, its efforts and its resources are
almost entirely turned toward its internal well-being and are not liable to
be dissipated in a vain mirage of glory. Moreover, as the powers of each
person are generally limited, so are the desires. The mediocrity of fortunes makes conditions there more or less equal; mores have a simple
and peaceful appearance. Thus, all things considered, and taking into
account the different degrees of morality and enlightenment, one ordinarily encounters in small nations more prosperity, more population,
and more tranquility than in great ones.

  When tyranny establishes itself within a small nation, it is more troublesome there than anywhere else, because, acting within a smaller circle, it extends to everything within this circle. Unable to give itself over
to some grand object, it busies itself with a multitude of small ones; it
proves to be at the same time violent and harrassing. From the political
world, which is, properly speaking, its domain, it penetrates into private
life. After actions, it aspires to dictate tastes; after the State, it wants to
govern families. But that rarely happens; liberty constitutes, in truth, the

natural condition of small societies. The government there offers too little temptation to ambition, and the resources of the individuals in it are
too limited, for the sovereign power to be easily concentrated in the
hands of a single person. Should this happen, it is not difficult for the
governed to unite, and, by means of a common effort, to overthrow at
the same time the tyrant and the tyranny.

Small nations have therefore always been the cradle of political liber- [163]
ty. As it happens, most of them have lost this liberty by growing bigger,
which well shows that it is due to the small size of the people and not to
the people itself.

The history of the world does not furnish an example of a great nation which remained a republic for long,[38] which has made men say that
the thing was impracticable. For myself, I think that it is very imprudent
for man to want to set limits to what is possible and to judge the future
when reality and the present elude him every day, and he finds himself
constantly surprised without warning in the matters that he knows the
best. What one can say with certainty is that the existence of a great republic will always be infinitely more precarious than that of a small one.

All the passions fatal to republics increase with the extent of its territory, whereas the virtues which serve to support them do not increase in
the same measure.

The ambition of individuals increases with the power of the State; the
strength of parties, with the importance of the aim that they set themselves; but the love of the fatherland, which must struggle against these
passions, is not stronger in a vast republic than in a small one. It would
even be easy to show that it is less developed and less powerful there.
Great riches and profound poverty, great cities, the depravity of morals,
individual egoism, the complexity of interests are so many perils which
almost always arise from the greatness of the State. Several of these
things are not harmful to the existence of a monarchy; some may even
contribute to its survival. Besides, in monarchies, the government has a
strength which belongs to itself; it makes use of the people and does not
depend on it; the more the people is great, the more the prince is strong;
but republican government can only oppose to these dangers the support
of the majority. Now, this element of strength is not more powerful, proportionately, in a vast republic than in a small one. Thus, whereas the
means of attack increase without letup in number and in power, the
strength of resistance remains the same. One may even say that it diminishes, because the more numerous the people and the more diverse the

---

38. I am speaking here not of a confederation of small republics, but of a great
consolidated republic.

nature of men's minds and interests, the more difficult it is, in consequence, to form a compact majority.

[164] It has also been pointed out that human passions acquire intensity not only due to the greatness of the aim they want to achieve, but also due to the multitude of individuals who feel them simultaneously. There is no one who is not more moved in the midst of an agitated crowd which shares his emotion, than if he were the only one to feel it. In a great republic, political passions become irresistible, not only because the object they pursue is immense, but also because millions of men feel them in the same way and in the same moment.

One may therefore say in a general way that nothing is so contrary to the well-being and the liberty of men as great empires.

Nevertheless, great States have their own particular advantages which it is necessary to recognize.

Just as the desire for power among ordinary men is more ardent there than elsewhere, the love of glory is also more developed in certain souls who find in the applause of a great people an object worthy of their efforts and fit for lifting them in a way above themselves. Thought receives a more rapid and powerful impulse there, ideas circulate more freely, great cities are like vast intellectual centers where all the rays of the human mind shine and combine with one another: this fact explains for us why great nations produce more rapid progress in enlightenment and in the general cause of civilization than small ones. One must add that important discoveries often require a development of national strength of which the government of a small people is incapable; in great nations, the government has more general ideas, it frees itself more completely from the routine of antecedents and the egoism of localities. There is more genius in its conceptions, more daring in its comportment.

Internal well-being is more complete and widespread in small nations, so long as they keep themselves at peace, but the state of war is more harmful to them than to the great. In the latter, the extent of their frontiers sometimes allows the majority of the people to remain far from danger for centuries. For them, war is a cause of uneasiness rather than of ruin.

There is also, in this matter as in many others, a consideration which dominates all the rest: that of necessity.

If there were only small nations and no great ones, humanity would certainly be freer and happier, but one cannot arrange for there to be no great nations.

[165] This introduces into the world a new element of prosperity, namely strength. Of what importance is it that a people presents the picture of prosperity and liberty, if it is visibly exposed each day to being ravaged or conquered? Of what importance is it that it is a manufacturing and

trading nation, if another dominates the seas and makes law for all the markets? Small nations are often poor not because they are small but because they are weak; the great ones prosper not because they are great but because they are strong. For nations, strength is therefore one of the first conditions of happiness and even of existence. From this it results that apart from exceptional circumstances, small peoples always end up by being united violently to great ones or by uniting among themselves. I know of no condition more deplorable than that of a people which can neither defend itself nor be self-sufficient.

It is in order to unite the different advantages that result from the great and the small size of nations that the federative system was created.

It suffices to cast a glance at the United States of America to see all the goods that result for them from the adoption of this system.

In centralized great nations, the legislator is obliged to give a uniform character to the laws which does not encompass the diversity of places and mores; never being informed about special cases, he can only proceed by general rules; men are then obliged to bend themselves to the necessities of legislation because legislation cannot accommodate itself to the needs and the mores of men, which is a great cause of unrest and misery.

This disadvantage does not exist in confederations: the congress decides on the principal acts which regulate the life of the society; all of their details are left to provincial legislation.

One cannot imagine to what extent this division of sovereignty serves the well-being of each of the States which compose the Union. In these small societies which are not preoccupied with the care for defending or enlarging themselves, all public power and all individual energy are turned to internal improvements. The central government of each State, being placed right beside the governed, is alerted daily to needs which make themselves felt: one therefore sees new plans presented each year which, discussed in the municipal assemblies or before the legislature of the State, and then reproduced by the press, excite the universal interest and zeal of the citizens. This need to make improvements continually agitates the American republics without troubling them; the ambition for power gives way there to the love of well-being, a passion more vulgar but less dangerous. This is a widely held opinion in America, that the [166] existence and the survival of republican forms in the New World depends on the existence and the survival of the federative system. A great part of the miseries into which the new States of South America are plunged is attributed to the fact that they tried to establish great republics there instead of dividing up sovereignty.

It is incontestable, in fact, that in the United States the taste and the habit of republican government were born in the townships and in the bosom of the provincial assemblies. In a small nation, like Connecticut, for example, where the great political business is the opening of a canal and the laying out of a road, where the State has no army to pay nor a war to sustain, and cannot give to those who govern it either much riches or much glory, one cannot imagine anything more natural and more appropriate to the nature of things than the republic. Now, it is this same republican spirit, it is these mores and these habits of a free people, which, having arisen and grown in the different States, are then easily applied to the whole of the country. The public spirit of the Union is itself in a way only a summary of provincial patriotism. Each citizen of the United States so to speak transports the interest which his small republic inspires in him into love of the common fatherland. By defending the Union, he defends the growing prosperity of his corner of the country, the right to govern its affairs, and the hope of making prevail there plans of improvement which will surely make him richer: all things which, ordinarily, touch more men than the general interests of the country and the glory of the nation.

On the other hand, if the spirit and the mores of the inhabitants make them more fit than others for making a great republic flourish, the federative system has made the task much less difficult. The confederation of all the American States does not present the usual disadvantages of large conglomerations of men. The Union is a great republic with respect to its extent, but one may in a way assimilate it to a small republic because of the few objects which are the responsibility of its government. Its acts are important, but they are infrequent. Since the sovereignty of the Union is encumbered and incomplete, the utilization of this sovereignty is not dangerous for liberty. Nor does it excite those immoderate desires for power and éclat that are so disastrous for great republics. Since everything there does not necessarily end up at a common center, one sees neither vast cities nor immense riches, great poverty, or sudden revolutions. Political passions, instead of spreading in an instant like a [167] sheet of flames over the whole surface of the country, break themselves against the interests and the individual passions of each State.

In the Union, however, things and ideas circulate freely, as they do among a single and identical people. Nothing there stops the development of the spirit of enterprise. Its government calls to itself talents and enlightenment. Within the frontiers of the Union a profound peace reigns, as in the interior of a country subject to the same empire; beyond them, it ranks among the most powerful nations of the earth; it offers to foreign commerce more than eight hundred leagues of coastline; and holding in its hands the keys to a whole world, it makes its flag respected to the outermost limits of the seas.

The Union is free and happy like a small nation, glorious and strong like a great one.

• • •

VOLUME ONE, PART TWO

PREFACE   [176]

Up to now I have examined the institutions, covered the written laws, and described the present forms of political society in the United States.

But above all the institutions, and beyond all the forms, resides a sovereign power, that of the people, which destroys or modifies them at its pleasure.

It remains for me to point out in what ways this power, ruler over the laws, proceeds; what are its instincts, its passions; what secret springs propel it, slow it down, or direct it in its irresistible march; what effects its omnipotence produces, and what future is reserved for it.

CHAPTER 1   [177]

HOW IT CAN BE STRICTLY SAID THAT IN
THE UNITED STATES IT IS THE PEOPLE THAT GOVERN

In America, the people designate the one who makes the law and the one who executes it. The people itself composes the jury that punishes infractions of the law. The institutions are democratic not only in their principle but also in all their elaborations. Thus, the people *directly* designates its representatives and chooses them in general *each year* in order to keep them more fully dependent upon itself. It is therefore really the people that governs, and although the form of government is representative, it is obvious that there are no lasting obstacles that can prevent the opinions, prejudices, interests, and even the passions of the people from manifesting themselves in the daily direction of the society.

In the United States, as in all countries where the people reigns, it is the majority that governs in the name of the people.

This majority is composed principally of peaceful citizens who, either by taste or by interest, sincerely desire the good of the country. About them, in constant agitation, are the parties, who seek to attract them into their midst and to acquire their support.

[178]

CHAPTER 2

PARTIES IN THE UNITED STATES

*One must make a great distinction between parties.—Parties
which are in relation to each other like rival nations.—Parties
properly so-called.—Difference between great and small
parties.—In what periods they arise.—Their different
characters.—America has had great parties.—She no longer
has them.—Federalists.—Republicans.—Defeat of the
Federalists.—Difficulty of creating parties in the United
States.—What is done to succeed in creating them.—
Aristocratic or democratic character which reappears in
all the parties.—Fight of General Jackson against the Bank.*

I must first establish a great distinction between parties.

There are countries so vast that the different groups that inhabit them, although united under the same sovereignty, have opposed interests, from which there arises between them a permanent opposition. The different fractions of a single people do not then form, properly speaking, parties, but distinct nations; and if civil war happens to break out, there is a conflict between rival peoples rather than a struggle between factions.

But when the citizens differ among themselves over points that interest all portions of the country equally, as, for example, the general principles of government, then one sees come into being what I will call genuine parties.

Parties are an evil inherent in free governments, but they do not have at all times the same character and the same instincts.

There are times in which nations feel themselves tormented by evils so great that the idea of a total change in their political constitution presents itself to their thought. There are others in which the uneasiness is still more profound and when the social state itself is exposed to risk. This is the age of great revolutions and great parties.

Between these ages of disorders and miseries, there are others in which societies rest and during which the human race seems to catch its
[179] breath. That is, in truth, only an appearance; time does not suspend its march for peoples any more than for men; both of them advance each day toward a future of which they are ignorant; and when we believe them to be stationary, it is because we do not notice their movements. These are men who are walking; they seem immobile only to those who are running.

Whatever the case may be, there are times when the changes that are occurring in the political constitution and social state of peoples are so slow and so imperceptible that men think they have arrived at a final state; the human mind then believes itself firmly seated on certain foundations and does not cast its glance beyond a certain horizon.

This is the age of intrigues and of small parties.

What I am calling the great political parties are those that are attached to principles more than to their consequences, to generalities and not to particular cases, to ideas and not to men. These parties have, in general, traits that are more noble, passions that are more generous, beliefs that are more real, a bearing that is more open and more intrepid than the others. Particular interest, which always plays the greatest role in political passions, hides itself more skillfully here beneath the veil of the public interest; sometimes it even succeeds in going unnoticed by those whom it inspires and causes to act.

Small parties, on the contrary, are, in general, without political faith. Since they do not feel uplifted and sustained by great objects, their character is marked by an egoism that manifests itself obviously in each of their actions. They become heated without genuine emotion; their speech is violent, but their steps are timid and uncertain. The means that they employ are contemptible like the end itself that they have in view. From this it results that when a time of calm follows a violent revolution, great men seem to suddenly disappear, and the souls of men withdraw into themselves.

Great parties turn society upside down, small ones agitate it; the first tear it apart, and the second corrupt it; the first sometimes save it by shaking it up, the second always trouble it without profit.

America has had great parties. Today they no longer exist: it has gained much in the way of happiness by this, but not in morality.

When the War of Independence came to an end, and it was a matter of establishing the foundations of the new government, the nation found itself divided between two opinions. These opinions were as old as the world; they recur under different forms and under different names in all free societies. The one wished to restrain popular power, the other to extend it indefinitely.

The struggle between these two opinions never took on the character [180] of violence among the Americans that has often been its signpost elsewhere. In America, the two parties were in agreement on the most essential points. Neither of them, in order to defeat the other, had to destroy an old order or overturn a whole social state. In neither case, consequently, were a great number of individual lives affected by the triumph of its principles. But they touched nonmaterial interests of the first order, such as the love of equality and of independence. That was enough to arouse violent passions.

The party that wanted to restrain the people's power sought particularly to apply its doctrines to the Constitution of the Union, which caused it to acquire the name of *Federal*.

The other, which claimed to be the exclusive lover of liberty, took the title of *Republican*.

America is the land of democracy. The Federalists were therefore always in the minority, but they counted among their ranks almost all the great men to which the War of Independence had given rise, and their moral authority was very extensive. The circumstances were also favorable to them. The ruin of the first confederation* made the people afraid of falling into anarchy, and the Federalists profited from this momentary disposition. For ten or twelve years, they directed public affairs and were able to apply not all their principles but some of them; for the opposing current became day by day too violent for one to dare to struggle against it.

In 1801, the Republicans finally seized hold of the government. Thomas Jefferson was chosen President. He brought them the support of a famous name, a great talent, and an immense popularity.

The Federalists had never been maintained in power except by artificial means and with the help of momentary resources; it was the virtue or the talents of their leaders, as well as the luck of circumstances, that had propelled them into power. When the Republicans arrived there in their turn, the opposition party was as much as enveloped by a sudden deluge. An immense majority declared itself against it, and the party saw itself at once in such a small minority that it immediately despaired of itself. From this moment, the republican, or democratic, party marched from conquest to conquest and seized hold of the entire society.

The Federalists, feeling themselves to be defeated, without resources, and seeing themselves isolated in the heart of the nation, split apart: some joined their vanquishers; the others put down their banner and changed their name. It is now a great many years since they have entirely ceased to exist as a party.

[181]   The accession of the Federalists to power is, in my view, one of the luckiest events that accompanied the birth of the great American Union. The Federalists struggled against the irresistible tendency of their time and of their country. Whatever the excellence or weakness of their theories, they had the defect of not being applicable in their entirety to the society that the Federalists wished to govern. What happened under Jefferson would thus have happened sooner or later. But their government at least gave the new republic time to set itself on a firm foundation and allowed it afterward to bear without harmful consequences the rapid

---

* The Articles of Confederation.

growth of the doctrines against which they had fought. In addition, a great number of their principles ended up entering into the creed of their adversaries, and the Federal Constitution, which still survives in our day, is a lasting monument to their patriotism and wisdom.

In this way, therefore, today there are no great political parties to be seen in the United States. There are many parties there that constitute a danger to the future of the Union, but there exist none that appear to attack the present form of the government and the general direction of the society. The parties that present a danger to the Union are based not on principles but on material interests. These interests constitute, within the different regions of such a vast empire, rival nations rather than parties. We have thus lately seen the North defending the system of commercial prohibitions, and the South taking up arms on behalf of the liberty of commerce, for the sole reason that the North is industrial and the South agricultural, and the restrictive system acts to the benefit of the first and to the detriment of the second.

For want of great parties, the United States swarms with small ones, and public opinion splits into an infinite number of pieces over questions of detail. It is impossible to imagine the trouble that is taken there to create parties; this is not an easy thing to do today. In the United States, there is no religious hatred, because religion is universally respected and no sect is dominant; no class hatred, because the people is everything, and nobody dares any more to fight with it; and finally, no public misery to exploit, because the material state of the country offers such an immense career to industry that it suffices to leave a man to himself for him to produce prodigies. Ambition must nevertheless succeed in creating parties, for it is difficult to topple the one who holds power for the sole reason that one wants to take his place. All the skill of politicians thus consists in forming parties: a politician in the United States first seeks to discern his own interest and to see what the similar interests are that could be grouped around his own; he then attends to discovering whether there does not by chance exist in the world some doctrine or some [182] principle that could be suitably placed at the head of the new grouping in order to give it the right to show itself and circulate freely. This is sort of like the authorization of the king that our forefathers used to print on the first page of their works, and that they incorporated into the book even though it was not part of it.

This done, the new power is introduced into the political world.

To a foreigner, almost all the domestic quarrels of the Americans appear, at first sight, incomprehensible or childish, and one does not know if one ought to pity a people that occupies itself seriously with such trifles or envy it the luck of being able to do so.

But when one comes to study with care the secret instincts that, in America, govern the factions, one easily discovers that the majority of them are more or less attached to one or the other of the two great parties that have divided men for as long as there have been free societies. As one penetrates more deeply into the intimate thoughts of these parties, one perceives that the one works to narrow the use of public power, the other to expand it.

I am not saying that American parties always have for their open aim or even hidden purpose to make aristocracy or democracy prevail in the country. I am saying only that aristocratic or democratic passions are easily rediscovered at the bottom of all the parties and that, although they escape notice there, they constitute as it were the parties' point of sensitivity and their soul.

I will cite a recent example: the President attacks the Bank of the United States; the country is aroused and becomes divided; the enlightened classes line up in general on the side of the Bank, the people in favor of the President. Do you think that the people was able to discern the reasons for its opinion in the midst of the complex turns of such a difficult question and about which experienced men hesitate? In no way. But the Bank is a great establishment that has an independent existence; the people, which destroys or raises up all powers, can do nothing to it, and this astonishes it. In the midst of the universal movement of the society, this fixed point is shocking to the people's eyes, and it wants to see if it can succeed in shaking it like everything else.

[183]   **The Remnants of the Aristocratic Party in the United States**

. . .

It sometimes happens, among a people divided in opinion, that the equilibrium between the parties comes to be broken, and one of the two acquires an irresistible preponderance. It smashes all obstacles, crushes its adversary, and runs the entire society for its own benefit. The vanquished, losing all hope of success, conceal themselves or keep quiet. A motionlessness and universal silence ensue. The nation seems united in a single way of thinking. The conquering party rises up and says: "I have brought peace to the country; I am owed expressions of thanks."*

But beneath this apparent unanimity are still hidden profound divisions and a real opposition.

---

* *On me doit des actions de grâces.* An *action de grâce* is an expression of thanks that is normally given to God. The French words for Thanksgiving Day, which commemorates the day the Plymouth colonists gave thanks to God for their first harvest, are *Jour d'action de grâce.*

That is what happened in America: when the democratic party had achieved predominance, one saw it seize hold of the exclusive direction of public affairs. Since then, it has not ceased to shape the mores and the laws according to its desires.

Today one can say that in the United States the wealthy classes of the society are almost entirely out of political affairs and that wealth, far from being an entitlement, is a real cause of disfavor and an obstacle to attaining power.

The wealthy thus prefer to abandon the lists than to sustain an often unequal struggle against the poorest of their fellow citizens. Unable to attain a rank in public life similar to that which they occupy in private life, they abandon the first in order to focus on the second. They form in the heart of the State a kind of private society with its own separate tastes and pleasures.

The wealthy person submits to this state of things as to an irremediable evil; he carefully avoids even showing that it offends him; thus he is heard to praise in public the appealing qualities of republican government and the advantages of democratic forms. For, next to hating their enemies, what is more natural to men than to flatter them?

Do you see this wealthy citizen? Would you not take him for a Jew of the Middle Ages who feared to allow men to suspect his wealth? His dress is simple, his gait is modest. Between the four walls of his house luxury is worshipped. He allows to enter into this sanctuary only a few chosen guests whom he arrogantly calls his equals. There is no noble- [184] man in Europe who proves to be more exclusive in his pleasures, and more jealous of the least advantages that a privileged position secures, than he. But here he is, leaving his house to go to work in a dusty nook that he occupies in the center of town and of business, and where anyone is free to come and approach him. In the middle of the road, his shoemaker happens to pass, and they stop: they both then start to chat. What can they be saying? These two citizens are dealing with the affairs of the State, and they will not take leave of one another without shaking hands.

At the bottom of this enthusiasm for convention, and in the midst of these obsequious proprieties regarding the dominant power, it is easy to perceive in the wealthy a great disgust for the democratic institutions of their country. The people is a power that they fear and that they despise. If the bad government of democracy were one day to bring about a political crisis, if monarchy were ever to present itself in the United States as a feasible thing, the truth of my argument would soon be revealed.

The two great weapons employed by the parties in order to succeed are newspapers and associations.

CHAPTER 3

LIBERTY OF THE PRESS IN THE UNITED STATES

*Difficulty of limiting liberty of the press.—Particular reasons
some peoples have for being attached to this liberty.—Liberty of
the press is a necessary consequence of the sovereignty of the
people as it is understood in America.—Violent language of the
periodical press in the United States.—The periodical press has
instincts that are its own; the example of the United States proves
this.—Opinion of the Americans on the judicial repression of the
offenses of the press.—Why the press is less powerful in the
United States than in France.*

Liberty of the press makes its power felt not only on political opinions,
but also on all the opinions of men. It modifies not only laws, but mores.
In another part of this work, I will try to determine the degree of influence that liberty of the press has exercised on civil society in the United
States; I will try to discern the direction that it has given to ideas, and the
habits it has caused the minds and sentiments of the Americans to pick
up. At this time, I want to examine only the effects produced by liberty
of the press in the political world.

I admit that I do not bear toward liberty of the press that complete
and immediate love that is given to things supremely good in their nature. I love it out of consideration for the evils it prevents much more
than for the goods it provides.

If someone were to show me, between the complete independence
and the complete enslavement of thought, an intermediate position
where I might hope to hold fast, I would perhaps settle myself there; but
who will discover this intermediate position? You start with the licentiousness of the press, and you become a partisan of order: what do you
do? First you send the writers before juries; but the juries acquit, and
what was only the opinion of an isolated man becomes the opinion of the
country. You have thus done too much and too little; it is necessary to go
further. You hand over the authors to permanent judges; but the judges
are obliged to hear before condemning; what one was afraid to avow in
[186] the book, one openly proclaims with impunity in the defense's pleading;
what was obscurely said in a single account is thereby repeated in a thousand others. Expression is the external form and, if I can speak in this
way, the body of thought, but it is not thought itself. Your tribunals arrest
the body, but the soul escapes them and subtly slips between their hands.
You have thus done too much and too little; it is necessary to continue to

go further. You finally deliver the writers over to the censors. Very fine! We're getting closer. But isn't the political forum free? You have thus again accomplished nothing; I am wrong, you have increased the harm. Do you by chance take thought to be one of those material powers that increases by means of the number of its agents? Do you count writers like the soldiers of an army? Contrary to all material powers, the power of thought is often increased precisely by the small number of those who express it. The speech of one forceful man, which penetrates alone into the depths of the passions of a silent assemblage, has more power than the confused shouting of a thousand orators; and if one may speak freely in a single public place, it's as if one were speaking publicly in every village. You must therefore destroy liberty of speech as well as that of writing. This time, you have arrived in port: everyone is silent. But where have you arrived? You had started with the abuses of liberty, and I find you now under the heel of a despot.

You have been from the utmost independence to the utmost servitude, without finding, over such a long distance, a single place where you could stop.

There are peoples who, independently of the general reasons I have just enunciated, have particular reasons which ought to attach them to the liberty of the press.

Among some nations who claim to be free, each of the agents of power can violate the law with impunity without the constitution of the country giving to the oppressed person the right to bring a complaint before a court. Among these peoples, one must no longer consider the independence of the press as one of the guarantees, but as the sole remaining guarantee of the liberty and security of the citizens.

If therefore the men who govern these nations were to talk about taking away the independence of the press, the whole people might respond to them: "Allow us to prosecute your crimes in the ordinary courts, and perhaps we will then consent to not appeal to the court of opinion."

In a country where the dogma of the sovereignty of the people openly reigns, censorship is not only a danger, but also a great absurdity.

When each person is granted a right to govern the society, it is neces- [187] sary to grant him the capacity to choose between the different opinions that agitate his contemporaries, and to evaluate the different facts the knowledge of which can guide him.

The sovereignty of the people and the liberty of the press are thus two things that are entirely correlative: censorship and universal suffrage are on the contrary two things that are in contradiction with each other and cannot be joined together for long in the political institutions of a single people. Among the twelve million men who live on the territory of the

United States, there is not *a single one* who has yet dared to suggest limiting the liberty of the press.

. . .

CHAPTER 5

THE GOVERNMENT OF DEMOCRACY IN AMERICA

. . .

Universal Suffrage

I have said previously that all the States of the Union had accepted universal suffrage. It is found among populations placed on different rungs of the social scale. I have had the chance to view its effects in diverse places and among races of men whose language, religion, or mores makes them almost strangers to one another; in Louisiana as well as in New England, [203] in Georgia as well as in Canada. I saw that universal suffrage was far from producing, in America, all the goods and all the evils that are expected from it in Europe, and that its effects were in general different than what they are assumed to be.

The Choices of the People and the Instincts of American Democracy in Its Choices

In the United States the most remarkable men are rarely called to the direction of public affairs.—Causes of this phenomenon.— The envy that animates the inferior classes of France against the superior ones is not a French sentiment, but a democratic one.— Why, in America, distinguished men often deliberately eschew political careers.

Many men in Europe believe without saying, or say without believing, that one of the great advantages of universal suffrage is to call to the direction of affairs men worthy of public confidence. The people cannot itself govern, it is said, but it always sincerely wills the good of the State, and its instinct does not fail to point out to it those who are animated by the same desire and who are the most capable of taking power well in hand.

For me, I must say, what I have seen in America does not justify my thinking that this is the case. Upon my arrival in the United States, I was struck with surprise upon discovering to what extent merit was common among the governed, and how little this was the case among the governors. It is invariably the case that, in our day, in the United States, the most remarkable men are rarely called to public office, and one is obliged to recognize that this has been the case to the degree that democracy has gone beyond all its former limits. It is obvious that the race of American statesmen has gotten much smaller over the last half century.

Several causes of this phenomenon may be pointed out.

It is impossible, no matter what one does, to raise the enlightenment of the people above a certain level. However much access to human knowledge is facilitated, methods of instruction improved and learning made a bargain, men will never be made to learn and develop their intelligence without their devoting time to it.

The greater or less ease with which the people can live without working therefore sets the necessary limit of its intellectual progress. This [204] limit is situated further out in certain countries, less far out in others, but in order for it not to exist at all, it would be necessary for the people not to have to be occupied with the material cares of life, that is to say that it would no longer be the people. It is therefore as difficult to conceive of a society in which all men are very enlightened, as it is to conceive of a State in which all the citizens are rich; these are two correlative difficulties. I will readily admit that the mass of citizens very sincerely wills the good of the country; I will go even further and say that the inferior classes of the society seem to me, in general, to mix with this desire fewer schemes of personal interest than the higher classes; but what they always lack, more or less, is the art of judging the means while sincerely willing the end. What long study, what diverse ideas are necessary in order to acquire an exact idea of the character of a single man! As if the multitude might succeed where the greatest geniuses lose their way! The people never finds the time and the means to engage in this work. It must always judge hastily and attach itself to the objects which stand out the most. This is why charlatans of all kinds know so well the secret of pleasing it, whereas, most often, its true friends fail to do so.

Moreover, it is not always the ability to choose men of merit which democracy lacks, but the desire and the taste.

We must not conceal from ourselves the fact that democratic institutions make the sentiment of envy grow in the human heart to a very high degree. It is not so much because they give to each the means of equaling the others, but because these means continually fail those who employ them. Democratic institutions awaken and flatter the passion for equality without ever being able to satisfy it completely. This complete equality always eludes the grasp of the people at the moment they believe they have gotten hold of it, and recedes, as Pascal says, in an eternal flight; the people is excited by the pursuit of this good which is all the more precious for being close enough to be known, and far enough away that it has not been tasted. The chance of succeeding excites it, the uncertainty of success irritates it; it agitates itself, it tires itself out, it becomes embittered. Everything which at some point surpasses it then appears to it as an obstacle to its desires, and there is no superiority so legitimate that the sight of it is not an annoyance to its eyes.

Many men imagine that this secret instinct which causes the inferior classes among us to cut the superior classes off as much as they can from the direction of public affairs is only found in France. This is an error: the instinct I am speaking about is not French, it is democratic; political circumstances may have given it a particular quality of bitterness, but they did not give rise to it.

[205]

In the United States, the people has no hatred for the higher classes of the society, but it feels little goodwill for them and is careful to keep them out of power; it does not fear great talents, but it has little taste for them. In general, one notices that everything which raises itself up without its help has difficulty obtaining its favor.

Whereas the natural instincts of democracy cause the people to keep distinguished men out of power, an instinct not less strong causes the latter to eschew the career of politics, in which it is so difficult for them to remain completely themselves and to engage in it without demeaning themselves. It is this thought which is very simply expressed by Chancellor Kent. The celebrated author of whom I speak, after having given great praise to that part of the Constitution which gives the nomination of judges to the executive power, adds: "It is probable, in fact, that the men who are the most fit to fill these places, would have manners too reserved, and principles too severe, to ever be able to attract the majority of votes in an election based on universal suffrage." (Kent's Commentaries, v. I, p. 272.) That was printed without contradiction in America in the year 1830.

I take it as proven that those who regard universal suffrage as a guarantee of the goodness of the choices are deluding themselves completely. Universal suffrage has other advantages, but not that one.

Causes That May Partially Correct These Instincts of Democracy

. . .

When great dangers threaten the State, the people are often seen to choose felicitously the citizens who are most fit to save it.

It has been observed that the man in urgent danger rarely remains at [206] his usual level: he rises well above it or falls below. This happens to peoples themselves. Extreme dangers, instead of uplifting a nation, sometimes complete its fall. They excite its passions without guiding them and cloud its intelligence instead of illuminating it. The Jews were still cutting each other's throats amid the smoking ruins of the Temple. But it is more common to see, in nations as in men, extraordinary virtues arise from the very imminence of dangers. Great characters then appear in relief like those monuments that were obscured by the darkness of night and that one sees suddenly stand out in the glow of a fire. Genius no longer disdains to show itself in its own image, and the people, stupefied by their own peril, temporarily forget their envious passions. Then it is not unusual to see famous names emerge from the ballot box. I said above that in America the statesmen today seem very inferior to those who appeared, fifty years ago, at the head of public affairs. This does not result only from the laws, but from circumstances. When America fought for the most just of causes, that of a people escaping the yoke of another people, when it was a question of bringing forth a new nation into the world, all the people lifted themselves up to reach the height of the goal of their efforts. In this general enthusiasm, the superior men rushed forward to meet the people, and the people, taking them in its arms, placed them at its head. But such events are rare; one must judge on the basis of the normal aspect of things.

• • •

The Corruption and the Vices of the Governors in Democracy; [229] The Effects on Public Morality That Result from It

In aristocracies, the governors sometimes try to corrupt.—Often, in democracies, they themselves prove to be corrupt.—In the first, vices attack the morality of the people directly.—In the second, they exercise an influence on it that is still more fearsome.

Aristocracy and democracy mutually reproach one another for facilitating corruption. One must make a distinction:

In aristocratic governments, the men who go into political affairs are rich men who only want power. In democracies, the statesmen are poor and have yet to make their fortune.

It follows that, in aristocratic states, the governors are little susceptible to corruption and have only a very modest taste for money, whereas the opposite happens among democratic peoples.

But, in aristocracies, those who want to reach the head of public affairs dispose of great wealth, and since the number of those who can enable them to reach it is often circumscribed within clear limits, the government is in a way up for auction. In democracies, on the contrary, those who angle eagerly for power are almost never rich, and the number of those who participate in granting it is very great. There may not be fewer men for sale in democracies, but one finds almost no buyers there; and besides, it would be necessary to buy too many people at one time in order to achieve the goal.

Among the men who have held power in France during the last forty years, several have been accused of having gotten rich at the expense of the State and its allies, a reproach which was rarely addressed to the officials of the former monarchy. But, in France, one almost never buys the vote of an elector in return for money, whereas the thing is notoriously and publicly done in England.

I have never heard it said that in the United States anyone employed wealth to win over the governed, but I have often seen the honesty of the officials placed in doubt. Still more often I have heard their success attributed to base intrigues or culpable maneuvers.

[230]   If, therefore, the men who govern aristocracies sometimes seek to corrupt, the leaders of democracies prove themselves to be corrupt. In the former, the morality of the people is attacked directly; in the latter, there is an indirect effect on the public conscience which must be dreaded even more.

Among democratic peoples, because those who are at the head of the State are almost always the butt of disagreeable suspicions, they in a way give the support of the government to the crimes of which they are accused. They thus offer dangerous examples to virtue which is still struggling and furnish glorious comparisons to hidden vice.

It is futile to say that dishonest passions are found in all ranks; that they often mount the throne by right of birth; that one may thus encounter very comtemptible men at the head of aristocratic nations as well as in the bosom of democracies.

This response does not satisfy me: in the corruption of those who come to power by chance, there is something crude and vulgar which makes it contagious for the crowd; on the contrary, there prevails, even in the depravity of great lords, a certain aristocratic refinement, an air of grandeur which often prevents it from being communicated to others.

The people will never penetrate the obscure labyrinth of the spirit of the court; it will always have difficulty seeing the baseness which is hidden beneath the elegance of manners, the pursuit of taste, and the charms of language. But stealing from the public treasury, or selling the favors of the State in return for money, the least wretch understands that and can flatter himself that he can do as much in his turn.

Besides, what one must fear is not so much the sight of the immorality of the great as that of immorality leading to greatness. In democracy, the simple citizens see a man who emerges from their ranks and achieves wealth and power in a few years; this spectacle provokes their surprise and their envy; they try to find out how he who was yesterday their equal today is invested with the right to govern them. To attribute his rise to his talents or to his virtues is inconvenient because that would be to admit that they themselves are less virtuous and less capable than he. They therefore locate the principal cause of his rise in some of his vices, and often they are right to do so. In this way, some sort of odious mixing takes place between the ideas of baseness and power, of unworthiness and success, of utility and dishonor.

. . .

CHAPTER 6   [241]

**WHAT ARE THE REAL ADVANTAGES THAT AMERICAN
SOCIETY DERIVES FROM DEMOCRATIC GOVERNMENT**

. . .

**The General Tendency of the Laws under the Dominion of
American Democracy and the Instinct of Those Who Apply Them**

> *The vices of democracy are immediately visible.—Its advantages
> are only perceived in the long run.—American democracy is often
> inept, but the general tendency of the laws is beneficial.—Public
> officials, under American democracy, have no permanent interests
> that differ from those of the majority.—What results from this.*

The vices and weakness of democratic government are easily seen; they are demonstrated by patent facts whereas its salutary influence is exercised in a way that is imperceptible and in a manner of speaking occult. Its defects strike one from the very beginning, but its virtues come to light only in the long run.

The laws of American democracy are often defective or incomplete;   [242]
sometimes they violate vested rights or ratify dangerous ones: if they were good, their frequency would be an even greater evil. All of this is evident at first glance.

How does it thus happen that the American republics survive and prosper?

One must distinguish carefully, in laws, the aim they pursue and the manner in which they march toward this aim, their absolute goodness from that which is only relative.

Assume that the object of the legislator is to favor the interests of the minority at the expense of those of the majority; his measures are combined in such a way that he obtains the result he intends in the least amount of time and with the least possible effort. The law will be well made, its aim bad; it will be dangerous in proportion to its very effectiveness.

The laws of democracy tend, in general, to the good of the greatest number because they emanate from the majority of all the citizens, which may make a mistake but which cannot have an interest contrary to itself.

Those of aristocracy tend, on the contrary, to monopolize wealth and power in the hands of the minority because it is of the nature of aristocracy always to consitute a minority.

One may therefore say, in a general way, that the object of democracy, in its legislation, is more useful to humanity than the object of aristocracy in its own legislation.

But there democracy's advantages end.

Aristocracy is infinitely more skillful in the science of the legislator than democracy is capable of being. Master of itself, it is not subject to transient impulses; it has long-term goals which it knows how to mature until the favorable opportunity presents itself. Aristocracy proceeds skillfully; it knows the art of making the collective force of all its laws converge at the same time toward the same point.

It is not the same with democracy: its laws are almost always defective or ill-timed.

Democracy's means are therefore more imperfect than those of aristocracy: often it works against itself without wishing to, but its goal is more useful.

Imagine a society which nature, or its constitution, had organized in such a manner as to withstand the transient influence of bad laws and which could await without peril the result of the *general tendency* of the laws, and you will see that democratic government, despite its faults, is still the most suitable of all to make this society prosper.

[243]   That is precisely what happens in the United States. I will repeat here what I have already expressed elsewhere: the great privilege of the Americans is to be able to make reparable mistakes.

I will say something analogous about the public officials.

It is easy to see that American democracy often errs in the choice of the men in whom it confides power, but it is not as easy to say why the State prospers in their hands.

Notice first that if, in a democratic State, the governors are less honest or less capable, the governed are more enlightened and more attentive.

The people in democracies, occupied constantly, as it is, with its affairs and jealous of its rights, prevents its representatives from straying from a certain general line that its interest traces for it.

Notice also that if the democratic magistrate makes worse use of power than another, he possesses it, in general, for less time.

But there is a reason more general and more satisfying than that.

It is without doubt important for the good of nations that those who govern have virtues or talents, but what is perhaps even more important to them is that the governors not have interests contrary to the mass of the governed, because, in this case, the virtues could become almost useless and the talents disastrous.

I have said that it was important that the governors not have interests contrary to or different than the mass of the governed; I have not said that it was important that they have interests similar to those of *all* the governed because I do not know that the thing has ever existed.

Up to now the political form has not been found which furthers equally the development and the prosperity of all the classes which compose society. These classes have continued to form, as it were, so many distinct nations within the same nation, and experience has proven that it was almost as dangerous to completely entrust the fate of the other classes to any one of them as to make one people the arbiter of the destiny of another people. When the rich alone govern, the interest of the poor is always in danger; and when the poor make the law, that of the rich runs great risks. What therefore is the advantage of democracy? The real advantage of democracy is not, as has been said, to further the prosperity of all, but only to serve the well-being of the greatest number.

Those who are charged, in the United States, with the direction of the affairs of the public, are often inferior in capacity and in morality to the [244] men whom aristocracy places in power, but their interest is merged and identified with that of the majority of their fellow citizens. They may therefore commit frequent acts of faithlessness and grave errors, but they will never systematically follow a tendency hostile to this majority; and it is impossible for them to give an exclusive and dangerous appearance to the government.

The bad administration of a magistrate, under democracy, is also an isolated fact which only has influence during the short duration of this administration. Corruption and incompetence are not common interests which can link men with one another in a permanent manner.

A corrupt or incompetent magistrate will not combine his efforts with another magistrate, for the single reason that the latter is as incompetent and as corrupt as he is, and these two men will never work in concert to make corruption and incompetence flourish among their posterity. The ambition and maneuvers of the one will serve, on the contrary, to unmask the other. The vices of the magistrate, in democracies, are, in general, entirely personal to him.

But public men under aristocratic government have a class interest which, if it sometimes merges with that of the majority, often remains distinct from it. This interest forms a common and durable link between them; it encourages them to unite and to combine their efforts toward a goal which is not always the happiness of the greatest number: it not only links the governors to each other, it also links them to a considerable portion of the governed because many citizens, without having any office, belong to the aristocracy.

The aristocratic magistrate therefore finds constant support within the society at the same time that he finds it in the government.

This common object which, in aristocracies, unites the magistrates with a portion of their contemporaries, also identifies them with, and as it were subjects them to, the interest of future generations. They work for the future as well as for the present. The aristocratic magistrate is therefore pushed at the same time toward a single point by the passions of the governed, by his own passions, and, I might almost say, by the passions of his posterity.

Why should we be surprised if he does not resist? In consequence, in aristocracies the spirit of class often carries along even those whom it does not corrupt and makes them unwittingly adapt the society little by little to their usage, and prepare it for their descendents.

I do not know if an aristocracy as liberal as that of England has ever existed, and which has, without interruption, furnished to the goverment of the country men as worthy and as enlightened.

[245]   It is, however, easy to see that in English legislation the good of the poor has often ended up being sacrificed to that of the rich, and the rights of the greatest number to the privileges of some: therefore England, in our day, brings together in its bosom the greatest extremes of fortune, and there is poverty in it that almost equals its power and its glory.

In the United States, where the public officials have no class interest to make prevail, the general and continuous course of the government is salutary, although the governments are often inept and sometimes contemptible.

There is, therefore, at the bottom of democratic institutions, a hidden tendency which often makes men contribute to the general prosperity despite their vices or errors, whereas in aristocratic institutions, there is sometimes a secret inclination which leads men, despite their talents and virtues, to contribute to the misery of their fellows. Thus it may happen that, in aristocratic governments, public men do evil without wanting to, and in democracies they do good without having given it a thought.

Public Spirit in the United States

Instinctive love of the fatherland.—Thoughtful patriotism.— Their different characters.—That peoples must strive with all their might toward the second when the first disappears.— Efforts that the Americans have made in order to succeed at this.—The interest of the individual intimately connected to that of the country.

There exists a love of the fatherland which has its source principally in that unreflective sentiment, disinterested and undefinable, which connects the heart of man to the place where he was born. This instinctive love is mixed with the taste for ancient customs, the respect for ancestors and the memory of the past; those who experience it cherish their country as one loves the paternal house. They love the tranquility that they enjoy there; they keep to the peaceful habits that they have acquired there; they become attached to the memories that it offers them and even find some sweetness in living there in obedience. Often this love of the fatherland is stimulated still more by religious zeal, and then one sees it accomplish prodigies. It is itself a sort of religion; it does not reason, it believes, it feels, it acts. There are peoples who have, in a certain way, personified the fatherland, and who glimpsed it in their prince. They [246] thus invested him with a portion of the sentiments of which patriotism is composed; they were proud of his triumphs and proud of his power. There was a time, under the former monarchy, when the French experienced a kind of joy at feeling themselves abandoned without recourse to the arbitrariness of the monarch and said with pride: "We live under the most powerful king in the world."

Like all unreflective passions, this love of country prompts great but fleeting efforts rather than continuity of effort. After having saved the State in time of crisis, this love of country often allows it to waste away in the midst of peace.

When peoples are still simple in their mores and firm in their belief, when society rests mildly upon an ancient order of things whose legitimacy is not questioned, this instinctive love of the fatherland reigns supreme.

There is another love of country that is more rational than that one: less generous, perhaps less ardent, but more fertile and more durable. This one is born of enlightenment; it develops with the help of laws, it grows with the exercise of rights, and it ends, in a way, by merging with personal interest. A man understands the influence that the well-being of the country has upon his own; he knows that the law permits him to contribute to producing this well-being, and he takes an interest in the prosperity of his country, at first as a thing which is useful to him and then as his own piece of work.

But a moment sometimes arrives, in the life of peoples, when the old customs are changed, mores destroyed, beliefs shaken, the prestige of memories vanished, and when, however, enlightenment has remained incomplete and political rights poorly secured or restricted. Then men no longer see the fatherland except in a weak and uncertain light; they no longer place it either in the soil, which has become in their eyes inanimate earth, or in the customs of their ancestors, which they have been taught to regard as a yoke; or in religion, which they doubt; or in the laws, which they do not make; or in the legislator, whom they fear and despise. They therefore do not see it anywhere, either under its own proper features or under any other, and they withdraw into a narrow and unenlightened egoism. These men are free of prejudices without recognizing the empire of reason; they have neither the instinctive patriotism of monarchy nor the thoughtful patriotism of the republic, but they have come to a stop between the two, in the midst of confusion and misery.

What to do in such a state? Step back. But peoples do not return to the sentiments of their youth any more than men return to the innocent tastes of their childhood; they may long for them but they cannot revive [247] them. It is therefore necessary to go forward and hasten to unite in the eyes of the people individual interest with the interest of the country, for the disinterested love of the fatherland is disappearing forever.

I am certainly far from claiming that in order to arrive at this result one must all at once grant the exercise of political rights to all men; but I do say that the most powerful means, and perhaps the only one which is left to us, for interesting men in the fate of their fatherland, is to arrange for them to participate in its government. In our day, civic spirit seems to me inseparable from the exercise of political rights; and I think that henceforth one will see the number of citizens in Europe increase or decrease in proportion to the extension of these rights.

How does it come about that in the United States, where the inhabitants only recently arrived on the soil that they occupy, where they brought to it neither customs nor memories; where they meet for the first time without knowing one another; where, to put it in a word, the instinct for the fatherland can barely exist; how does it come about that everyone takes an interest in the affairs of his township, his region, and the State altogether as his very own? It is because everyone, in his sphere, takes an active part in the government of the society.

The man of the people, in the United States, has understood the influence which the general prosperity exercises upon his happiness, an idea so simple and yet so little familiar to the people. In addition, he is accustomed to regard this prosperity as his own work. He therefore sees in the public fortune his own, and he works for the good of the State, not only out of duty or pride, but I would almost dare to say out of greed.

There is no need to study the institutions and history of the Americans to appreciate the truth of the foregoing; mores inform one about it sufficiently. The American, taking part in everything which is done in this country, thinks he has an interest in defending everything that is criticized in it; for in this case it is not only his country that is attacked, it is he himself; and so we see his national pride recur to all strategems and stoop to all the childishness of individual vanity.

There is nothing more disagreeable in the habits of daily life than this irritable patriotism of the Americans. The foreigner would indeed be willing to praise much in their country; but he would want to be allowed to blame something, and it is that which is absolutely refused to him.

America is thus a country of liberty where, in order not to wound anyone, the foreigner must not speak freely about either private individuals, or the State, or the governed, or the governors, or public undertakings, or private undertakings; of nothing, finally, that one comes across there, except perhaps the climate or the soil; but there are also Americans ready to defend both, as if they had contributed to making them.

In our day, one must know how to make up one's mind and dare to [248] choose between the patriotism of all and government by the minority, for one cannot combine at the same time the strength and the social activity that the first gives, with the guarantees of tranquility that the second sometimes provides.

The Idea of Rights in the United States

There are no great peoples without an idea of rights.—What is the means of giving to the people the idea of rights.—Respect for rights in the United States.—Its source.

After the general idea of virtue, I know of none more beautiful than that of rights, or rather, these two ideas merge with one another. The idea of rights is nothing other than the idea of virtue introduced into the political world.

It is by means of the idea of rights that men have defined license and tyranny. Enlightened by it, each could be independent without arrogance and submissive without baseness. The man who submits to violence stoops and abases himself, but when he submits to the right to command which he recognizes in his fellow man, he raises himself in a way above the very one who commands him. There are no great men without virtue; there is no great people without respect for rights: one may almost say that there is no society; for what is a union of rational and intelligent human beings whose only linkage is force?

I ask myself what is, in our day, the means of inculcating in men the idea of rights and of making it, so to speak, self-evident to them; and I see only one, to give to all of them the peaceful exercise of certain rights: this is very evident in children, who are men, but without the strength and experience of men. When the child begins to move amid exterior objects, instinct makes him put to use everything that he finds to hand; he does not have the idea of the property of others, not even that of their existence, but as he is made aware of the value of things and discovers that one may, in turn, strip him of them, he becomes more circumspect and ends up respecting in his fellows what he wants one to respect in him.

What happens to the child with regard to his toys, happens later on to the man with regard to all the objects which belong to him. Why is it that in America, the democratic country par excellence, no one hears [249] those complaints against property in general which often resound in Europe? Is there any need to say it? It is that in America there are no proletarians. Since everyone has private property to protect, they recognize in principle the right of property.

It is the same in the political world. In America, the man of the people has conceived a lofty idea of political rights because he has political rights; he refrains from attacking those of others so that his own will not be violated. And whereas in Europe this same man refuses to recognize even the sovereign authority, the American submits without a murmur to the power of the lowest magistrate.

This truth is visible even in the smallest details of the life of peoples. In France, there are few pleasures reserved exclusively for the higher classes of the society; the poor man is admitted almost everywhere where the rich man may enter; therefore one sees him conduct himself with decency and respect everything that serves the rights which he shares. In England, where riches possess the privilege of enjoyment as well as the monopoly of power, one complains that when the poor man succeeds in entering surreptitiously the place reserved for the pleasures of the rich, he takes pleasure in causing pointless damage there: why be surprised by this? One has seen to it that he has nothing to lose.

Democratic government brings the idea of political rights down to the lowest citizen, just as the division of property places the idea of the right of property in general within the reach of all men. In my eyes, that is one of its greatest merits.

I am not saying that it is an easy thing to teach all men to make use of political rights; I am only saying that, when that is possible, the effects which result from it are great.

And I add that if there is any time in which such an undertaking must be attempted, that time is our own.

Do you not see that the religions are becoming weaker and that the divine notion of rights is disappearing? Do you not see that morals are being corrupted and that with them the moral notion of rights is fading?

Do you not see that on all sides belief is giving way to argument, and sentiments to calculations? If, in the midst of this universal tremor, you do not succeed in linking the idea of rights to personal interest, which presents itself as the sole fixed point in the human heart, what then will you be left with for governing the world, except fear?

When, therefore, I am told that the laws are weak and the governed turbulent, that passions are keen and virtue without power, and that in this situation one must not contemplate increasing democratic rights, I respond that it is because of these very things that I believe one must contemplate it; and, in truth, I think that governments have an even [250] greater interest in this than society, because governments perish, and society can never die. Besides, I do not want to overuse the example of America.

In America, the people were invested with political rights at a time when it was difficult to use them badly because the citizens were few in number and simple in their mores. In growing, the Americans have not increased, as it were, the powers of democracy; rather they have increased its fields of activity.

No doubt the moment when political rights are granted to a people who up to then has been deprived of them is a moment of crisis, an often necessary but always dangerous crisis.

The child inflicts death when he is ignorant of the value of life; he takes away the property of others before he knows that one may rob him of his own. The man of the people, at the moment when he is granted political rights, is, in relation to these rights, in the same position as the child *vis-à-vis* all of nature, and in this case the famous saying is applicable to him: *Homo puer robustus.**

This truth is visible even in America. The States where the citizens

---

*   *Man is a robust child.* The quote is from Thomas Hobbes, *De Cive*, Preface.

have enjoyed their rights the longest are those where they still know best how to make use of them.

One cannot say it too often: there is nothing more productive of wonders than the art of being free; but there is nothing harder than the apprenticeship of liberty. This is not the case with despotism. Despotism often appears as the cure for all evils suffered; it is the supporter of just rights, helper of the oppressed, and founder of order. Peoples go to sleep in the bosom of the temporary prosperity to which it gives rise; and when they awaken, they are miserable. Liberty, on the contrary, is usually born in the midst of storms, it establishes itself with difficulty amid civil discord, and it is only when it is already old that one can appreciate its benefits.

Respect for the Law in the United States

Respect of the Americans for the law.—Paternal love that they feel for it.—Personal interest that each has in increasing the power of the law.

One is not always at liberty to call the whole people, either directly or [251] indirectly, to the making of law, but one cannot deny that, when that is feasible, the law acquires a great authority from it. This popular origin, which is often harmful to the goodness and wisdom of legislation, contributes very much to its power.

There is a prodigious force in the expression of the will of a whole people. When it is visible in broad daylight, the imagination even of those who would like to fight against it is, as it were, overwhelmed by it.

The truth of this is well known to the parties.

One therefore sees them contesting the validity of the majority everywhere they can. When it eludes them among those who voted, they place it among those who abstained from voting, and when there again it succeeds in eluding them, they find it again among those who did not have the right to vote.

In the United States, excepting the slaves, servants, and indigents provided for by the municipalities, there is no one who is not an elector and who does not by this right participate indirectly in making the law. Those who wish to attack the laws are therefore reduced to openly doing one of these two things: they must either change the opinion of the nation or crush its wishes underfoot.

Add to this first reason another more direct and more powerful one, that in the United States each one finds a kind of personal interest in the obedience of all to the laws because he who does not belong to the majority today will perhaps be in its ranks tomorrow; and the respect which he now professes for the wishes of the legislator, he will soon have occasion to demand for his own. However troublesome the law is, the inhabitant of the United States therefore submits to it without difficulty, not only as the work of the greatest number, but also as his very own; he considers it from the point of view of a contract to which he was a party.

Therefore one does not see, in the United States, a numerous and always turbulent crowd, which, regarding the law as a natural enemy, casts only glances of fear and suspicion at it. It is impossible, on the contrary, not to see that all the classes show a great confidence in the legislation which governs the country and feel for it a kind of paternal love.

I am wrong to say all the classes. In America, the European scale of powers being reversed, the rich are in a position analogous to that of the poor in Europe; it is they who often distrust the law. I have said it elsewhere: the real advantage of democratic government is not to guarantee the interests of all, as has sometimes been claimed, but only to protect those of the greatest number. In the United States, where the poor man [252] governs, the rich always have to fear that he will abuse his power against them.

This disposition in the mind of the rich may produce a muted discontent, but the society is not violently disturbed by it because the same reason which prevents the rich man from giving his confidence to the legislator prevents him from defying his orders. He does not make the law because he is rich, and because of his riches he does not dare to violate it. In civilized nations, it is only those, in general, who have nothing to lose who revolt. Consequently, therefore, if the laws of democracy are not always respectable, they are almost always respected, because those who, in general, violate the laws cannot fail to obey those that they have made and from which they benefit, and the citizens who might have an interest in infringing them are brought by character and by position to submit to whatever are the wishes of the legislator. Besides, the people in America do not obey the law only because it is their work, but also because they can change it when by chance it harms them; they submit to it at first as to an ill which they have imposed on themselves and then as to a temporary ill.

The Activity Prevailing in All the Parts of the Political Body in the United States: The Influence That It Exercises upon Society

It is more difficult to conceive of the political activity prevailing in the United States than the liberty or the equality which is found there.—The great movement which incessantly agitates the

legislatures is only an episode, a continuation of this universal
movement.—The difficulty which the American finds in being
occupied only with his own affairs.—The political agitation
spreads to the civil society.—The industrial activity of the
Americans arising partly from this cause.—The indirect
advantages which the society draws from democratic
government.

When one passes from a free country into another which is not, one is struck by a very extraordinary sight: there, everything is activity and movement; here, everything seems calm and immobile. In the one, the only concern is with improvement and progress; in the other, one would think that the society, after having acquired all goods, only aspired to repose in order to enjoy them. However, the country which gives itself so much agitation in order to be happy is in general richer and more prosperous than the one which appears so satisfied with its lot. And in con-
[253] sidering them both, it is hard to conceive how so many new needs make themselves felt each day in the first, whereas so few of them seem to be felt in the second.

If this remark is applicable to free countries which have retained the monarchical form and to those in which aristocracy dominates, it is even more so to democratic republics. There, it is no longer a part of the people which undertakes to improve the state of the society; the whole people takes up this care. It is a matter of providing for the needs and conveniences not only of a class, but of all the classes at the same time.

It is not impossible to conceive of the immense liberty which the Americans enjoy; one may also conceive an idea of their extreme equality; but what one cannot comprehend without having already seen it is the political activity which prevails in the United States.

Scarcely have you set foot on the soil of America when you find yourself in the midst of a kind of tumult; a thousand voices reach your ears simultaneously; each of them expresses some social need or other. Around you, everything is in motion: here, the people of one quarter are gathered together in order to know if a church must be built; there, one works at the choice of a representative; further afield, the representatives of a county* are hastening to town in order to see to some local improvements; in another place, it is the farmers of a village who abandon their

---

*   The French word is *canton* and has no direct American equivalent. In Tocqueville's comparison of French and American political subdivisions, it would lie somewhere between the American county and the township or municipality. See Vol. 1, Part 1, Chap. 5 [60]. But in this context, county seems apt.

fields in order to go debate the plan for a road or a school. Some citizens assemble with the sole purpose of declaring that they disapprove of the course of the government, whereas others get together in order to proclaim that the men in office are the fathers of the country. Here are still others who, regarding drunkenness as the principal source of the ills of the State, come to commit themselves solemnly to set an example of temperance.[1]

The great political movement which incessantly agitates the American legislatures, the only one that one notices on the outside, is only an episode and a sort of continuation of this universal movement which begins in the last ranks of the people and then gradually penetrates all the classes of the citizenry. One cannot work more laboriously to be happy.

It is hard to say what place political concerns occupy in the life of a man in the United States. To take part in the government of the society and to talk about it is the greatest business and as it were the only plea- [254] sure that an American knows. This is seen even in the smallest habits of his life: women themselves often go to public meetings and divert themselves from the troubles of housework by listening to political speeches. For them, the clubs to a certain extent take the place of theatrical entertainments. An American does not know how to converse, but he debates; he does not talk, he speechifies. He speaks to you always as if to a meeting, and if by chance he happens to become excited, he will say: "Sirs," in addressing his interlocutor.

In certain countries, the inhabitant only accepts with a sort of repugnance the political rights which the law grants him; it seems that occupying him with common interests takes his time away from him, and he likes to shut himself up in a narrow egoism whose exact limit is formed by four ditches topped off by a hedgerow.

From the moment, on the contrary, that the American was reduced to being occupied only with his own affairs, half of his life would be taken from him; he would feel as if there were an immense emptiness in his life, and he would become incredibly unhappy.[2]

---

1. Temperance societies are associations whose members commit themselves to abstain from strong liquors. When I visited the United States, temperance societies already had more than 270,000 members, and their effect had been to diminish, in the State of Pennsylvania alone, the consumption of strong liquors by 500,000 gallons per year.

2. The same thing was already observed in Rome under the first Caesars.

Montesquieu remarks somewhere that nothing equaled the despair of certain Roman citizens who, after the agitations of a political life, suddenly returned to the calm of private life.

I am persuaded that if despotism ever succeeds in being established in America, it will find it still more difficult to conquer the habits which liberty has brought into being than to overcome the love of liberty itself.

This continually recurring agitation, which democratic government introduced into the political world, passes afterward into the civil society. I do not know if, all things considered, this is not the greatest advantage of democratic government, and I praise it much more because of what it causes to be done than because of what it does.

It is incontestable that the people often manage public affairs very badly, but the people cannot participate in public affairs without extending the circle of its ideas and without its mind going outside its ordinary routine. The man of the people who is called to the government of society conceives a certain regard for himself. As he is then one of the authorities, very enlightened intellects are placed in the service of his own. He is constantly asked for his help, and in seeking to deceive him in a thousand different ways, one enlightens him. In politics, he takes part in enterprises which he did not conceive but which give him the general taste for enterprises. Every day new improvements to be made to the common property are pointed out to him, and he feels the desire awaken [255] to improve that which is personal to him. He is neither more virtuous nor happier perhaps, but more enlightened and more active than his predecessors. I do not doubt that democratic institutions, joined to the physical nature of the country, are the cause, not direct, as many men say, but the indirect cause of the prodigious development of industry that one notices in the United States. It is not the laws which give rise to it, but the people learns to produce it by making the law.

When the enemies of democracy claim that a single man accomplishes whatever he takes on better than the government of all, it seems to me that they are right. The government of a single man, assuming an equality of enlightenment on both sides, puts more follow-through into his undertakings than the multitude; he demonstrates more perseverence, a better grasp of the whole, more perfection of detail, and more accurate discernment in his choice of men. Those who deny these things have never seen a democratic republic or have made their judgment only on the basis of a small number of examples. Democracy, even when the local circumstances and the dispositions of the people allow it to survive, does not present the appearance of administrative regularity and methodical order in the government; that is true. Democratic liberty does not execute each of its undertakings with the same perfection as intelligent despotism; often it abandons them before having gotten results from them or takes a risk on dangerous ones. But in the long term it produces more than despotism; it does each thing less well, but it does more things. Under its empire, it is not so much what the public administration executes that is great, it is what is executed without it and outside of it. Democracy does not give the people the most skillful government, but it accomplishes what the most skillful government is often powerless to create; it spreads throughout the whole social body a restless activity, an overabundant force, an energy which never exists without it, and which, if the circumstances are favorable, can bring forth wonders. There are its true advantages.

In this century, when the fate of the Christian world appears in suspense, some hasten to attack democracy as an enemy power while it is still growing; others are already worshipping it like a new god who arises out of nothing; but both of them understand only imperfectly the object of their hate or their desire; they are fighting in the dark and only achieve a hit by chance.

What are you asking of society and of its government? It is necessary to be clear about this.

Do you want to give to the human mind a certain elevation, a generous way of envisioning the things of this world? Do you want to inspire in [256] men a sort of contempt for material goods? Do you desire to bring into being profound convictions and lay the ground for great acts of devotion?

Are you concerned with refining morals, elevating manners, making the arts shine? Do you want poetry, éclat,* glory?

Do you intend to organize a people so that they act strongly on all the others? Do you mean it to attempt great enterprises and, whatever the result of these efforts, to leave an immense mark in history?

If such is, according to you, the principal aim which a society must set for itself, do not choose democratic government; it would not lead you with certainty to the goal.

But if it seems to you useful to turn the intellectual and moral activity of man toward the necessities of material life and to use it to produce well-being; if reason appears to you more profitable to men than genius; if your object is not to create heroic virtues but peaceful habits; if you prefer vices to crimes and prefer that there be fewer great deeds on condition that there be fewer crimes; if, instead of acting in the midst of a brilliant society, it is enough for you to live in the midst of a prosperous society; if, finally, the principal object of government is not, according to you, to give to the entire body of the nation the greatest strength or the greatest glory possible, but to obtain the greatest well-being for all of the individuals who compose it and to spare them the greatest misery; then equalize conditions and constitute democratic government.

---

* *du bruit*. See the note on *bruit* at [66], page 54 of this translation.

But if there is no longer time to make a choice, and a force superior to man is already carrying you, without consulting your desires, toward one of the two governments, at least seek to draw from it all the good that it can do, and, knowing its good instincts as well as its bad tendencies, strive to restrain the effect of the second and to develop the first.

CHAPTER 7

**THE OMNIPOTENCE OF THE MAJORITY IN THE
UNITED STATES AND ITS EFFECTS**

> *Natural force of the majority in democracies.—The majority of the
> American constitutions have increased artificially this natural
> force.—How.—Compulsory mandates.*—Moral empire of the
> majority.—Opinion of its infallibility.—Respect for its rights.—
> What increases it in the United States.*

It is of the very essence of democratic governments that the empire of the majority be absolute in them; for outside of the majority, in democracies, there is nothing which resists.

The majority of the American constitutions have further sought to increase artificially this natural force of the majority.[1]

The legislature is, of all the political powers, the one which most willingly obeys the majority. The Americans wanted the members of the legislature to be elected *directly* by the people, and for a *very short* term, in order to oblige them to abide by not only the general views but even the daily passions of their constituents.

They drew from the same classes and elected in the same manner the members of the two Chambers, so that the movements of the legislative

---

* *Mandats impératifs.* These words were translated as "pledged delegates" by Tocqueville's own translator, Henry Reeve, almost certainly in reference to the American political parties' practice of requiring delegates to nominating conventions and electors to the electoral college to pledge in advance to vote for a certain candidate. However, Tocqueville's choice of the words *mandats impératifs*, and his explanation of them in the third paragraph of [258], go beyond the simple example of pledged delegates.

1. We have seen, when examining the Federal Constitution, that the legislators of the Union made contrary efforts. The result of these efforts was to make the Federal Government more independent in its sphere than that of the States. But the Federal Government is concerned almost exclusively with external affairs; it is the State governments that really govern American society.

body are almost as rapid and not less irresistible than those of a single assembly.

Having thus constituted the legislature, they gathered within it almost all the government.

At the same time that the law increased the force of powers that were naturally strong, it weakened more and more those which were naturally weak. It gave to the representatives of the executive power neither stability nor independence, and, by submitting them completely to the whims of the legislature, it deprived them of the little influence which the nature [258] of democratic government would have permitted them to exercise.

In several states, the law gave the judicial power over to election by the majority, and in all of them it made its existence dependent, in a way, upon the legislative power by giving to the representatives the right to fix the salary of the judges annually.

The customs have gone even further than the laws.

A custom is spreading more and more in the United States which will end by making the guarantees of representative government empty: it happens very frequently that the electors, in electing a representative, map out a course of action for him and impose on him a certain number of positive obligations from which he can in no way deviate. Short of a tumult, it is as if the majority itself were deliberating in the public square.

Several particular circumstances also tend to make the power of the majority in America not only predominant, but irresistible.

The moral empire of the majority is based in part on this idea, that there is more enlightenment and wisdom in many men who are brought together than in one alone, more enlightenment and wisdom in the number than in the choice of legislators. This is the theory of equality applied to the intellect. This doctrine attacks the pride of man in its last refuge: therefore the minority has a hard time accepting it; it becomes accustomed to it only in the long run. Like all the powers, and more perhaps than any of them, the power of the majority therefore needs to last for a long time in order to appear legitimate. When it starts to establish itself, it makes itself obeyed by force; it is only after having lived for a long time under its laws that one begins to respect it.

The idea that the majority possesses the right, by its enlightenment, to govern the society was brought to the soil of the United States by its first inhabitants. This idea, which was alone sufficient for creating a free people, has today passed into the mores, and it is visible even in the smallest habits of daily life.

The French, under the former monarchy, took it as given that the king was infallible; and when he happened to act badly, they thought that the fault lay with his advisors. This facilitated obedience wonderfully. One could grumble against the law without ceasing to love and respect the legislator. The Americans have the same opinion of the majority.

The moral empire of the majority is based on this principle, that the interests of the greatest number must be preferred to those of the minority. Now, it is easy to see that the respect which is professed for this right of the greatest number naturally increases or diminishes according to the state of the parties. When a nation is divided between several great irrec- [259] oncilable interests, the right of the majority is often refused acceptance because it becomes too difficult to submit to it.

If there existed in America a class of citizens which the legislature was trying to strip of certain exclusive advantages, possessed for centuries, and wished to bring down from an elevated position in order to bring it back into the ranks of the multitude, it is probable that the minority would not easily submit to its laws.

But since the United States was settled by men equal among themselves, there is not yet enough natural and permanent divergence among the interests of its different inhabitants.

There are some social states in which the members of the minority cannot hope to attract to themselves the majority because it would be necessary to abandon the very object of the struggle that they are sustaining against it. An aristocracy, for example, cannot become a majority while conserving its exclusive privileges, and it cannot let go of those privileges without ceasing to be an aristocracy.

In the United States, political questions cannot arise in such a general and absolute manner, and all the parties are ready to recognize the rights of the majority because they all hope to be able one day to exercise them for their own advantage.

The majority thus has in the United States an immense power in fact and a power of opinion almost as great; and once a majority has formed on a question, there are virtually no obstacles which can, never mind stop, but even slow down its march and allow it the time to listen to the complaints of those it crushes in passing.

The consequences of this state of things are disastrous and dangerous for the future.

How the Omnipotence of the Majority Increases, in America, the Legislative and Administrative Instability Which Is Natural in Democracies

How the Americans increase legislative instability, which is natural to democracy, by changing the legislature each year and by arming it with a power almost without limits.—The same effect

produced in administration.—In America, one brings to social
improvements a force which is infinitely greater but less
continuous than in Europe.

I spoke earlier of the vices which are natural to democratic government; there is not one of them which does not grow simultaneously with the power of the majority.

And to begin with the most apparent of all: [260]

Legislative instability is an evil inherent in democratic government because it is in the nature of democracies to bring new men to power. But this evil is more or less great depending on the power and the means of action that are granted to the legislature.

In America, the authority which makes the laws is given a sovereign power. It can abandon itself rapidly and irresistibly to every one of its desires, and every year it is given different representatives. Which is to say that precisely that combination was adopted which most favors democratic instability and which allows democracy to apply its changing desires to the most important objects.

Because of this, America is the country in the world today where the laws last the shortest time. Almost all the American constitutions have been amended in the last thirty years. There is thus no American State which has not, during this period, modified the foundation of its laws.

As for the laws themselves, it is sufficient to glance at the archives of the different States of the Union in order to be convinced that in America the action of the legislature never slows down. It is not that American democracy is by its nature more unstable than any other, but it has been given the means to follow, in making the laws, the natural instability of its inclinations.[2]

The omnipotence of the majority, and the rapid and absolute manner in which its desires are complied with in the United States, not only makes the law unstable, it also exercises the same influence on the execution of the law and on the action of public administration.

Since the majority is the sole power which it is important to please, one participates with zeal in the works it undertakes; but from the moment that

---

2. The legislative acts promulgated in the state of Massachusetts alone, from 1780 to the present, already fill three fat volumes. One also has to note that the collection I am talking about was revised in 1823 and that many ancient or pointless laws were removed from it. Now the state of Massachusetts, which is not more populous than one of our *départements,* may be said to be the most stable in the whole Union and the one which puts the most continuity and wisdom into its undertakings.

its attention is drawn elsewhere, all efforts cease, whereas in the free States of Europe, where the administrative power has an independent existence and a secure position, the desires of the legislator continue to be complied with even while he is occupied with other objects.

In America, one brings to certain improvements much more zeal and activity than elsewhere.

[261]   In Europe, one employs for these same things a social force which is infinitely less great but more continuous.

Some religious men undertook, several years ago, to improve the state of the prisons. The public was moved by their plea, and the rehabilitation of criminals became a popular cause.

New prisons were then built. For the first time, the idea of the reform of the criminal as well as his punishment penetrated the prisons. But the happy revolution with which the public had associated itself with so much ardor, and which the simultaneous efforts of the citizens made irresistible, could not be accomplished in an instant.

Alongside the new prisons, whose construction was hastened by the wishes of the majority, the old prisons still remained and continued to house a great number of criminals. The old ones seemed to become more unhealthy and more corrupting as the new ones became more reformative and healthier. This double effect is easy to understand: the majority, preoccupied with founding the new type of establishment, had forgotten the one which already existed. Since every one then turned his eyes from the object which no longer attracted the attention of the master, oversight had ceased. The salutary ties of discipline were first relaxed and then, soon afterward, broken. And next to the prison, the lasting monument to the mildness and enlightenment of our time, stood a dungeon reminiscent of the barbarity of the Middle Ages.

The Tyranny of the Majority

How the principle of the sovereignty of the people must be understood.—Impossibility of conceiving of a mixed government.—Sovereign power must exist somewhere.— Preventive measures that must be taken to moderate its action.—These measures were not taken in the United States.—What results from this.

I regard as impious and detestable the maxim that in matters of government the majority of a people has the right to do everything, and nevertheless I place the origin of all powers in the wishes of the majority. Am I in contradiction with myself?

There exists a general law which has been made, or at least adopted, not only by the majority of this or that people but by the majority of all men. This law is justice.

Justice thus forms the limit to the right of each people.

A nation is like a jury charged with representing universal society and applying justice, which is its law. Must the jury, which represents [262] society, have more power than the society itself whose laws it applies?

When, therefore, I refuse to obey an unjust law, I do not deny to the majority the right to command; I am only appealing from the sovereignty of the people to the sovereignty of mankind.

There are men who do not fear to say that a people, with respect to the matters that interest only itself, cannot entirely go beyond the limits of justice and reason and that therefore one should not fear giving all power to the majority which represents it. But that is the language of slaves.

What therefore is a majority, taken collectively, except an individual who has opinions and most often interests contrary to another individual whom one calls the minority? Now, if you admit that a man invested with absolute power may abuse it against his adversaries, why do you not admit the same thing for a majority? Have men, by being brought together, changed character? Have they become more patient before obstacles in becoming stronger?[3] For myself, I cannot believe it, and the power to do everything, which I refuse to a single one of my fellow men, I will never grant to several.

It is not that, in order to conserve liberty, I believe that one can mix several principles in the same government in such a manner that they are really opposed to one another.

What is called mixed government has always seemed to me a chimera. In truth, mixed government (in the sense that is given to this word) does not exist, because in each society one ends up finding a principle of action which dominates all the others.

England in the last century, which has been particularly cited as an example of this sort of government, was essentially an aristocratic state, although large elements of democracy existed within it, because the laws and mores were ordered in such a way that, in the long run, aristocracy would always prevail and manage public affairs as it wished.

The error is due to the fact that, constantly seeing the interests of the

---

3. Nobody would wish to claim that a people cannot abuse its power vis-à-vis another people. Now, parties are like so many small nations within a great one; their relation to one another is like that of foreign countries.

   If one agrees that a nation may be tyrannical toward another nation, how can one deny that a party may be the same way toward another party?

great in battle with those of the people, one only thought about the struggle instead of paying attention to the result of this struggle, which [263] was the important point. When a society comes to really have a mixed government, that is to say equally divided between contrary principles, it has a revolution, or it breaks up.

I think, therefore, that a social power superior to all the others must always be placed somewhere, but I think liberty in danger when this power finds no obstacle before it which can check its march and give it the time to moderate itself on its own.

Absolute power seems to me in itself a bad and dangerous thing. Its exercise appears to me to be beyond the powers of man, no matter who he is, and I see only God who can be all-powerful without danger, because his wisdom and justice are always equal to His power. There is therefore no authority on earth so respectable in itself, or invested with a right so sacred, that I wish to let it act without control and to dominate without obstacles. Therefore, the moment I see the right and the capability to do everything granted to any power whatsoever, whether one calls it people or king, democracy or aristocracy, whether it is exercised in a monarchy or in a democracy, I say: there is the germ of tyranny, and I try to go live under other laws.

What I reproach the most in democratic government, as it has been organized in the United States, is not, as many men claim in Europe, its weakness, but on the contrary its irresistible force. And what I find most repugnant in America is not the extreme liberty which prevails there; it is the little guarantee against tyranny which one finds there.

When a man or party suffers from an injustice in the United States, to whom do you want him to appeal? To public opinion? It is that which forms the majority. To the legislative body? It represents the majority and obeys it blindly. To the executive power? It is chosen by the majority and serves as its passive instrument. To public force? The public force is nothing other than the majority under arms. To the jury? The jury is the majority invested with the right to pronounce sentence: the judges themselves, in certain states, are elected by the majority. However unjust or irrational the measure which strikes you, you must therefore submit to it.[4]

---

4. In Baltimore, during the War of 1812, there was a striking example of the excess to which the despotism of the majority may lead. At this time the war was very popular in Baltimore. A newspaper which displayed strong opposition to it provoked with this conduct the indignation of the inhabitants. The people gathered together, broke the presses, and attacked the journalists' house. An effort was made to assemble the militia, but it did not respond to the call. In order to save

Suppose, on the contrary, a legislative body composed in such a way [264] that it represents the majority without being necessarily the slave of its passions, an executive power possessed of a strength which is its own, and a judicial power independent of the two other powers; you will still have a democratic government, but there will be almost no chance any longer of tyranny.

I am not saying that in the present time in America tyranny occurs frequently; I am saying that there is no guarantee there against it and that the causes of the mildness of government there must be sought in the circumstances and in the mores rather than in the laws.

Effects of the Omnipotence of the Majority on the Arbitrary Power of American Public Officials

Liberty that the law allows to American officials within the limits it has marked out.—Their power.

---

the unfortunates whom the public furor was menacing, the decision was made to put them in prison, as if they were criminals. This precaution was futile: during the night, the people gathered again; the magistrates having failed to assemble the militia, the prison was broken into, one of the journalists was killed on the spot, and the others left for dead: the offenders brought before the jury were acquitted.

I once said to an inhabitant of Pennsylvania:

"Explain to me, please, how, in a State founded by Quakers, and famous for its tolerance, free Negroes are not permitted to exercise the rights of citizens. They pay taxes, isn't it just for them to have the vote?"

"Don't insult us," he answered me, "by thinking that our legislators have committed such a gross act of injustice and intolerance."

"So, in your State, blacks have the right to vote?"

"Without any doubt."

"Then, how does it happen that at the electoral college this morning I did not notice a single one in the gathering?"

"That is not the fault of the law," the American told me; "the Negroes have, it is true, the right to take part in elections, but they abstain from appearing voluntarily."

"That is very modest of them."

"Oh! it's not that they refuse to go there, but they are afraid of being mistreated there. In our State, it sometimes happens that the law lacks force when the majority does not support it. Now, the majority is imbued with the greatest prejudices against the Negroes, and the magistrates do not feel that they have the force to guarantee them the rights which the legislature has granted them."

"What! The majority, which has the privilege of making the law, also wants to have the privilege of disobeying the law?"

It is necessary to distinguish well between arbitrary power and tyranny. Tyranny may be exercised by means of the law itself, and then it is not arbitrary; arbitrary power may be exercised in the interest of the governed, and then it is not tyrannical.

Tyranny usually makes use of arbitrary power, but if necessary it knows how to do without it.

[265]   In the United States, the omnipotence of the majority, at the same time that it facilitates the legal despotism of the legislature, also facilitates the arbitrary power of the magistrate. The majority, being absolute master of the making of law and of the supervision of its execution, having an equal control over the governors and the governed, regards public officials as its passive agents and willingly relies on them for the task of carrying out its intentions. It therefore does not go into the detail of their duties in advance and barely takes the trouble to define their rights. It treats them as a master might treat his servants if, seeing them act at all times under his eyes, he could direct or correct their conduct at each moment.

In general, the law leaves American officials much freer than ours within the limits it has marked out for them. Sometimes it even happens that the majority allows them to go beyond those limits. Backed by the opinion of the majority and confident of its support, they then dare things that astonish even a European accustomed to the sight of arbitrary power. Habits are thus formed in the bosom of liberty that may become disastrous for it.

The Power That the Majority in America Exercises over Thought

In the United States, when the majority is irrevocably fixed on any question, there is no more debate.—Why.—Moral power that the majority exercises over thought.—Democratic republics spiritualize despotism.*

When one comes to examine the exercise of thought in the United States, it is then that one sees very clearly to what extent the power of the majority surpasses all the powers that we know in Europe.

Thought is an invisible power, and one almost impossible to seize

*   *immatérialisent le despotisme:* literally, "make despotism immaterial." Tocqueville does not mean that democracy makes despotism into something *negligible.* He means that democracy exercises a despotic power over men's ideas rather than directly over their actions.

hold of,* which mocks all tyrannies. In our day, the most absolute sovereigns of Europe cannot prevent certain thoughts hostile to their authority
from circulating silently in their States and even in the heart of their
courts. It is not the same in America: to the extent that the majority is in
doubt, one speaks; but as soon as it has irrevocably decided, each one
falls silent, and friends as well as enemies seem then to attach themselves together to its chariot. The reason for this is simple: there is no
monarch so absolute that he can unite in his hands all the forces of society and vanquish resistance, as a majority can when it is invested with   [266]
the right to make the laws and to execute them.

In addition, a king has only a material power which acts upon behavior
and cannot reach wills, but the majority is invested with a force at once
material and moral which acts upon the will as much as upon actions and
which prevents at one and the same time the act and the desire to act.

I know of no country where there prevails, in general, less independence of mind and less true freedom of discussion than in America.

There is no religious or political theory which cannot be preached
freely in the constitutional States of Europe and which does not penetrate the others; for there is no country in Europe so subject to a single
power that he who wishes to speak the truth there cannot find some support in it capable of securing him against the consequences of his independence. If he has the misfortune to live under an absolute government,
he often has the people on his side; if he lives in a free country, he can
take refuge if necessary behind the royal power. The aristocratic fraction
of the society supports him in democratic countries, and the democratic
fraction does so in the others. But in an organized democracy like that of
the United States, there is only a single power, a single element of
strength and success, and nothing outside of it.

In America, the majority draws a formidable ring around thought.
Within these limits, the writer is free; but woe to him if he dares to go outside of it. It is not that he has to fear being burnt at the stake, but he is exposed to all kinds of execrations and daily persecutions. A political career
is closed to him: he has offended the only power which has the capability
of opening it up to him. Everything is refused to him, even glory. Before
publishing his opinions, he believed that he had partisans; it seems to
him that he no longer has any now that he has opened himself up to
everyone, because those who condemn him express themselves loudly,
and those who think like him, without having his courage, fall silent and

---

* The word translated as "impossible to seize hold of" is *insaisissable*. *Insaisiss-*
able, whose literal translation would be "unseizable," can mean "impalpable"; "elusive"; "unfathomable"; or, in law, "not subject to seizure" (as of property or goods).

withdraw. He gives in, he bows in the end beneath the effort of each day, and he becomes silent again, as if he felt remorse at having told the truth.

Chains and executioners: those are the crude instruments which tyranny formerly employed, but in our day civilization has perfected even despotism itself, which seemed to have nothing more to learn.

The princes had, so to speak, materialized violence; the democratic republics of our day have made it as intellectual as the human will that it wishes to constrain. Under the absolute government of a single man, despotism, in order to reach the soul, crudely strikes the body, and the [267] soul, escaping these blows, rises gloriously above it, but in the democratic republics, tyranny does not proceed in this way; it leaves the body alone and goes straight to the soul. The master no longer says to it: "You will think like me, or you will die;" he says: "You are free to not think like me; your life, your property, all stays with you; but from this day you are a stranger among us. You will keep your political rights, but they will be useless to you; because if you seek the vote of your fellow citizens, they will not give it to you, and if you demand only their esteem, they will still feign refusing it to you.* You will remain among men, but you will lose your rights to humanity. When you approach your fellow men, they will avoid you like an impure being; and those who believe in your innocence, those very same ones will abandon you, because they would be avoided in their turn. Go in peace, I leave you your life, but I leave it to you in a condition worse than death."

The absolute monarchies brought despotism into disrepute; let us take care that the democratic republics do not rehabilitate it and that in making it more oppressive for some, they do not take away from it, in the eyes of the majority, its odious appearance and degrading character.

In the proudest nations of the Old World, works were published which were intended to depict faithfully the vices and absurdities of contemporaries; La Bruyère was living in the palace of Louis XIV when he composed his chapter on the great, and Molière criticized the court in plays he arranged to have performed before the courtiers.† But the power that holds sway in the United States does not intend to be made a fool of in this way. The slightest reproach offends it, the smallest of stinging truths shocks it; it must be praised, from the forms of its language to its most solid virtues. No writer, no matter what his renown, can escape this

---

* *ils feindront encore de vous la refuser.* That is to say: they will feel constrained to refuse you their esteem even though that refusal does not reflect their true feelings of esteem for you.

† The courtiers (*courtisans*) were those who frequented and were attached to the court (*cour*). Because they sought to curry favor with the powerful, *courtisan* also came to mean flatterer or sycophant.

obligation to shower praise upon his fellow citizens. The majority thus lives amid a perpetual adoration of itself; only foreigners or experience can make certain truths reach the ears of the Americans.

If America does not yet have great writers, we need not look for the reasons elsewhere: literary genius does not exist without freedom of mind, and there is no freedom of mind in America.

The Inquisition was never able to prevent the circulation in Spain of books contrary to the religion of the majority. The empire of the majority does better in the United States: it has removed even the thought of publishing them. One meets unbelievers in America, but unbelief has virtually no voice there.

One sees governments which try hard to protect morals by condemning the authors of licentious books. In the United States, no one is con- [268] demned for these sorts of works, but no one is tempted to write them. It is not, however, that all citizens have pure morals, but the majority is regular in its own.

Here, the use of power is without doubt good: but I was only speaking of the power in itself. This irresistible power is a constant fact, and its good use is only an accident.

Effects of the Tyranny of the Majority on the National Character of the Americans; The Courtier Spirit in the United States

The effects of the tyranny of the majority have been felt up to now more in the mores than in the conduct of the society.—They arrest the growth of great characters.—Democratic republics organized like those of the United States place the courtier spirit within reach of a great many.—Evidence of this spirit in the United States.—Why there is more patriotism in the people than in those who govern in its name.

The influence of what I have just discussed still makes itself felt only weakly in the political society, but one already notices its unfortunate effects upon the national character of the Americans. I think that the small number of outstanding men that are visible today on the political scene must be attributed above all to the continually increasing influence of the despotism of the majority in the United States.

When the American Revolution broke out, a crowd of them appeared; public opinion at that time guided the wills of men but did not tyrannize them. The famous men of that time, while freely taking part in the movement of ideas, had a grandeur that was their own: they spread their brilliance over the nation and did not borrow from it.

In absolute governments, the great men who are close to the throne flatter the passions of the master and bend themselves readily to his caprices. But the mass of the nation does not lend itself to servitude; it submits often out of weakness, out of habit, or out of ignorance; sometimes out of love of royalty or of the king. Some peoples have invested a sort of pleasure and pride in the sacrifice of their will to that of the prince and have thus placed a kind of independence of soul in the very midst of obedience. Among these peoples, there is much less degradation than misery. There is, in addition, a great difference between doing what one does not approve of and feigning to approve of what one does: the former belongs to a weak man, but the latter belongs only to the habits of a valet.

[269]

In free countries, where each is more or less called to give his opinion on the affairs of State; in democratic republics, where public life is constantly mixed with private life, where the sovereign is approachable from all sides, and where one only needs to raise one's voice in order to reach its ear, there are many more men who seek to speculate on its weaknesses and to make their living at the expense of its passions than in absolute monarchies. It is not that men there are naturally worse than elsewhere, but the temptation there is at the same time stronger and open to more men. There results from this a much more general abasement in men's souls.

Democratic republics place the courtier spirit within reach of a great number and cause it to penetrate all the classes at the same time. This is one of the principal reproaches which one can make against them.

That is above all true in democratic States organized like the American republics, where the majority possesses an empire so absolute and so irresistible that it is necessary in a way to renounce one's rights as a citizen, and, so to speak, one's standing as a man, when one wishes to deviate from the path which the majority has marked out.

Among the immense crowd which in the United States rushes into the career of politics, I have seen very few men who exhibit the virile candor, the manly independence of thought, which often distinguished the Americans in former times, and which, everywhere where it is found, forms the outstanding trait of great characters. One would think at first glance that in America minds were all formed on the same model, so much do they follow exactly the same paths. The foreigner, it is true, sometimes meets Americans who deviate from the rigor of the accepted formulas; sometimes they deplore the defect of the laws, the fickleness of democracy, and its lack of enlightenment; often they even notice the defects which corrupt the national character, and they point out the measures which one could take in order to correct them; but no one, except you, listens to them; and you, to whom they confide these secret thoughts, you are only a foreigner, and you are passing through. They readily reveal truths to you which are useless to you, and, when they go down into the public square, they use a different language.

If these lines ever reach America, I am certain of two things: first, that all readers will raise their voice to condemn me; second, that many of them will absolve me in the depths of their conscience.

I have heard men speak of the fatherland in the United States. I have [270] found true patriotism in the people; I have often looked for it in vain in those who govern them. This is easily understood by analogy: despotism corrupts much more he who submits to it than he who imposes it. In absolute monarchies, the king often has great virtues, but the courtiers are always base.

It is true that courtiers in America do not say: "Sire" and "Your Majesty," as if this were a great and capital difference, but they speak incessantly of the natural enlightenment of their master; they do not put to the test the question of knowing which of the prince's virtues is most worthy of admiration because they guarantee that he possesses all the virtues without having acquired them and, so to speak, without wishing to do so; they do not give him their wives and their daughters in order that he deign to raise them to the rank of his mistresses, but, by sacrificing their opinions to him, they prostitute themselves.

The moralists and the philosophers in America are not obliged to wrap their opinions in the veils of allegory, but, before hazarding a disagreeable truth, they say: "We know that we are speaking to a people too far above human weaknesses not to remain always master of itself. We would not express ourselves in this way, if we were not addressing men whose virtues and enlightenment make them alone, among all others, worthy of remaining free."

How could the flatterers of Louis XIV have done better?

For myself, I believe that in all governments, no matter what they are, baseness will become attached to force, and flattery to power. And I know only one way of preventing men from becoming degraded: that is to grant to no one, along with absolute power, the sovereign power to debase them.

The Greatest Danger to the American Republics Comes from the Omnipotence of the Majority

It is by the bad use of their power, and not by impotence, that democratic republics are imperiled.—The government of the American republics more centralized and more energetic than the monarchies of Europe.—The danger which results from this.—Opinions of Madison and Jefferson on this subject.

Governments ordinarily perish from impotence or from tyranny. In the first case, power escapes them; in the other, it is forcibly taken from them.

[271]   Many men, seeing democratic States fall into a state of anarchy, have thought that the government in these States was naturally weak and impotent. The truth is that, once war breaks out between the parties there, the government loses its influence over the society. But I do not think that it is the nature of a democratic power to lack strength and resources; I believe, on the contrary, that it is almost always the abuse of its powers and the bad use of its resources which imperil it. Anarchy arises almost always from its tyranny or from its incapacity, but not from its impotence.

One must not confuse stability with strength or the grandeur of a thing with its longevity. In democratic republics, the power which directs[5] the society is not stable, because it often changes hands and aim. But everywhere it is brought to bear, its force is almost irresistible.

The government of the American republics appears to me to be as centralized and more energetic than that of the absolute monarchies of Europe. I do not think that it will perish from weakness.[6]

If liberty is ever lost in America, the blame will have to be placed on the omnipotence of the majority which will have brought the minorities to the point of despair and constrained them to make an appeal to physical force. Then one will see anarchy, but it will occur as a consequence of despotism.

President James Madison expressed the same thoughts. (See *The Federalist*, N° 51.)

"It is of great importance in republics," he said, "not only to defend the society against the oppression of those who govern it, but also to safeguard one part of the society against the injustice of the other part. Justice is the end to which any government must aspire; this is the end which men intend by uniting with one another. Peoples have made and will always make efforts toward this end, until they have succeeded in attaining it, or they have lost their liberty.

"If there existed a society in which the most powerful party was able to easily unite its forces and oppress the weakest, one could conclude that anarchy prevails in such a society just as it does in the state of nature, where the weakest individual has no guarantee against the violence

---

5. Power can be centralized in an assembly; then it is strong but not stable; it can be centralized in a man: then it is less strong, but it is more stable.

6. It is not necessary, I think, to warn the reader that here, as in the rest of the chapter, I am speaking not of the Federal government, but of the particular governments of each State which the majority governs despotically.

of the strongest; and just as in the state of nature the disadvantages of an [272] uncertain and precarious fate persuade the strongest to submit to a government which protects the weak as well as themselves, in an anarchic government the same motives will lead the strongest parties gradually to wish for a government which can protect equally all parties, the strong and the weak. If the State of Rhode Island were separated from the Confederation and handed over to a popular government, acting with sovereign power and within narrow limits, it cannot be doubted that the tyranny of the majorities would render the exercise of rights so uncertain, that one would come to call for a power altogether independent of the people. The factions themselves, which would have made it necessary, would hasten to call for it."

Jefferson also said: "The executive power, in our government, is not the only, is perhaps not the principal object of my concern. The tyranny of the legislature is presently, and will be for many more years, the danger most to be feared. That of the executive power will come in its turn, but at a more distant time."[7]

On this subject, I prefer to cite Jefferson more than anyone else because I consider him the most powerful apostle that democracy has ever had.

CHAPTER 8   [273]

WHAT TEMPERS THE TYRANNY OF THE MAJORITY IN THE UNITED STATES

Absence of Administrative Centralization

• • •

I distinguished previously between two kinds of centralization: I have called the one governmental and the other administrative.

Only the first exists in America; the second is almost unknown there.

If the power that governs American societies had at its disposal both of these means of government and joined the capability and the habit of executing everything by itself to the right of commanding everything; if, after having established the general principles of government, it entered into the details of their application, and after having settled the great interests of the country, it was able to descend to the threshold of individual interests, liberty would soon be banished from the New World.

---

7. Letter of Jefferson to Madison, 15 March 1789.

But, in the United States, the majority, which often has the tastes and the instincts of a despot, still lacks the most refined instruments of tyranny.

In all of the American republics, the central government is only responsible for a small number of objects, whose importance has attracted its attention. It has not undertaken to regulate the secondary matters of society. Nothing indicates that it has even conceived the desire to do so. The majority, while becoming more and more absolute, has not increased the prerogatives of the central power; it has only made it all-powerful within its sphere. Thus despotism may weigh very heavily on one point, but it cannot be extended to all.

[274] Besides, however carried away the national majority may be by its passions, however ardent it is in its designs, it cannot make all the citizens bend to its desires everywhere, in the same manner, and at the same time. When the central government that represents it has given an order with sovereign authority, it must rely, for the execution of its commands, on agents who often are not dependent on it and whom it cannot direct at every moment. The municipal bodies and the county administrations thus form, as it were, so many hidden reefs that slow down or break up the overflowing current of the public will. Were the law oppressive, liberty would still find refuge in the manner in which the law was executed, and the majority could not descend into the details, and, if I dare say it, into the puerilities of administrative tyranny. It does not even imagine that it may do so, for it does not have complete consciousness of its power. It still only knows its natural powers, and it is ignorant of how far art may extend their limits.

This is worth thinking about. If a democratic republic like that of the United States ever comes to be established in a country where the power of a single man had already been established and had caused administrative centralization to enter into the habits, as well as into the laws, I am not afraid to say that, in such a republic, despotism would become more intolerable than in any of the absolute monarchies of Europe. One would have to go to Asia to find something comparable to it.

The Spirit of the Legal Profession in the United States, and How It Serves as a Counterweight to Democracy

Utility of investigating what are the natural instincts of the legal spirit.—Lawyers are called to play a great role in the society that is striving to be born.—How the kind of work lawyers engage in gives an aristocratic turn to their ideas.—Accidental causes that may pose obstacles to the development of these ideas.—Ease with

*which aristocracy unites with lawyers.—Use that a despot may
make of lawyers.—How lawyers form the only aristocratic
element that is liable to be combined with the natural elements of
democracy.—Particular causes which tend to give an aristocratic
turn to the English and American legal spirit.—The American
aristocracy is on the lawyers' benches and in the judges' seats.—
Influence exercised by lawyers on American society.—How their
spirit penetrates the legislatures and the administration and ends
up by giving the people itself something of the instincts of judges.*

When one visits the Americans and studies their laws, one sees that the authority that they have given to lawyers, and the influence that they [275] have allowed them to have in the government, forms today the most powerful barrier against the excesses of democracy. This effect seems to me to result from a general cause that it is useful to investigate, for it may recur elsewhere.

Lawyers have been involved in all the movements of political society, in Europe, for the last five hundred years. Sometimes they have served as instruments of the political powers, sometimes they have made the political powers their instruments. In the Middle Ages, lawyers contributed wonderfully to expanding the domination of the kings; since then, they have worked powerfully to restrain this same power. In England, they united themselves closely with the aristocracy; in France, they proved to be its most dangerous enemies. Do lawyers thus give way to sudden and momentary impulses, or do they obey more or less, according to the circumstances, instincts that are natural to them, and that always recur? I would like to be clear about this point; for it may be that lawyers are called upon to play the principal role in the political society that is striving to be born.

The men who have made the laws their particular study have drawn from this work habits of order, a certain taste for forms, a sort of instinctive love for the regular sequence of ideas, that makes them naturally strongly opposed to the revolutionary spirit and the thoughtless passions of democracy.

The particular knowledge that lawyers acquire by studying the law assures them a separate rank in the society; they form a sort of privileged class among the intellectual classes. They reencounter the idea of this superiority every day in the exercise of their profession; they are the masters of a necessary science, knowledge of which is not widespread; they serve as arbiters between citizens, and the habit of directing the blind passions of parties to a litigation toward their objective gives them a certain contempt for the judgment of the crowd. Add to that that they form naturally *a corporate body.*[*] It is not that they have an understanding among themselves and move in concert toward a single goal, but their common studies and identity of methods link their minds, just as interest might link their wills.

A portion of the tastes and the habits of aristocracy thus reappears, hidden in the depths of the souls of lawyers. Like it, they have an instinctive inclination for order, a natural love of forms; like it, they conceive a great distaste for the actions of the multitude and secretly disdain the government of the people.

I do not mean that these natural inclinations of lawyers are strong enough to constrain them irresistibly. What is dominant in lawyers, as in all men, is particular interest, and especially the interest of the moment.

[276]   Take a society in which men of law cannot assume a rank in the political world analogous to that which they occupy in private life: one may be assured that, in a society organized in this manner, lawyers will be very active agents of revolution. But one must investigate whether the cause that then leads them to destroy or change, arises in them from a permanent disposition or from something accidental. It is true that lawyers contributed very much to overthrowing the French monarchy in 1789. It remains to determine if they acted in this way because they studied law or because they could not participate in making it.

Five hundred years ago, the English aristocracy stood at the head of the people and spoke in its name; today it supports the throne and makes itself the defender of royal authority. Aristocracy nevertheless has instincts and inclinations that are its own.

One must also take care not to take the isolated members of the corporate body for the body itself.

In all free governments, whatever their form, there are lawyers in the first ranks of all the parties. This same remark is also applicable to aristocracy. Almost all the democratic movements that have agitated the world have been led by nobles.

An elite body can never satisfy all the ambitions that it contains: there are always more talents and more passions in it than employments, and there never fails to be a great number of men in it who, unable to rise quickly enough by making use of the privileges of the body, seek to do so by attacking those privileges.

---

* The word translated as *"corporate body"* here (the italics are Tocqueville's), and "body" elsewhere, is *corps*, which means "body" in the usual physical sense, but also, as here, in the sense of a group of persons that can be considered to form a whole. French synonyms for *corps* in this sense are *communauté* ("community"), *corporation* ("corporate body" or "profession"), and *métier* ("trade" or "profession").

Thus, I am claiming neither that *all* lawyers at some time, nor that the majority of them at *all* times, will prove to be friends of order and enemies of change.

I am saying that in a society in which lawyers occupy without dispute the high position that naturally belongs to them, their spirit will be eminently conservative and will prove to be antidemocratic.

• • •

• • •   [277]

Democratic government is favorable to the political power of lawyers. When the rich man, the noble, and the prince are excluded from government, the lawyers arrive there, as it were by rights, for they are then the only enlightened and skillful men that the people can choose who are outside itself.

If lawyers are borne naturally by their tastes toward the aristocracy and the prince, they are thus borne naturally toward the people by their interest.

In this way, lawyers like democratic government, without sharing its inclinations and without repeating its weaknesses, a double cause of their being powerful through it and over it.

The people, in democracy, does not distrust lawyers, because it knows that their interest is to serve its cause; it listens to them without anger because it assumes they have no hidden motives. In fact, the lawyers do not wish to overturn the government that democracy has given to itself, but they continually make every effort to direct it according to a propensity that is not its own and by means that are foreign to it. The lawyer belongs to the people by his interest and his birth and to aristocracy by his habits and his tastes; he is, so to speak, the natural link between these two things, as it were the band that unites them.

The body of lawyers forms the only aristocratic element that can be mixed with the natural elements of democracy without difficulty, and be [278] combined with them in a happy and lasting manner. I am not unaware of the defects inherent in the legal spirit; nevertheless, without this mixture of the legal spirit with the democratic spirit, I doubt that democracy could govern the society for long, and I cannot believe that in our day a republic could hope to maintain its existence if the influence of lawyers in public affairs did not increase in proportion to the power of the people.

• • •

• • •   [279]

In America, there are neither nobles nor men of letters, and the people distrust the wealthy. The lawyers thus compose the higher political class and the most intellectual part of the society. Thus, they could only lose by innovating: this adds a conservative interest to the natural taste that they have for order.

[280] If I were asked where I situate the American aristocracy, I would answer without hesitating that it is not among the wealthy, who have no common tie that brings them together. The American aristocracy is on the lawyers' benches and in the judges' seats.

The more one reflects on what happens in the United States, the more one feels convinced that the body of lawyers forms in that country the most powerful and, as it were, the only counterweight to democracy.

It is in the United States that one sees easily the extent to which the legal spirit, by its virtues, and I will even say by its defects, is suited to neutralize the vices inherent in popular government.

When the American people allows itself to become intoxicated by its passions or abandons itself to the forward thrust of its ideas, the lawyers make it feel an almost invisible brake that moderates and stops it. To its democratic instincts, they secretly oppose their aristocratic inclinations; to its love of novelty, their superstitious respect for what is old; to the immensity of its designs, their narrow views; to its disdain for rules, their taste for forms; and to its ardor, their habit of proceeding slowly.

The courts are the most visible organs that the lawyers make use of to act upon democracy.

The judge is a lawyer who, independently of the taste for order and rules that he has contracted in his study of the laws, also acquires the love of stability from his irremovability from office. His legal knowledge had already assured him a high position among his fellow men; his political power completes the process of placing him in a separate rank and giving him the instincts of the privileged classes.

Armed with the right of declaring the laws unconstitutional, the American judge constantly enters into political affairs.[1] He cannot force the people to make laws, but at least he constrains it to not be unfaithful to its own laws and to remain in accord with itself.

I am not unaware that there exists in the United States a secret tendency that leads the people to diminish the judicial power. In the majority of the State constitutions, the government, at the demand of the two Houses, can remove judges from office. Some constitutions make the members of their courts *elective* and subject them to frequent elections. I dare to predict that these innovations will sooner or later have disastrous results and that one day it will be seen that by diminishing

---

1. See what I said about the judicial power in the first volume.

the independence of the judges in this way, not only was the judicial power attacked, but the democratic republic itself.

It must not be thought, moreover, that in the United States the legal spirit is found only within the confines of the courts: it extends well be- [281] yond them.

The lawyers, forming the only enlightened class that the people does not distrust, are naturally called to occupy most of the political offices. They fill the legislatures and are at the head of the administrations; they thus exercise a great influence on the formation of the law and on its execution. The lawyers are still obliged to yield to the current of public opinion that carries them along, but it is easy to find the indications of what they would do if they were free. The Americans, who have innovated so much in their political laws, have introduced only slight changes, and those with great difficulty, into their civil laws, even though some of those laws are very repugnant to their social state. That is due to the fact that in matters of civil right the majority is always obliged to depend on lawyers, and American lawyers, left to their own judgment, do not innovate.

It is a very odd experience for a Frenchman to listen to the complaints that are made in the United States against the stationary spirit and the prejudices of lawyers in favor of what is established.

The influence of the legal spirit extends even further than the precise limits I have just traced.

There is almost no political question, in the United States, that does not sooner or later resolve itself into a judicial question. Due to this, the parties find themselves obliged, in their daily polemics, to borrow from the law its ideas and its language. Since the majority of the politicians are or have been lawyers, they cause the habitual practices and the turn of mind that are proper to them to pass into the handling of public affairs. The jury completes the process of making all the classes familiar with them. The language of the judiciary thus becomes, in a way, the common language; the legal spirit, born within the schools and the courts, thus spreads gradually beyond their confines; it as it were infiltrates the whole society, it descends into the lowest ranks, and the entire people ends up contracting a portion of the habits and the tastes of the judge.

The lawyers form, in the United States, a power that is little feared, that is scarcely perceived, that has no banner of its own, that bends itself flexibly to the exigencies of the times and abandons itself without resistance to all the movements of the social body; but it envelops the whole society, penetrates each of the classes that compose it, works on it in secret, constantly acts upon it without its being aware of it, and ends up by shaping it according to its desires.

The Jury in the United States
Considered as a Political Institution

• • •

• • •

. . . . To limit oneself to considering the jury as a judicial institution
would be to narrow one's thought greatly; for if it exercises a great influence on the outcome of trials, it exercises an influence on the very destiny of the society that is very much greater still. The jury is thus above all
a political institution. This is the point of view from which one must always judge it.

[284]   I understand by a jury a certain number of citizens chosen at random
and temporarily invested with the right to judge.

To apply the jury to the punishment of crime appears to me to introduce
into the government an eminently republican institution. I will explain:

The institution of the jury may be aristocratic or democratic according to the class from which the jurors are taken, but it still retains a republican character in that it places the real direction of the society in the
hands of the governed or of a portion of them, and not in those of the
governors.

Force is never more than a passing element of success: the idea of
right comes immediately after it. A government reduced to being unable
to reach its enemies except on the field of battle would soon be destroyed. The true sanction for the political laws thus resides in the penal
laws, and if the sanction is lacking, the law sooner or later loses its
force. The man who judges in *criminal proceedings* is therefore the real
master of the society. Now, the institution of the jury places the people
itself, or at least a class of citizens, on the judge's bench. The institution
of the jury thus places the real direction of the society in the hands of the
people or of this class.[5]

In England, the jury comes from the aristocratic portion of the nation. The aristocracy makes the laws, applies the laws, and judges the

---

5. It is necessary, however, to make an important remark:

The institution of the jury gives to the people, it is true, a general right of
control over the actions of the citizens, but it does not furnish it with the means
of exercising this control in all cases nor in a manner that is always tyrannical.

When an absolute prince has the power of making his representatives the
judges of crimes, the fate of the accused is, so to speak, settled in advance. But
even if the people were set on condemning, the composition of the jury and its
lack of accountability would offer more favorable chances to an innocent man.

infractions of the laws. Everything is consistent: therefore England is in truth an aristocratic republic. In the United States, the same system is applied to the whole people. Each American citizen is an elector, eligible to hold office, and may be a juror. The system of the jury, as it is understood in America, appears to me to be a consequence of the dogma of the sovereignty of the people that is as direct and as extreme as universal suffrage. These are two equally powerful means of ensuring the predominance of the majority.

All the sovereigns who wanted to draw the sources of their authority from themselves, and to direct the society instead of allowing themselves to be directed by it, have destroyed or weakened the institution of the jury. The Tudors sent to prison the jurors who refused to convict, and Napoleon arranged for them to be chosen by his agents.

· · ·

· · ·   [285]

In whatever way one utilizes the jury, it cannot fail to exercise a great influence on the national character, but its influence increases immea- [286] surably the further it is introduced into civil matters.

The jury, and especially the civil jury, serves to impart to the minds of all the citizens a portion of the habits of mind of the judge; and these habits are precisely those that best prepare the people to be free.

Respect for judicial decision and the idea of right is spread throughout all classes. Take away these two things, and the love of independence will be no more than a destructive passion.

It teaches men the practice of equity. Each one, in judging his neighbor, thinks that he may be judged in his turn. That is especially true of the jury in civil matters: there is almost no one who fears one day to be the object of a criminal prosecution, but everyone may be a party to a lawsuit.

The jury teaches every man not to shrink from responsibility for his own actions: a manly disposition without which there cannot be political virtue.

It invests every citizen with a sort of judicial authority; it makes all of them feel that they have duties to be filled toward society and that they take part in its government. By forcing men to take responsibility for something other than their own affairs, it combats individual egoism, which is, as it were, the rust of societies.

The jury serves amazingly to form the judgment and increase the natural enlightenment of the people. That, in my opinion, is its greatest advantage. It must be considered as a school that is free and always open, where each juror comes to learn about his rights, where he enters into daily contact with the most learned and most enlightened members of the higher classes, where the laws are taught to him in a practical manner and are placed within his reach by the efforts of lawyers, the opinions of the judge, and the very passions of the parties. I think that the practical intelligence and the political good sense of the Americans must be attributed principally to the long use that they have made of the jury in civil matters.

I do not know if the jury is useful to those who are parties to lawsuits, but I am certain that it is very useful to those who judge them. I regard it as one of the most effective means that the society can use for the education of the people.

The foregoing applies to all nations; but here is what is particular to the Americans and to democratic peoples in general.

I said above that in democracies the lawyers, and among them the judges, form the only aristocratic body that can moderate the movements of the people. This aristocracy is not invested with any material [287] power; it exercises its conservative influence only over minds. Now, it is in the institution of the civil jury that it finds the principal sources of its power.

In criminal trials, where the society fights a single man, the jury is led to see in the judge the passive instrument of social power, and it distrusts his opinions. In addition, criminal trials depend entirely on simple facts that common sense easily succeeds in judging. On this terrain, the judge and the jurors are equal.

It is not the same in civil trials. The judge then appears as a disinterested arbiter between the passions of the parties. The jurors view him with confidence, and they listen to him with respect, for here his understanding completely dominates their own. It is he who unfolds before them the different arguments that have worn out their memory and who takes them by the hand in order to lead them through the convolutions of procedure. It is he who restricts them to points of fact and teaches them the response that they must make to the question of right. His influence over them is almost without limits.

Finally, is it necessary to say why I feel little moved by arguments drawn from the incompetence of jurors in civil matters?

In civil trials, at all times at least that do not involve questions of fact, the jury has only the appearance of being a judicial body.

The jurors pronounce the judgment that the judge has made. They give to this judgment the authority of the society that they represent, and he gives to it that of reason and of the law.

In England and America, the judges exercise an influence over the outcome of criminal trials that the French judge has never known. It is easy to understand the reason for this difference: it is in civil matters that the English or American judge has established his power; afterward, he is only exercising it in another theater; he does not acquire it there.

There are some cases, and these are often the most important, where the American judge has the right to pronounce judgment alone.[7] He then finds himself by chance in the situation that the French judge is in normally. But his moral power is much greater: the recollection of the jury still attaches to him, and his voice has almost as much power as that of the society whose organ was the jurors.

His influence even extends well beyond the confines of the courts: in the relaxations of private life as well as in the work of political life, in the public square as well as in the legislatures, the American judge is constantly surrounded by men who are accustomed to view his intelligence as superior to their own; and, after having been brought to bear on court cases, his power influences all the habits of mind and even the [288] very souls of those who have participated with him in judging them.

The jury, which seems to diminish the rights of the judiciary, thus in reality gives a foundation to its power,[*] and there is no country where the judges are as powerful as those in which the people share in their prerogatives.

It is above all by means of the jury in civil matters that the American judge causes what I have called the legal spirit to penetrate even into the lowest ranks of society.

In this way the jury, which is the most powerful means of ensuring that the people rules, is also the most effective means of teaching it to rule.

CHAPTER 9   [289]

PRINCIPAL CAUSES THAT TEND TO MAINTAIN
THE DEMOCRATIC REPUBLIC IN THE UNITED STATES

• • •

---

7. The Federal judges almost always decide alone those questions that touch the government of the country most closely.

* The word translated as "gives a foundation to" is *fonde*. *Fonder* means to found, or establish on a base, often in the sense of justifying something, rendering it legitimate or reasonable. Tocqueville's point here is that the jury gives the power of the judge a solid foundation precisely by lending it a legitimacy that derives directly from the people.

The Influence of the Laws on the Maintenance
of a Democratic Republic in the United States

*Three principal causes of the maintenance of a democratic
republic.—Federal form.—Municipal institutions.—Judicial power.*

The principal aim of this book was to make known the laws of the United States; if this aim has been achieved, the reader has already been
able himself to judge which of these laws really tend to maintain a democratic republic and which ones endanger it. If I have not succeeded in
doing this in the whole course of the book, still less will I succeed in
one chapter.

I therefore do not want to go back over the ground which I have already covered, and a few lines must suffice for a summary.

[300]   Three things seem to contribute more than all others to the maintenance of a democratic republic in the New World:

The first is the Federal form that the Americans have adopted and that
permits the Union to enjoy the power of a large republic and the security
of a small one.

I find the second in the municipal institutions which, in tempering the
despotism of the majority, give the people at the same time the taste for
liberty and the art of being free.

The third is found in the constitution of the judicial power. I have
shown to what extent the courts serve to correct the excesses of democracy and how, without ever being able to arrest the movements of the
majority, it succeeds in slowing them down and giving them direction.

The Influence of Mores upon the Maintenance
of a Democratic Republic in the United States

I said above that I considered mores to be one of the great general causes
to which one can attribute the maintenance of a democratic republic in
the United States.

I understand here the expression *mores* in the sense which the ancients attached to the word *mores:*[*] I apply it not only to moral habits
properly so-called, which one might call the habits of the heart, but to
the different notions men have, to the different opinions which have currency among them, and to the whole body of ideas from which the habits of the mind are formed.

I therefore understand by this word the whole moral and intellectual

---

* Tocqueville uses here the Latin word *mores*.

state of a people. My aim is not to give a description of American mores. I am limiting myself for the moment to seeking which among them is favorable to the maintenance of its political institutions.

Religion Considered as a Political Institution, and How It Serves Powerfully to Maintain a Democratic Republic among the Americans [301]

North America peopled by men who professed a democratic and republican Christianity.—Arrival of the Catholics.—Why today the Catholics form the most democratic and republican class.

Alongside each religion is a political opinion which is joined to it by affinity.

Allow the human mind to follow its inclination, and it will arrange the political society and the divine city in a uniform manner; it will seek, dare I say it, to *harmonize* earth with heaven.

The largest portion of English America was peopled by men who, after having freed themselves from the authority of the Pope, did not submit to any religious supremacy; they therefore brought to the New World a Christianity which I cannot describe better than to call it democratic and republican: this particularly furthered the establishment of a republic and democracy in political affairs. From the beginnning, politics and religion were in accord, and ever since they have not ceased to be so.

About fifty years ago Ireland began to pour out a Catholic population into the bosom of the United States. For its part, American Catholicism made converts: there are today more than a million Christians in the Union who profess the beliefs of the Roman church.

These Catholics show great fidelity in the observances of their faith and are full of ardor and zeal for their beliefs; however, they form the most republican and most democratic class that exists in the United States. This fact is surprising at first glance, but upon reflection the hidden causes are easily discovered.

I think it is wrong to regard the Catholic religion as a natural enemy of democracy. Among the different Christian doctrines, Catholicism appears to me on the contrary one of the most favorable to the equality of conditions. Among Catholics, religious society is composed of only two elements: the priest and the people. The priest alone is raised above the faithful: all are equal below him.

In matters of dogma, Catholicism puts all intellects on the same level; it constrains the learned as well as the ignorant, the man of genius as [302] well as the common man, to the details of the same beliefs; it imposes the same observances upon the rich as well as the poor, imposes the same austere practices upon the powerful as well as the weak; it compromises with no mortal, and by applying the same measure to all men, it likes to mix together all the classes of society at the foot of the same altar, as they are mixed together in the eyes of God.

If Catholicism disposes the faithful to obey, it does not thereby prepare them for inequality. I will say the opposite of Protestantism, which, in general, carries men much less toward equality than toward independence.

Catholicism is like an absolute monarchy. Remove the prince, and the conditions there are more equal than in republics.

It has often happened that the Catholic priest leaves the sanctuary to enter the society as a power and that he succeeds in establishing himself in the midst of the social hierarchy; sometimes he has then used his religious influence to assure the duration of a political order to which he belonged: then one could also see Catholics who were partisans of aristocracy out of religious spirit.

But once the clergy are removed or remove themselves from government, as they do in the United States, there are no men who, by their beliefs, are more disposed than the Catholics to transport the idea of the equality of conditions into the political world.

If, therefore, the Catholics of the United States are not powerfully drawn by the nature of their beliefs toward democratic and republican opinions, at least they are not naturally opposed to them, and their social position, as well as their small number, requires them to embrace those opinions.

The majority of Catholics are poor, and they have need that all citizens govern in order to accede to government themselves. The Catholics are in a minority, and they need to have all rights respected in order to be assured of the free exercise of their own. These two causes push them, without their even being aware of it, toward political doctrines which they would adopt with perhaps less ardor if they were rich and predominant.

The Catholic clergy of the United States has not tried to struggle against this political tendency; it seeks instead to justify it. The Catholic priests of America have divided the intellectual world into two parts: in the one, they have left the revealed dogmas, and they submit to them without debate; in the other, they have placed political truth, and they [303] think that God has there left it to the free inquiries of men. Thus, the Catholics of the United States are at the same time the most submissive faithful and the most independent citizens.

One can therefore say that in the United States there is not a single religious doctrine that appears hostile to democratic and republican institutions. All the clergy there speak the same language; the opinions there are in accord with the laws, and there prevails, so to speak, only a single current in the human mind.

I was residing temporarily in one of the largest cities of the Union, when I was invited to a political meeting whose purpose was to come to the aid of the Poles and to have arms and money sent to them.

There were thus two or three thousand persons brought together in a vast hall which had been set up to receive them. Soon thereafter, a priest, wearing his ecclesiastical habits, advanced to the edge of the speakers' dais. Those present, after taking off their hats, remained standing in silence, and he spoke in these terms:

"Almighty God! Lord of Hosts! Thou who steadied the hearts and guided the arms of our fathers, when they asserted the sacred rights of their national independence; Thou who made them triumph over an odious oppression, and granted to our people the benefits of peace and liberty, O Lord! turn a kind eye toward the other hemisphere; look with pity upon a heroic people who struggle today as we did in former times and for the defense of the same rights! Lord, who made all men on the same model, do not allow despotism to succeed in deforming Thy work and maintaining inequality on earth. Almighty God! watch over the fate of the Poles, make them worthy of being free; may Thy wisdom prevail in their councils, may Thy power be in their arms; spread terror over their enemies, divide the powers which plot their ruin, and do not allow the injustice to which the world was witness fifty years ago to be consummated today. Lord, who hold in Thy powerful hand the heart of peoples as well as of men, make allies rise up in the sacred cause of just right; make the French nation finally rise up and, emerging from the slumber in which its leaders keep it, come to fight once more for the liberty of the world.

"O Lord! never turn Thy face away from us; allow us always to be the most religious as well as the most free people.

"Almighty God, answer today our prayer; save the Poles. We ask this of Thee in the name of your well-loved Son, Our Lord Jesus Christ, who died on the cross for the salvation of all men. *Amen*."

The whole assemblage repeated *Amen* with reverence.

The Indirect Influence That Religious Beliefs Exercise   [304]
on the Political Society in the United States

Christian morality is found in all the sects.—Influence of religion on the moral habits of the Americans.—Respect for the marriage bond.—How religion keeps the imagination of the Americans within certain limits and moderates their passion to innovate.— Opinion of the Americans on the political utility of religion.— Their efforts to extend and secure its influence.

I have just shown what is, in the United States, the direct influence of religion on politics. Its indirect influence seems to me even more powerful, and it is when it does not speak about liberty that it best teaches Americans the art of being free.

There is an innumerable multitude of sects in the United States. All are different regarding the worship which must be made to the Creator, but all are in agreement regarding the duties of men toward each other. Each sect thus worships God in its manner, but all sects preach the same morality in the name of God. If it is very useful to man as an individual that his religion be true, it is not the same for society. Society has nothing to fear nor to hope from the other life; and what is most important to it is not so much that all citizens profess the true religion, but that they profess some religion. In addition, all the sects in the United States are reunited in the great Christian community, and the morality of Christianity is everywhere the same.

One may think that a certain number of Americans follow, in the worship that they make to God, their habits more than their convictions. In the United States, in addition, the sovereign is religious, and in consequence hypocrisy ought to be common; but America is nevertheless still the place in the world where the Christian religion has retained the greatest true power over souls, and nothing shows better how much it is useful and natural to man, since the country where it exercises today the greatest influence is at the same time the most enlightened and the most free.

I have said that the American clergy pronounce themselves in a general manner in favor of civil liberty, without excepting even those among them who do not accept freedom of religion; nevertheless, one does not see them lend their support to any particular political system. They take care to keep themselves out of political affairs and do not take part in the scheming of parties. Therefore, one cannot say that in the United States [305] religion exercises an influence on the laws or on the details of political opinions, but it governs moral habits, and it is by regulating the family that it works to regulate the state.

I do not doubt for one instant that the great severity of morals one sees in the United States has its principal source in beliefs. Religion there is often powerless to hold back the man in the midst of the numberless temptations that fortune presents to him. It cannot moderate in him the passion to become rich which everything stimulates, but it reigns with sovereign authority over the soul of the woman, and it is the woman who forms moral habits. America is undoubtedly the country in the world where the marriage bond is the most respected and where they have conceived the highest and most just idea of conjugal happiness.

In Europe, almost all the disorders of the society are born around the domestic hearth and not far from the nuptial bed. It is there that men conceive the contempt for natural ties and permitted pleasures, the taste for disorder, the restlessness of heart, the instability of desires. Agitated by tumultuous passions which have often troubled his own home, the European submits only with difficulty to the legislative power of the State. When, upon leaving the agitations of the political world, the American returns to the bosom of his family, he immediately finds there the picture of order and peace. There, all his pleasures are simple and natural, his joys innocent and tranquil; and since he arrives at happiness by way of the regularity of his life, he becomes habituated to regulate his opinions as well as his tastes.

Whereas the European seeks to escape his domestic distress by disturbing the society, the American draws from his home the love of order, which he then brings into the affairs of the State.

In the United States, religion regulates not only morals, it extends its influence even over the intellect.

Among the Anglo-Americans, some profess Christian dogmas because they believe in them, others because they fear not giving the impression of believing in them. Christianity thus reigns without obstacles, acknowledged by all.* It results from this, just as I have already said elsewhere, that all is certain and fixed in the moral world, although the political world seems abandoned to the debate and experiments of men. Thus the human mind never sees before it a field without limits: however audacious it is, it senses from time to time that it must stop in front of insurmountable barriers. Before innovating, it is obliged to accept certain principal givens and to subject the most daring of its conceptions to certain forms that slow it down and stop it.

The imagination of the Americans, in its greatest excesses, thus has only a circumspect and uncertain course; its pace is encumbered and its works incomplete. These habits of reserve are also found in the political [306] society and are extremely favorable to the tranquility of the people, as well as to the duration of the political institutions that they have given to themselves. Nature and circumstances have made the inhabitant of the United States a man of daring; this is easy to judge when one sees in what manner he seeks his fortune. If the mind of the Americans were free of all shackles, it would not be long before one found among them

---

* *de l'aveu de tous. Aveu* has the primary meaning of an "acknowledgment," "avowal," or "confession." It can also mean "consent." During the Middle Ages, the vassal made an *aveu* (acknowledgment, avowal), or *hommage,* of service to a lord in return for the property (called a *fief*) and the protection that he received from the lord. Later, a man *sans aveu*—a man without avowal or acknowledgment of any tie or bond—came to mean someone without scruple, whose word could not be trusted.

the most daring innovators and the most implacable logicians in the
world. But American revolutionaries are obliged to profess visibly a certain respect for morality and Christian equity, which does not allow
them to easily violate their laws when those laws are opposed to the carrying out of their intentions; and if they were able to rise above their
scruples, they would still feel hindered by those of their partisans. Up to
the present, no one in the United States has dared advance this maxim:
that everything is permitted in the interest of society. An impious maxim, which seems to have been invented in an age of liberty in order to legitimate all the tyrants to come.

In this way, therefore, at the same time that the law allows the American people to do everything, religion prevents them from imagining everything and keeps them from daring everything.

Religion, which among the Americans never takes part directly in the
government of society, must therefore be considered as the first of their
political institutions; for if it does not give them the taste for liberty, it
greatly facilitates their use of it.

The inhabitants of the United States themselves also consider religious beliefs from this point of view. I do not know if the Americans
have faith in their religion, for who can read the bottom of men's hearts?
But I am certain that they believe it necessary to the maintenance of republican institutions. This opinion does not belong to a particular class
of citizens or to a particular party, but to the entire nation; it is found in
all classes.

In the United States, when a politician attacks a particular sect, this is
not a reason for the adherents themselves of that sect not to support him,
but if he attacks all the sects together, every one shuns him, and he remains alone.

While I was in America, a witness presented himself at the assizes of
the county of Chester (State of New York) and declared that he did not
believe in the existence of God and in the immortality of the soul. The
presiding judge refused to accept his oath, seeing, he said, that the witness had destroyed in advance all the faith that one could have put in his
words.[3] The newspapers reported the fact without commentary.

---

3. Here are the terms in which *New York Spectator* of 23 August 1831 reported the fact: "The court of common pleas of Chester county (New York) a few
days since rejected a witness who declared his disbelief in the existence of God.
The presiding judge remarked that he had not before been aware that there was a
man living who did not believe in the existence of God; that this belief constituted the sanction of all testimony in a court of justice and that he knew of no cause
in a Christian country where a witness had been permitted to testify without
such a belief." [Tocqueville makes use here of the original English text.]

The Americans mix together Christianity and liberty so completely in [307] their mind that it is almost impossible to make them conceive of the one without the other, and among them this is not one of those sterile beliefs that the past bequeaths to the present and that seem less to live than to vegetate at the bottom of the soul.

I have seen Americans form associations for sending clergy into the new States in the West and for founding schools and churches there; they fear that religion will come to be lost in the middle of the woods and that the people who are arising may not be as free as the people from which they have issued. I have met rich inhabitants of New England who were abandoning the region of their birth with the aim of going to establish, on the banks of the Missouri or on the prairies of Illinois, the foundations of Christianity and of liberty. In this way, in the United States religious zeal warms itself continually at the hearth of patriotism. If you think that these men act only with a view to the other life, you are mistaken: eternity is only one of their concerns. If you question these missionaries of Christian civilization, you will be very surprised to hear them speak so often about the goods of this world and to find politicians where you thought you saw only religious people. "All the American republics stand together," they will tell you; "if the republics in the West were to fall into anarchy or be subjected to the yoke of despotism, the republican institutions that are flourishing on the Atlantic coast would be in great danger; therefore we have an interest that the new States be religious so that they allow us to remain free."

Such are the opinions of the Americans, but their error is obvious: for every day I am shown with great erudition that everything is fine in America except for precisely this religious spirit which I admire, and I learn that the only thing lacking for the liberty and happiness of mankind, on the other side of the ocean, is to believe with Spinoza in the eternity of the world* and to affirm with Cabanis that the brain secretes thought. To that I have nothing to respond, in truth, except that those who talk this way have not been in America and have not seen religious peoples any more than free ones. I will therefore await them upon their return.

There are men in France who consider republican institutions as a [308] temporary instrument of their own grandeur. They measure with their eyes the immense distance that separates their vices and their distress from power and riches, and they would like to pile ruins into this abyss in order to fill it up. Those men are in relation to liberty what the free companies of the Middle Ages were to the kings; they make war for their own account even though they are bearing the kings' colors: the

---

* That is, not to believe that the world was created.

republic will always last long enough to pull them up out of their present servility. It is not to them that I am speaking, but there are others who see in a republic a permanent and tranquil state, an unavoidable goal toward which ideas and mores are each day drawing modern societies and who sincerely wish to prepare men to be free. When these men attack religious beliefs, they follow their passions and not their interests. It is despotism that can do without faith, but not liberty. Religion is much more necessary in the republic which they advocate than in monarchy which they attack, and in democratic republics more than in all the others. How will society avoid perishing if, while the political bond is loosened, the moral bond is not tightened? And what can be done with a people that is master of itself, if it is not subject to God?

The Principal Causes That Make Religion Powerful in America

> *The care taken by the Americans to separate the church from the state.—The laws, public opinion, the efforts of the clergy themselves contribute to this result.—It is to this cause that one must attribute the power exercised by religion over souls in the United States.—Why.—What is in our day the natural state of men with respect to religion.—The particular and accidental cause which in certain countries poses an obstacle to the conformity of men with this state.*

The philosophers of the 18th century explained in a very simple way the gradual weakening of belief. Religious zeal, they said, must abate in proportion as liberty and enlightenment increase. It is annoying that the facts are not in accord with this theory.

There is a portion of the population in Europe whose unbelief is equaled only by their brutishness and ignorance, whereas in America one sees one of the most free and enlightened peoples in the world carry out ardently all the external duties of religion.

[309]   Upon my arrival in the United States, it was the religious aspect of the country which first struck me. As I extended my stay, I perceived the large political consequences which flowed from these new facts.

I have seen among us the spirit of religion and the spirit of liberty almost always march in opposite directions. Here, I found them intimately united with each other: they reigned together on the same soil.

Each day I felt my desire grow to know the cause of this phenomenon.

In order to learn it, I questioned the faithful of each denomination; above all, I sought out the company of clergy, who are the depositories of the different beliefs and who have a personal interest in their survival.

The religion which I profess brought me especially close to the Catholic clergy, and I wasted no time in striking up a certain intimacy with several of its members. To each of them, I expressed my astonishment, and I exposed my doubts: I found that all these men differed among themselves only over details, but all attributed the peaceful empire that religion exercises in their country principally to the complete separation of church and state. I am not afraid to assert that, during my stay in America, I did not meet a single man, priest or layman, who was not in agreement on this point.

This led me to examine more attentively than I had done up to then the position which the American clergy occupies in the political society. I recognized with surprise that they filled no public office.[4] I did not see a single one of them in the administration, and I discovered that they were not even represented in the assemblies.

The law, in several states, has closed a political career to them;[5] opinion has done the same in all the others.

When finally I came to investigate the mind of the clergy itself, I saw [310] that most of its members willingly kept themselves apart from power and maintained a sort of professional pride in remaining outside of it.

I heard them condemn ambition and bad faith, whatever the political opinions with which they took care to cover themselves. But I learned, listening to them, that men cannot be worthy of condemnation in the eyes of God because of these same opinions, when they are sincere, and that there is not more sin in erring in matters of government than there is in making a mistake about the way to build one's house or plow one's field.

I saw them separate themselves with care from all the parties and shun contact with them with all the passion of personal interest.

---

4. Unless one gives this name to the functions that many of them fill in the schools. The greatest part of education is entrusted to the clergy.

5. See the Constitution of New York, art. 7, § 4.
   Idem of North Carolina, art. 31.
   Idem of Virginia.
   Idem of South Carolina, art. I, § 23.
   Idem of Kentucky, art. 2, § 26.
   Idem of Tennessee, art. 8, § 1.
   Idem of Louisiana, art. 2, § 22.
   The article of the Constitution of New York is composed in these terms:
   "The ministers of the Gospel being by their profession devoted to the service of God, and charged with the responsibility for directing men's souls, must not be disturbed in the exercise of these important duties; in consequence, no minister of the Gospel or priest, no matter which sect he belongs to, can be invested with any public office, civil or military."

These facts proved conclusively to me that I had been told the truth. Then I wanted to go back from facts to causes: I wondered how it could happen that in diminishing the apparent strength of religion, one succeeded in increasing its real power, and I believed that it was not impossible to find out how.

The short space of sixty years will never contain the whole imagination of man; the incomplete joys of this world will never be sufficient for his heart. Alone among all beings, man displays a natural disgust for existence and an immense desire to exist: he despises life and fears nothingness. These different instincts push his soul unceasingly toward the contemplation of another world, and it is religion which leads him there. Religion is therefore only a particular form of hope, and it is as natural to the human heart as hope itself. It is through a kind of aberration of the intellect, and with the aid of a sort of moral violence exercised upon their own nature, that men abandon religious belief; an irresistible penchant brings them back to it. Unbelief is an accident; faith alone is the permanent state of humanity.

In considering religions only from a purely human point of view, one may therefore say that all religions draw from man himself an element of strength which they can never be without, because it results from one of the constitutive principles of human nature.

I know that there are times when religion can add to this influence which is proper to itself the artificial power of the laws and the support of the material powers which govern the society. We have seen religions, linked intimately to earthly governments, dominate souls by terror and by faith at the same time; but when a religion contracts such an alliance, I do not fear to say it, it acts as a man might act: it sacrifices the future with [311] a view to the present, and by obtaining a power which is not its due, it puts its legitimate power at risk.

When a religion seeks to found its influence only upon the desire for immortality which torments the heart of all men equally, it may aspire to universality, but when it links itself to a government, it must adopt maxims which are only applicable to certain peoples. In this way, therefore, by allying itself with a political power, religion increases its power over some and loses the hope of reigning over all.

As long as religion bases itself only on the sentiments which are the consolation of all miseries, it can attract to itself the heart of mankind. Mixed with the bitter passions of this world, it is sometimes forced to defend allies which interest more than love have handed to it, and it must push away as adversaries men who often still love it, even while they are fighting against those with whom it is united. Religion cannot therefore share in the material force of governments without taking on some of the hatreds which they bring into being.

The political powers which appear the best established have as a guarantee of their duration only the opinions of a generation, the interests of a century, often the life of a single man. A single law can modify the social state which seems the most irrevocable and most firmly established, and with it everything changes.

The powers of society are all more or less fleeting, like our lives on earth; they rapidly succeed one another like the different cares of life; and a government has never been seen which based itself on an invariable disposition of the human heart or which was able to found itself on an immortal interest.

As long as religion finds its strength in the sentiments, the instincts, and the passions which are seen to recur in the same way in all periods of history, it defies the force of time, or at least it can only be destroyed by another religion. But when religion wishes to base itself on the interests of this world, it becomes almost as fragile as all the earthly powers. Alone, it can hope for immortality; linked to ephemeral powers, it follows their fortune and often falls along with the passions of a day which support them.

By linking itself to the different political powers, religion can therefore only contract a burdensome alliance. It has no need of their aid in order to live, and by aiding them it may die.

The danger which I have just pointed out exists at all times, but it is not always as visible.

There are times in which governments appear immortal, and others in which one would think that the existence of society is more fragile than that of a man.

Certain constitutions keep their citizens in a sort of lethargic slumber, [312] and others abandon them to a feverish agitation.

When governments seem so strong and the laws so stable, men do not see the risk that religion may incur by linking itself to power.

When governments appear so weak and the laws so changeable, the danger strikes everyone's eyes, but often there is then no longer time to escape. It is therefore necessary to learn to notice it from a distance.

To the degree that a nation assumes a democratic social state, and societies are seen to incline toward a republic, it becomes more and more dangerous to link religion to authority; for the time is approaching when power will pass from hand to hand, when political theories will succeed one another, when men, laws, and constitutions themselves will disappear or be modified every day, and this state of things will last not for a particular time but forever. Agitation and instability result from the nature of democratic republics, just as immobility and somnolence form the law of absolute monarchies.

If the Americans, who change their chief of State every four years, choose new legislators every two years, and replace their provincial administrators each year; if the Americans, who have abandoned the political world to the experiments of innovators, had not placed their religion somewhere outside of that world, what would their religion be able to hold onto in the ebb and flow of human opinions? In the midst of party struggle, where would be the respect which is due to it? What would become of its immortality when everything around it perished?

The American clergy have perceived this truth before all others, and they conform their conduct to it. They saw that it was necessary to give up religious influence if they wished to acquire any political power, and they have preferred to lose the support of power than to share in its vicissitudes.

In America, religion is perhaps less powerful than it has been at certain times and among certain peoples, but its influence is more durable. It has been reduced to its own strengths, which no one can take away from it; it acts only within a single sphere, but it covers it completely and dominates it effortlessly.

I hear voices in Europe which are raised everywhere; the absence of belief is deplored, and one wonders what is the means of giving back to religion some vestige of its former power.

It seems to me that it is first necessary to carefully look into what ought to be, in our day, the *natural state* of men with respect to religion. [313] Knowing then what we may hope and what we have to fear, we would see clearly toward what end our efforts must tend.

Two great dangers threaten the existence of religions: schisms and indifference.

In times of fervor, it happens sometimes that men abandon their religion, but they break free of its yoke only to submit themselves to that of another one. Faith changes its object, it does not die. The former religion then excites in all hearts ardent love or implacable hatred; the ones leave it in anger, the others become attached to it with a new ardor: the beliefs differ, irreligion is unknown.

But it is not the same when a religious belief is silently undermined by doctrines which I will call negative, since in affirming the falsity of one religion they do not establish the truth of any other.

Then prodigious revolutions take place in the human mind without man giving the impression of aiding them with his passions and almost without his suspecting anything. One sees men, as if out of forgetfulness, allowing the object of their dearest hopes to get away from them.

Drawn by an imperceptible current against which they do not have the courage to struggle, and to which they nevertheless give in with regret, they abandon the faith which they love in order to follow the doubt which leads them to despair.

During the times which we have just described, beliefs are given up out of indifference instead of hatred; they are not rejected, they desert you. While ceasing to believe in the true religion, the unbeliever continues to judge it useful. Considering religious beliefs from a human point of view, he recognizes their influence over morals, their influence over the laws. He understands how they can cause men to live in peace and prepare them gently for death. He therefore misses his faith after having lost it, and deprived of a good whose whole value he knows, he fears taking it away from those who still possess it.

For his part, he who continues to believe does not fear exposing his faith to all eyes. In those who do not share in his hopes, he sees wretched men rather than adversaries; he knows that he can win their esteem without following their example; he is therefore not at war with anyone; and since he does not think of the society in which he lives as an arena where religion must struggle incessantly against a thousand relentless enemies, he loves his contemporaries at the same time that he condemns their weaknesses and is grieved by their errors.

With unbelievers concealing their unbelief and believers showing their faith, a public opinion in favor of religion is created; it is loved, affirmed, and honored, and one has to penetrate all the way to the bottom [314] of souls in order to discover the wounds it has received.

The mass of men, whom religious sentiment never abandons, see nothing then which pulls them away from established beliefs. The instinct for another life leads them without difficulty to the foot of the altars and delivers their hearts to the precepts and the consolations of faith.

Why does this picture not apply to us?

I see among us men who have ceased to believe in Christianity without becoming attached to any other religion.

I see others who are arrested in a state of doubt and are already feigning that they no longer believe.

Further on, I come across Christians who still believe and dare not say it.

In the midst of these lukewarm friends and ardent adversaries, I discover finally a small number of faithful ready to confront all obstacles and despise all dangers for the sake of their beliefs. These have done violence to human weakness in order to rise above common opinion. Carried away by this very effort, they no longer know precisely where they ought to stop. As they have seen that, in their fatherland, the first use that man has made of independence has been to attack religion, they are fearful of their contemporaries and draw back with terror from the liberty which the latter chase after. Unbelief appearing to them a novel thing, they envelop everything that is new in a single hatred. They are therefore at war with their time and their country, and in each of the opinions professed there they see a necessary enemy of faith.

This should not be in our day the natural state of men with respect to religion.

There is therefore among us an accidental and particular cause which prevents the human mind from following its inclination and pushes it beyond the limits within which it ought naturally to stop.

I am profoundly convinced that this particular and accidental cause is the intimate link between politics and religion.

The unbelievers in Europe pursue the Christians like political enemies rather than as religious adversaries: they hate faith as the opinion of a party much more than as a mistaken belief; and it is less the representative of God whom they find repugnant in the priest than the friend of power.

In Europe, Christianity has allowed itself to be intimately linked with the earthly powers. Today these powers are falling, and Christianity is, as it were, buried beneath their debris. One has tried to attach a living thing to dead ones: cut the ties which hold it back, and it will get back up.

[315]   I do not know what it would be necessary to do in order to give back to European Christianity the energy of youth. Only God could do it; but at least it depends on men to allow to faith the use of all the strength which it still retains.

· · ·

[319]   · · ·

The Laws Serve to Maintain a Democratic Republic in the United States More Than Physical Causes, and Mores Do So More Than Laws

All the peoples of America have a democratic social state.—
However, democratic institutions are only maintained among the
Anglo-Americans.—The Spanish of South America, as favored
by physical nature as the Anglo-Americans, cannot support a
democratic republic.—Mexico, which has adopted the constitution
of the United States, cannot do it.—The Anglo-Americans of the
West support it with more difficulty than those of the East.—
Reasons for these differences.

I have said that it was necessary to attribute the maintenance of the democratic institutions of the United States to circumstances, laws, and mores.[8]

The majority of Europeans only know the first of these three causes, and they give it a preponderant importance which it does not have.

It is true that the Anglo-Americans brought the equality of conditions into the New World. One never comes across either commoners or nobles among them; the prejudices of birth have been as unknown there as the prejudices of profession. The social state thus being democratic, democracy had no difficulty in establishing its empire.

But this fact is not particular to the United States; almost all the colo- [320] nies of America were founded by men equal among themselves or who became equal while living in them. There is not a single part of the New World where the Europeans have been able to create an aristocracy.

Nevertheless, democratic institutions flourish only in the United States.

The American Union has no enemies to combat. It is alone in the middle of the wilderness like an island in the middle of the ocean.

But nature had isolated the Spanish of South America in the same manner, and this isolation did not prevent them from maintaining standing armies. They made war against each other when they lacked foreigners. Up to the present, only Anglo-American democracy has been able to remain at peace.

The territory of the Union presents a field without limits to human activity; it offers inexhaustible nourishment for industry and work. There, love of riches thus takes the place of ambition, and well-being extinguishes the ardor of parties.

But in what part of the world is there more fertile wilderness, greater rivers, more intact and inexhaustible riches than in South America? Nevertheless, South America cannot support democracy. If it sufficed to peoples, in order to be happy, to have been placed in some corner of the universe and to be able to expand at will into uninhabited terrain, the Spanish of southern America would have no reason to complain of their fate. And if they did not enjoy the same happiness as the inhabitants of the United States, they ought to at least make themselves the envy of the peoples of Europe. Nevertheless, there are no nations on the earth more miserable than those of South America.

Thus, not only are physical causes unable to produce analogous results among the South Americans and the North Americans, but they

---

8. Here I remind the reader of the general sense in which I take the word *mores:* I mean by this word the whole body of intellectual and moral dispositions that men bring into the state of society.

cannot even produce among the former something not inferior to what one sees in Europe, where they act in a contrary direction.

Physical causes therefore do not have the influence upon the fate of nations that one supposes.

I met men in New England ready to abandon a fatherland where they could have found a comfortable living in order to seek their fortune in the wilderness. Nearby, I saw the French population of Canada crowd into a space too narrow for it when the same wilderness was nearby; and whereas the emigrant from the United States acquired a great domain at the price of several days' work, the Canadian paid as much for land as if he still lived in France.

Thus nature, in delivering to the Europeans the solitary expanses of [321] the New World, offers them goods which they do not always know how to use.

I see among other peoples of America the same conditions of prosperity as among the Anglo-Americans without their laws and their mores, and these peoples are wretched. The laws and the mores of the Anglo-Americans form, therefore, the specific reason for their greatness and the predominant cause for which I am searching.

I am far from claiming that there is an absolute goodness in American laws: I do not believe that they are applicable to all democratic peoples; and among them, there are several that even in the United States seem to me dangerous.

Nevertheless, one cannot deny that the legislation of the Americans, taken as a whole, is well adapted to the genius of the people which it must govern and to the nature of the country.

American laws are thus good, and one must grant them a great share in the success that democratic government achieves in America, but I do not think that they are its principal cause. If they appear to me to have more influence on the social happiness of the Americans than the nature of the country itself, on the other hand I see reason to believe that they exercise less influence on it than mores.

Federal laws certainly form the most important part of the legislation of the United States.

Mexico, which is as happily situated as the Anglo-American Union, has appropriated these same laws for itself, and it cannot accustom itself to democratic government.

There is, therefore, a reason independent of physical causes and of the laws which enables democracy to govern the United States.

But here is what proves this even more. Almost all the men who inhabit the territory of the United States spring from the same stock. They speak the same language, pray to God in the same way, are subject to the same material causes, and obey the same laws.

From whence, therefore, arise the differences that one cannot fail to notice between them?

Why, in the eastern part of the Union, does republican government show itself strong and regular and proceed with maturity and slowly? What cause gives to all its acts a character of wisdom and durability?

How is it that, on the contrary, in the West the powers of society seem to function haphazardly?

Why does there prevail, in the activity of public affairs, something disordered, passionate, one might almost say feverish, which does not presage a long future?

I am no longer comparing the Anglo-Americans to foreign peoples; I [322] am now comparing the Anglo-Americans to one other, and I am looking into why they do not resemble each other. Here, all the arguments drawn from the nature of the country and the difference in the laws are unavailable to me. It is necessary to recur to some other cause, and where will I discover this cause if not in mores?

It is in the East that the Anglo-Americans have made the longest use of democratic government and have formed the habits and conceived the ideas that are most favorable to its maintenance. Democracy there has gradually penetrated into the customs, opinions, and conventions; it is found in all the details of social life as well as in the laws. It is in the East that the literary instruction and practical education of the people have been most perfected and that religion has been best mixed together with liberty. What are all these habits, these opinions, these customs, these beliefs, if not what I have called mores?

In the West, on the contrary, a portion of the same advantages are still missing. Many Americans in the States of the West are born in the woods, and they mix with the civilization of their fathers the ideas and customs of a savage life.* Among them, passions are more violent, religious morality less powerful, ideas less fixed. Men there exercise no control over each other for they scarcely know each other. The nations of the West reveal, therefore, to a certain extent, the inexperience and the disordered habits of nascent peoples. Nevertheless, these societies in the West are formed of ancient elements; however, the amalgam is new.

---

*   la vie sauvage. Sauvage can of course mean "savage" in the sense of ferocious or bestial. But its primary meaning is simply "to be in a natural state unmodified by human action." Hence: uncivilized, uncultivated, undomesticated (or wild or untamed); or, of places, solitary or uninhabited. A person is sauvage if he eschews human company and prefers to live alone and apart. La vie sauvage is the solitary way of life characteristic of the uncivilized or untamed wilderness.

It is therefore especially their mores which make the Americans of the United States, alone among all Americans, capable of supporting the empire of democracy; and it is also they which cause the different Anglo-American democracies to be more or less well regulated and prosperous.

Thus, in Europe the influence that the geographic position of the country exerts on the duration of democratic institutions is exaggerated. Too much importance is attributed to laws, too little to mores. These three great causes serve without doubt to regulate and direct American democracy, but if it were necessary to classify them, I would say that the physical causes contribute less than the laws, and the laws less than mores.

I am convinced that the happiest situation and the best laws cannot maintain a constitution in spite of mores, whereas the latter draw advantage even from the most unfavorable situations and the worst laws. The importance of mores is a universal truth to which study and experience [323] constantly lead back. It seems to me that it is set in my mind as a central point; I perceive that it is where all my ideas end up.

I have only one more word to say on this subject.

If I have not succeeded in making the reader feel in the course of this work the importance which I attribute to the practical experience of the Americans, to their habits, to their opinions, in a word to their mores, for the maintenance of their laws, I have failed in the principal aim which I set for myself in writing it.

• • •

[331]   CHAPTER 10

SOME CONSIDERATIONS ON THE PRESENT STATE
AND PROBABLE FUTURE OF THE THREE RACES
THAT INHABIT THE TERRITORY OF THE UNITED STATES

The principal task that I set for myself is now finished. I have shown, as far as I was able, what were the laws of American democracy. I have shown what were the mores. I could stop here, but the reader might perhaps feel that I had not satisfied his expectation.

There are other things in America in addition to an immense and complete democracy; the peoples who inhabit the New World can be viewed from more than one point of view.

In the course of this work, my subject has often led me to speak of the Indians and Negroes, but I have never had the time to stop in order to show what position was occupied by these two races in the midst of the democratic people that I was busy describing. I have described according to what spirit, and by means of what laws, the Anglo-American confederation was formed. I was able to indicate only in passing, and in a very incomplete way, the dangers that threaten this confederation, and it was impossible for me to show in detail what were, independently of the laws and mores, its chances of enduring. In speaking of united republics, I hazarded no conjecture on the permanence of republican forms in the New World, and in making frequent allusion to the commercial activity that prevails in the Union, I was nevertheless unable to deal with the future of the Americans as a commercial people.

These objects touch upon my subject but do not enter into it; they are American without being democratic, and it is above all democracy whose portrait I wanted to make. Initially, therefore, I had to put them aside, but I must return to them in finishing.

The territory occupied or claimed by the American Union today extends from the Atlantic Ocean to the shores of the Pacific. In both the [332] East and the West, its limits are thus those of the continent itself. In the South it approaches the edge of the tropics and then ascends back up to the middle of the northern ice fields.

The men spread over this surface do not form, as in Europe, so many offshoots of a single family. Among them one sees, at first glance, three naturally distinct, and I might almost say enemy, races. Education, law, origins, and even the external form of their features have raised an almost insurmountable barrier between them. Chance has brought them together on the same ground, but it has mixed them up together without being able to merge them, and each one pursues his destiny separately.

Among such different men, the first which attracts attention, the first in enlightenment, power, and happiness, is the white man, the European, man par excellence. Below him appear the Negro and the Indian.

These two unlucky races have in common neither birth nor features nor language nor mores; only their misfortunes are similar. Both occupy an equally inferior position in the country they inhabit; both suffer the effects of tyranny, and if their sufferings are different, they can blame the same agents for them.

Might one not say, seeing what happens in the world, that the European is to the men of the other races what man himself is to the animals? He makes them serve his use, and when he cannot make them bend, he destroys them.

Oppression has taken away from the descendents of the Africans in one blow almost all the privileges of humanity! The Negro in the United States has lost even the memory of his country; he no longer understands the language his forefathers spoke; he has renounced their religion and forgotten their mores. While thus ceasing to belong to Africa, he has not acquired any right to the benefits of Europe; but he has come to a stop between the two societies; he has remained isolated between the two peoples, sold by one and repudiated by the other; in the entire universe, only the home of his master offers him the fragmentary image of a fatherland.

The Negro man has no family; he is unable to see in woman anything other than the temporary companion of his pleasures, and, as soon as they are born, his children are his equals.

Shall I call it an act of grace by God or a final malediction of His anger, this disposition of the soul that makes man insensitive to extreme sufferings and often even gives him a sort of depraved liking for the cause of his misfortunes?

Plunged into this abyss of evils, the Negro barely feels his misfortune; violence put him in slavery, the habit of servitude has given him [333] the thoughts and ambition of a slave; he admires his tyrants even more than he hates them and finds his joy and his pride in the servile imitation of those who oppress him.

His intelligence is degraded to the level of his soul.

The Negro enters into servitude and enters into the world at the same moment. What am I saying? He is often bought from the moment he is in his mother's womb, and he begins, as it were, to be a slave before being born.

Without either need or pleasure, useless to himself, he understands, with the first notions he gets from life, that he is the property of another, whose interest it is to look after his life; he perceives that the concern for his own fate does not devolve upon himself; the use of thought itself seems to him a useless gift of Providence, and he peacefully enjoys all the privileges of his servility.

If he becomes free, independence often appears to him to be a heavier shackle than slavery itself, for in the course of his life, he has learned to submit to everything except to reason; and when reason becomes his only guide, he is unable to recognize its voice. A thousand new appetites lay seige to him, and he lacks the enlightenment* and the energy to resist them. Appetites are masters that must be combatted, and he has learned only to submit and to obey. He thus arrives at this height of wretchedness, that servitude brutalizes him and liberty destroys him.

Oppression has not exercised less influence over the Indian races, but its effects are different.

Before the arrival of the whites in the New World, the men who inhabited North America lived peacefully in the woods. Abandoned to the

---

*   *connaissances:* acquired knowledge—"learning," "culture," or "enlightenment."

usual vicissitudes of the savage life,* they exhibited the vices and the virtues of uncivilized peoples. The Europeans, after having dispersed the Indian tribes far into the wilderness, condemned them to a life of wandering and vagabondage, full of inexpressible miseries.

Savage nations are governed only by opinions and mores.

By weakening the sentiment of the fatherland among the Indians of North America, by dispersing their families, by obscuring their traditions, by breaking the chain of their memories, by changing all their habits, and by increasing excessively their appetites, the European tyranny made them more disordered and less civilized than they already were. At the same time, the moral condition and physical state of these peoples did not cease to worsen, and they became more barbaric in proportion as they were more wretched. Nevertheless, the Europeans were unable to entirely change the character of the Indians, and while they had the power to destroy them, they never had the power to civilize and subdue them.

The Negro is placed at the extreme limits of servitude; the Indian, at [334] the extreme limits of liberty. The effect of slavery on the first is hardly less catastrophic than the effect of independence on the second.

The Negro has even lost the ownership of his body, and he cannot dispose of his own life without committing a kind of larceny.

The savage is left to himself as soon as he is capable of acting. He barely recognizes the authority of the family; he has never bent his will before that of his fellows; no one has taught him to distinguish a voluntary obedience from a shameful subjection, and he is ignorant of even the name of the law. For him, to be free is to escape almost all the ties of societies. He delights in this barbaric independence, and he would prefer to die rather than give up the smallest part of it. Civilization has little hold over such a man.

The Negro makes a thousand futile efforts to gain admittance to a society that rejects him. He adapts himself to the preferences of his oppressors, adopts their opinions, and aspires, by imitating them, to merge with them. He has been told from his birth that his race is naturally inferior to that of the whites, and he is not far from believing it; he is thus ashamed of himself. In each of his traits he discovers a trace of slavery, and if he were able to do so, he would consent with pleasure to repudiate himself entirely.

The Indian's imagination, on the contrary, is entirely filled with the alleged nobility of his origin. He lives and dies in the midst of these dreams of his pride. Far from wanting to adapt his mores to ours, he is attached to

* *la vie sauvage.* See the note on *la vie sauvage* at [322].

barbarism as to a distinctive mark of his race, and he rejects civilization perhaps less from hatred of it than from fear of resembling Europeans.

[335]   To the perfection of our arts, he tries to oppose only the resources of the wilderness: to our tactics, only his undisciplined courage; to the depth of our plans, only the spontaneous instincts of his savage nature. In this unequal struggle, he succumbs.

The Negro would like to merge with the Europeans, and he cannot do it. The Indian might up to a certain point succeed in doing so, but he disdains to try. The servility of the one delivers him into slavery, and the pride of the other to death.

I recall that, while passing through the forests that still cover the State of Alabama, I arrived one day at the cabin of a pioneer. I did not wish to enter the American's dwelling, but I went to rest for a few moments on the bank of a spring not far from there in the woods. While I was at this spot, an Indian woman arrived (we were then very near to the territory occupied by the nation of the Creeks). She held by the hand a small girl of five to six years, belonging to the white race, and whom I assumed to be the daughter of the pioneer. A Negro woman followed them. The dress of the Indian woman showed a kind of barbarous splendor: metal rings hung from her nostrils and her ears; her hair, mixed with glass beads, fell freely on her shoulders, and I saw that she had no husband, for she still wore the necklace of shells that it was the custom of virgins to place upon the nuptial bed. The Negro woman was dressed in European clothing that was almost in rags.

All three came and sat down on the banks of the spring, and the young savage woman, taking the infant in her arms, lavished her with caresses that one might have believed to be inspired by the heart of a mother. On her side, the Negro woman sought with a thousand innocent artifices to attract the attention of the little creole. The latter displayed in its slightest movements a sentiment of superiority that contrasted strangely with its weakness and its age; she looked as if, in receiving the attentions of her companions, she was exercising a kind of condescension.

Crouching before her mistress, anticipating each of her desires, the Negro woman seemed equally divided between an almost maternal attachment and a servile fear, whereas even in the savage woman's outpouring of tenderness there reigned visibly an air that was free, proud, and almost savage.[*]

---

[*]   The word translated as "savage" is *farouche,* which can mean "fierce," "wild" or "undomesticated," and also "shy"—shy of society because of being wild or undomesticated.

I had come near and was contemplating this scene in silence. My cu- [336]
riosity without doubt displeased the Indian woman, for she got up
abruptly, pushed the infant away from her brusquely, and, after giving
me an angry look, plunged into the woods.

I often happened to see individuals belonging to the three human races
that people North America brought together in the same places. I had already recognized in a thousand different effects the predominance exercised by the whites. But there was something particularly touching in the
scene I have just described: a tie of affection here united the oppressed
with the oppressors, and nature, by making every effort to bring them
nearer to one another, made all the more striking the immense distance
that the prejudices and the laws had put between them.

The Present State and the Probable Future of the Indian
Tribes That Inhabit the Territory Possessed by the Union

· · ·

· · ·   [354]

From whatever side one considers the fate of the natives of North
America, one sees only irremediable evils: if they remain savage, we
drive them before us on our march; if they try to become civilized, the
contact with men more civilized than they delivers them over to oppression and misery. If they continue to wander from wilderness to wilderness, they perish; if they try to settle somewhere, they perish anyway.
They can become enlightened only with the help of the Europeans, and
the approach of the Europeans corrupts them and drives them back toward barbarism. As long as they are left in their solitary expanses, they
refuse to change their mores, and when they are finally constrained to
try, there is no longer time to do it.

The Spanish loose their dogs on the Indians as on savage beasts; they
pillage the New World like a city taken by assault, without discrimina-
tion and without pity. But one cannot destroy everything; furor has a
limit: the remnant of the Indian populations that escaped the massacres
ends up becoming mixed with its conquerors and adopting their religion
and their mores.[28]

The conduct of the Americans of the United States toward the natives

---

28. One must not moreover honor the Spanish for this result. If the Indian tribes
had not already been fixed to the soil by agriculture at the moment the Europeans arrived, they would no doubt have been destroyed in South America as they
have been in North America.

exudes on the contrary the purest love of forms and of legality. Provided that the Indians remain in the savage state, the Americans do not interfere in their affairs and treat them as independent peoples; they do not permit themselves to occupy their lands without having duly acquired them by means of a contract; and if by chance an Indian nation can no longer live on its land, they take them fraternally by the hand and lead them to die far from the country of their forefathers.

[355]   The Spanish, by means of unprecedented monstrosities, covering themselves with an indelible shame, were not able to succeed in exterminating the Indian race nor even in preventing them from sharing their rights. The Americans of the United States attained this double result with a marvelous facility, tranquilly, legally, philanthropically, without shedding blood, without violating a single one of the great principles of morality in the eyes of the world. It is not possible to destroy men while respecting better the laws of humanity.

The Position Occupied by the Black Race in the United States; The Dangers That Its Presence Presents to the Whites

. . .

The Indians will die as they have lived, in isolation; but the fate of the [356] Negroes is in a way bound up with that of the Europeans. The two races are connected to each other, without thereby being mixed together; it is as difficult for them to separate completely as to unite.

The most fearsome of all the evils that threaten the future of the United States arises from the presence of the blacks on their soil. When one seeks the cause of the present troubles and the future dangers to the Union, one almost always arrives at this fundamental fact, no matter where one begins.

In general, men need to make great and continual efforts in order to create lasting evils. But there is one evil that penetrates into the world furtively. At first it is scarcely noticed amid the normal abuses of power; it begins with an individual whose name history does not preserve; it is deposited like an accursed seed in some spot of ground; then it nourishes itself on its own, spreads without effort, and grows naturally with the society that has accepted it. This evil is slavery.

Christianity had destroyed slavery; the Christians of the 16th century reestablished it. They never accepted it, however, save as an exception in their social system, and they took care to restrict it to a single one of the human races. They thus opened a wound in humanity that was less wide but infinitely more difficult to heal.

One must distinguish carefully between two things: slavery in itself and its consequences.

The immediate evils produced by slavery were more or less the same among the ancients as they are among the moderns, but the consequences of these evils were different. Among the ancients, the slave belonged to the same race as his master, and he was often superior to him in education and enlightenment.[31] Liberty alone separated them; liberty being granted, they easily merged together.

The ancients thus had a very simple means of liberating themselves from slavery and its consequences; this means was manumission, and as [357] soon as they applied it in a general manner, they succeeded.

It is not that, in antiquity, the traces of servitude did not still subsist for a time after servitude was destroyed.

There is a natural prejudice that leads man to look down on the one who was his inferior, for a long time after the latter has become his equal; the real inequality produced by wealth or law is always succeeded by an imaginary inequality that has its roots in mores. But among the ancients, this secondary effect of slavery had a term. The freedman so strongly resembled those men who were born free that it soon became impossible to distinguish him in the midst of the others.

What was most difficult among the ancients was to modify the law. Among the moderns, it is to change the mores, and, for us, the real difficulty begins where that of antiquity ended.

The reason for this is that among the moderns the spiritual and transient fact of slavery is combined in the most lethal manner with the material and permanent fact of racial difference. The memory of slavery dishonors the race, and race perpetuates the memory of slavery.

No African arrived upon the shores of the New World of his own free will, from which it follows that all those that are found there today are slaves or freedmen. Thus, the Negro transmits to all his descendents, along with life, the external sign of his dishonor. The law can destroy servitude, but only God alone can obliterate its traces.

The modern slave differs from the master not only in his lack of liberty, but also in his origin. You can make the Negro free, but you cannot cause him not to be in the position of a foreigner vis-à-vis the European.

This is still not all: this man who is born in servility, this foreigner whom slavery has introduced among us, we barely recognize in him the general traits of humanity. His face appears hideous to us, his intelligence

---

31. It is known that several of the most celebrated authors of antiquity were or had been slaves: Aesop and Terence, for example. Slaves were not always taken from barbarian nations: war placed some very civilized men in slavery.

seems to us limited, his tastes are low. We almost take him for a being intermediary between brute and man.[32]

The moderns, after having abolished slavery, thus still have to destroy three prejudices that are much more elusive and tenacious than slavery itself: the prejudice of the master, the prejudice of race, and finally the prejudice of the white.

[358]   It is very difficult for us, who have had the good fortune to be born in the midst of men whom nature has made similar to us and the law has made our equals; it is very difficult for us, I say, to understand the unbridgeable gap that separates the American Negro from the European. But we can have a remote idea of it in reasoning by analogy.

We have in former times seen among us great inequalities that had their origins only in law. What is more fictitious than a purely legal inequality! What more contrary to the instinct of man than permanent differences established between obviously similar men! These differences nevertheless lasted for centuries; they still subsist in a thousand places; everywhere they have left traces that are imaginary but that time is barely able to efface. If the inequality created only by law is so hard to uproot, how can one destroy that which seems, in addition, to have immutable foundations in nature itself?

For myself, when I consider with what difficulty aristocratic bodies, of whatever nature, succeed in establishing themselves within the mass of the people, and the extreme care they take to conserve through centuries the ideational barriers[*] that separate themselves from them, I despair of seeing an aristocracy founded on visible and imperishable signs disappear.

Those who hope that the Europeans will one day merge with the Negroes thus seem to me to be entertaining a fantasy. My reason does not lead me to believe it, and I see nothing in the facts that suggests it to me.

To this point, everywhere the whites have been the stronger ones, they have held the Negroes in degradation or slavery. Everywhere the Negroes have been stronger, they have destroyed the whites. This is the only reckoning that has ever been made between the two races.

If I consider the United States today, I see well that, in some parts of the country, the legal barrier that separates the two races is tending to be lowered, but not that of mores: I see slavery retreat; the prejudice that it has brought into being is immobile.

---

32. In order for the whites to abandon the opinion they have conceived of the intellectual and moral inferiority of their former slaves, the Negroes would have to change, and they cannot change as long as this opinion subsists.

* *barrières idéales:* the barriers that are in the realm of ideas, that are purely intellectual.

In the part of the Union where the Negroes are no longer slaves, have they come closer to the whites? Any man who has lived in the United States will have noticed that the opposite occurred.

The prejudice of race appears to me stronger in the States that abolished slavery than in those where slavery still exists, and nowhere does it show itself to be as intolerant as in the States that have never known slavery.

It is true that in the northern part of the Union the law allows Negroes and whites to enter into legal marriages. But opinion declares the white who unites with a Negro woman disgraceful, and it would be very hard to give an example of such an occurrence.

In almost all the States where slavery is abolished, the Negroes have [359] been given electoral rights, but if they show up to vote, they risk their lives. If they are oppressed, they may complain, but only whites are to be found among the judges. The law opens the jurors' bench to him, but prejudice keeps him out of it. His son is excluded from the school where the descendent of Europeans comes to learn. In the theaters, he cannot, for the price of gold, buy the right to take his place beside his former master. In the hospitals, he sleeps separately. The black is allowed to pray to the same God as the whites, but not to pray to him at the same altar. He has his own clergy and his own churches. The doors of heaven are not closed to him: nevertheless, inequality hardly ceases at the border of the other world. When the Negro is no longer, his bones are cast aside, and the disparity of conditions persists even in the equality of death.

Thus the Negro is free, but he cannot share either the rights or the pleasures or the work or the sufferings or even the tomb of him whose equal he has been declared to be. There is no point at which they can touch, either in life or in death.

In the South, where slavery still exists, less care is taken to keep the Negroes apart; they sometimes share the work and the pleasures of the whites; one consents to mix with them up to a certain point; the law regarding them is harsher; the habits are more tolerant and milder.

In the South, the master does not fear raising his slave up to his level because he knows that he can always, if he wants to, throw him back down into the dust. In the North, the white man no longer sees clearly the barrier that ought to separate him from a debased race, and he distances himself from the Negro with all the more care as he fears that one day he may happen to merge with him.

Among the Americans of the South, nature, from time to time regaining its rights, succeeds for a moment in reestablishing equality between the whites and the blacks. In the North, pride silences even the most imperious passion of man. The American of the North would perhaps consent to make of the Negro woman the temporary companion of his pleasures, if the legislators had declared that she must not aspire to share his bed; but she may become his wife, and he withdraws from her with a sort of horror.

It is in this way that in the United States the prejudice that rejects the Negroes seems to grow in proportion as the Negroes cease to be slaves and that inequality engraves itself in the mores as it disappears in the laws.

But if the relative position of the two races that inhabit the United States is as I have just shown, why have the Americans abolished slavery in the North of the Union, why do they maintain it in the South, and why do they increase its harshness there?

[360]   It is easy to answer. It is not in the interest of the Negroes but in that of the whites that slavery is being destroyed in the United States.

The first Negroes were imported into Virginia around the year 1621. In America, as everywhere else on earth, servitude was thus born in the South. From there, it spread gradually; but as slavery worked its way north, the number of slaves decreased; there have always been very few Negroes in New England.

The colonies were founded; a century had by now elapsed, and an extraordinary fact began to strike everyone's eyes. The regions that possessed virtually no slaves grew in population, wealth, and well-being more rapidly than those that possessed them.

In the first, however, the inhabitant was obliged to cultivate the soil himself or to hire the services of another. In the second, he had at his disposition workers whose efforts he did not remunerate. There was therefore work and expenses on one side, leisure and economy on the other: nevertheless, the advantage remained with the first.

This result seems all the more difficult to explain since the emigrants, all belonging to the same European race, had the same habits, the same civilization, and the same laws, and differed only in barely perceptible nuances.

Time continued to march on: leaving behind the coast of the Atlantic Ocean, the Anglo-Americans penetrated every day further into the solitudes of the West; there they found new lands and new climates; they had to overcome obstacles of a diverse nature; their races mixed together, men of the South went up to the North, men of the North went down to the South. In the midst of all these causes, the same thing occurred at

[361] each step; and, in general, the colony where there were no slaves became more populous and more prosperous than the one where slavery was in force.

As they advanced, one began, therefore, to see that servitude, so cruel to the slave, was fatal to the master.

But this truth received its final proof when one reached the banks of the Ohio.

The river to which the Indians had given the name par excellence of Ohio, or Beautiful River, waters one of the most magnificent valleys in which man has ever made his home. On both banks of the Ohio stretches rolling countryside where the soil offers every day inexhaustible treasures to the laborer. On both banks, the air is equally healthy and the climate temperate. Each of them forms the extreme frontier of a vast state: the one south of the river which follows the thousand bends that the Ohio makes in its course is called Kentucky; the other has borrowed its name from the river itself. The two states differ only in one respect: Kentucky has admitted slaves, the State of Ohio has refused to allow any of them within its borders.

The traveler who, placed in the middle of Ohio, allows himself to be carried by its current down to the mouth of the river in the Mississippi, thus sails, as it were, between liberty and servitude; and he only has to look around him in order to judge in an instant which is the more favorable for humanity.

On the southern bank of the river, the population is sparse; from time to time one sees a troop of slaves walking across half-deserted fields with a casual air; virgin forest constantly reappears; one would think that the society was asleep; man seems idle, and nature presents the image of activity and life.

On the northern bank, on the contrary, a confused hum proclaims in the distance the presence of industry; rich harvests cover the fields; elegant dwellings speak of the taste and care of the laborer; prosperity is visible everywhere; man appears wealthy and content: he works.

The State of Kentucky was founded in 1775, the State of Ohio came into being only twelve years later: twelve years in America is more than a half century in Europe. Today the population of Ohio already exceeds [362] that of Kentucky by 250,000 inhabitants.

These different effects of slavery and liberty are easy to understand; they suffice for explaining many of the differences that exist between ancient civilization and that of our day.

On the southern bank of the Ohio, work is mixed up with the idea of slavery; on the northern bank, with that of well-being and progress; there it is abased, here it is honored. On the southern bank of the river, one cannot find workers belonging to the white race; they are afraid of resembling the slaves. One must rely on the Negroes to take care of doing the work. On the northern bank, one would look in vain for an idler: the white man extends his activity and his intelligence to all his tasks.

In this way, therefore, the men who in Kentucky are responsible for exploiting the natural riches of the soil have neither zeal nor enlightenment, whereas those who might have these two things do nothing or pass into Ohio in order to make use of their industry and to be able to exercise it without shame.

It is true that in Kentucky the masters make the slaves work without being obliged to pay them, but they derive little profit from their efforts, whereas the money that they gave to free workers would be recouped with interest in the value of their work.

The free worker is paid, but he does his work more quickly than the slave, and rapidity of execution is one of the great elements of economy. The white sells his services, but they are purchased only when they are useful. The black cannot claim anything for the value of his services, but one is obliged to feed him at all times; he must be supported in his old age as well as in adulthood, in his unproductive childhood as well as during the fertile years of his youth, during sickness as well as in health. It is therefore only by paying that one obtains the work of these two men: the free worker receives a wage; the slave, an education, nourishment, care, clothes. The money that the master spends for the maintenance of the slave flows gradually and in small amounts; it is scarcely perceived. The wages given to the worker are given in a lump sum, and it seems to enrich him who receives it, but in reality the slave has cost more than the free man, and his work has been less productive.

[363]   The influence of slavery extends even further. It penetrates even into the soul itself of the master and gives a particular direction to his ideas and tastes.

On the two banks of the Ohio, nature has given to man an enterprising and energetic character; but on each side of the river he makes a different use of this common quality.

The white man of the northern bank, obliged to live by his own efforts, has made material well-being the principal aim of his life; and since the country he inhabits offers inexhaustible resources to his industry and offers never ending lures to his activity, his ardor to acquire has exceeded the normal limits of human cupidity: tormented by the desire for wealth, one sees him boldly enter all the paths that fortune opens up to him; he is equally liable to become a sailor, pioneer, manufacturer, or farmer, bearing the work or the dangers attached to these different occupations with an unchanging steadfastness. There is something wonderful in the resourcefulness of his nature and a sort of heroism in his enthusiasm for gain.

The American of the southern bank disdains not only work, but all the enterprises that work causes to succeed. Living in idle comfort, he has the tastes of idle men. Money has lost a portion of its worth in his eyes; he pursues not so much fortune as excitement* and pleasure, and he brings to this side of things the energy that his neighbor deploys elsewhere. He loves hunting and war with a passion; he takes pleasure in the most violent bodily exercises; he is familiar with the use of arms, and from his childhood he has learned to risk his life in individual combat. Slavery thus not only prevents the whites from making their fortune, it turns them away from wishing to do so.

The same causes, acting continually for two centuries in opposite directions in the English colonies of North America, have ended up creating an enormous gap between the commercial capability of the Southerner and that of the Northerner. Today, it is only the North that possesses ships, factories, railroads, and canals.

This gap is noticeable not only in comparing the North and the South, [364] but in comparing the inhabitants of the South to one another. Almost all the men in the southernmost states of the Union who engage in commercial enterprises and seek to profit from slavery have come from the North. Every day, Northerners spread into this part of the American territory where they have less competition to fear. They discover resources there that the inhabitants have not noticed, and in adapting themselves to a system of which they disapprove, they succeed in getting more profit out of it that those who founded it and still support it.

Were I inclined to press the parallel further, I could easily show that almost all the differences that are visible between the character of Southern and Northern Americans have their origin in slavery. But that would be to go beyond my subject: at this point I am not investigating all the effects of slavery, but what effects it produces on the material prosperity of those who have accepted it.

This influence of slavery on the production of wealth could only have been imperfectly understood in antiquity. Slavery then existed throughout the civilized world, and the peoples who were not familiar with it were barbarians.

In consequence, Christianity destroyed slavery only by asserting the rights of the slave. In our time one may attack it in the name of the master: on this point, interest and morality are in accord.

As these truths became manifest in the United States, one saw slavery gradually retreat before the enlightenment born of experience.

· · ·

---

* The word translated as "excitement" is *agitation*. *Agitation* can also mean "restlessness" or "turbulence"; and, politically, "unrest."

[371]   • • •

By leaving the Negro in slavery, he can be kept in a state akin to that of a brute; free, he cannot be prevented from learning enough to appreciate the extent of his afflictions and to glimpse their remedy. There is, in addition, a singular principle of relative justice that is very deeply embedded in the human heart. Men are struck much more by inequality that exists within a single class than by inequalities that are visible between the different classes. One understands slavery; but how to conceive of the existence of several million citizens forever bent beneath disgrace and abandoned to hereditary wretchedness? In the North, a population of [372] freed Negroes experiences these afflictions and feels these injustices, but it is weak and small; in the South, it would be numerous and strong.

From the moment that one admits that the whites and the emancipated Negroes are placed on the same soil as peoples who are foreign to one another, one will easily understand that there are only two possibilities for the future: the Negroes and the whites must either merge together completely or separate.

I have already expressed above my belief regarding the first possibility. I do not think that the white race and the black race will succeed in living anywhere on a footing of equality.

But I think that the difficulty will be even greater in the United States than anywhere else. One man may put himself outside of the prejudices of religion, of country, or of race, and if this man is king, he may effect surprising changes in the society: an entire people cannot in this way put itself, as it were, above itself.

                                       • • •

[376]   • • •

I confess that when I consider the South, I see only two ways of acting for the white race that inhabits these regions: to free the Negroes and merge them with itself, or to remain isolated from them and keep them in slavery as long as possible. The intermediate solutions seem to me to soon lead to the most horrible of all civil wars and perhaps to the ruin of one of the two races.

[377]   The Americans of the South see the matter in this way, and they act accordingly. Not wishing to merge with the Negroes, they refuse to set them free.

It is not that all the inhabitants of the South regard slavery as necessary to the wealth of the master. On this point, many of them are in agreement with the Northerners and readily admit with the latter that slavery is an evil; but they think that it is necessary to maintain this evil in order to live.

Enlightenment, in increasing in the South, has made the inhabitants in this part of the country see that slavery is harmful to the master, and this same enlightenment shows them, more clearly than they had seen up until then, the near impossibility of abolishing it. From this a remarkable contrast results: slavery is increasingly embedded in the laws, even as its utility is more in dispute; and while its principle is gradually being abolished in the North, in the South increasingly harsh conclusions are being drawn from this same principle.

The legislation of the southern States relative to the slaves presents today a kind of unprecedented atrocity, which by itself shows some profound disturbance in the laws of humanity. It suffices to read the legislation of the southern States in order to judge the desperate position of the two races that inhabit them.

It is not that the Americans of this part of the Union have exactly increased the severity of slavery; on the contrary, they have eased the material condition of the slaves. The ancients knew only about shackles and death for maintaining slavery; the Americans of the South of the Union have discovered more intellectual guarantees for the perpetuation of their power. They have, if I may express myself thus, spiritualized despotism and violence. In antiquity, one sought to prevent the slave from breaking his shackles; in our day, one has tried to deprive him of the desire to do so.

The ancients enchained the body of the slave, but they left his spirit free and permitted him to acquire learning. In that, they were consistent with themselves; there was at that time a natural end to servitude: one day or other the slave might become free and equal to his master.

The Americans of the South, who do not think that the Negroes can ever merge with them, have forbidden them, under severe penalties, to be taught to read and write. Not wishing to raise them to their level, they keep them as close as possible to the brutes.

. . .

. . .   [378]

From the moment that the Europeans took their slaves from a race of men different from their own, one that many among them viewed as inferior to the other human races and with which all of them viewed the idea of ever assimilating with horror, they have supposed slavery to be permanent. For between the extreme inequality that slavery creates and the complete equality that independence naturally produces among men, there is no intermediate state that is durable. The Europeans have vaguely sensed this truth, but without admitting it. Every time the question involves the Negroes, one sees them obey sometimes their interest or pride, sometimes their pity. They have violated all the rights of humanity toward the black man, and then they have taught him the worth and inviolability of these rights. They opened their ranks to their slaves, and when the latter tried to enter them, they ignominiously drove them out. Wanting slavery, they have allowed themselves to be drawn, despite themselves or without their being aware of it, toward liberty, without having the courage to be either completely unjust or completely just.

[379]   If it is impossible to anticipate a time when the Americans of the South will mix their blood with that of the Negroes, can they, without running the risk of perishing, allow the latter to become free? And if they are obliged, in order to save their own race, to try to keep them in shackles, must they not be excused for choosing the most effective means for succeeding in doing so?

What is occuring in the South of the Union seems to me to be at once the most horrible and the most natural consequence of slavery. When I see the order of nature overturned, when I hear humanity crying out and struggling in vain under the laws, I confess that I do not find in myself the indignation to denounce the men of our day who are responsible for these outrages, but I concentrate all my hatred against those who, after more than a thousand years of equality, have introduced slavery once again into the world.

Besides, whatever the efforts of the Americans of the South to conserve slavery, they will not succeed forever. Slavery, narrowed to a single point on the globe, attacked by Christianity as unjust, by political economy as disastrous; slavery, in the midst of the democratic liberty and enlightenment of our age, is not an institution that can last. It will end by the act of the slave or by that of the master. In both cases, great misfortunes must be expected.

If liberty is refused to the Negroes of the South, they will end by seizing it themselves violently. If it is granted to them, they will not be long in abusing it.

[380]   **What Are the Chances of Survival of the**
American Union? What Dangers Threaten It?

· · ·

[391]   · · ·

The men who inhabit the immense territory of the United States are almost all the issue of a common stock, but over time the climate and above all slavery have introduced marked differences between the character of the English of the South of the United States and the character of the English of the North.

It is generally believed among us that slavery gives to one part of the Union interests opposed to those of the other. I have never noticed that to be the case. Slavery in the South has not created interests opposed to those of the North, but it has modified the character of the inhabitants of the South and given them different habits.

I have described elsewhere what influence slavery had exercised on the commercial aptitude of the Americans of the South; this same influence also extends to their mores.

The slave is a servant who does not argue and submits to everything without a murmur. Sometimes he murders his master, but he never resists him. In the South there are no families so poor that they do not have slaves. The American of the South, from his birth, finds himself invested with a sort of domestic dictatorship; the first notions that he receives about life announce to him that he is born to command, and the first habit that he acquires is that of easily dominating. Education thus tends powerfully to make of the southern American a man haughty, rash, iras- [392] cible, violent, ardent in his desires, impatient of obstacles, but easy to discourage if he cannot triumph at the first try.

The American of the North sees no slaves running around his cradle. He does not even encounter free servants because most often he is constrained to provide for his own needs by himself. Scarcely is he in the world when the idea of necessity comes from all directions to present itself to his mind. He thus learns early to recognize exactly, through his own efforts, the natural limit to his power; he does not expect to bend by force the wills that are opposed to his own, and he knows that in order to obtain the aid of his fellow men, he must above all win their good will. He is therefore patient, thoughtful, tolerant, slow to act, and persevering in his goals.

In the southern States, the most pressing needs of man are always satisfied. Thus the southern American is not preoccupied by the material cares of life; another is responsible for thinking about them for him. Free on this point, his imagination is directed toward other, greater, and less precisely defined objects. The southern American loves above all grandeur, luxury, glory, éclat,* pleasures, idleness. Nothing constrains him to make efforts in order to live, and since he has no necessary work, he falls into a slumber and does not even attempt anything useful.

---

*   *le bruit*. See the note on *bruit* at [66], page 54 of this translation.

Equality of wealth prevails in the North, and since slavery no longer exists there, man there finds himself, as it were, absorbed by the same material cares that the white man disdains in the South. From his child-hood he is occupied with struggling against poverty, and he learns to put material comfort above all the pleasures of the mind and heart. Concen-trated upon the small details of life, his imagination fades, his ideas are fewer and less general, but they become more practical, clearer, and more precise. Since he directs all the efforts of his mind to the study of well-being alone, he is not long in excelling in it. He knows wonderfully how to profit from nature and men in order to produce wealth. He under-stands marvelously the art of making society contribute to the prosperity of each of its members and of extracting from individual egoism the happiness of all.

The Northerner has not only experience but knowledge. Neverthe-less, he does not prize science as a pleasure, he esteems it as a means, and he seizes eagerly only its useful applications.

The Southerner is more spontaneous, more full of spirit[*], more open, more generous, more intellectual, and more dazzling.

The Northerner is more active, more reasonable, more enlightened, and more adroit.

[393]   The one has the tastes, prejudices, weaknesses, and grandeur of all aristocracies.

The other, the virtues and defects that characterize the middle class.

Bring together two men in society, give to these two men the same in-terests and in part the same opinions; if their character, their enlighten-ment, and their civilization differ, there is a strong chance that they will not be in harmony with one another. The same observation applies to a society of nations.

Slavery does not therefore attack the American confederation directly by way of its interests, but indirectly by way of its mores.

• • •

[412]   **On Republican Institutions in the United States; What Are Their Chances of Survival?**

• • •

What is meant by republic in the United States is the slow and quiet action of the society upon itself. It is a regular state really founded upon the enlightened will of the people. It is a conciliating government, where

---

[*]   *spirituel. Spirituel* implies a sharp and even mischievous humor.

decisions ripen for a long time, are debated slowly, and are carried out when they have reached maturity.

Republicans, in the United States, prize morals, respect beliefs, and [413] recognize rights. They profess this opinion, that a people must be moral, religious, and moderate, in the degree that it is free. What is called "re-public" in the United States is the tranquil reign of the majority. The majority, after it has had the time to find itself and to recognize its existence, is the common source of all powers. But the majority itself is not all-powerful. Above it, in the moral world, are humanity, justice, and reason; in the political world, acquired rights. The majority recognizes these two limits, and if it happens to overstep them, it is because it has passions, like each man, and because, like him, it may do evil while discerning the good.

. . .

. . .   [414]

In the United States, the dogma of the sovereignty of the people is not an isolated doctrine that has no connection with habits or the body of predominant ideas. On the contrary, one may view it as the last link of a chain of opinions that envelops the entire Anglo-American world. Providence has given to each individual, whoever he may be, the degree of reason necessary for him to be able to govern himself in the things that interest him exclusively. Such is the great maxim on which, in the United States, civil and political society rests: the father in a family applies it to his children, the master to his servants, the township to those who come under its jurisdiction, the province to the townships, the State to the provinces, the Union to the States. Extended to the whole body of the nation, it becomes the dogma of the sovereignty of the people.

In this way, in the United States the generative principle of the republic is the same one that governs the majority of human actions. The republic thus penetrates, if I may thus express myself, into the ideas, the [415] opinions, and all the habits of the Americans at the same time that it is established in their laws; and in order to succeed in changing the laws, they would have to succeed in changing themselves in a sense in their entirety. In the United States, the religion of the majority is itself republican: it submits the truths of the other world to individual reason, just as politics leaves the care for the interests of this one to the good sense of all, and it grants that every man may freely choose the path that will lead him to heaven, in the same way that the law recognizes in each citizen the right to choose his government.

• • •

• • •

There are men among us who expect to see aristocracy come into being in America and who already foresee exactly the moment when it will
seize hold of power.

I have already said, and I repeat, that the present trend of American
society seems to me more and more democratic.

However, I do not claim that the Americans will not one day come to
restrict the sphere of political rights in their country or take away these
same rights in the interest of a single man. But I cannot believe that they
will ever confide the exclusive exercise of them to a particular class of
citizens or, in other words, that they will found an aristocracy.

[417]   An aristocratic body is composed of a certain number of citizens
who, without being placed very far from the crowd, are nevertheless elevated above it in a permanent manner; a body that one touches and that
one cannot hit, with which one mixes every day and with which one
cannot merge.

It is impossible to imagine anything more contrary to the nature and
the secret instincts of the human heart than a subjection of this kind: left
to themselves, men always prefer the arbitrary power of a king to the
regular administration of the nobles.

An aristocracy, in order to last, needs to base inequality on principle, to
legalize it in advance, and to introduce it into the family at the same time
that it propagates it within the society, all things that are so repugnant to
natural equity that one cannot obtain them from men except by force.

Since the existence of human societies, I do not believe that one can
cite the example of a single people who, left to itself and through its own
efforts, has created an aristocracy within itself: all the aristocracies of
the Middle Ages are the fruit of conquest. The conqueror was the noble,
the conquered was the serf. At that time, force imposed inequality,
which, once it penetrated into the mores, persisted on its own and passed
naturally into the laws.

There have been societies that, due to events preceding their existence, were, so to speak, born aristocratic and that each century afterward led back toward democracy. That was the fate of the Romans and
of the barbarians who followed them. But a people that, beginning with
civilization and democracy, by degrees moved closer to the inequality of
conditions and ended up establishing within itself inviolable privileges
and exclusive classes, that would be new in the world.

Nothing indicates that America is destined to be the first to offer such
a spectacle.

Some Considerations Concerning the Causes of [418]
the Commercial Greatness of the United States

. . .

The American sailor leaves Boston to go and buy tea in China. He ar- [421]
rives in Canton, remains there a few days, and returns. He has covered in
less than two years the entire circumference of the globe, and he has
seen land only once. During a crossing of eight to ten months, he has
drunk brackish water and lived on salted meat; he has struggled constantly against the sea, against disease, against boredom; but upon his
return, he can sell his pound of tea for a penny less than the English
merchant: the goal is achieved.

I cannot express my thought better than by saying that the Americans
put a kind of heroism into their way of engaging in commerce.

It will always be very hard for the European merchant to follow his
American competitor in the same course. The American, in acting in the
manner that I have described above, is not only following a calculation,
he is obeying above all his nature.

The inhabitant of the United States feels all the needs and desires that
an advanced civilization brings into being, and he does not find about
him, as in Europe, a society cleverly organized to satisfy them. He is
therefore often obliged to procure for himself through his own efforts
the different objects that his education and his habits have made necessary to him. In America, it sometimes happens that the same man works
his field, builds his house, produces his tools, makes his shoes, and
weaves with his own hands the crude cloth that will cover him. This hinders the improvement of industry but serves powerfully to develop the
mind of the worker. There is nothing that tends more than the great division of work to treat man as if he were mere matter* and deprive his
works of all trace of the soul. In a country like America, where special-
ists are so rare, one cannot demand a long apprenticeship of those who
take up a profession. The Americans therefore find it very easy to
change their state, and they take advantage of this, depending on the
needs of the moment. One comes across those that have been successively lawyers, farmers, merchants, evangelical ministers, and doctors.
If the American is less skillful than the European in each profession,
there are almost none of them that are entirely foreign to him. His ability [422]
is more general, the reach of his mind is wider. The inhabitant of the

---

* The words translated as "to treat man as if he were mere matter" are *matérialiser*
l'homme. *Matérialiser* in this context means to treat something as if it had only a material nature.

United States is thus never handcuffed by any professional axiom; he is free of all professional prejudices; he is not more attached to one system of operation than another; he does not feel more attached to an old method than to a new one; he has not created any habit for himself, and he easily escapes the influence that foreign habits might exercise on his mind, for he knows that his country does not resemble any other and that his situation is new in the world.

The American inhabits a land of wonders, around him everything is in constant motion, and each movement seems a progress. The idea of the new is thus intimately connected in his mind to the idea of improvement. Nowhere does he perceive the limit that nature may have placed on the efforts of man; to his eyes, what does not exist is that which has not yet been attempted.

This universal movement which prevails in the United States, these frequent reversals of fortune, this unpredictable movement of public and private wealth, all combine to keep the soul in a sort of feverish agitation that wonderfully disposes it to all efforts and maintains it, as it were, above the common level of humanity. For an American, the whole of life is passed as if it were a hand in a game, a time of revolution, a day of battle.

These same causes, by acting at the same time on all individuals, end up imparting an irresistible impulse to the national character. The American picked at random will therefore be a man ardent in his desires, enterprising, adventurous, above all innovative. This spirit reappears, in fact, in all his works: he introduces it into his political laws, his religious doctrines, his theories of social economy, his individual occupation; he carries it with him everywhere, in the depths of the woods as well as in the midst of the cities. It is this same spirit that, applied to maritime commerce, causes the American to cross the seas more quickly and more cheaply than any other merchants in the world.

· · ·

PREFACE

The Americans have a democratic social state which has naturally suggested to them certain laws and certain political mores.

This same social state has, in addition, brought into being among them a multitude of sentiments and opinions that were unknown in the old aristocratic societies of Europe. It has destroyed or modified relations which formerly existed and established new ones. The appearance of civil society is not less changed than the physiognomy of the political world.

I have treated the first subject in the work I published five years ago on American democracy. The second is the object of this book. These two parts complement one another and form a single work.

I must immediately warn the reader against an error which would be very prejudicial to me.

In seeing me attribute so many different effects to equality, he might conclude that I consider equality as the unique cause of all that happens in our day. This would be to assume that I have a very narrow viewpoint.

There are, in our time, a host of opinions, sentiments, and instincts which owe their birth to circumstances that have nothing to do with, or are even contrary to, equality. Thus, if I were to take the United States for an example, I would easily prove that the nature of the country, the origin of its inhabitants, the religion of the original founders, their acquired learning, and their former habits have exercised and still exercise, independently of democracy, an immense influence on their manner of thinking and feeling. Different causes, but just as distinct from the fact of equality, would be found in Europe and would explain a great portion of what happens there.

I recognize the existence of all these different causes and their power, but they are not my subject. I have not undertaken to show the reason for all our inclinations and all our ideas; I have only wanted to show in what part equality had modified both of them.

Perhaps it will be surprising that, while being firmly of the opinion [8] that the democratic revolution that we are witnessing is an irresistible fact against which it would be neither desirable nor wise to fight, it has often been the case in this book that I address such severe remarks to the democratic societies that this revolution has created.

I will simply respond that it is because I was not an adversary of democracy that I wanted to be honest with it.

Men do not receive the truth from their enemies, and their friends scarcely offer it to them; that is why I have spoken it.

I thought that many men would take care of announcing the new goods which equality promises to men but that few would dare point out the perils with which it threatens them from afar. It is therefore principally toward these perils that I have directed my attention, and believing I saw them clearly, I have not had the cowardice to be silent about them.

I hope that the impartiality that was apparently noticed in the first work will be found again in this second one. Placed in the midst of the contradictory opinions that divide us, I have tried to temporarily destroy in my heart the favorable sympathies or contrary instincts that each of them inspires in me. If those who read my book find in it a single phrase whose purpose is to flatter one of the great parties which have agitated our country or one of the small factions which, in our day, torment and annoy it, let these readers raise their voices and accuse me.

The subject that I wished to encompass is immense because it comprehends most of the sentiments and ideas that the new state of the world brings into being. Such a subject certainly exceeds my powers; in treating it, I have not succeeded in satisfying myself.

But if I have not been able to attain the goal to which I aspired, readers will at least render me this justice, that I have conceived and pursued my undertaking in the spirit that could make me worthy of succeeding in it.

[11]   PART ONE

INFLUENCE OF DEMOCRACY ON INTELLECTUAL
ACTIVITY IN THE UNITED STATES

CHAPTER 1

THE PHILOSOPHIC METHOD OF THE AMERICANS

I think that there is not, in the civilized world, a country where philosophy is paid less attention than in the United States.

The Americans have no philosophic school which is their own, and they pay very little mind to those which divide Europe; they scarcely know their names.

Nevertheless, it is easy to see that almost all the inhabitants of the United States govern their minds in the same manner and direct them according to the same rules; that is to say that they possess, without ever having taken the trouble to define its rules, a certain philosophic method which is common to all of them.

Avoiding the spirit of system, the yoke of habit, the maxims of family, the opinions of class, and, up to a certain point, national prejudices; taking tradition only as a piece of information, and present facts only as useful preparatory work for doing differently and better; seeking the reason for things by oneself and in oneself alone, aiming for the result without allowing oneself to be shackled to the means, and setting one's sights on the substance beneath the form: such are the principal traits that characterize what I will call the philosophic method of the Americans.

If I go still further, and among these diverse traits I look for the principal one, and the one that can summarize almost all the others, I find that, in most of the operations of the mind, each American appeals only to the individual effort of his reason.

America is thus one of the countries in the world where the precepts of Descartes are least studied and best followed. This should not be surprising.

The Americans do not read the works of Descartes, because their social state diverts them from speculative studies, and they follow his maxims because this same social state disposes their minds naturally to adopt them.

In the midst of the continual movement which prevails within a democratic society, the tie which unites the generations with each other is loosened or broken; everyone in it easily loses all trace of the ideas of his ancestors or pays them scarcely any mind. [12]

The men who live in such a society can no longer draw their beliefs from the opinions of the class to which they belong because there are no longer, as it were, any classes, and those that still exist are composed of such unstable elements that the body can never exercise any true power over its members.

As for the influence that the intellect of one man may have over that of another, it is necessarily very limited in a country where the citizens, having become almost alike, see each other from very close up and, not perceiving the signs of an indisputable grandeur and superiority in anyone among them, are continually led back toward their own reason as toward the most visible and nearest wellspring of truth. Then it is not only the confidence in any particular man that is destroyed, but the disposition to believe any man whatsoever on the basis of his word.

Each one therefore closes up narrowly within himself and claims to judge the world from there.

The Americans' habitual practice of taking the rule for their judgment only from themselves leads their mind to other habits.

As they see that they succeed in resolving without help all the little difficulties that their practical life presents, they easily conclude from it that everything in the world is explicable and that nothing in it is beyond the limits of the intelligence.

In this way, they readily deny what they cannot understand: that gives them little faith in the extraordinary and an almost invincible aversion to the supernatural.

Since they are accustomed to relying on the evidence of their own perceptions, they like to see very clearly the object that they are concerned with; they therefore rid it, as much as they can, of its covering; they take away everything that separates them from it and remove everything that conceals it from their view in order to see it at closer range and in the light of day. This disposition of their mind soon leads them to have contempt for forms, which they consider as useless and inconvenient veils placed between themselves and truth.

The Americans therefore have not needed to draw their philosophic method from books; they have found it in themselves. Much the same thing has occurred in Europe.

This same method has been established and popularized in Europe only to the extent that the conditions there have become more equal and men more similar.

[13]   Let us consider for a moment the sequence of epochs:

In the 16th century, the reformers submit some of the dogmas of the ancient faith to individual reason, but they continue to prohibit it from examining all the others. In the 17th century, Bacon, in the natural sciences, and Descartes, in philosophy proper, abolish the received formulas, destroy the influence of traditions, and overturn the authority of the master.

The philosophers of the 18th century, finally generalizing the same principle, undertake to submit to the individual examination of each man the object of all his beliefs.

Who does not see that Luther, Descartes, and Voltaire all made use of the same method and that they differed only in the greater or lesser use that they claimed should be made of it?

Why did the reformers keep themselves within such narrow limits in the sphere of religious ideas? Why did Descartes, wishing to make use of his method only with respect to certain matters even though he had made it fit to be applied to all, declare that one must judge matters only of philosophy and not of politics? How did it happen that in the 18th century, general applications suddenly were drawn from this method which Descartes and his predecessors had not seen or had refused to uncover? Finally, how did it happen that at this time the method we are talking about suddenly emerged from the schools to penetrate the society and become the universal rule of the intellect, and that after having become popular among the French, it was openly adopted or secretly followed by all the peoples of Europe?

The philosophic method in question could come into being in the 16th century and be clarified and generalized in the 17th, but it could not be universally adopted in either of them. The political laws, the social state, and the habits of mind which flow from these first causes were opposed to it.

It was discovered at a time when men were beginning to become more equal and more similar to one another. It could be generally followed only in the times when conditions had finally become more or less equal and men almost alike.

The philosophic method of the 18th century is therefore not just French but democratic, which explains why it was so easily accepted in the whole of Europe, whose face it has contributed so much to change. It is not because the French changed their old beliefs and modified their former mores that they turned the world upside down: rather, it is because they were the first ones to generalize and clarify a philosophic method with the help of which all the old things could be attacked and [14] the way to all the new ones could be opened.

If I am now asked why, in our day, this same method is more rigorously followed and more often applied among the French than among the Americans, among whom equality is nevertheless as complete and more long standing, I will answer that this is due in part to two circumstances that it is first necessary to explain.

It is religion which gave birth to the Anglo-American societies: one must never forget it. In the United States, religion is therefore mixed together with all the national habits and all the sentiments that the fatherland brings into being. That gives it a special force.

To that powerful reason add this other equally powerful one: in America, religion has, so to speak, set limits for itself on its own; the religious order there has remained entirely distinct from the political order, so that the old laws could easily be changed without shaking the former beliefs.

Christianity has thus conserved a great influence over the minds of the Americans, and, what I want above all to remark is that it prevails not only as a philosophy that is adopted after examination, but as a religion that is believed without debate.

In the United States, the Christian sects are of an infinite variety and modify themselves incessantly, but Christianity itself is an established and irresistible fact that one undertakes neither to attack nor to defend.

The Americans, having accepted without examination the principal dogmas of the Christian religion, are obliged to accept in the same manner a great number of moral truths which flow from them and are attached to them. This compresses individual action and analysis within narrow limits and removes from it several of the most important matters of human opinion.

The other circumstance I am talking about is this:

The Americans have a democratic social state and Constitution, but they have not had a democratic revolution. They arrived more or less just as we see them on the land that they occupy. This is very remarkable.

There are no revolutions that do not shake old beliefs, weaken authority, and obscure common ideas. Every revolution therefore has more or less the effect of abandoning men to themselves and opening before the mind of each of them a space that is empty and almost without limits.

[15] When conditions become equal following a prolonged struggle between the different classes which composed the old society, envy, hate and disdain for one's neighbor, pride and exaggerated confidence in oneself, invade, so to speak, the human heart and make it for a time their domain. This, independently of equality, contributes powerfully to divide men, to cause them to distrust one another's judgment and seek enlightenment only in themselves.

Each then tries to be self-sufficient and glories in fashioning for himself beliefs about everything which are his own. Men are no longer connected by ideas but only by interests, and it is as if human opinions were no longer anything but a sort of intellectual dust which is stirred up everywhere, without being able to gather itself together and fix itself.

Thus the independence of mind that equality supposes is never so great and never appears so excessive as in the moment when equality begins to establish itself and during the painful process that establishes it. One must thus distinguish with care the kind of intellectual liberty which equality is capable of producing from the anarchy to which revolution leads. Each of these two things must be considered separately so as not to conceive exaggerated hopes and fears about the future.

I believe that the men who live in the new societies will often make use of their individual reason, but I am far from believing that they will often abuse it.

This results from a cause more generally applicable to all democratic countries and which, in the long run, should keep individual independence of thought within fixed, and sometimes narrow, limits.

I will discuss this in the chapter which follows.

CHAPTER 2

THE PRINCIPAL SOURCE OF BELIEFS AMONG DEMOCRATIC PEOPLES

Dogmatic beliefs are more or less numerous depending upon the times. They are born in different ways and can change form and object, but one cannot make it so that there are no dogmatic beliefs, that is to say opinions which men accept on trust and without debate. If each one undertook by himself to form all his opinions and to pursue the truth in isolation down paths cleared by him alone, it is unlikely that any great number of men would ever unite under any common belief.

Now, it is easy to see that no society is capable of prospering without common beliefs, or rather that there is none which can survive in this manner; for without common ideas, there is no common action, and without common action, men still exist, but not a social body. In order for there to be a society, and, even more, in order for this society to prosper, it is therefore necessary that all the minds of the citizens always be united and held together by some principal ideas; and that cannot be unless each of them sometimes derives his opinions from the same source and consents to accept a certain number of beliefs ready made.

If I now consider man by himself, I find that dogmatic beliefs are not less indispensable to him for living alone than for acting in common with his fellows.

If man were forced to prove to himself all the truths that he makes use of each day, he would never finish with it; he would exhaust himself in preliminary demonstrations without advancing. Since he does not have the time to act in this way, due to the short space of his life, nor the ability to do so, due to the limits of his mind, he is reduced to holding as certain a mass of facts and opinions that he has neither the leisure nor the ability to examine and verify by himself but that more intelligent men have found out or that the crowd adopts. It is upon this first founda- [17] tion that he himself erects the edifice of his own thoughts. It is not his will which leads him to proceed in this manner; the inflexible law of his condition forces him to do it.

There is no philosopher in the world so great that he does not believe a million things on the word of others and who does not assume many more truths than he has proven.

This is not only necessary but desirable. A man who would undertake to examine everything by himself would be able to give only a little time and attention to each thing; this labor would keep his mind in a perpetual agitation that would prevent him from penetrating deeply into any truth and fixing himself solidly in any certitude. His mind would be at the same time independent and weak. It is thus necessary that, among the diverse objects of human opinions, he make a choice and that he adopt many beliefs without debate in order to delve more deeply into a small number of them that he has reserved for examination.

It is true that any man who accepts an opinion on the word of others puts his mind in servitude, but it is a salutary servitude that allows him to make good use of liberty.

It is therefore always necessary, no matter what the circumstances are, that authority exist somewhere in the intellectual and moral world. Its role is variable, but it necessarily has a role. Individual independence may be more or less great; it cannot be without limits. Thus, the question is not to know whether there exists an intellectual authority in democratic times, but only where it is located and how far it will extend.

I have shown in the preceding chapter how the equality of conditions made men conceive a kind of instinctive disbelief in the supernatural and a very high and often very exaggerated idea of human reason.

The men who live in times of equality are therefore not easily led to place the intellectual authority to which they submit outside of and above humanity. It is in themselves or in their fellows that they usually seek the sources of truth. This would be sufficient to prove that a new religion cannot be established during these times and that all attempts to to bring it into being would be not only impious but ridiculous and irrational. One may predict that democratic peoples will not easily believe in divine missions, that they will readily laugh at new prophets, and that they will want to find within the limits of mankind, and not outside it, the principal arbiter of their beliefs.

When conditions are unequal and men are different from one another, there is a small number of individuals who are very enlightened, very [18] learned, and very powerful by virtue of their intelligence, and a multitude who are very ignorant and very limited. The men who live in aristocratic times are therefore naturally led to take as a guide for their opinions the superior reason of a man or a class, whereas they are little disposed to acknowledge the infallibility of the mass of men.

The opposite occurs in times of equality.

To the extent that the citizens become more equal and more alike, the inclination of each to believe blindly a certain man or a certain class diminishes. The tendency to believe the mass increases, and it is opinion which increasingly leads the world.

Not only is common opinion the sole guide which remains for individual reason among democratic peoples, but it has, among these peoples, a power infinitely greater than among any other people. In times of equality, men have no faith in one another, due to their similarity, but this same similarity gives them an almost unlimited confidence in the judgment of the public; for it does not appear to them likely that, all of them having a similar level of enlightenment, the truth will not be found on the side of the greatest number.

When the man who lives in a democratic country compares himself individually to all those who surround him, he feels with pride that he is equal to each of them, but when he comes to envisage the whole body of his fellows and place himself alongside this great body, he is immediately overwhelmed by his own insignificance and weakness.

This same equality which renders him independent of each of his fellow citizens individually, abandons him, isolated and without defense, to the influence of the greatest number.

The public thus has, among democratic peoples, a remarkable power of which aristocratic nations could not even conceive the idea. It does not persuade men of its beliefs, it imposes them and makes them penetrate the souls of men by a sort of immense pressure of the mind of all on the intellect of each.

In the United States, the majority takes care of supplying individuals with a host of ready-made opinions and thus relieves them of the obligation of forming their own. There are a great number of theories of philosophy, morality, or politics which everyone there adopts in this way without examination, on the word of the public, and if one looks closely, one will see that religion itself prevails there much less as revealed doctrine than as common opinion.

I know that among the Americans the political laws are such that the majority there governs the society with sovereign power, which greatly increases the influence that it naturally exercises there over the intellect. For there is nothing more usual for man than to acknowledge a superior [19] wisdom in what oppresses him.

This absolute political power of the majority in the United States in fact increases the influence over the mind of each citizen that public opinion would obtain there without it. But it is not the foundation of that influence. It is in equality itself that one must seek the sources of this influence, and not in the more or less popular institutions that equal men may give themselves. It is plausible that the intellectual influence of the greatest number would be less complete among a democratic people subject to a king than in the midst of a pure democracy, but it will always be very complete, and no matter what laws govern men during times of equality, we can foresee that the faith in common opinion will there become a sort of religion whose prophet is the majority.

Thus intellectual authority will be different, but it will not be less; and, far from believing that it must disappear, I foresee that it may easily become too great and that it may happen that it finally confines the action of individual reason within limits that are narrower than befits the grandeur and happiness of mankind. I see clearly two tendencies in equality: one that carries the mind of each man to new thoughts and the other that readily reduces it to no longer thinking at all. And I see how, under the influence of certain laws, democracy may extinguish the intellectual liberty that the democratic social state favors, so that after having broken all the shackles once imposed upon it by classes or by individual men, the human mind would shackle itself tightly to the general will* of the majority.

If, in place of all the different powers that encumbered or hampered excessively the activity of individual reason, democratic peoples substituted the absolute power of a majority, the evil would only have changed character. Men would not have found the means to live independently; they would only have discovered—something not easy to do—a new physiognomy of servitude. This, I cannot repeat too often, is matter for profound reflection on the part of those who see in liberty of mind something sacred and who hate not only the despot but despotism. For myself, when I feel the hand of power weighing heavily upon my head, it is of little importance for me to know who oppresses me, and I am not more disposed to place my head in the yoke because a million arms present it to me.

· · ·

[27]   **CHAPTER 5**

**HOW, IN THE UNITED STATES, RELIGION IS ABLE
TO MAKE USE OF DEMOCRATIC INSTINCTS**

In the preceding chapters, I have shown that men cannot do without dogmatic beliefs and that it was even very desirable that they have such beliefs. I will add here that, among all dogmatic beliefs, the most desirable seem to me to be dogmatic beliefs in matters of religion; that is very clearly demonstrated even if we pay attention only to the interests of this world alone.

There is almost no human action, no matter how out of the ordinary one supposes it to be, that does not originate in a very general idea that men have conceived of God, of His relations with mankind, of the nature of their souls and of their duties toward their fellow men. These

---

* Tocqueville uses the plural expression *volontés générales,* "general wills."

ideas cannot be prevented from being the common source from which all the rest flows.

Men thus have an enormous interest in forming for themselves well-settled ideas about God, their soul, their general duties toward their Creator, and their fellow men; for doubt about these first points would abandon all their actions to chance and condemn them in a way to disorder and impotence.

This is therefore the question about which it is most important that each of us has settled ideas, and unfortunately it is also the one about which it is most difficult for each, left to himself and through the sole effort of his reason, to finally settle his ideas.

Only minds very free from the ordinary preoccupations of life, very penetrating, very subtle, very well trained, can, with much time and attention, pierce through to these very necessary truths.

Still, we see that these philosophers themselves are almost always surrounded by uncertainties, that at each step the natural light which informs them darkens and threatens to go out, and that, despite all their efforts, they have still only been able to discover a small number of [28] contradictory ideas, in the midst of which the human mind has wandered continually for thousands of years without being able to get a firm grasp on the truth nor even to find new errors. Such studies are far above the average capacity of men, and even if the majority of men were capable of engaging in them, it is obvious that they would not have the leisure for it.

Settled ideas about God and human nature are indispensable to the daily conduct of their lives, but this very activity prevents them from being able to acquire those ideas.

This difficulty appears to me unique. Among the sciences, there are some which, useful to the masses, are within their reach; others are accessible only to a few persons and are not cultivated by the majority, who have need only of their most far-removed applications; but the daily practice of this latter science is indispensable to all, even though its study is inaccessible to the greatest number.

General ideas relative to God and human nature are therefore, among all ideas, those which it is most suitable to remove from the habitual action of individual reason and regarding which there is most to gain and least to lose in acknowledging an authority.

The first object, and one of the principal advantages of religions, is to supply, for each of these fundamental questions, a solution that is clear, precise, intelligible to the mass of men, and very durable.

There are religions that are very false and very absurd; nevertheless, one can say that every religion that remains within the sphere I have just pointed out and does not claim to go outside it—as several have tried to do in order to put a stop everywhere to the free flight of the human mind—imposes a salutary yoke upon the intellect, and it must be acknowledged that, if it does not save men in the other world, it is at least very useful to their happiness and grandeur in this one.

That is above all true of men who live in free countries.

When religion is destroyed among a people, doubt takes over the highest regions of the intellect, and it halfway paralyzes all the others. Everyone becomes used to having only confused and unstable notions about the matters that most interest his fellow men and himself; men defend their opinions badly or abandon them, and since they despair of being able, by themselves alone, to resolve the greatest problems that human fate presents, they are reduced in cowardly fashion to not giving them any thought.

Such a state cannot fail to weaken souls; it relaxes the springs of the will, and it prepares citizens for servitude.

[29]   Not only does it then happen that these men allow their liberty to be taken, but often they give it away.

Just as in matters of politics, when authority in matters of religion no longer exists men are soon frightened by the sight of this independence without limits. This perpetual agitation of all things worries and exhausts them. Since everything is in motion in the intellectual world, they wish at least that everything be firm and stable in the material order, and since they are no longer able to recover their former beliefs, they give themselves a master.

For myself, I doubt that man can ever support at the same time complete religious independence and complete political liberty, and I am led to think that if he has no faith, he must serve, and if he is free, he must believe.

I do not know, however, if this great utility of religions is not still more visible among peoples whose conditions are equal than among all the others.

It must be acknowledged that equality, which introduces great goods into the world, nevertheless suggests to men, as will be shown hereafter, some very dangerous instincts; it tends to isolate them from one another, leading each of them to be concerned only with himself alone.

It opens their soul excessively to the love of material pleasures.

The greatest advantage of religions is to inspire completely opposite instincts. There is no religion which does not place the object of man's desires beyond and above earthly goods and which does not raise his soul naturally toward regions far superior to his own. Nor are there any which do not impose upon each man some duties toward mankind, or to be performed in common with it, and which do not in this way draw him away, from time to time, from the contemplation of himself. This is true of the most false and most dangerous religions.

Religious peoples are thus naturally strong precisely where democratic peoples are weak, which shows well how important it is that men keep their religion while becoming equal.

I have neither the right nor the wish to examine the divine means God uses to make a religious belief achieve a place in the heart of man. At this time I am considering religions only from a purely human point of view; I am looking for the manner in which they can most easily conserve their influence during the democratic times that we are entering.

I have shown how, in times of enlightenment and equality, the human mind consents only with difficulty to accept dogmatic beliefs and only [30] feels the need of them strongly with respect to religion. This indicates first that during those times, religions must keep themselves more discreetly than in all others within the limits that are proper to them and not seek to go outside those limits; for, in wanting to extend their power beyond religious matters, they risk no longer being believed in any matter. They must thus mark out with care the sphere within which they claim to decide the human mind, and beyond this leave it entirely free to be entrusted to itself.

Mohammed brought down from Heaven and placed in the Koran not only religious doctrines, but political maxims, civil and criminal laws, and scientific theories. The Gospel, on the contrary, speaks only about the general relations of men with God and among themselves. Beyond that, it teaches nothing and does not oblige belief about anything. That alone, among a thousand other reasons, suffices to show that the first of these two religions cannot rule for long during times of enlightenment and democracy, whereas the second is destined to reign during these times as in all others.

If I proceed further in this same direction, I find that, in order for religions to be able, humanly speaking, to maintain themselves during democratic times, it is not only necessary that they confine themselves carefully within the sphere of religious matters; their power depends still more upon the nature of the beliefs that they profess, the external forms that they adopt, and the obligations that they impose.

What I said earlier, that equality leads men to very general and vast ideas, must be understood principally with respect to religion. Men who are alike and equal easily conceive the notion of a unique God, imposing on each of them the same rules and granting them future happiness at the same price. The idea of the unity of mankind leads them back continually to the idea of the unity of the Creator, whereas, on the contrary, men who are very separated from one another and very different readily come to create as many divinities as there are peoples, castes, classes, and families, and to mark out a thousand particular paths for reaching Heaven.

It cannot be denied that Christianity itself has been subjected in a way to the influence that the social and political state exercises on religious beliefs.

At the moment when the Christian religion appeared on the earth, Providence, which without doubt was preparing the world for its coming, had brought together a great portion of mankind, like an immense flock, under the authority of the Caesars. The men who composed this [31] multitude differed greatly from one another, but they nevertheless had this feature in common, that they all obeyed the same laws, and each of them was so weak and so small in relation to the grandeur of the prince that they all appeared equal when they were compared to him.

It must be acknowledged that this new and particular state of humanity must have disposed men to accept the general truths that Christianity teaches and serves to explain the easy and rapid manner with which it penetrated the human mind at that time.

The verification of this occurred after the destruction of the Empire.

The Roman world being then broken, so to speak, into a thousand pieces, each nation reverted to its original character. Soon, within these nations, ranks were infinitely divided; races were distinguished; castes divided each nation into several peoples. In the midst of this universal effort which seemed to lead human societies to subdivide themselves into as many fragments as it was possible to conceive of, Christianity did not lose sight of the principal general ideas that it had brought to light. But it appeared nonetheless to lend itself, as much as it could, to the new tendencies that the fragmentation of mankind brought into being. Men continued to adore only a single God, creator and preserver of all things, but each people, each city, and, as it were, each man believed they could obtain some separate privilege and create for themselves special protectors before the sovereign master. Unable to divide Divinity, they rather multiplied it and increased the importance of its agents to a point of excess; the homage due to the angels and the saints became, for most Christians, an almost idolatrous cult, and one could have feared for a moment that the Christian religion would move backward toward the religions that it had vanquished.

It seems to me obvious that the more the barriers which separate the nations within humanity and the citizens within each people, tend to disappear, the more the human mind is directed, as if by itself, toward the idea of a unique and all-powerful being, dispensing the same laws equally and in the same manner to each man. It is therefore especially in democratic times that it is important not to allow the homage rendered to secondary agents to be confused with the worship which is due only to the Creator.

Another truth appears to me to be very clear: it is that religions must be less concerned with external practices in democratic times than in all others.

I have shown, with respect to the philosophic method of the Americans, that nothing is more revolting to the human mind during times of equality than the idea of submitting to forms.* The men who live in these [32] times do not have much patience for figures;† symbols appear to them childish artifices used for concealing or adorning truths that it would be more natural to show to them completely naked and in broad daylight; the spectacle of ceremonies leaves them cold, and they are naturally led to attach only a secondary importance to the details of worship.

Those who are responsible for determining the external form of religions in democratic times must pay close attention to these natural instincts of the human intellect so as to avoid struggling against them without necessity.

I believe firmly in the necessity of forms; I know that they fix the human mind in the contemplation of abstract truths, and, helping it to grasp them firmly, makes it embrace them with fervor. I do not imagine that it is possible to maintain a religion without external practices; but, on the other hand, I think that, in the times we are entering, it would be particularly dangerous to multiply them excessively, that it is necessary instead to limit them, and that only those must be retained that are absolutely necessary for the perpetuation of belief itself, which is the substance of religions,[1] of which worship is only the form. A religion that became more detailed, more inflexible, and more encumbered with

---

*   *les formes. Les formes* are the conventions, proprieties, or etiquette, necessarily rule-bound, which may govern any or all human activities, from social and political conduct to speech, to dancing, etc.

†   *Figures* derives from the Latin word for "form" (*figura*). *Les figures* for Tocqueville's reader would have comprised an entire world of conventions, of which "figures of speech" or (in ice skating) "compulsory figures" are contemporary remnants, and would have included, for example, forms of speech and writing from grammar to rhetoric, forms of thought, positions and steps in dance and in fencing, and musical notation.

1. In all religions, there are ceremonies that are inherent in the very substance of belief and about which one must be very careful to change nothing. This is particularly clear in Catholicism, where often the form and the substance are so tightly linked that they are only one.

small observances at the same time that men are becoming more equal would soon see itself reduced to a troop of passionate zealots in the midst of an unbelieving multitude.

I know that someone will certainly object that religions, all of which take for their object general and eternal truths, cannot bend themselves in this way to the changing instincts of each century without losing their quality of certitude in the eyes of men: I will answer here once more that it is necessary to distinguish very carefully the principal opinions that constitute a belief and that compose what theologians call its articles of faith from the incidental notions that are connected to it. Religions are obliged always to hold firm with respect to the former, no matter what the particular spirit of the times, but they must be careful to avoid being linked in the same way to the latter during times when everything is constantly changing position and when the mind, accustomed to the changing spectacle of human things, tolerates being fixed with reluctance. Lack of change in external and secondary things appears to me to have a chance of enduring only when the civil society itself is immobile; everywhere else, I am led to believe that it is dangerous.

[33]   We will see that among all the passions that equality brings into being or favors, there is one that it makes especially strong and that it places at the same time in the hearts of all men: that is the love of well-being. The taste for well-being is the outstanding and indelible characteristic of democratic times.

One may believe that a religion that undertook to destroy this mother-passion would in the end be destroyed by it; if it wanted to tear men away completely from the contemplation of the goods of this world in order to deliver them over solely to thought about those of the other one, it can be expected that their souls would in the end slip through its hands in order to throw themselves, far away from it, into material and present pleasures alone.

The principal business of religions is to purify, regulate, and restrain the too ardent and too exclusive taste for well-being that men experience in times of equality, but I believe that they would be wrong to try to subjugate it completely and destroy it. They will not succeed in turning men away from the love of riches, but they can still persuade them to enrich themselves only by honest means.

This leads me to a final consideration which includes, in a way, all the others. To the extent that men become more alike and more equal, it is more important that religions, while carefully keeping themselves at a distance from the activity of daily affairs, not offend without necessity generally accepted ideas and the permanent interests which hold sway among the mass; for common opinion appears more and more as the

One of the most usual weaknesses of the human mind is to want to reconcile opposite principles and to purchase peace at the expense of [36] logic. Thus, there have always been and there always will be men who, after having subjected some of their religious beliefs to an authority, will want to withdraw from it several others and allow their minds to float haphazardly between obedience and liberty. But I am led to believe that their number will be less great in democratic times than in other times and that our descendents will tend more and more to be divided into only two parts, the ones abandoning Christianity entirely and the others entering into the bosom of the Roman Church.

. . .

CHAPTER 8 [39]

HOW EQUALITY SUGGESTS TO AMERICANS THE IDEA OF THE INDEFINITE PERFECTIBILITY OF MAN

Equality suggests to the human mind several ideas which would not have come to mind without it, and it modifies almost all of those it already had. I will take as an example the idea of human perfectibility because it is one of the principal ones that the mind can conceive and because it constitutes in itself a grand philosophical theory whose consequences are visible at each moment in the conduct of human affairs.

Although man resembles the animals in several respects, one trait is particular to him alone: he perfects himself, and the animals do not perfect themselves. Mankind could not fail to reveal this difference from the beginning. The idea of perfectibility is therefore as old as the world; equality did not bring it into being, but it gives it a new character.

When citizens are classed according to rank, profession, birth, and when all are constrained to follow the path on which they are placed by chance, each one believes he sees the outer limits of human power close to himself, and no one seeks any longer to struggle against an inevitable fate. It is not that aristocratic peoples absolutely deny to man the faculty of perfecting himself. They do not think it is without definite limits; they conceive of improvement, not change; they imagine the condition of future societies as better, but not different; and while admitting that humanity has made great progress and that it is capable of making still more, they confine it in advance within certain insurmountable limits.

Therefore they do not think that they have arrived at the supreme good and the absolute truth (what man or what people has ever been insane enough to imagine they have?), but they like to persuade themselves that they have attained roughly the degree of grandeur and knowledge that our imperfect nature allows, and since nothing around them moves, [40] they readily imagine that everything is in its place. It is at such times that the legislator claims to promulgate eternal laws, that peoples and kings wish to raise only monuments meant for the ages, and that the present generation assumes the responsibility of sparing future generations the care of deciding their own destinies.

As castes disappear, as classes move closer to each other, as men (mixing themselves together tumultuously), habitual practices, customs, and laws change, as new facts arise, as new truths are brought to light, as old opinions disappear and as others take their place, the image of an ideal and always elusive perfection presents itself to the human mind.

Then constant changes occur at each instant under the eyes of each man. Some worsen his position, and he understands only too well that a people or an individual, no matter how enlightened, is not infallible. Others improve his lot, and he concludes from them that man, in general, is endowed with the indefinite capability of perfecting himself. His setbacks show him that no one can flatter himself that he has discovered the absolute good; his successes fire him up to pursue it without respite. Thus, always seeking, falling, getting back up, often disappointed, never discouraged, he strives continually toward this immense grandeur which he glimpses in a confused manner at the end of the long path which humanity must still traverse.

It is impossible to believe how many facts flow naturally from this philosophical theory according to which man is indefinitely perfectible and the prodigious influence that it exercises on those very ones who, always involved only with acting and not thinking, seem to conform their actions to it without acknowledging it.

I meet an American seaman, and I ask him why the vessels of his country are constructed in such a way that they do not last, and he answers me without hesitating that the art of navigation is every day making such rapid progress that the most beautiful boat would soon become almost useless if it lasted more than a few years.

In these words spoken at random and regarding an unusual fact by a coarse man, I perceive the general and systematic idea according to which a great people conducts all its affairs.

Aristocratic nations are naturally led to tighten the limits of human perfectibility too much, and democratic nations sometimes stretch them to a point of excess.

. . .

CHAPTER 10   [46]

WHY THE AMERICANS ARE MORE DEVOTED TO
THE PRACTICE OF THE SCIENCES THAN TO THEIR THEORY

If the democratic social state and institutions do not stop the flight of the human mind, it is at least indisputable that they steer it in one direction rather than in another. Their effects, while circumscribed in this way, are still very great, and one will pardon me, I hope, for stopping for a moment to contemplate them.

We have made several remarks regarding the philosophical method of the Americans that we must take advantage of here.

Equality makes grow in each man the desire to judge everything by himself; it gives him, in all things, the taste for the tangible and the real, the disdain for traditions and forms. These general instincts reveal themselves principally in the particular subject of this chapter.

Those who cultivate the sciences among democratic peoples are always afraid of losing themselves in utopias. They distrust systems; they like to keep themselves very close to the facts and to study them by themselves; since they do not easily allow themselves to be impressed by the reputation of any of their fellow men, they are never inclined to swear to anything on the word of the master, but, on the contrary, we see them constantly looking for the weak point of his doctrine. Scientific traditions have little influence over them; they do not pause for long among the subtleties of a school and are not easily satisfied by grand words; they penetrate, as far as they can, into the principal parts of the subject with which they are occupied, and they like to set them forth in ordinary language. At such times the sciences have a bearing that is freer and more certain, but less high.

The mind, it seems to me, may divide science into three parts.

The first contains the most theoretical principles, the most abstract notions, those whose application is not known or is very remote.

The second is composed of general truths which, while still coming under pure theory, nevertheless lead, by a direct and short path, to practice.   [47]

The methods of application and the means of execution make up the third.

Each of these different parts of science may be cultivated separately although reason and experience show us that none of them can prosper for long when it is absolutely separated from the other two.

In America, the purely practical part of the sciences is admirably cultivated, and the portion of theory that is immediately necessary for application is treated with care; here, the Americans display an intelligence that is always clear, free, original, and fertile; but almost no one in the United States devotes himself to the essentially theoretical and abstract portion of human knowledge. In this the Americans exhibit the excess of a tendency that reappears, I think, although to a lesser degree, in all democratic peoples.

Nothing is more necessary to the cultivation of the higher sciences, or of the higher portion of all sciences, than reflection, and there is nothing less suitable to reflection than the interior of a democratic society. One does not come across there, as one does among aristocratic peoples, a large class that remains at rest because it feels itself to be well-off and another that does not bestir itself because it despairs of improving its lot. Everyone is in constant restless motion: some want to attain power, others to get hold of riches. In the midst of this universal tumult, of this repeated clash of contrary interests, of this constant march of men toward wealth, where can one find the calm necessary to the profound constructions of the mind? How can one make thought stop at any one point, when everything around one is in motion and when one is oneself swept up and tossed about every day in the impetuous current that moves all things?

It is necessary to clearly distinguish the kind of permanent agitation that exists in the midst of a tranquil and already constituted democracy, from the tumultuous and revolutionary movements that almost always accompany the birth and development of a democratic society.

When a violent revolution takes place among a very civilized people, it cannot fail to give a sudden impulsion to sentiments and ideas.

This is true above all of democratic revolutions, which, in shaking up all at once all the classes which compose a people, simultaneously causes immense ambitions to be born in the heart of each citizen.

[48]   If the French suddenly made such admirable progress in the exact sciences at the very moment that they were completing the destruction of the remnants of the old feudal society, this sudden fecundity must be attributed not to democracy but to the unprecedented revolution that accompanied its growth. What happened then was an unusual occurrence; it would be unwise to see in it the sign of a general law.

Great revolutions are not more common among democratic peoples than among the other peoples; I am even inclined to believe that they are less so. But there prevails in these nations a slight bothersome movement, a sort of incessant turnover of men one after another, which troubles and distracts the mind without inspiring or elevating it.

Not only do the men who live in democratic societies have difficulty devoting themselves to reflection, they also have naturally little esteem for it. The democratic social state and democratic institutions lead most men to act constantly. Now, the habits of mind that are suitable for action are not always suitable for thought. The man who acts is often reduced to being satisfied with approximations because he would never accomplish his intention if he wanted to perfect every detail. He must continually depend upon ideas that he has not had the leisure to examine thoroughly, for he is helped much more by the opportunity afforded by the idea that he makes use of than he is by its strict soundness; and all things considered, there is less risk for him in making use of some false principles than in consuming his time in establishing the truth of all his principles. It is not by means of long and learned demonstrations that the world is led. The rapid glance at a particular fact, the daily study of the changing passions of the crowd, the momentary chance and the skill to seize it decide all affairs there.

In times when almost everyone is engaged in action, one is therefore generally led to attach an excessive value to the rapid bounds and superficial conceptions of the mind and, on the contrary, to depreciate excessively its profound and slow working.

This public opinion influences the judgment of men who cultivate the sciences; it persuades them that they can succeed in them without reflection, or it pushes them away from those sciences that require it.

There are several ways of studying the sciences. There is in a great number of men a selfish, venal, and industrial taste for the discoveries of the mind that must not be confused with the disinterested passion that is aroused in the heart of a small number; there is a desire to make use of knowledge and a pure desire to know. I do not doubt that from time to time, in some men, a passionate and inextinguishable love of truth is born, which is self-sufficient and takes pleasure continually without ever [49] being able to satisfy itself. It is this passionate, proud, and disinterested love of the true which leads men up to the abstract sources of truth in order to draw from them mother ideas.*

If Pascal had envisaged only some great gain, or even if he had been moved only by the desire for glory alone, I cannot believe that he would have ever been able to bring together, as he did, all the powers of his mind in order to better discover the most obscure secrets of the Creator. When I see him, in a way, tear his soul from the cares of life in order to bind it in its entirety to this pursuit and, prematurely breaking the ties that hold it to the body, die of old age before forty years, I stop, speechless, and I comprehend that it is no ordinary cause that is capable of producing such extraordinary efforts.

The future will show whether these passions, so rare and so fertile, are born and grow as easily in the midst of democratic societies as in

---

* *les idées mères.* See the note in Vol. 1, Introduction [13].

the midst of aristocracies. As for me, I admit that I have difficulty believing it.

In aristocratic societies, the class that governs opinion and conducts public affairs, being placed in a permanent and hereditary manner above the crowd, naturally conceives a high idea of itself and of man. It readily imagines glorious pleasures for itself, and it sets magnificent goals for its aspirations. Aristocracies often take very tyrannical and very inhuman actions, but they rarely conceive base thoughts, and they show a certain prideful disdain for petty pleasures, even when they indulge themselves in them: that gives a very high tone to all souls. In aristocratic times, very vast ideas of the dignity, power, and grandeur of man are generally formed. These opinions influence those who cultivate the sciences just as they do all others; they facilitate the natural flight of the mind toward the highest regions of thought and dispose it naturally to form a notion of the sublime and almost divine love of truth.

The learned men of these times are thus drawn toward theory, and it even frequently happens that they conceive an ill-considered disdain for practice. "Archimedes," said Plutarch, "had such a high heart that he never deigned to leave behind any written work on the manner of constructing all these machines of war; and, considering as contemptible, base, and mercenary this whole science of inventing and putting together machines and generally any art that contributes something useful to putting it into practice, he employed his mind and his study in writing only about things whose beauty and subtlety were not mixed in any way with necessity." That is the aristocratic view of the sciences.

[50]   It cannot be the same among democratic nations.

The majority of men who compose these nations are very desirous of material and present pleasures. Since they are always discontented with the position that they occupy and always free to leave it, they think only about the means of changing their fortune or improving it. For minds disposed in this way, every new expedient that leads to riches by a shorter road, every machine that shortens work, every instrument that diminishes the costs of production, every discovery that facilitates the pleasures and augments them, seems the most magnificent work of the human intellect. It is principally from this direction that democratic peoples become attached to the sciences, understand them, and honor them. In aristocratic times, one demands from the sciences the pleasures of the mind especially; in democracies, those of the body.

You can assume that the more a nation is democratic, enlightened, and free, the more the number of self-interested appreciators of scientific genius will increase, and the more discoveries immediately applicable to industry will bring profit, glory, and even power to their authors, because in democracies the class that works* takes part in public affairs, and those who aid it can expect honors from it as well as money.

One may easily imagine that, in a society organized in this manner, the human mind will be led imperceptibly to neglect theory and that it must, on the contrary, feel pushed toward application with an unparalleled energy, or at least toward that portion of theory that is necessary to those who engage in its application.

It is in vain that an instinctive inclination raises the mind toward the highest spheres of the intellect; interest leads it back toward the middling spheres. It is there that it deploys its force and its restless activity and gives birth to marvels. These same Americans, who have not discovered a single one of the general laws of mechanics, have introduced into navigation a new machine that is changing the face of the world.

Certainly, I am far from claiming that the democratic peoples of our day are destined to watch the transcendent lights of the human mind be extinguished nor even that they will not give rise to new ones in their midst. At the current age of the world, and among so many educated nations that are continually agitated by the ardor of industry, one cannot fail to be struck by the links that unite the different parts of science; and the taste for practice itself, if it is enlightened, should lead men to not neglect theory. In the midst of so many attempts at application, of so many experiments occurring every day, it is all but impossible that, of- [51] ten, very general laws will not happen to emerge in such a way that great discoveries would be frequent, even though great inventors are rare.

Besides, I believe in high scientific vocations. If democracy does not lead men to cultivate the sciences for their own sake, on the other hand it immensely increases the number of those who cultivate them. It is not plausible that, among such a great multitude, there will not be born from time to time some speculative genius inflamed by the love of truth alone. One may be assured that he will make every effort to penetrate the profoundest mysteries of nature, no matter what the spirit of his country and his time. There is no need to aid the upsurge of his development; it suffices to not stop it. All I want to say is this: the permanent inequality of conditions leads men to confine themselves to the proud and sterile search for abstract truths, whereas the democratic social state and institutions dispose them to demand from the sciences only their immediate and useful applications.

This tendency is natural and inevitable. Becoming aware of it is curious, and it may be necessary to spell it out.

---

* *la classe qui travaille:* not to be confused with what we mean by "the working class." Tocqueville is contrasting the "working" merchant and manufacturing classes to the "leisured" ruling class in the aristocracy that he has just described.

If those who are called to govern the nations of our times perceived clearly and from a long way off these new instincts that will soon be irresistible, they would understand that with enlightenment and liberty, the men who live in democratic times cannot fail to perfect the industrial portion of the sciences and that henceforth all the effort of the social power should be given over to supporting higher studies and creating great scientific passions.

In our day, one must keep the human mind to theory; it runs by itself to practice, and instead of constantly leading it back to the detailed examination of secondary effects, it is sometimes good to distract it from them in order to raise it up all the way to the contemplation of first causes.

Because Roman civilization perished following the invasion of the barbarians, we are perhaps too inclined to believe that civilization cannot otherwise perish.

If the learning that enlightens us ever came to be extinguished, it would darken gradually and as if by itself. By dint of confining ourselves to application, we would lose sight of principles, and when we had entirely forgotten principles, we would follow badly the methods that derive from them; we would no longer be able to invent new ones, and we would use without intelligence and without art learned procedures that we would no longer understand.

[52]   When Europeans first arrived in China, three hundred years ago, they found there almost all the arts arrived at a certain degree of perfection, and they were astonished that having arrived at this point, the Chinese had not advanced any further. Later, they discovered the vestiges of some higher knowledge that had been lost. The nation was industrial; most of the scientific methods had been conserved in it, but science itself no longer existed there. That explained to them the sort of remarkable immobility in which they had found the mind of this people. The Chinese, while following in the tracks of their fathers, had forgotten the reasons that had guided the latter. They still made use of the formula without looking for its meaning; they kept the instrument and no longer possessed the art of modifying and reproducing it. The Chinese were therefore unable to change anything. They had to give up on improvement. They were forced to imitate their ancestors always and in everything in order to avoid throwing themselves into impenetrable darkness, were they to stray for an instant from the path that the latter had marked out. The wellspring of human knowledge had nearly run dry, and although the river continued to flow, it could no longer either increase its flow or change its course.

Nevertheless, China survived peacefully for centuries; its conquerors had taken up its mores; order reigned in it. A sort of material well-being was visible everywhere in it. Revolutions were very rare there, and war virtually unknown.

We must not therefore reassure ourselves with the thought that the barbarians are still far away from us; for if there are peoples who allow the light to be torn out of their hands, there are others who snuff it out under their feet.

. . .

CHAPTER 14   [66]

THE INDUSTRY OF LITERATURE

Democracy not only makes the taste for letters penetrate into the industrial classes, it introduces the industrial spirit into the bosom of literature.

In aristocracies, readers are demanding and few in number; in democracies, they are less difficult to please, and their numbers are prodigious. It results from this that among aristocratic peoples, one must not hope to succeed without immense efforts and that these efforts, which may produce much glory, can never furnish much wealth, whereas among democratic nations a writer can hope to obtain with little effort a modest renown and a great fortune. For that, it is not necessary that he be admired, it suffices that he be liked.

The constantly increasing crowd of readers and the perpetual need that they have something new guarantees sales for a book that they hardly esteem at all.

In democratic times, the public often treats authors the way kings usually treat their courtiers; it enriches and despises them. What else is appropriate for the venal souls that arise in courts or who are worthy of living in them?

Democratic literature always abounds with those writers who see in letters only an industry, and for the few great writers that one sees there, one counts sellers of ideas by the thousands.

CHAPTER 15   [67]

WHY THE STUDY OF GREEK AND LATIN LITERATURE IS ESPECIALLY USEFUL IN DEMOCRATIC SOCIETIES

What one called the people in the most democratic republics of antiquity hardly resembled what we call the people. In Athens, all the citizens took part in public affairs, but there were only twenty thousand citizens among more than three hundred and fifty thousand inhabitants; all the others were slaves and performed most of the functions that in our day belong to the people and even to the middle classes.

Athens, with its universal suffrage, was thus, after all, only an aristocratic republic where all the nobles had an equal right in the government.

The conflict between the patricians and the plebeians of Rome must be understood in the same light and seen only as an internal quarrel between the younger and older members of the same family. All belonged in fact to the aristocracy and had its spirit.

One must, in addition, remark that in all of antiquity books were rare and expensive and that their reproduction and circulation were very difficult. These circumstances, by concentrating the taste for and the customary use of letters in a small number of men, created something like a small literary aristocracy of the elite of a great political aristocracy. There is thus no indication that, among the Greeks and the Romans, letters were ever treated like an industry.

These peoples, who not only formed aristocracies but who were also very civilized and very free nations, thus of necessity gave to their literary productions the particular vices and special virtues that characterize literature in aristocratic times.

[68] It suffices, in fact, to cast a glance at the writings that antiquity has left us in order to see that, if writers then sometimes lacked variety and fecundity in their subjects, and daring, movement, and generalization in their thought, they always demonstrated an admirable art and care in the details; nothing in their works seems done in haste or by chance; everything there is written for connoisseurs, and the search for ideal beauty is revealed there constantly. There is no literature that places in greater relief than that of the ancients the qualities that are naturally lacking in writers in democracies. There is therefore no literature that it is more needful to study in democratic times. This study is, of all studies, the most suitable for combating the literary defects inherent in these times; as for the qualities that are natural to these times, they will come forth on their own without it being necessary to learn to acquire them.

It is here that I need to be well understood.

A study may be useful to the literature of a people and not be appropriate to its social and political needs.

If one insisted on teaching only *belles-lettres** in a society where each person is normally led to make fierce efforts to increase his fortune or to

---

* *belles-lettres:* the great classic literature of the humanities.

maintain it, one would have citizens that are very well bred and very dangerous; for since the social and political state would give them, every day, needs that their education would never teach them to satisfy, they would disturb the state, in the name of the Greeks and the Romans, instead of enriching it by their industry.

It is obvious that, in democratic societies, the interest of the individuals, as well as the security of the state, demand that the education of the majority be scientific, commercial, and industrial rather than literary.

Greek and Latin should not be taught in all the schools, but it is important that those who by their temperament or fortune are destined to cultivate letters or are predisposed to appreciate them find schools where one can make oneself absolutely the master of ancient literature and absorb its spirit completely. Several excellent universities would be better for achieving the goal than a multitude of bad schools where superfluous studies that are done badly prevent the necessary studies from being done well.

In democratic nations, all those who have the ambition to excel in letters should often nourish themselves on the works of antiquity. This is a salutary hygiene.

It is not that I consider the literary productions of the ancients as beyond reproach. I think only that they have special qualities that can serve wonderfully to counterbalance our particular defects. They right us on the side where we list.

• • •

CHAPTER 20   [89]

**SOME PARTICULAR TENDENCIES
OF HISTORIANS IN DEMOCRATIC TIMES**

Historians who write in aristocratic times usually make all events depend on the particular will and temper of certain men, and they readily link the greatest revolutions to the slightest accidents. They sagaciously highlight the smallest causes, and often do not perceive the greatest ones.

Historians who live in democratic times display completely opposite tendencies.

The majority of them attribute almost no influence to the individual over the destiny of the species or to the citizens over the destiny of the people. But in return they give great general causes to all the small particular facts. These opposite tendencies can be explained.

When historians in aristocratic times cast their eyes over the world's theater, they see to begin with a very small number of principal actors who lead the whole play. These great personages, who occupy the front of the stage, arrest their attention and fix it: while they apply themselves to uncovering the secret motives that make the latter act and speak, they forget the rest.

The magnitude of the things they see a few men do gives them an exaggerated idea of the influence that a single man can exercise and naturally disposes them to believe that it is always necessary to go back to the particular action of an individual in order to explain the movements of the mass.

When, on the contrary, all the citizens are independent of one another, and each one of them is weak, none are seen to exercise a very great, nor above all a very lasting, power over the mass. At first sight, individuals seem absolutely powerless over it, and it is as if the society moves all alone by means of the free and spontaneous cooperation of all the men who compose it.

[90]   This naturally leads the human mind to look for the general cause that could have affected so many minds in this way and turned them simultaneously in the same direction.

I am quite convinced that, in democratic nations themselves, the character, the vices, or the virtues of certain individuals slow down or speed up the natural course of the destiny of the people. But these kinds of accidental and secondary causes are infinitely more varied, more hidden, more complicated, less powerful, and in consequence more difficult to disentangle and follow in times of equality than in aristocratic times, when it is only a matter of analyzing, in the midst of the general facts, the particular influence of a single man or a few men.

The historian is soon fatigued by this kind of effort. His mind gets lost in the midst of this labyrinth, and, being unable to clearly perceive and shed sufficient light on individual influences, he denies them. He chooses instead to talk to us about the nature of the races, the physical constitution of the country, or the spirit of the civilization. This shortens his work and, at less expense, better satisfies the reader.

M. de La Fayette said somewhere in his *Memoirs* that the overblown system of general causes furnishes wonderful consolations for mediocre public men. I will add that it gives admirable ones to mediocre historians. It always furnishes them with a few great reasons that promptly get them out of trouble at the most difficult place in their book and serve the weakness or laziness of their mind, while doing honor to its depth.

For myself, I think that there is no time in which it is not necessary to attribute a portion of the events of this world to very general facts and another portion to very particular influences. These two causes exist always; only their relation is different. The general facts explain more things in democratic times than in aristocratic times, and particular influences less. In aristocratic times, the opposite is the case: particular influences are stronger, and general causes weaker, unless one considers as a general cause the very fact of the inequality of conditions, which permits a few individuals to oppose the natural tendencies of all the others.

The historians who seek to depict what happens in democratic societies are thus right in giving a large role to general causes and in trying principally to uncover them. But they are wrong to deny completely the particular influence of individuals because it is difficult to find and follow it.

Not only are historians who live in democratic times led to give to every fact a great cause, but they are also led to link the facts with each other and to make a system emerge from them. [91]

In aristocratic times, since the attention of the historians is at every moment diverted to individuals, the concatenation of events escapes them, or rather they do not believe in such a concatenation. The thread of the story seems to them broken at each moment by the passage of a single man.

In democratic times, on the contrary, the historian, noticing the actors much less and the acts much more, can easily establish a relationship and a methodical order between the latter.

Ancient literature, which has left us such beautiful histories, offers not a single great historical system, whereas the most wretched modern writings abound with them. It seems that ancient historians did not make enough use of these general theories that ours are always on the verge of abusing.

Those who write in democratic times have another, more dangerous tendency.

When the trace of the influence of individuals on nations is lost, it often happens that the world is seen to move without the driving force being discovered. Since it becomes very difficult to perceive and to analyze the reasons which, acting separately on the will of each citizen, end up producing the movement of the people, one is tempted to believe that this movement is not voluntary and that societies unwittingly obey a superior force that rules them.

Even if the general fact that directs the particular will of the individuals must be discovered on the earth, this does not save human liberty. A cause vast enough to be applicable to millions of men at the same time, and strong enough to incline all of them together in the same direction, easily seems irresistible: after having seen that one gives in to it, one is very close to believing that one cannot resist it.

Historians who live in democratic times thus not only deny to a few citizens the power to influence the destiny of the people, they also deprive the peoples themselves of the power to alter their own destiny, and they subject them either to an inflexible providence or to a sort of blind fate. According to them, each nation is irresistibly attached, by its situation, its origin, its past, and its nature, to a particular destiny that all its efforts cannot change. They make the generations dependent on one another, and going back in this way, from one age to another and from one inevitable event to another, all the way back to the origin of the world, [92] they create a tight and immense chain that envelops the whole of mankind and binds it together.

It is not enough for them to show how events happened; it also pleases them to show that they could not have happened otherwise. They consider a nation as it has arrived at a certain point in its history, and they assert that it was constrained to follow the path that led it to that point. That is easier than teaching how it might have acted in order to take a better path.

It seems, in reading the historians of aristocratic ages and particularly those of antiquity, that in order to become master of one's fate and to govern one's fellow men, man has only to be able to master himself. One would think, perusing the histories written in our day, that man has no power, either over himself or over what is around him. The ancient historians taught men to command; those of our day teach them scarcely anything except to obey. In their writings, the author often appears great, but humanity is always small.

If this doctrine of fatalism, which has so many attractions for those who write history in democratic times, by passing from the writers to their readers, were thus to penetrate the whole mass of citizens and seize hold of the public mind, one can predict that it would soon paralyze the movement of new societies and reduce the Christians to Turks.

I will say furthermore that such a doctrine is particularly dangerous in our time. Our contemporaries are only too inclined to have doubts about free will because each one of them feels himself limited on all sides by his weakness, but they also readily accord strength and independence to men united in a social body. We must be careful not to obscure this idea, for it is necessary to uplift men's souls and not to complete the process of demoralizing them.

· · ·

VOLUME TWO, PART TWO   [99]

INFLUENCE OF DEMOCRACY ON THE
SENTIMENTS OF THE AMERICANS

CHAPTER 1   [101]

WHY DEMOCRATIC PEOPLES SHOW A MORE ARDENT AND
MORE LASTING LOVE FOR EQUALITY THAN FOR LIBERTY

The first and the strongest of the passions that equality of conditions causes to be born, it is not necessary for me to say, is the love of this very equality. It will thus not be surprising if I talk about it before all the others.

Everyone has noticed that in our time, and especially in France, this passion for equality occupies every day a larger place in the human heart. It has been said a hundred times that our contemporaries have a much more ardent and much more tenacious love for equality than for liberty, but I do not think that we have gone far enough back to the causes of this fact. I am going to try to do it.

One can imagine an extreme point where liberty and equality touch one another and merge together.

I assume that all the citizens participate in the government and that everyone has an equal right to participate in it.

Since no one then differs from his fellow men, no one will be able to exercise a tyrannical power; men will be perfectly free because they will all be entirely equal; and they will all be perfectly equal because they will be entirely free. It is toward this ideal that democratic peoples tend.

This is the most complete form that equality can take on earth, but there are a thousand others, which, without being as perfect, are scarcely less dear to these peoples.

Equality may be established in the civil society and not reign in the political world. One may have the right to indulge in the same pleasures, to enter the same professions, and to get together in the same places; in a word, to live in the same manner and pursue wealth by the same means, without everyone taking the same part in government.

A sort of equality may even be established in the political world, al- [102]
though there is no political liberty there. One is the equal of all one's fellow men, save one, who is, without exception, the master of all and who picks the agents of his power from among all men equally.

It would be easy to make several other hypotheses according to which a very great equality might easily be combined with more or less free institutions or even with institutions that are not at all free.

Although men cannot become absolutely equal without being completely free, and consequently equality, in its most extreme degree, merges with liberty, we are nevertheless justified in distinguishing the one from the other.

The taste that men have for liberty and that which they feel for equality are, in fact, two distinct things, and I am not afraid to add that, among democratic peoples, they are two unequal things.

If one wishes to pay attention, one will find in each age a particular and dominant fact to which the others are attached; this fact almost always gives birth to a mother thought,* or to a principal passion that then ends up attracting to itself and sweeping along in its course all sentiments and all ideas. It is like a great river toward which each of the surrounding streams seems to flow.

Liberty manifests itself to men in different times and under different forms; it is not attached exclusively to one social state, and it is found in other places besides democracies. It cannot thus form the distinctive characteristic of democratic times.

The particular and dominant fact that makes these times stand out is the equality of conditions; the principal passion that agitates men in these times is the love of that equality.

Do not ask what singular charm the men of democratic ages find in living as equals nor the particular reasons they may have for being so obstinately attached to equality rather than to the other goods that society offers them: equality forms the distinctive characteristic of the epoch in which they live; that alone suffices to explain why they prefer it to all the rest.

But, independently of this reason, there are several others that, in all times, normally lead men to prefer equality to liberty.

If a people were ever able itself to destroy or even diminish within itself the equality that prevails there, it would succeed in doing so only by means of long and difficult effort. It would have to modify its social state, abolish its laws, make over its ideas, change its habits, and alter its [103] mores. But, in order to lose political liberty, it suffices to not hold onto it, and it slips away.

Men are therefore attached to equality not only because it is dear to them; they are also attached to it because they believe it is bound to last forever.

---

* *une pensée mère.* See the note in Vol. 1, Introduction [13].

There are no men so limited and so thoughtless that they do not see that political liberty may, in its excesses, endanger the tranquility, the patrimony, and the life of private individuals. On the contrary, only attentive and farsighted men perceive the perils with which equality threatens us, and ordinarily they avoid pointing them out. They know that the calamities they fear are a long way off, and they flatter themselves that they will touch only the generations to come, about which the present generation scarcely troubles itself. The evils to which liberty sometimes leads are immediate; they are visible to all, and all, more or less, feel them. The evils that extreme equality can produce only manifest themselves little by little; they insinuate themselves into the social body gradually; they are only seen from time to time, and, at the moment when they become most violent, habit has already made it so that they are no longer felt.

The goods that liberty procures are only visible in the long term, and it is always easy to misconstrue the cause that produces them.

The advantages of equality make themselves felt from the beginning, and every day we see them flow from their source.

Political liberty gives, from time to time, to a certain number of citizens, sublime pleasures.

Equality furnishes every day a multitude of small pleasures to every man. The charms of equality are felt at every moment, and they are within the reach of everyone; the most noble hearts are not insensible to them, and the most ordinary souls delight in them. The passion that equality causes to be born is therefore bound to be at once powerful and general.

Men cannot enjoy political liberty without purchasing it by means of some sacrifices, and they never take full possession of it except by much effort. But the pleasures that equality procures offer themselves of their own accord. Each of the small incidents of private life seems to give rise to them, and in order to savor them, it is necessary only to live.

Democratic peoples love equality in all times, but it is in certain epochs that they push the passion that they feel for it to the point of delirium. This occurs at the moment that the old social hierarchy, under threat for a long time, is completely destroyed after a final internal struggle, and the barriers that separate the citizens are finally overturned. Men then throw themselves upon equality as upon a conquest, and they become attached to it as to a precious good that one wants to take from them. The passion for equality penetrates into every part of the human heart, it spreads there, and it fills it completely. Do not tell men that by so [104] blindly giving way to an exclusive passion, they endanger their most precious interests; they are deaf. Do not point out to them the liberty that is slipping from their hands while they are looking elsewhere; they are blind, or rather they perceive in the entire universe only a single good worthy of desire.

The foregoing applies to all democratic nations. What follows only relates to us.*

In the majority of modern nations, and in particular among the peoples of the European continent, the taste for and the idea of liberty only began to appear and grow at the moment when conditions began to become more equal and as a consequence of this very equality. It was the absolute monarchs who did the most work to level ranks among their subjects. Among these peoples, equality preceded liberty; equality was thus an old reality when liberty was still a new thing; the one had already created opinions, customs, and laws that were suited to itself, when the other appeared alone and, for the first time, in the light of day. Thus, the second still only existed in ideas and tastes, while the first had already penetrated into habits, taken possession of mores, and given a particular turn to the slightest actions of life. Why be surprised if the men of our day prefer the one to the other?

I think that democratic peoples have a natural taste for liberty; left to themselves, they seek it, they love it, and they feel pain if it is taken away from them. But they have an ardent, insatiable, eternal, invincible passion for equality; they want equality in liberty, and, if they cannot obtain it, they still want it in slavery. They will put up with poverty, servitude, barbarism, but they will not put up with aristocracy.

This is true in all times, and above all in ours. All the men and all the powers that try to struggle against this irresistible power will be overthrown and destroyed by it. In our day, liberty cannot be established without its support, and despotism itself cannot prevail without it.

[105]   CHAPTER 2

INDIVIDUALISM IN DEMOCRATIC COUNTRIES

I have shown how, in times of equality, each man looks within himself for his beliefs; I wish to show how, in these same times, he turns all his sentiments toward himself alone.

Individualism is a recent expression that a new idea has brought into being. Our fathers only knew about egoism.

Egoism is a passionate and exaggerated love of oneself, which leads man to relate everything only to himself alone and to prefer himself over all things.

---

* i.e., to the French people.

Individualism is a reflective and peaceful sentiment that disposes each citizen to isolate himself from the mass of his fellow men and to draw himself off to the side with his family and his friends in such a way that, after having thus created for himself a small society for his own use, he willingly abandons the larger society to itself.

Egoism is born from a blind instinct; individualism proceeds from an erroneous judgment rather than a depraved sentiment. It has its source in the defects of the mind as much as in the vices of the heart.

Egoism dries up the germ of all the virtues; individualism at first only dries up the source of the public virtues, but over the long term it attacks and destroys all the others and eventually becomes absorbed in egoism.

Egoism is a vice as old as the world. It scarcely belongs more to one form of society than to another.

Individualism is in origin democratic, and it risks growing as conditions become more equal.

Among aristocratic peoples, families remain in the same state for centuries and often in the same place. That makes all generations, so to speak, contemporaries. A man almost always knows his ancestors and honors them; he believes he already sees his great-grandchildren, and he loves them. He willingly sets himself duties toward both of them, and he frequently comes to sacrifice his personal pleasures to these beings who no longer exist or do not yet exist.

Aristocratic institutions have, in addition, the effect of tightly connecting each man to several of his fellow citizens.

Since the classes within an aristocratic people are very distinct and [106] immobile, each of them becomes for its members a sort of small fatherland, more visible and more precious than the larger one.

Since in aristocratic societies all citizens are placed in a fixed post, some above the others, it again results that each of them always sees above him a man whose protection he needs, and below he sees another whose aid he may invoke.

The men who live in aristocratic times are therefore almost always connected in a close way to something that is placed outside of themselves, and they are often disposed to forget themselves. It is true that, in these same times, the general notion of *one's fellow man* is obscure and that one scarcely thinks of sacrificing oneself for the cause of humanity, but one often sacrifices oneself for certain men.

In democratic times, on the contrary, when the duties of each individual toward the species are much clearer, devotion to one man becomes rarer: the tie of human affections is stretched and loosened.

Among democratic peoples, new families are constantly emerging from nowhere, other ones fall back into obscurity all the time, and all those that remain change their aspect; the thread of the past is broken at every moment, and the vestige of prior generations is effaced. You easily forget those who have preceded you, and you have no idea of those who will follow you. One takes an interest only in those who are closest to you.

Since each class comes to be similar to the others and is mingled with them, its members become indifferent and like strangers to each other. Aristocracy had made of all its citizens a long chain that went up from the peasant to the king; democracy breaks the chain and separates each link from the others.

As conditions become more equal, there are a larger number of individuals who, while no longer being rich enough or powerful enough to exercise a large influence on the fate of their fellow men, have nonetheless acquired or conserved enough enlightenment and property to be able to be self-sufficient. These men owe nothing to anyone; they expect almost nothing from anyone; they are accustomed to always consider themselves in isolation, and they readily imagine that their whole destiny is in their hands.

In this way, democracy not only makes each man forget his forefathers, but it conceals his descendents from him and separates him from his contemporaries; it leads him back constantly toward himself alone and threatens finally to confine him entirely within the solitude of his own heart.

・ ・ ・

Chapter 4

How the Americans Combat Individualism by Free Institutions

Despotism, which by its nature is fearful, sees in the isolation of men the surest guarantee of its own duration, and it ordinarily devotes all of its attention to isolating them. There is no vice of the human heart that suits it as much as egoism: a despot easily pardons his subjects for not loving him, provided that they do not love one another. He does not demand that they help him to govern the State; it is enough that they do not aspire to govern it themselves. He calls turbulent and restless spirits those who claim to unite their efforts in order to create mutual prosperity, and, changing the natural sense of the words, he calls good citizens those who confine themselves narrowly within themselves.

Thus, the vices that despotism brings into being are precisely those that equality promotes. These two things complement one another and help one another in a way that is lethal.

Equality places men beside each other, without a common link to hold them. Despotism raises barriers between them and separates them. The former disposes them to not think about their fellow men, and the latter makes indifference into a kind of public virtue.

Despotism, which is dangerous at all times, is thus especially to be feared in democratic times.

It is easy to see that in these same times men have a particular need for liberty.

When citizens are forced to assume responsibility for public affairs, they are necessarily removed from the milieu of their individual interests and drawn away, from time to time, from looking at themselves.

From the moment that one treats common affairs in common, every man sees that he is not as independent of his fellow men as he imagined himself to be at first and that, in order to obtain their help, he must often lend them his active support.

When the public governs, there is no one who does not sense the value [110] of public goodwill and who does not seek to capture it by attracting to himself the esteem and the affection of those in whose midst he must live.

Several of the passions that turn hearts cold and divide them are then obliged to withdraw to the bottom of the soul and conceal themselves there. Pride conceals itself, contempt dares not show itself. Egoism is afraid of itself.

Under a free government, since most public offices are elective, the men for whom the largeness of their soul or the restlessness of their desires leaves them too little space in private life, are aware every day that they cannot do without the population that surrounds them.

It then occurs that one thinks of one's fellow men out of ambition and that often one finds, in a sense, one's interest in forgetting oneself. I know that one can confront me here with all the intrigues that an election occasions, the shameful methods that candidates often make use of, and the calumnies that their enemies spread. These occasion hatreds, and they recur all the more often as elections become more frequent.

These evils are great, without doubt, but they are passing, while the goods that come into being with them remain.

The desire to be elected may momentarily lead certain men to make war on each other, but this same desire leads all men in the long term to lend one another mutual support; and if it happens that an election accidentally divides two friends, the electoral system brings together in a permanent manner a multitude of citizens who would have remained forever strangers to one another. Liberty creates some individual hatreds, but despotism creates general indifference.

The Americans have combated by means of liberty the individualism that equality brought into being, and they have vanquished it.

The lawmakers of America did not believe that in order to cure a malady so natural to the social body in democratic times, and so lethal, it was sufficient to accord the nation as a whole a representation of itself; they thought that, in addition, it was necessary to give a political life to each portion of the territory in order to infinitely multiply the chances for the citizens to act together and to make them feel every day that they depend on one another.

In so doing they conducted themselves wisely.

The general affairs of a country occupy only the leading citizens. Those men are only periodically brought together in the same places, and since it often happens that afterward they lose sight of one another, [111] lasting ties are not established between them. But when it is a matter of having the particular affairs of a county* settled by the men who live in it, the same individuals are always in contact, and they are in a way forced to get to know one another and to accommodate one another.

It is difficult to draw a man out of himself in order to interest him in the fate of the whole State because he understands poorly the influence that the fate of the State may exercise on his own lot. But if it is necessary to make a road pass the end of his property, he will see with a glance that there is a relation between this small public affair and his most important private affairs, and he will see, without being shown, the tight link that unites at this point the particular interest and the general interest.

It is therefore by charging the citizens with the administration of small public matters, much more than by handing over to them the government of great ones, that one interests them in the public good and makes them see the continual need that they have of one another in order to produce it.

One may, by an act of brilliance, gain at one stroke the favor of a people; but in order to win the love and respect of the population that surrounds you, a long succession of small services rendered, obscure good offices, a constant habit of kindness, and a well-established reputation for disinterestedness are necessary.

Local liberties, which cause a great number of citizens to value the affection of their neighbors and their close relations, thus continually lead men back toward each other, despite the instincts that draw them apart, and force them to help one another.

---

* The French word is *canton*. See the note at Vol. 1, Part 2, Chap. 6 [253].

In the United States, the wealthiest citizens take great care not to isolate themselves from the people; on the contrary, they approach them constantly, they listen to them willingly and talk to them every day. They know that rich men in democracies always need the poor and that, in democratic times, one attaches the poor to oneself by one's manners more than by largesse.* The very magnitude of the largesse, which illuminates the difference of conditions, causes a secret irritation in those who derive advantage from it. But simplicity of manners has almost irresistible charms: their familiarity is captivating and their very lack of refinement does not always displease.

This truth does not penetrate the mind of the rich at first. They ordinarily put up a resistance to it as long as the democratic revolution lasts, and they even refuse to accept it immediately after this revolution is accomplished. They willingly consent to do good to the people, but they want to continue carefully to keep it at a distance. They believe that that is sufficient; they are mistaken. This way, they would bankrupt themselves without warming the heart of the population that surrounds them. [112] It is not the sacrifice of their money that is required of them; it is the sacrifice of their pride.

One has the impression that in the United States there is no imagination that does not exhaust itself in inventing means of increasing the wealth and satisfying the needs of the public. The most enlightened inhabitants of each county constantly make use of their learning in order to discover new secrets suited for increasing the common prosperity, and when they have found some, they hasten to hand them over to the crowd.

When we examine closely the vices and weaknesses that are often exhibited in America by those who govern, we are surprised by the growing prosperity of its people, but we are wrong to be surprised. It is not the elected magistrate who makes American democracy prosper; rather, it prospers because the magistrate is elective.

It would be unfair to think that the patriotism of the Americans and the zeal each of them shows for the well-being of his fellow citizens is not real. Although private interest governs most human actions, in the United States as well as elsewhere, it does not decide all of them.

I must say that I have often seen Americans make great and true

---

* The words translated as "by one's manners more than by largesse" are *par les manières plus que par les bienfaits. Manières* ("manners") must be understood broadly: it refers to how one comports or conducts oneself vis-à-vis others. *Bienfaits* ("largesse") are acts of kindness or generosity; some synonyms are liberality, favors, and charity.

sacrifices for the republic,[*] and I have noticed a hundred times that when necessary they almost never fail to give reliable support to one another.

The free institutions that the inhabitants of the United States possess, and the political rights of which they make so much use, remind each citizen, and in a thousand ways, that he lives in society. At every moment they lead his mind back toward this idea, that it is the duty as well as the interest of men to make themselves useful to their fellow men; and, as he sees no particular reason to hate them, since he is never either their slave or their master, his heart easily inclines in the direction of altruism.[†] At first one assumes responsibility for the general interest by necessity, and then by choice; what was a calculation becomes an instinct; and, by dint of working for the good of one's fellow citizens, one finally acquires the habit and the taste for helping them.

Many men in France consider equality of conditions as a pre-eminent evil, and political liberty as a second. When they are obliged to suffer the one, they try hard at least to escape the other. And myself, I say that in order to combat the evils that equality may produce, there is only one effective remedy: that is political liberty.

[113]   CHAPTER 5

THE USE THAT THE AMERICANS MAKE OF THE ASSOCIATION IN CIVIL LIFE

I do not wish to discuss those political associations by means of which men defend themselves against the despotic action of a majority or against the encroachments of royal power. I have already treated this subject elsewhere. It is clear that if each citizen, in the degree that he becomes individually weaker, and consequently less capable of preserving his liberty individually, were not to learn the art of uniting with his fellow men in order to defend it, tyranny would necessarily increase along with equality. I am concerned here only with the associations that are formed in civil life and whose purpose is not political.

---

*   The phrase is *la chose publique,* which is the literal equivalent in French of the Latin *res publica,* "the public thing," from which the words *république* and republic are directly derived. Other possible translations are "polity" or "commonwealth."

†   *bienveillance. Bienveillance,* also translatable as "benevolence," means literally "goodwill" or "wishing (others) well," and as such its synonym *altruisme* ("altruism") is especially apt, since its opposite in Tocqueville's argument as well as linguistically is *egoïsme. Bienveillance* also has a less egalitarian usage: *bienveillance,* as benevolence, favor, or grace, was solicited by inferiors and freely granted by superiors.

The political associations that exist in the United States make up one detail in the midst of an immense tableau that the whole body of associations presents there.

Americans of all ages, all conditions, and all minds constantly unite together. Not only do they have commercial and industrial associations in which all take part, but they also have a thousand other types: religious, moral, solemn, frivolous, very general and very particular, immense and very small. The Americans form associations in order to hold holiday celebrations, found seminaries, build hostels, erect churches, disseminate books, and send missionaries to the ends of the earth; in this manner they create hospitals, prisons, and schools. Finally, if it is a question of bringing a truth to light or developing a sentiment with the aid of a great example, they form associations. Everywhere, where, at the head of a new enterprise, you see in France the government and in England some great lord, count on seeing in the United States an association.

I have come across types of associations in America that I confess I did not even conceive of, and I have often admired the infinite art with which the inhabitants of the United States succeed in establishing a [114] common goal for a great number of men and in making them march toward it voluntarily.

I have since traveled through England, where the Americans picked up some of their laws and many of their customs, and it appeared to me that the English were very far from making as constant and as skillful a use of the association.

It often happens that some Englishmen accomplish very great things as isolated individuals, whereas there is hardly any enterprise so small that the Americans do not join together for it. It is obvious that the first consider the association as a powerful means of action; but the second seem to see in it the sole means that they have for acting.

Thus the most democratic country on the earth is found to be out of all of them the one where men have most perfected, in our day, the art of pursuing in common the object of their common desires and have applied this new science to the greatest number of objects. Is this the result of some accident, or might it be that there exists in fact a necessary relationship between associations and equality?

Aristocratic societies always contain within themselves, in the midst of a multitude of individuals who can do nothing by themselves, a small number of very powerful and very rich citizens; each of these latter individuals can accomplish great enterprises by themselves alone.

In aristocratic societies, men do not need to join together in order to act because they are held together strongly.

Each citizen, rich and powerful, is like the head of a permanent and obligatory association composed of all those whom he holds in his dependence and whom he makes contribute to the execution of his intentions.

Among democratic peoples, on the contrary, all the citizens are independent and weak; they can do almost nothing by themselves, and none among them can oblige his fellows to lend him their support. Therefore they all lapse into impotence if they do not learn to help one another voluntarily.

If the men who live in democratic countries had neither the right nor the disposition to unite with each other for political aims, their independence would incur great dangers, but they would be able to conserve their riches and their enlightenment for a long time; whereas if they had not acquired the custom of associating with one another in ordinary life, civilization itself would be in danger. A people among whom private individuals lost the power to accomplish great things individually without acquiring the capability of producing them in common would soon go back toward barbarism.

[115]   Unfortunately, the same social state that makes associations so necessary to democratic peoples makes them more difficult for those peoples than for all others.

When several members of an aristocracy wish to unite with one another, they succeed easily in doing so. Since each of them contributes a great force to the society, the number of members can be very small, and when the members are small in number, it is very easy for them to know one another, to understand one another, and to establish fixed rules.

The same facility does not exist in democratic nations, where it is always necessary for the members to be very numerous in order for the association to have some power.

I know there are many of my contemporaries who are not troubled by this. They claim that to the extent that the citizens become weaker and more incapable, the government must be rendered more skillful and active so that the society can accomplish what the individuals can no longer do. They believe they have answered all objections by saying that. But I think that they are mistaken.

A government might take the place of some of the largest American associations, and, within the Union, several particular States have already tried to do it. But what political power could ever suffice for the innumerable multitude of small undertakings that American citizens accomplish every day by means of the association?

It is easy to foresee that the time is approaching when man will be less and less able to produce by himself alone the things that are the most common and most necessary for his life. The role of the social power will therefore continually grow, and its very efforts will make it more vast each day. The more it puts itself in the place of associations, the more the individuals, losing the idea of associating with one another, will need it to come to their aid: these are causes and effects that beget one another without letup. Will the public administration end up managing all the industries for which an individual citizen cannot suffice? And if a time finally arrives when, as a consequence of the extreme division of landed property, the earth is infinitely divided up so that it can no longer be cultivated except by associations of laborers, will it be necessary for the head of the government to quit the helm of the State in order to come take up the plow?

The morality and intelligence of a democratic people would not be less at risk than its commerce and industry, were the government to take the place of the associations everywhere in it.

Sentiments and ideas renew themselves, the heart grows, and the human mind develops only by the reciprocal action of men upon one another. [116]

I have shown that this action is almost nonexistent in democratic countries. It is therefore necessary to create it there artificially. Associations alone are capable of doing this.

When the members of an aristocracy adopt a new idea or conceive a new sentiment, they place it, in a fashion, alongside them on the grand stage that they themselves occupy, and exposing it in this way to the view of the crowd, they easily introduce it into the minds or hearts of all those who surround them.

In democratic countries only the social power is naturally in a position to act in this way, but it is easy to see that its action is always insufficient and often dangerous.

A government is no more capable of sufficing by itself for maintaining and renewing the movement of sentiments and ideas among a great people than of conducting all the industrial enterprises in it. As soon as it tries to leave the political sphere in order to rush headlong in this new direction, it will exercise, without even wishing to do so, an intolerable tyranny; for a government only knows how to dictate exact rules; it imposes the sentiments and ideas that it favors, and it is always difficult to distinguish its counsel from its orders.

It will be very much worse if it believes that it is in its real interest that nothing move. Then it will hold itself motionless and allow itself to weigh down upon everything by means of a deliberate lethargy.

It is therefore necessary that it not act alone.

It is associations that, among democratic peoples, must take the place of the powerful individuals that the equality of conditions has caused to disappear.

As soon as some number of the inhabitants of the United States have conceived a sentiment or an idea that they want to realize in the world, they seek out one another, and when they have found one another, they join together. From that moment, they are no longer isolated men, but a power visible from a distance, and whose actions serve as an example, one which speaks and is listened to.

The first time that I heard it said in the United States that one hundred thousand men had promised publicly not to drink hard liquor, the thing appeared to me more amusing than serious, and I did not see at first why such temperate citizens were not content to drink water within their own households.*

I finally understood that these hundred thousand Americans, frightened by the progress that drunkenness was making around them, had [117] wanted to give their patronage to sobriety. They had acted just like a great lord who dresses very simply in order to inspire the contempt for luxury in simple citizens. You can believe that if these hundred thousand men had lived in France, each of them individually would have addressed himself to the government in order to beg it to supervise the taverns in every part of the kingdom.

To my mind, there is nothing that merits our attention more than the intellectual and moral associations of America. The political and industrial associations of the Americans are immediately obvious to us, but we overlook the others; and if we notice them, we understand them poorly because we have almost never seen anything like them. One must recognize, however, that they are as necessary to the American people as the first, and perhaps more so.

In democratic countries, the science of association is the mother science; the progress of all the others depends on its progress.

Among the laws that govern human societies, there is one that seems more precise and more clear than all others. In order that men remain or become civilized, it is necessary that the art of forming associations grow and be improved among them in proportion as the equality of conditions increases.

· · ·

---

* *liqueurs fortes* ("hard liquor"), the words Tocqueville uses here to refer to *all* alcoholic beverages, normally refer only to distilled spirits, not wine or beer.

CHAPTER 7 [122]

RELATIONSHIPS BETWEEN CIVIL AND POLITICAL ASSOCIATIONS

There is only one nation on the earth where use is made each day of the unlimited liberty to form associations with political aims. This same nation is the only one in the world whose citizens have conceived of making constant use of the right of association in civil life and have succeeded in procuring for themselves in this manner all the goods that civilization can offer.

Among all peoples where the political association is prohibited, the civil association is rare.

It is scarcely likely that this is the result of an accident, but one ought rather to conclude from it that there exists a natural and perhaps necessary relationship between these two kinds of associations.

Some men have by chance a common interest in a certain affair. It involves directing a commercial enterprise, or agreeing on an industrial transaction; they meet one another and join together; in this way they gradually become familiar with the association.

The more the number of these small common affairs increases, the more that men acquire, without their even being aware of it, the capability of pursuing great affairs in common.

Civil associations therefore facilitate political associations; but, on the other hand, political association develops and improves civil association very much.

In civil life, each man can, if necessary, imagine that he is able to be self-sufficient. In politics, he can never imagine it. When a people has a public life, the idea of the association and the desire to join together are therefore present every day in the minds of all the citizens: whatever natural reluctance men have to act in common, they will always be ready to do it in the interest of a party.

In this way politics generalizes the taste for and the habit of association; it causes a host of men who would have otherwise lived alone to want to join together, and it teaches them the art of doing so.

Politics not only causes many associations to come into being, it cre- [123] ates very immense associations.

In civil life it is rare for a single interest to naturally draw a great number of men to a common action. It is only with much art that one succeeds in creating such a thing.

In politics, the opportunity offers itself of its own accord at every moment. Now, it is only in great associations that the general value of the association appears. Individually weak citizens do not form in advance a clear idea of the force that they can acquire by uniting; they must be shown it for them to understand it. For this reason a multitude is often easier to bring together in a common purpose than a few men; a thousand citizens do not see the interest that they have in uniting; ten thousand see it. In politics, men unite together for great undertakings, and the advantage they obtain from association in important affairs teaches them, in a practical manner, the interest that they have in helping one another in the smallest ones.

A political association draws a multitude of individuals outside of themselves; however separated they are naturally by age, spirit, or fortune, it brings them nearer and puts them in contact. They meet one another once and learn to find each other again forever.

One cannot enter into most civil associations without exposing a portion of one's patrimony; that is the way things are for all industrial and commercial companies. When men are still but little versed in the art of forming associations and are ignorant of their principal rules, they are afraid, in joining together for the first time in this way, of paying dearly for the experience. Therefore they prefer to deprive themselves of a powerful means of success rather than accept the risks that accompany it. But they hesitate less to take part in political associations, which appear to them without danger because they do not risk their money in them. Now, they cannot belong to these latter associations for long without discovering how one maintains order among a great number of men and by what means one succeeds in making them march, in agreement and methodically, toward the same goal. They learn there to submit their will to that of all the others and to subordinate their individual efforts to the common action, all things that are not less necessary to know how to do in civil associations than in political associations.

Political associations can thus be considered as great free schools, where all the citizens come to learn the general theory of associations.

[124]   Even if the political association did not directly serve the progress of the civil association, destroying the first would still damage the second.

When citizens may form associations only in certain cases, they regard the association as a rare and unusual means, and they barely have the temerity to consider it.

When they are allowed to form associations freely in everything, they end up seeing, in the association, the universal, and almost unique, means that men can use to attain the different ends that they propose to themselves. Each new need immediately awakens the idea in them. The art of the association then becomes, as I said above, the mother science; all study and apply it.

When certain associations are prohibited and others are permitted, it is difficult to distinguish in advance the first from the second. In a state of uncertainty, one refrains from all of them, and a kind of public opinion is established that tends to cause any association whatsoever to be considered as a daring and almost illicit enterprise.[1]

It is therefore chimerical to believe that the spirit of association, curtailed at one point, will nevertheless develop with the same vigor at all the others, and that it will be enough to allow men to carry out in common certain enterprises, in order for them to hasten to attempt to do so. When the citizens have the capability and habit of forming associations for all things, they will form associations as readily for the small as for the great. But, if they are only able to form associations for the small, they will not have the desire and the capability of doing even that. It will be futile for you to leave them the complete liberty to assume responsibility in common for their commerce: they will only make casual use of the rights they are granted; and after you have exhausted yourself in efforts to keep them away from the prohibited associations, you will [125] be surprised that you are unable to persuade them to form the permitted associations.

I am not saying that there cannot be civil associations in a country where the political association is prohibited; for men can never live in society without engaging in some common enterprise. But I maintain that, in such a country, civil associations will always be few in number, weakly conceived, ineptly led, and that they will never embrace vast purposes or will run aground in trying to accomplish them.

---

1. This is true above all when it is the executive power that is responsible for permitting or prohibiting associations according to its arbitrary will.

When the law limits itself to prohibiting certain associations and leaves to the courts the task of punishing those who disobey, the evil is much less great: then each citizen more or less knows in advance what he can count on; he judges himself in a way in advance of his judges, and, avoiding prohibited associations, he engages in permitted associations. It is in this way that all free peoples have always understood that one might limit the right of association. But if the legislator were to charge a man with clarifying in advance which are the dangerous associations and which the useful and leave him free to destroy all associations in their bud or allow them to come into being, since no one will be able any longer to foresee in advance in what case one may form an association and in what other case one must refrain from doing so, the spirit of association would be completely seized by inertia. The first of these two laws attacks only certain associations; the second is aimed at society itself and wounds it. I can conceive of a legitimate government having recourse to the first, but I admit to no government the right to apply the second.

This naturally leads me to think that liberty of association in political matters is not as dangerous for the public tranquility as one supposes and that it might happen that, after having shaken the State for a time, it strengthens it.

In democratic countries, political associations form, so to speak, the only powerful individuals that aspire to govern the State. Therefore governments in our day view these kinds of associations in the same spirit that the kings of the Middle Ages regarded the great vassals of the crown: they feel a kind of instinctive horror of them, and they oppose them every time they encounter them.

They have, on the contrary, a natural goodwill toward civil associations because they have easily seen that these, instead of directing the mind of the citizens toward public affairs, serve to distract them from them and, engaging them more and more in projects that cannot be accomplished without public peace, turn them away from revolutions. But they are not attentive to the fact that political associations multiply and enormously facilitate civil associations and that in avoiding a dangerous evil they deprive themselves of an effective remedy. When you see the Americans form associations freely, every day, with the goal of making a political opinion prevail, putting a statesman into government, or taking power away from another, you have difficulty comprehending that such independent men do not fall at any moment into license.

On the other hand, if you come to consider the infinite number of industrial enterprises that are pursued in common in the United States, and see Americans everywhere working without respite to carry out some important and difficult purpose which the slightest revolution may cause to run aground, you understand easily why such busy men are not tempted to trouble the State or destroy a public peace from which they profit.

Is it enough to perceive these things separately, and isn't it necessary to see the concealed knot that ties them together? It is in the bosom of [126] political associations that Americans of all the States, of all minds,* and of all ages pick up every day the general taste for the association and familiarize themselves with its use. There, they see each other in great numbers, talk with one another, listen to one another, and inspire each other in common to all sorts of enterprises. They then transfer to civil life the notions that they have thus acquired and put them to a thousand uses.

It is therefore by enjoying a dangerous liberty that the Americans learn the art of making the dangers of liberty less great.

---

* *esprits. Esprit* can mean "spirit" or "mind"; as such, it can also refer to someone's "mentality" or "opinion" (as in the expression "like-minded").

If one chooses a certain moment in the life of a nation, it is easy to show that political associations trouble the State and paralyze industry; but let one take the life of a people as a whole, and it will perhaps be easy to demonstrate that liberty of association in political matters is favorable to the well-being and even to the tranquility of the citizens.

I said in the first part of this work: "The unlimited liberty of association cannot be confused with the liberty to write: the first is at the same time less necessary and more dangerous than the second. A nation may place limits on it without ceasing to be master of itself; sometimes it must do it in order to continue to be so." And further on I added: "One may not delude oneself that the unlimited liberty of association in political matters is not, of all liberties, the last that a people is able to bear. If it does not make them fall into anarchy, it brings them almost to the verge of it at every moment."

Thus, I do not believe that a nation is always free to allow to its citizens the absolute right of forming political associations, and I even doubt that there is any country and any time in which it is wise to place no limits on the liberty of association.

Such and such a people, it is said, cannot maintain peace in its midst, inspire respect for the laws, nor secure lasting government if it does not confine the right of association within narrow limits. Such goods are doubtless precious, and I understand that a nation, in order to acquire or to conserve them, may consent to temporarily impose on itself great constraints, but it is still good for it to know precisely what these goods are costing it.

That, in order to save the life of a man, one may cut off one of his arms, I understand; but I refuse to be told that he will be as dexterous as if he were not one-armed.

CHAPTER 8   [127]

HOW THE AMERICANS COMBAT INDIVIDUALISM BY THE DOCTRINE OF INTEREST RIGHTLY UNDERSTOOD*

When the world was led by a small number of powerful and rich individuals, these men liked to fashion for themselves a sublime idea of the duties of man; they took pleasure in professing that it is glorious to forget oneself and that it is proper to do good disinterestedly, like God himself. This was the official doctrine of that time in matters of morality.

---

* Tocqueville's words are *intérêt bien entendu*. This famous phrase is usually translated as "self-interest rightly understood."

I doubt that men were more virtuous in aristocratic times than in others, but it is certain that they spoke constantly of the beauties of virtue then; they only studied in secret the respect in which it is useful. But as the imagination takes a less high flight and everyone concentrates on himself, moralists take fright at this idea of sacrifice, and they no longer dare to place it before the human mind. They are therefore reduced to inquiring whether it is not to the individual advantage of the citizens to work for the happiness of all, and when they have discovered one of those points where the individual interest happens to see eye to eye with the general interest and merge with it, they hasten to bring it to light. Such observations are gradually multiplied. What was only an isolated observation becomes a general doctrine, and in the end men think they perceive that man, in helping his fellow men, helps himself, and that his individual interest is to do right.

I have already shown in several places in this work how the inhabitants of the United States almost always know how to combine their own well-being with that of their fellow citizens. What I want to remark here is the general theory by means of which they succeed in doing so.

In the United States, it is almost never said that virtue is beautiful. It is maintained that it is useful, and that is proven every day. The American moralists do not claim that it is necessary to sacrifice oneself to [128] one's fellow men because it is grand to do it, but they say boldly that such sacrifices are as necessary to the one who imposes them on himself as they are to the one who profits from them.

They saw that, in their country and in their time, man had been led back toward himself by an irresistible force, and losing hope of stopping it, they no longer thought about anything other than directing it.

Therefore they do not deny that each man may follow his interest, but they strive to prove that the interest of each man is to be decent.

I do not want to go into their reasons in detail here, which would take me away from my subject; let it suffice to say that they have convinced their fellow citizens.

A long time ago Montaigne said: "When I do not follow the right path because of its rightness, I follow it because I have found, by experience, that in the end it is usually the happiest and the most useful."

The doctrine of interest rightly understood is therefore not new, but among the Americans of our day, it has been universally accepted. It has become popular there: one finds it at the bottom of all their actions; it comes through in everything they say. One does not hear it less from the poor man than from the rich.

In Europe, the doctrine of interest is much cruder than in America, but it is at the same time less widespread and, above all, less exhibited, and one still feigns every day great devotions* that one no longer feels.

The Americans, on the contrary, like to explain by means of interest rightly understood almost all the acts of their life; they obligingly show how the enlightened love of oneself leads them constantly to help one another and disposes them to willingly sacrifice to the good of the State a portion of their time and their riches. I think that in this regard it is often the case that they do not do justice to themselves; for one sometimes sees in the United States, as elsewhere, the citizens give themselves over to the disinterested and unreflective impulses that are natural to man; but the Americans hardly admit that they give way to impulses of this sort; they prefer to honor their philosophy rather than themselves.

I could stop here and not try to judge what I have just described. The extreme difficulty of the subject would be my excuse. But I will not make use of it, and I prefer that my readers, seeing clearly my purpose, refuse to follow me rather than leave them in suspense.

Interest rightly understood is a not very high doctrine, but it is clear and certain. It does not seek to attain great objects, but it attains without too much effort all those at which it aims. Since it is within the reach of [129] all intellects, everyone grasps it easily and retains it without difficulty. By accommodating itself wonderfully to the weaknesses of men, it easily obtains a great influence, and it is not difficult for it to conserve that influence because it turns personal interest around against itself and makes use of the stimulus that arouses the passions in order to direct them.

The doctrine of interest rightly understood does not produce great devotions,† but every day it suggests small sacrifices; by itself alone, it cannot make a man virtuous, but it forms a multitude of citizens who are orderly, sober, moderate, provident, and in control of themselves; and, if it does not lead directly to virtue by means of the will, it approaches it imperceptibly by means of habits.

If the doctrine of interest rightly understood were to succeed in dominating the moral world entirely, extraordinary virtues would be without doubt rarer. But I also think that crude depravities would then be less common. The doctrine of interest rightly understood perhaps prevents some men from rising far above the ordinary level of humanity, but a great number of others who were falling below that level encounter this doctrine and hold onto it. If you consider some individuals, it pulls them down. If you consider the species, it elevates it.

---

* *dévouements. Dévouements* might also be translated as "altruistic commitments." *Dévouements* are acts of devotion, heroism, or self-sacrifice for a person, community, or cause.

† *dévouements.* See the preceding note.

I am not afraid to say that the doctrine of interest rightly understood seems to me, of all philosophical theories, the best suited to the needs of the men of our time, and that I see in it the most powerful guarantee that is left for them against themselves. It is therefore principally toward it that the mind of the moralists of our day ought to turn. Even if they were to judge it to be imperfect, they would still have to adopt it as necessary.

I do not believe, all things considered, that there is more egoism among us than in America; the only difference is that there it is enlightened and here it is not. Every American knows how to sacrifice a portion of his individual interests in order to save the rest. We want to keep it all, and often it all gets away from us.

I see around me only men who seem to want to teach their contemporaries every day, by their word and their example, that the useful is never indecent. Will I not then finally find some who undertake to make them understand how the decent can be useful?

There is no power on earth that can prevent the increasing equality of conditions from leading the human mind toward the pursuit of the useful and disposing every citizen to close up within himself.

It is thus necessary to expect that individual interest will become more than ever the principal, if not the only, motive for the actions of [130] men; but it remains to find out how each man will understand his individual interest.

If the citizens, in becoming equal, were to remain ignorant and crude, it is hard to foresee to what stupid excess their egoism might lead them, and one cannot say in advance into what shameful wretchedness they would throw themselves out of fear of sacrificing something of their well-being to the prosperity of their fellow men.

I do not believe that the doctrine of interest, as it is preached in America, is self-evident in all of its parts, but it includes a great number of truths that are so evident that it suffices to enlighten men in order for them to see them. Enlighten them, therefore, at any cost; for the age of blind devotions and instinctive virtues is already receding far away from us, and I see the time approaching when liberty, public peace, and social order itself will not be able to do without enlightenment.

[131]   **CHAPTER 9**

HOW THE AMERICANS APPLY THE DOCTRINE OF INTEREST RIGHTLY UNDERSTOOD IN MATTERS OF RELIGION

If the doctrine of interest rightly understood had in view only this world, it would be far from sufficient; for there are a great number of sacrifices that can only find their reward in the other; and no matter what effort of mind is made to prove the utility of virtue, it will always be hard to make a man who does not want to die live well.

It is thus necessary to find out if the doctrine of interest rightly understood can easily be reconciled with religious beliefs.

The philosophers who teach this doctrine say to men that, in order to be happy in life, one must watch over one's passions and carefully constrain their excess, that one can only acquire lasting happiness by denying oneself a thousand fleeting pleasures, and finally that one must triumph over oneself constantly in order to best serve oneself.

The founders of almost all religions talked in more or less the same way. Without showing men a different path, they only made its end recede; instead of placing the reward for the sacrifices they impose in this world, they put it in the other.

However, I refuse to believe that all those who practice virtue out of religious spirit only act with a view to a reward.

I have met zealous Christians who constantly forget themselves in order to work with more ardor for the happiness of all, and I have heard them claim that they act in this way only in order to deserve the goods of the other world; but I cannot prevent myself from thinking that they delude themselves. I respect them too much to believe them.

Christianity tells us, it is true, that one must prefer others to oneself in order to gain Heaven, but Christianity also tells us that one must do good to one's fellow men out of love of God. That is a magnificent expression: man penetrates the divine way of thinking by means of his intellect; he sees that the purpose of God is order; he freely associates himself with this great purpose; and, while sacrificing his individual interests to this admirable order of all things, he expects no other reward than the pleasure of contemplating it. [132]

Therefore I do not believe that the only motive of religious men is interest; but I think that interest is the principal means that religions themselves use in order to lead men, and I do not doubt that it is from this angle that they get hold of the crowd and become popular.

So I do not see clearly why the doctrine of interest rightly understood takes men away from religious beliefs, and it seems to me, on the contrary, that I am clarifying how it brings them closer to those beliefs.

Assume that in order to attain happiness in this world, a man resists instinct at every point and coldly reasons out all the actions of his life, that instead of blindly giving way to the ardor of his first desires, he learned the art of combating them, and that he habituated himself to sacrifice without effort the pleasure of the moment to the permanent interest of his whole life.

If such a man has faith in the religion he professes, it will hardly cost him anything to submit to the constraints that it imposes. Reason itself advises him to do it, and habit has prepared him in advance to tolerate it.

Even if he has conceived doubts about the object of his hopes, he will not easily allow himself to stop there, and he will judge that it is wise to hazard some of the goods of this world in order to conserve his rights to the immense inheritance that he is promised in the other.

"To be mistaken in believing the Christian religion to be true," said Pascal, "there is not a great deal to lose in that; but what misfortune to be mistaken in believing it to be false!"

The Americans do not affect a crude indifference toward the other life; they do not take a childish pride in despising the perils they hope to evade.

They thus practice their religion without shame and without weakness; but one sees ordinarily, even in the midst of their zeal, something so tranquil, so methodical, and so calculated that it seems to be reason much more than the heart that leads them to the foot of the altars.

Not only do the Americans follow their religion out of interest, but they often place in this world the interest that one may have in following it. In the Middle Ages, the priests talked only about the other life: they scarcely troubled themselves to prove that a sincere Christian may be a happy man here below.

[133]   But the American preachers come back constantly to the earth, and they cannot turn their eyes away from it without great difficulty. In order to best touch their listeners, they make them see each day how religious beliefs promote liberty and public order, and it is often hard to know, in listening to them, if the principal object of religion is to procure eternal happiness in the other world or well-being in this one.

[134]   **CHAPTER 10**

THE TASTE FOR MATERIAL WELL-BEING IN AMERICA

In America, the passion for material well-being is not always the only one, but it is general; if all do not experience it in the same manner, all feel it. The concern to satisfy the slightest needs of the body and to provide the small conveniences of life preoccupies every mind there.

Something similar is more and more visible in Europe.

Among the causes that produce these similar effects in the two worlds, several are close to my subject, and I ought to point them out.

When wealth is fixed by heredity in the same families, there are a great number of men who enjoy material well-being, without feeling the exclusive taste for well-being.

What most engages the human heart is not the peaceful possession of a precious object, it is the imperfectly satisfied desire to possess it and the constant fear of losing it.

In aristocratic societies, the rich, having never known any state different from their own, have no fear of changing it; they hardly imagine any other one. Material well-being is therefore not for them the aim of life; it is a manner of living. They consider it, as it were, like life itself, and enjoy it without thinking about it.

The natural and instinctive taste that all men feel for well-being, being thus satisfied without difficulty and without fear, their soul heads elsewhere and becomes attached to some more difficult and grander enterprise, which inspires it and carries it off.

It is thus that in the midst of material pleasures the members of an aristocracy often show a proud contempt for these same pleasures and find remarkable strength when it is finally necessary to do without them. All the revolutions that have disturbed or destroyed aristocracies have shown with what ease men accustomed to superabundance could do [135] without necessities, whereas men who have laboriously attained a level of prosperity can barely live after having lost it.

If I pass from the upper ranks to the lower classes, I see analogous effects produced by different causes.

In nations where the aristocracy dominates the society and keeps it immobile, the people end up becoming used to poverty just as the rich become used to their opulence. The latter are not preoccupied with material well-being because they possess it without effort; the former does not think about it because it despairs of acquiring it and because it is not familiar enough with it to desire it.

In these sorts of societies the imagination of the poor person is driven back toward the other world. The miseries of real life press in on it, but it escapes them and goes to seek its pleasures beyond it.

When, on the contrary, the ranks are mixed together and privileges destroyed, when patrimonies are broken up and enlightenment and liberty spread, the desire to acquire well-being presents itself to the imagination of the poor person, and the fear of losing it to the mind of the rich one. A multitude of mediocre fortunes are established. Those who possess them have enough material pleasures to conceive the taste for these pleasures, and not enough to be content with what they have. They never obtain them without effort and never indulge in them without trembling with fear.

They thus become attached to constantly pursuing or keeping such precious, incomplete, and fleeting pleasures.

I seek a passion that is natural to men who are stimulated and limited by the obscurity of their origins or the mediocrity of their fortune, and I find none more appropriate than the taste for well-being. The passion for material well-being is in essence a middle class passion. It increases and spreads with this class; it becomes preponderant with it. It is from there that it spreads to the upper ranks of the society and descends into the midst of the people.

I met no citizen in America so poor that he did not look with hope and envy on the pleasures of the rich, and whose imagination did not take hold in advance of the goods that fate stubbornly refused to him.

On the other hand, I never saw among the rich of the United States that proud disdain for material well-being that is sometimes shown even the midst of the most opulent and dissolute aristocracies.

Most of these rich men have been poor. They have felt the sting of want. For a long time they have struggled against a hostile fortune, and [136] now that the victory is won, the passions that accompanied the struggle outlive it. These men remain, as it were, drunk in the midst of these small pleasures that they have pursued for forty years.

It is not that in the United States, as elsewhere, there are not a rather large number of rich men who, holding their property by inheritance, possess without effort an opulence that they have not acquired. But even these do not show themselves to be less attached to the pleasures of the material life. The love of well-being has become the national and dominant taste. The great current of human passions leads in this direction, and it carries along everything in its course.

[137]   **CHAPTER 11**

THE PARTICULAR EFFECTS THAT THE LOVE OF MATERIAL PLEASURES PRODUCES IN DEMOCRATIC TIMES

One might believe, after the foregoing, that the love of material pleasures is bound to carry the Americans constantly toward moral disorder, disturb families, and finally endanger the future of the society itself.

But it is not like that: the passion for material pleasures produces in democracies different effects than it does among aristocratic peoples.

It happens sometimes that weariness with public affairs, the excess of riches, the destruction of beliefs, and the decadence of the State turn the heart of an aristocracy gradually toward material pleasures alone. Other times, the power of the prince or the weakness of the people, without stripping the nobles of their wealth, forces them to step aside from power and, blocking their way to great undertakings, abandons them to the restlessness of their desires; they then fall back heavily upon themselves, and they seek to forget their past grandeur in the pleasures of the body.

When the members of an aristocratic body thus turn exclusively to the love of material pleasures, they usually concentrate in this single direction all the energy that the long-standing habit of exercising power has given them.

For men like this, the pursuit of well-being does not suffice; they need sumptuous depravity and brilliant corruption. They make a magnificent cult of material things, and they seem to vie with one another in wishing to excel in the art of degrading themselves.

The stronger, more glorious, and freer the aristocracy, the more it will prove to be depraved, and no matter what the splendor of its virtues, I dare predict that it will always be surpassed by the brilliance of its vices.

The taste for material pleasures does not lead democratic peoples to [138] such excesses. The love of well-being among them proves to be a tenacious, exclusive, universal, but contained passion. It is not a question of building vast palaces, of conquering or fooling nature, of exhausting the universe in order to better satisfy the passions of one man; it is a question of adding some land to one's fields, of planting an orchard, of enlarging a house, of always making life easier and more convenient, of averting trouble and satisfying the slightest needs without effort and almost without cost. These objects are small, but the soul attaches itself to them: it thinks about them every day and from very close up; they end up obscuring the rest of the world from it, and they sometimes come to be placed between it and God.

This, it will be said, only applies to those citizens whose fortune is mediocre; the rich will display tastes analogous to those they displayed in aristocratic times. I dispute this.

In regard to material pleasures, the most opulent citizens of a democracy do not display very different tastes from those of the people, either because, having emerged from the people's midst, they really share those tastes, or because they believe they have to submit to them. In democratic societies, the sensuality of the public has taken on a certain moderate and tranquil appearance to which all souls are constrained to conform. There, it is as hard for vices as for virtues to escape the common rule.

The rich who live in the midst of democratic nations thus aim at the satisfaction of their slightest needs rather than at extraordinary pleasures; they satisfy a multitude of small desires and do not abandon themselves to any great disordered passion. In this way they lapse into softness rather than debauchery.

This particular taste that men in democratic times conceive for material pleasures is not naturally opposed to order; on the contrary, it often has need of order to satisfy itself. Nor is it opposed to regularity in morals, because good morals are useful for public tranquility and promote industry. Often it is even combined with a sort of religious morality; one wants to be as well off as possible in this world, without giving up one's chances in the next.

Among material goods, there are some whose possession is criminal; care is taken to abstain from them. There are others whose use is allowed by religion and morality; to those, one's heart, imagination, and life are given without reserve, and sight is lost, in endeavoring to get hold of them, of those more precious goods that constitute the glory and grandeur of mankind.

[139]   What I reproach equality for is not that it leads men to pursue prohibited pleasures; it is that it absorbs them entirely in the pursuit of permitted pleasures.

In this way, a sort of decent materialism might be established in the world that would not corrupt souls but that would soften them and end up silently relaxing all their moral forces.

[140]   **CHAPTER 12**

WHY CERTAIN AMERICANS DISPLAY SUCH AN INTENSE* SPIRITUALISM

Although the desire to acquire the goods of this world is the dominant passion of Americans, there are moments of respite when their soul seems suddenly to break the material bonds that hold it back and escape impetuously toward heaven.

In all the States of the Union, but principally in the half-populated regions of the West, one sometimes comes across preachers who spread the word of God from place to place.

Entire families, old people, women, and children, cross difficult terrain and push through forest wildernesses in order to come from afar to hear them; and, when they are in meetings with them, for several days and nights, while listening to them, they forget their care for their affairs and even the most pressing needs of the body.

One finds here and there, in the midst of American society, men quite filled with an intense and almost savage spiritualism, which one scarcely encounters in Europe. From time to time bizarre sects arise there that make great efforts to open up extraordinary paths to eternal happiness. Religious madnesses are very common there.

---

*   *Exalté. Exalté* has the sense of "overexcited," "enthusiastic," "frenzied." *Un exalté* is "a fanatic."

This should not surprise us.

It is not man who has given himself the taste for the infinite and the love of what is immortal. These sublime instincts do not spring from a caprice of his will: they have their immovable foundation in his nature; they exist despite his efforts. He can hinder them and deform them but not destroy them.

The soul has needs that must be satisfied, and no matter what care one takes to distract it from itself, it is soon bored, uneasy, and restless in the midst of the pleasures of the senses.

If the minds of the great majority of mankind are ever focused on the exclusive pursuit of material goods, one may expect that there would be a prodigious reaction in the souls of some men. The latter would throw [141] themselves madly into the world of spirits, for fear of remaining encumbered within the excessively narrow fetters that the body wishes to impose on them.

It would therefore not be surprising if, in the midst of a society that thought only about the earth, one came across a small number of individuals who wished to think only about Heaven. I would be surprised if, among a people solely preoccupied with its well-being, mysticism did not soon make progress.

It is said that it was the persecutions of the emperors and the butchery of the circus that peopled the deserts of the Thebaid; I think myself that it was instead the pleasures of Rome and the Epicurean philosophy of Greece.

If the social state, the circumstances, and the laws did not hold the American mind so closely within the pursuit of well-being, it is plausible that, when it came to concern itself with immaterial things, it would show more reticence and more experience, and that it would restrain itself easily. But it feels imprisoned within limits that one seems unwilling to allow it to go beyond. As soon as it passes beyond these limits, it does not know where to settle down, and it often runs, without stopping, beyond the limits of common sense.

CHAPTER 13   [142]

**WHY THE AMERICANS PROVE TO BE SO UNEASY
IN THE MIDST OF THEIR WELL-BEING**

One still sometimes finds, in certain remote areas of the Old World, small populations who have, as it were, been forgotten in the midst of the universal tumult and who have remained fixed when everything was shifting around them. Most of these peoples are very ignorant and very poor; they do not take part in the affairs of government, and often governments oppress them. However, they ordinarily show a serene face, and they often display good humor.

In America I have seen the freest and the most enlightened men, placed in the happiest condition in the world; it seemed to me that a sort of cloud habitually covered their features; they appeared to me grave and almost sad even in the midst of their pleasures.

The principal reason for this is that the former do not think about the ills that they endure, whereas the latter think constantly of the goods that they do not have.

It is a strange thing to see with what feverish passion the Americans pursue well-being and how they prove to be constantly tormented by a vague fear of not having chosen the shortest route that may lead to it.

The inhabitant of the United States is attached to the goods of this world as if he were assured of not dying, and he is in such haste to seize those which pass within his reach that one would think that he was afraid at each moment of ceasing to live before having enjoyed them. He seizes hold of all of them, but without embracing them, and he soon allows them to slip from his hands in order to run after new pleasures.

A man in the United States builds a house with care in order to spend his last days there, and he sells it while the roof is being put on it; he plants a garden, and he lets it out just when he was about to enjoy its [143] fruits; he clears a field, and he leaves to others the job of harvesting its crops. He takes up an occupation, and he quits it. He settles down in a place that he leaves soon afterward in order to carry his changing desires elsewhere. If his private affairs give him some respite, he plunges himself immediately into the whirl of politics. And when, toward the end of a year filled with work, he still has some leisure, he takes his restless curiosity out here and there within the vast borders of the United States. He will in this way cover five hundred leagues* in several days, in order to better distract himself from his happiness.

Death finally occurs, and it stops him before he has become bored with this futile pursuit of a complete happiness that forever recedes from his grasp.

Contemplating this remarkable restlessness that is shown by so many happy men in the very midst of their affluence, one is initially astonished. This spectacle is nevertheless as old as the world; what is new is to see a whole people present it.

The taste for material pleasures must be considered the fundamental source of that secret uneasiness that is revealed in the actions of the Americans and of that changeableness of which they daily give example.

---

*   A league is about four kilometers or two and a half miles.

He who has confined his heart within the exclusive pursuit of the goods of this world is always pressed because he has only a limited time to find them, take possession of them, and enjoy them. The recollection of the brevity of life constantly goads him on. Apart from the goods that he possesses, at each moment he imagines a thousand others that death will prevent him from enjoying, if he does not hurry. This thought fills him with distress, fears, and regrets, and keeps his soul in a sort of continual agitation that leads him to constantly change his aims and his place.

If a social state in which neither law nor custom any longer keeps anyone in his place comes to be joined to the taste for material well-being, that is another great stimulus for this restlessness of mind: men will then be seen to continually change course for fear of missing the shortest path that will lead them to happiness.

Besides, it is easy to conceive that, if the men who passionately seek material pleasures desire keenly, they must be easily discouraged: their final object being to enjoy, the means of getting there must be quick and easy, without which the pain of acquiring the pleasure would surpass the pleasure. In this matter, most men are therefore at the same time ardent and without vigor,* impetuous and without energy. Often, death is less dreaded than continuity of effort toward a single goal.

Equality leads by a still more direct path to several of the effects that I have just described.

When all the prerogatives of birth and wealth are destroyed, when all [144] occupations are open to all, and when one can reach the summit of every one of them by one's own efforts, an immense and easy path seems to open up before the ambition of men, and they readily imagine that they are called to great destinies. But that is a mistaken opinion that experience corrects every day. The very equality that allows each citizen to conceive vast hopes renders all citizens individually weak. It limits their powers on all sides, at the same time that it allows their desires to expand.

Not only are they powerless by themselves, but they discover at each step immense obstacles that they had not at first perceived.

They destroyed the bothersome privileges of some of their fellow men; they encounter the competition of all. The limiting boundary has changed form rather than position. When men are more or less alike and follow the same path, it is very difficult for any of them to advance rapidly and break through the uniform crowd that surrounds them and presses in upon them.

---

* *mou.* See the note at Vol. 2 [244].

This constant opposition that prevails between the instincts that equality causes to be born and the means that it furnishes for satisfying them torments and exhausts the souls of men.

One can conceive of men arrived at a certain degree of liberty that satisfies them completely. They then enjoy their independence without uneasiness and without ardor. But men will never establish an equality that is enough for them.

No matter what efforts a people makes, it will never succeed in making conditions perfectly equal within it; and if it has the misfortune to arrive at an absolute and complete leveling, there would still remain the inequality of intelligence, which, coming directly from God, will always elude the laws.

No matter how democratic the social state and political constitution of a people, one can therefore reckon that each of its citizens will always notice several positions that look down on him, and one can foresee that he will obstinately turn his sights in this direction alone. When inequality is the common law of a society, the greatest inequalities do not strike the eye; when everything is more or less level, the least inequalities offend it. That is why the desire for equality always becomes more insatiable as equality increases.

Among democratic peoples, men easily acquire a certain level of equality; they cannot attain the equality that they wish for. This latter recedes each day before them but without ever leaving their sight, and in receding, it draws them to its pursuit. They believe constantly that they [145] are going to get hold of it, and it constantly eludes their grasp. They see it close enough to know its charms, they do not approach close enough to it to enjoy them, and they die before having fully savored its pleasures.

It is to these causes that one must attribute the remarkable melancholy that the inhabitants of democratic countries often display in the midst of their abundance, and the disgust with life that sometimes seizes them in the midst of a comfortable and tranquil existence.

In France one complains that the number of suicides is increasing; in America suicide is rare, but I am assured that insanity is more common there than anywhere else.

These are different symptoms of the same malady.

The Americans do not kill themselves, no matter how agitated they are, because religion forbids them to do it and because among them materialism is virtually nonexistent, even though the passion for well-being is universal.

Their will resists, but often their reason gives way.

In democratic times pleasures are more intense than in aristocratic times, and above all the number of those who partake of them is infinitely greater; but on the other hand it must be recognized that in those times, hopes and desires are more often disappointed, souls are more agitated and uneasy, and worries are keener.

• • •

CHAPTER 15   [149]

HOW RELIGIOUS BELIEFS SOMETIMES TURN THE SOUL OF AMERICANS TOWARD SPIRITUAL PLEASURES

In the United States, when the seventh day of each week arrives, the commercial and industrial life of the nation seems suspended; all commotion ceases. A profound quiet, or rather a sort of solemn meditation, follows it; the soul finally regains possession of itself and contemplates itself.

During this day, the places devoted to commerce are deserted; each citizen, surrounded by his children, goes to a temple; there strange speeches are made to him that seem little fashioned for his ear. He is told of the numberless evils caused by pride and covetousness. He is told of the necessity of regulating his desires, of the refined pleasures attached to virtue alone, and of the true happiness that accompanies it.

Upon his return home, one does not see him run to his business's books. He opens the book of Holy Scripture; there he finds sublime or touching images of the grandeur and goodness of the Creator, of the infinite magnificence of the works of God, of the high destiny reserved for men, of their duties, and of their rights to immortality.

It is in this way that, from time to time, the American escapes in a way from himself, and that, tearing himself away for a moment from the passions that agitate his life and the passing interests that fill it, he suddenly penetrates into an ideal world where everything is grand, pure, and eternal.

I have explored in another part of this work the causes to which one must attribute the maintenance of the political institutions of the Americans, and religion appeared to me one of the principal ones. Now that I am concerned with individuals, I come upon it and perceive that it is not less useful to each citizen than it is to the whole State.

The Americans show, by their practice, that they feel all the necessity [150] of improving the morals of democracy by means of religion. What they think about themselves in this regard is a truth in which every democratic nation ought to be steeped.

I do not doubt that the social and political constitution of a people disposes it to certain beliefs and tastes to which it then easily gives itself over, whereas these same causes turn it away from certain opinions and inclinations, without its making any effort of its own, and almost without its suspecting anything.

The whole art of the legislator consists of correctly discerning in advance these natural inclinations of human societies in order to know where it is necessary to aid the effort of the citizens and where it is necessary instead to slow it down. For these requirements are different depending on the times. There is nothing fixed except the goal toward which mankind must always strive; the means of making it arrive there vary constantly.

If I had been born in an aristocratic century, in the midst of a nation where the hereditary wealth of some and the irremediable poverty of others turned all men equally away from the idea of betterment and held men's souls, as if numbed, in the contemplation of another world, I would wish that it were possible for me to stimulate in such a people the consciousness of needs, I would think about discovering more rapid and easier means of satisfying the new desires that I would have caused to be born, and, turning the greatest efforts of the human mind toward physical studies, I would try to excite it to the pursuit of well-being.

If it happened that some men were thoughtlessly inflamed for the pursuit of wealth and displayed an excessive love for material pleasures, I would not be alarmed by it; these particular traits would soon disappear in the general aspect of the larger society.

The legislators of democracies have other concerns.

Give democratic peoples enlightenment and liberty, and let them act. They will easily succeed in drawing from this world all the goods that it can offer; they will improve each of the useful arts and make all of life's days easy, more comfortable, and milder; their social state pushes them naturally in this direction. I am not afraid of their stopping.

But while man takes pleasure in this honest and legitimate pursuit of well-being, it is to be feared that in the end he will lose the use of his most sublime faculties and that by wanting to improve everything around him, in the end he will himself become worse. That is where the danger lies, and not elsewhere.

It is therefore necessary that the legislators of democracies and all decent and enlightened men that live in them try continuously to lift up [151] the souls in democracies and keep them raised toward Heaven. It is necessary that all those who are interested in the future of democratic societies unite and that all, in concert, make continual efforts to spread within the bosom of these societies the taste for the infinite, the sentiment of greatness, and the love of spiritual pleasures.

If some of those pernicious theories that have a tendency to produce the belief that everything perishes with the body are encountered among the opinions of a democratic people, consider the men who profess them as the natural enemies of that people.

There are many things about the materialists that offend me. Their doctrines seem to me to be pernicious, and their pride revolts me. If their system were able to be of some use to man, it seems that it would be in giving to him a modest idea of himself. But they do not show that this is the case, and when they believe that they have proven sufficiently that men are brutes, they display as much pride as if they had demonstrated that they were gods.

In all nations materialism is a dangerous malady of the human mind; but it must be particularly dreaded in a democratic people because it combines marvelously with the vice of the heart that is the most usual one with those peoples.

Democracy promotes the taste for material pleasures. This taste, if it becomes excessive, soon disposes men to believe that everything is only matter; and materialism, in its turn, completes the process of carrying them off with a mad ardor toward these same pleasures. Such is the fatal circle into which democratic nations are pushed. It is good for them to see the danger and restrain themselves.

Most religions are only general, simple, and practical means of teaching men the immortality of the soul. That is the greatest advantage that a democratic people derives from religious beliefs, and one which makes them more necessary to such a people than to all others.

When, therefore, any religion whatsoever sinks deep roots into the heart of a democratic people, beware of shaking it, but conserve it instead with care as the most precious heritage of the aristocratic ages. Do not seek to tear men away from their former religious opinions in order to replace them with new ones, for fear that, in the passage from one faith to another, the soul being momentarily empty of beliefs, the love of material pleasures will come to expand within it and fill it completely.

Certainly, reincarnation is not more reasonable than materialism; nevertheless, if it were absolutely necessary for a democracy to make a [152] choice between the two, I would not hesitate, and I would consider that these citizens are at less risk of degrading themselves by thinking that their soul is going to pass into the body of a hog, than by believing that it is nothing.

The belief in an immaterial and immortal principle, united for a time to matter, is so necessary to the grandeur of man that it still produces beautiful effects when the idea of rewards and punishments is not joined to it and when one limits oneself to the belief that after death the divine

principle contained within man is absorbed in God or is going to animate another creature.

These same men consider the body as a secondary and inferior part
of our nature; and they despise it even though they are subject to its influence; whereas they have a natural esteem and a secret admiration for
the spiritual part of man, even though they sometimes refuse to submit
to its rule. This is enough to give a certain elevated turn to their ideas
and their tastes and to make them tend disinterestedly, and as it were of
themselves, toward pure sentiments and grand thoughts.

It is not certain that Socrates and his school had well-settled opinions
on what would happen to man in the other life, but the sole belief on
which they were fixed, that the soul had nothing in common with the
body and that it survived it, was sufficient to give to Platonic philosophy
the kind of sublime impetus that distinguishes it.

When we read Plato, we notice that in the times before him, and in
his time, there existed many writers who advocated materialism. These
writers have not come down to us or have come down to us only very incompletely. It has been like this in almost all times: the majority of the
great literary reputations are connected to spiritualism. The instinct and
taste of mankind sustain this doctrine; they often save it despite men
themselves and cause the names of those who are devoted to it to survive. Therefore one must not believe that in any time, and no matter
what the political state, the passion for material pleasures and the opinions that are connected with it can suffice for a whole people. The heart
of man is more vast than we suppose; it can at the same time contain the
taste for the goods of the earth and the love for those of Heaven; sometimes it seems to abandon itself madly to one of the two, but it never
goes for long without thinking of the other.

If it is easy to see that especially in democratic times it is important
to make spiritualist opinions prevail, it is not easy to say how those who
govern democratic peoples should act so that they will prevail.

[153]   I do not believe in the success or the longevity of official philoso-
phies, and as for State religions, I have always thought that if they were
sometimes temporarily able to serve the interests of political power,
sooner or later they always became fatal to the Church.

Nor am I among those who consider that in order to restore religion
in the eyes of peoples, and bring into favor the spiritualism that it professes, it is good to grant indirectly to its ministers a political influence
that the law denies to them.

I feel so impressed by the almost inevitable dangers to which beliefs
are exposed when their interpreters are mixed up in public affairs, and I
am so convinced that one must at any price maintain Christianity within

the bosom of the new democracies, that I would prefer to lock up the priests within the sanctuary than to allow them to leave it.

What means therefore remain to authority for leading men back toward spiritualist opinions or for keeping them within the religion that inspires those opinions?

What I am going to say is going to cause me much damage in the eyes of the politicians. I believe that the only effective means governments can use in order to bring into favor the dogma of the immortality of the soul is to act every day as if they believe in it themselves; and I think that it is only by scrupulously conforming themselves to religious morality in great matters that they can flatter themselves that they are teaching the citizens to understand it, to love it, and to respect it in small matters.

· · ·

CHAPTER 17 [155]

HOW, IN TIMES OF EQUALITY AND OF SKEPTICISM, IT IS IMPORTANT TO PLACE THE GOAL OF HUMAN ACTIONS AT A GREATER DISTANCE

In times of faith, the ultimate end of life is situated after life.

The men of these times are thus accustomed naturally, and as it were involuntarily, to contemplate for many years an immobile object toward which they are moving, and they learn, by imperceptible steps, to suppress a thousand small passing desires in order to better succeed in satisfying that great and permanent desire which agitates them. When the same men wish to concern themselves with earthly things, these habits reappear. They readily settle on a general and certain goal for their actions here below, toward which all their efforts are directed. They do not give way to new temptations every day; instead they have fixed goals that they pursue tirelessly.

This explains why religious peoples often accomplished such lasting things. It turns out that in concerning themselves with the other world, they had hit upon the great secret of success in this one.

Religions give men the general habit of comporting themselves with a view to the future. In this they are not less useful to happiness in this life than to happiness in the other. This is one of their greatest political qualities.

But as the light of faith is obscured, the view of men narrows, and it seems as if the object of human actions appears closer to them every day.

When once they are accustomed to no longer being concerned with what must happen after their life, they fall back easily into that complete and brutish indifference to the future which accords only too well with certain instincts of the human species. As soon as they have lost the habit of situating their principal hopes in the long term, they are naturally led to want to fulfill their slightest desires immediately, and it seems that [156] from the moment that they despair of living eternally, they are disposed to act as if they were only going to live for a single day.

In times of unbelief, therefore, it is always to be feared that men will constantly abandon themselves to their shifting chance desires and that, renouncing entirely whatever cannot be acquired without long effort, they will create nothing great, calm, and lasting.

If it happens that, in a people disposed in this way, the social state becomes democratic, the danger I am pointing out increases.

When each one seeks constantly to change his place, when an immense competition is open to all, when wealth is accumulated and dissipated in a few instants in the midst of the tumult of democracy, the idea of a sudden and easy fortune, of great wealth acquired and lost, the image of chance, in all its forms, presents itself to the human mind. The instability of the social state comes to encourage the natural instability of the desires. In the midst of these perpetual fluctuations of fate, the present looms larger. It obscures the future, which is effaced, and men want to think only of the next day.

In that country where, through an unhappy coincidence, irreligion and democracy join, the philosophers and the rulers must constantly make every effort to place the goal of human actions at a greater distance from men's eyes. This is their great business.

While remaining within the spirit of his time and his country, the moralist must learn to justify himself there. Let him endeavor every day to show his contemporaries how, in the very midst of the perpetual movement that surrounds them, it is easier than they suppose to conceive and realize lengthy undertakings. Let him show them that, although humanity has changed its aspect, the methods by means of which men can obtain prosperity in this world have remained the same, and that among democratic peoples, as elsewhere, it is only by resisting every day a thousand small particular passions that one can succeed in satisfying the general passion for happiness that agitates them.

The task of the rulers is not less well marked out.

In all times it is important that those who govern nations conduct themselves with a view to the future. But that is still more necessary in democratic and unbelieving times than in all others. By acting in this way, the leaders of democracies not only cause public affairs to prosper, but they also teach private individuals, by their example, the art of conducting private affairs.

Above all, they must make every effort to banish, as far as possible, chance from the political world.

The sudden and undeserved elevation of a courtier only makes a [157] fleeting impression in an aristocratic country because the whole body of its institutions and beliefs normally forces men to progress slowly within pathways that they cannot leave.

But there is nothing more pernicious than such examples placed before the eyes of a democratic people. They complete the process of precipitating its heart down a slope where everything is carrying it. It is therefore principally in times of skepticism and equality that one must carefully prevent the people's or prince's favor, with which you are helped or hindered by chance, from taking the place of knowledge and service. It is desirable that every advance appear to be the fruit of an effort so that no greatness is achieved too easily and ambition is forced to fix its eyes on the goal for a long time before attaining it.

It is necessary that governments work at giving back to men that taste for the future, which is no longer inspired by religion and the social state, and that, without saying so, they teach citizens in practice every day that wealth, renown, and power are the rewards of effort, that great successes are found at the end of long-standing desires, and that nothing lasting is obtained unless it is acquired with difficulty.

When men are accustomed to foresee from very far off what will happen to them on earth, and to nourish themselves there with hopes, it becomes hard for them always to stop their mind at the exact limits of life, and they are very close to breaching its limits, in order to cast their eyes beyond it.

I do not doubt that by habituating citizens to think of the future in this world, they are gradually brought closer, and without their being aware of it themselves, to religious beliefs.

In this way, the means that allows men, up to a certain point, to do without religion, is perhaps, after all, the only one that remains to us for leading mankind by way of a long detour back to faith.

CHAPTER 18   [158]

WHY, AMONG THE AMERICANS, ALL HONEST OCCUPATIONS ARE CONSIDERED HONORABLE

Among democratic peoples, where there is no hereditary wealth, each person works in order to live, or has worked, or is born to those who have worked. The idea of work as a necessary, natural, and honest condition of humanity is thus presented to the human mind on all sides.

Not only is work not dishonored among those peoples, it is honored; prejudice is not against it, it is for it. In the United States, a rich man believes he owes it to public opinion to dedicate his leisure to some work of industry, of commerce, or to some public duties. He would consider himself disreputable if he only employed his life in living. It is in order to evade this obligation to work that so many rich Americans come to Europe: there, they find some remnants of aristocratic societies among whom idleness is still honored.

Equality not only rehabilitates the idea of work, it restores the idea of work that procures a profit.

In aristocracies, it is not exactly work that is despised, it is work with a view to a profit. Work is glorious when it is ambition or virtue alone that causes one to undertake it. Under aristocracy, nevertheless, it constantly happens that he who works for honor is not insensible to the lure of gain. But these two desires only meet in the depths of his soul. He takes much care in concealing from all eyes the place where they join together. He readily hides it from himself. In aristocratic countries, there are scarcely any public officials who do not claim to serve the State disinterestedly. Their pay is a detail about which they sometimes think a little, and about which they always pretend to think not at all.

In this way, the idea of gain remains distinct from that of work. However much they are joined in deed, the aristocratic past separates them.

[159]   In democratic societies, these two ideas are, on the contrary, always visibly united. Since the desire for well-being is universal, since fortunes are mediocre and fleeting, and since each one needs to increase his resources or prepare new ones for his children, all see very clearly that it is gain that is, if not in whole, at least in part, what leads them to work. Even those who act principally with a view to glory inevitably get accustomed to the thought that they do not act solely with this in view, and they discover, no matter what they feel about it, that the desire to make a living is mixed up in them with the desire to make their lives illustrious.

From the moment when, on the one hand, work seems to all citizens an honorable necessity of the human condition and when, on the other, work is always visibly done, in whole or in part, in return for pay, the immense distance that separates the different occupations in aristocratic societies disappears. If they are not all alike, they have at least a similar character.

There is no occupation where one does not work for money. Pay, which is common to all of them, gives to all of them a family resemblance.

This serves to explain the opinions held by the Americans concerning the different occupations.

American servants do not think themselves degraded because they work, for everyone around them works. They do not feel abased by the idea that they receive pay, for the President of the United States also works for pay. He is paid for commanding, just as they are for serving.

In the United States, occupations are more or less laborious, and more or less lucrative, but they are never high or low. Every honest occupation is honorable.

CHAPTER 19   [160]

WHAT MAKES ALMOST ALL AMERICANS LEAN TOWARD INDUSTRIAL OCCUPATIONS

I do not know if, of all the useful arts, agriculture is not the one which improves the least quickly in democratic nations. Often one would even think that it is standing still, because several others seem to run.

On the contrary, almost all the tastes and habits that are born of equality lead men naturally toward commerce and industry.

I picture a man who is active, enlightened, free, comfortably well-off, full of desires. He is too poor to be able to live in idleness; he is wealthy enough to feel that he is above the immediate fear of need, and he thinks of improving his lot. This man has conceived the taste for material pleasures; a thousand others abandon themselves to this taste under his eyes; he himself has begun to abandon himself to it, and he burns to increase his means of satisfying it more. However, life is passing, time is pressing. What is he going to do?

The cultivation of the earth promises results to his efforts that are almost certain, but slow. One only enriches oneself little by little, and with difficulty. Agriculture only suits the rich who already have a great superabundance, or the poor who only ask to live. His choice is made: he sells his field, leaves his home, and goes to engage in some risky but lucrative occupation.

Now, democratic societies abound in men of this kind, and as the equality of conditions becomes greater, their host increases.

Democracy thus not only multiplies the number of workers, it leads men to one kind of work rather than another; and, whereas it makes agriculture distasteful to them, it directs them toward commerce and industry.[1]

This spirit is shown by the richest citizens themselves.   [161]

---

1. It has been remarked more than once that manufacturers and merchants are possessed of an immoderate taste for material pleasures, and commerce and

In democratic countries, a man, however rich he is assumed to be, is almost always dissatisfied with his fortune because he finds that he is less rich than his father and because he fears that his sons will be less rich than he. Most rich men in democracies therefore constantly dream of the means of acquiring riches, and they naturally turn their eyes toward commerce and industry, which appear to them to be the quickest and most powerful means of getting them. On this point they share the instincts of the poor man without having his needs, or rather they are impelled by the most imperious of all needs: that of not falling to an inferior state.

In aristocracies, the rich are at the same time the rulers. The attention that they continually give to great public affairs turns them away from the small cares that commerce and industry require. If by chance the will of one among them heads toward commerce, the will of the body soon comes to block his way; for however much one stands up against the influence of numbers, its yoke is never completely escaped, and in the very bosom of the aristocratic body that refuses with the greatest obstinacy to recognize the rights of the national majority, a particular majority forms which rules.[2]

In democratic countries, where money does not give its possessor access to power, but often keeps him out of it, the rich do not know what to do with their leisure. The restlessness and grandeur of their desires, the extent of their resources, the taste for the extraordinary that is almost always felt by those who rise, in whatever manner, above the crowd, press them to act. Commerce is the only route open to them. In democracies, there is nothing more grand or dazzling than commerce; this is what attracts the attention of the public and fills the imagination of the crowd;

---

industry are blamed for that. I believe that in this case the effect has been taken for the cause.

It is not commerce and industry which inspire in men the taste for material pleasures, but rather that taste which leads men toward industrial and commercial careers, where they hope to satisfy themselves more completely and more quickly.

If commerce and industry make the desire for well-being grow, that is because every passion becomes stronger as more attention is given to it, and increases with all the efforts that are made to satisfy it. All the causes that make the love of the goods of this world predominate in the human heart, develop industry and commerce. Equality is one of those causes. It promotes commerce, not only directly by giving men the taste for commerce, but indirectly by strengthening and generalizing in their souls the love of well-being.

2. See the note at the end of the volume.

all the energetic passions head toward it. Nothing can prevent the rich from abandoning themselves to it, neither their own prejudices, nor those of anyone else. The rich in democracies never form a body that [162] has its own mores and its own enforcement of those mores; the particular ideas of their class do not stop them, and the general ideas of their country push them forward. Since in addition the great fortunes that one sees in the midst of a democratic people almost always have a commercial origin, several generations in succession are needed before their possessors have entirely lost the habits of commerce.

Squeezed into the narrow space that is left to them by politics, the rich in democracies thus throw themselves into commerce from all sides; there they can stretch themselves out and make use of their natural advantages, and, in a way, it is by the very daring and grandeur of their industrial enterprises that one may judge in what little esteem they would have held industry if they had been born in an aristocracy.

A single remark is moreover applicable to all men in democracies, whether they are poor or rich.

Those who live in the midst of democratic instability have constantly before their eyes the image of chance, and they end up by liking all enterprises in which chance plays a role.

They are all therefore borne toward commerce, not only because of the gain that it promises them, but because of the love of the emotions that it affords them.

The United States of America only emerged a half century ago from the colonial dependence in which England held them; the number of great fortunes there is very small, and capital is still scarce. There is nevertheless no people on earth who have made as rapid progress in commerce and industry as the Americans. They are today the second maritime nation of the world, and even though their manufacturing has to struggle against almost insurmountable natural obstacles, they do not fail to make new progress every day.

In the United States, the greatest industrial enterprises are accomplished easily because the entire population takes part in industry, and in this the poorest as well as the richest citizen willingly unite their efforts. One is thus astonished to see immense works accomplished every day by a nation that contains almost no rich people. The Americans arrived only yesterday on the soil that they inhabit, and they have already turned the entire order of nature there upside down to their profit. They have linked the Hudson to the Mississippi and the Atlantic Ocean with the Gulf of Mexico, across more than five hundred leagues of mainland that separate their two seas. The longest lines of rail that have been laid up to our time are in America.

[163]   But what strikes me the most in the United States is not the extraordinary grandeur of a few industrial enterprises, it is the innumerable multitude of small enterprises.

Almost all the farmers in the United States have joined some commercial business to agriculture; most have made agriculture into a commercial business.

It is rare for an American farmer to settle forever on the soil that he occupies. In the new regions of the West principally, a field is cleared in order to be resold and not in order to be cultivated; a farm is built in the expectation that, since the condition of the country will soon change due to the increase in its population, one will be able to fetch a good price for it.

Every year a swarm of inhabitants from the North goes down to the South and settles in the regions where cotton and sugar cane grow. These men cultivate the earth with the goal of making it produce in a few years enough to enrich them, and they already glimpse the moment when they will be able to return to their region of origin to enjoy the prosperity thus acquired. The Americans thus transport the spirit of commerce into agriculture, and their industrial passions are shown there as elsewhere.

The Americans make immense progress in industry because they are all of them at the same time involved in industry; and for this same reason they are susceptible to very unexpected and very formidable industrial crises.

Since they all engage in commerce, among them commerce is subject to such numerous and complex influences that it is impossible to foresee in advance the troubles that may arise. Since each of them participates to some degree in industry, at the least shock experienced by business, all the individual fortunes totter at the same time, and the State becomes unsteady.

I believe that the recurrence of industrial crises is an endemic malady among the democratic nations of our day. It can be rendered less dangerous but not cured, because it is due not to an accident, but to the very temperament of those peoples.

[164]   **CHAPTER 20**

HOW ARISTOCRACY MAY EMERGE FROM INDUSTRY

I have shown how democracy favored the growth of industry and multiplied without limit the number of industrialists; we are going to see by what indirect path industry may indeed in its turn lead men back toward aristocracy.

It has been recognized that when a worker takes care of the same detail every day, the general production of the work is achieved more easily, more rapidly, and with more economy.

It has also been recognized that the more an industry is undertaken on a large scale, with great amounts of capital and a large amount of credit, the cheaper are its products.

These truths were glimpsed a long time ago, but they were demonstrated in our time. They are already applied to a number of very important industries, and one after another the least important ones are seizing hold of them.

I see nothing in the political world that ought to concern the legislator more than these two new axioms of industrial science.

When an artisan devotes himself continually and exclusively to the fabrication of a single object, he ends up carrying out this work with remarkable skill. But he loses, at the same time, the general capability of applying his mind to the overall direction of the work. Each day he becomes more adroit and less industrious, and one may say that in him the man declines as the worker improves.

What ought one to expect of a man who has employed twenty years of his life in the making of pinheads? And to what in him can that powerful human intelligence, which has often moved the world, henceforth be applied, except to finding the best means of making pinheads!

When a worker has consumed a considerable portion of his life in this way, his thought is arrested forever near the daily object of his labors; his body has contracted certain fixed habits from which it is no longer possible for him to depart. In a word, he no longer belongs to himself but to the occupation that he has chosen. It is in vain that laws and mores have taken care to break all the barriers surrounding this man and to open to him on all sides a thousand different paths to wealth; an industrial theory more powerful than mores and laws has attached him to a trade, and often to a place, that he cannot quit. It has assigned him a certain position in the society that he cannot leave. In the midst of universal movement, it has rendered him immobile. [165]

As the division of work is given a more complete application, the worker becomes weaker, more limited, and more dependent. The art makes progress, the artisan regresses. On the other hand, as it becomes clearer that the products of an industry are better and less expensive in the degree that the manufacturing is vaster and the capital greater, very rich and very enlightened men come forward to exploit industries which, up to then, had been left to ignorant or unprosperous* artisans. The magnitude of the efforts required and the immensity of the results to be obtained attract them.

In this way, therefore, at the same time that industrial science continually lowers the class of workers, it raises that of the masters.

Whereas the worker increasingly brings his intelligence back to the study of a single detail, the master casts his glance every day over a vaster whole, and his mind is expanded proportionately as that of the other is narrowed. Soon no more will be necessary to the second than physical strength without intelligence; the first needs knowledge, and almost genius, in order to succeed. The one resembles more and more the administrator of a vast empire, and the other a brute.

The master and the worker thus bear no resemblance to one another, and they differ more every day. They are only connected like the two extreme links of a long chain. Each occupies a place that is made for him and which he does not leave. The one is in a continual, tight, and necessary dependence upon the other and seems born in order to obey, as the latter is born to command.

What is this, if not aristocracy?

As conditions become increasingly equal in the body of the nation, the need for manufactured objects becomes more general and increases, and the low pricing that places these objects within the reach of modest fortunes becomes a greater element of success.

[166]   It thus happens every day that richer and more enlightened men devote their riches and their knowledge to industry and attempt, by opening great workshops and strictly dividing up their work, to satisfy the new desires that come forward from all sides.

In this way, as the mass of the nation turns to democracy, the particular class that is in charge of industry becomes more aristocratic. Men are increasingly alike in the first and increasingly different in the second, and inequality increases in the little society as it decreases in the large one.

It is in this way that, when one goes back to the source, it seems that aristocracy emerges by means of a natural process from the very heart of democracy.

But this aristocracy does not resemble those which preceded it.

It will be noticed first that, since it applies only to industry and to some of the industrial professions only, it is an exception, a monster, in the social state considered as a whole.

The small aristocratic societies that are formed by certain industries

---

* The word translated as "unprosperous" is *malaisés,* which means "not well-off" (but not poor).

in the midst of the immense democracy of our day contain, like the great aristocratic societies of former times, a few very rich men and a multitude that is very poor.

These poor have few means of escaping their condition and of becoming rich, but the rich are constantly becoming poor or leave commerce after having gained their wealth. In this way, the elements that compose the class of the poor are more or less fixed, but the elements that compose the class of the rich are not. In truth, although there may be rich men, the class of rich men does not exist; for these rich men do not have either a common spirit or purposes, or common traditions or hopes. There are thus members, but no body.*

Not only are the rich not solidly united among themselves, but one can say that there is no true connection between the poor man and the rich man.

They are not fixed near one another for life; at every moment interest brings them closer and pulls them apart. The worker depends on masters in general but not on some particular master. These two men see each other at the factory and are not acquainted with one another elsewhere, and while they touch one another at one point, they remain very far apart at all the others. The manufacturer only demands of the worker his work, and the worker only expects from the manufacturer his wages. The one does not commit to protect, nor the other to defend, and they are not connected in a permanent manner either by habit or by duty.

The aristocracy founded by commerce almost never settles in the [167] midst of the industrial population that it directs; its goal is not to govern the latter, but to make use of it.

An aristocracy constituted in this way cannot have a great hold over those whom it employs; and, if it succeeds for a moment in getting hold of them, they soon slip from its grasp. It does not know how to will, and cannot act.

The landed aristocracy of the past centuries was obliged by law, or believed itself to be obliged by mores, to come to the aid of its servants and to alleviate their misfortunes. But the manufacturing aristocracy of our day, after having impoverished and degraded the men whom it makes use of, in times of crisis hands them over to public charity to be fed. This results naturally from the foregoing. Between the worker and the master, the relations are frequent, but there is no true community.

---

* _Il y a donc des membres, mais point de corps. Membres,_ as in English, can mean (individual) "members" or it can mean "limbs." And _corps_ can mean "body" or "corporation" (the ensemble—the whole—of persons sharing the same _métier_ or occupation).

I think that all things considered, the manufacturing aristocracy that we see rising before our eyes is one of the hardest that has appeared on the earth, but it is at the same time one of the most restrained and least dangerous.

However, it is in this direction that the friends of democracy must constantly turn their eyes with anxiety; for if the permanent inequality of conditions and aristocracy ever enter the world once again, one may predict that they will come in through this door.

[169]   VOLUME TWO, PART THREE

INFLUENCE OF DEMOCRACY ON MORAL
HABITS* PROPERLY SO-CALLED

[171]   CHAPTER 1

HOW MORAL HABITS BECOME MILDER AS CONDITIONS
BECOME MORE EQUAL

We see that for several centuries conditions have been becoming more equal, and we find at the same time that moral habits have been becoming milder. Are these two things merely coincidental, or does there exist some secret link between them, so that the one cannot advance without causing the other to move forward?

There are several causes that can contribute to making the moral habits of a people less harsh, but among all these causes the most powerful appears to me to be the equality of conditions. The equality of conditions and the increasing mildness of moral habits are therefore not only coincidental events in my eyes, they are also correlative facts.

When the writers of fables wish to interest us in the acts of animals, they give the latter human ideas and passions. This is what the poets do when they speak of spirits and angels. There are no miseries as profound or joys as pure as those that can capture our minds and grab hold of our hearts when we are represented to ourselves under other features.

This applies very much to our present subject.

When all men in an aristocratic society are ranked in an irrevocable way, according to their occupation, wealth, and birth, the members of each class, considering themselves all as children of the same family,

---

* *moeurs.* See Vol. 1, Part 2, Chap. 9 [300]: *moeurs proprement dites,* "moral habits properly so-called," are *les habitudes du coeur,* "the habits of the heart."

feel a continual and active sympathy for one another that can never be found to the same degree among the citizens of a democracy.

But that is not the case for the different classes vis-à-vis one another.

Among an aristocratic people, each caste has its opinions, its sentiments, its rights, its moral habits, its separate existence. Thus the men who compose it bear no resemblance to any of the others; they do not [172] have the same way of thinking or of feeling, and if they believe themselves to belong to the same humanity, they do so just barely.

They therefore cannot well understand what the others feel nor judge the latter by themselves.

Nevertheless, they are sometimes seen to ardently lend one another mutual aid; but that is not contrary to what we have just said.

These same aristocratic institutions, which had made beings of a single species so different from one another, had nevertheless united them with one another by means of a very tight political bond.

Although the serf did not naturally interest himself in the fate of the nobles, he did not think himself less obliged to devote himself to the particular noble who was his chief; and although the noble believed himself to be of a different nature than the serf, he nevertheless judged that his duty and his honor constrained him to defend, at the risk of his own life, those who lived on his lands.

It is obvious that these mutual obligations did not arise out of natural right, but out of political right, and that the society obtained more than humanity alone could have done. It was not to the man that one believed oneself bound to lend support; it was to the vassal or to the lord. Feudal institutions made one very sensitive to the sufferings of certain men, not to the misfortunes of mankind. They gave generosity rather than mildness to moral habits, and although they called forth great sacrifices, they did not create genuine sympathies; for there is real sympathy only between men who are alike, and during aristocratic times, one saw one's own kind only in the members of one's caste.

When the chroniclers of the Middle Ages, who all, by their birth or their habits, belonged to the aristocracy, report the tragic death of a noble, they express infinite sorrows; whereas they recount in one breath and without batting an eye the massacre and tortures of the common people.

It is not that the writers felt a habitual hatred or a systematic contempt for the people. The war between the different classes of the State had not yet been declared. They were obeying an instinct rather than a passion; since they did not form a clear idea of the suffering of the poor man, their interest in his fate was weak.

The same was true of the common people as soon as the feudal tie came to be broken. The same centuries that saw so much heroic sacrifice on the part of the vassals for their lords, also witnessed unheard-of cruelties inflicted from time to time by the lower classes upon the higher.

It must not be thought that this mutual lack of feeling was due only to the lack of public order and enlightenment, for one finds traces of it [173] again in the following centuries, which, while becoming well-ordered and enlightened, still remained aristocratic.

In the year 1675, the lower classes of Brittany were moved to revolt by a new tax. These tumultuous movements were repressed with an unexampled cruelty. Here is how Mme de Sévigné, a witness of these horrors, gives an account of them to her daughter:

Aux Rochers, 30 October 1675.

"My God, my daughter, how amusing is your letter from Aix! At least re-read your letters before sending them. Allow yourself to be surprised by their charm and console yourself, with this pleasure, for the trouble you have in writing so many of them. Have you thus kissed all of Provence? There would be no satisfaction in kissing all of Brittany, unless one liked to smell of wine. Would you like to know the news from Rennes? A tax of one hundred thousand crowns was imposed, and if this sum is not received within twenty-four hours, it will be doubled and collectable by the soldiers. The entirety of one main street was driven out and banished, and its inhabitants prohibited, on pain of death, from being taken in; so that all these miserable people, women who have just given birth, old people, and children, upon leaving the town, wander about in tears, without knowing where to go, without food, or anything upon which they can sleep. The day before yesterday they broke on the wheel the violinist who started the dance and the theft of stamped paper; he was quartered, and his four quarters exposed in the four corners of the town. Sixty bourgeois were seized, and they will begin hanging them tomorrow. This province is a fine example for the others, and especially to respect the governors and their wives, and not to throw stones in their garden.[1]

"Mme de Tarente was in these woods yesterday during enchanting weather. There's no question of arranging for a room or light meal. She enters by the gate and leaves the same way. . . ."

In another letter she adds:

"You talk to me very pleasantly about our distress; but we are no longer breaking so many on the wheel; one in eight days, in order to uphold

---

1. To understand the pertinence of this last joke, one must recall that Mme de Grignan was the wife of the governor of Provence.

justice. It is true that hanging seems to me now a refreshment. I have an entirely different idea of justice, since I have been in this region. Your galley slaves seem to me a society of honest men who have withdrawn from the world in order to lead a quiet life."

One would be wrong to believe that Mme de Sévigné, who wrote these lines, was a selfish and barbaric creature: she loved her children [174] with passion and showed herself very sensitive to the sorrows of her friends; and we even notice, in reading her, that she treated her vassals and her servants with kindness and leniency. But Mme de Sévigné had no clear conception of what it was to suffer if one was not a noble.

In our day, the hardest man, writing to the most unfeeling person, would not dare to indulge cold-bloodedly in the cruel jesting that I have just quoted, and even if his particular moral habits allowed him to do it, the general moral habits of the nation would have forbidden him to do it.

What does this come from? Have we more sensitivity than our fore-fathers? I do not know; but, undoubtedly, our sensitivity is brought to bear on more objects.

When ranks are almost equal among a people, with all men having more or less the same manner of thinking and feeling, each of them can judge in an instant the feelings of all the others: he casts a rapid glance at himself; that suffices for him. There is thus no misery that he cannot easily conceive of and whose dimensions are not revealed to him by a secret instinct. It does not matter whether it is a question of strangers or enemies: his imagination puts him immediately in their place. It mixes something personal into his pity and makes him suffer himself when the body of his fellow man is torn apart.

In democratic times, men rarely sacrifice themselves for one another, but they show a general compassion for all the members of the human species. They are never seen to inflict gratuitous harm, and when, without much harm to themselves, they can alleviate the suffering of others, they take pleasure in doing so; they are not disinterested, but they are gentle.

Although the Americans have, so to speak, reduced egoism to a social and philosophical theory, they do not turn out to be less strongly susceptible to pity.

There is no country where criminal justice is administered with more mildness than in the United States. Whereas the English seem to wish to carefully preserve in their penal laws the bloody traces of the Middle Ages, the Americans have nearly eliminated the penalty of death from their codes.

North America is, I think, the only country on the earth where, for fifty years, they have not taken the life of a single citizen for political offenses.

What completes the proof that this remarkable mildness of the Americans derives principally from their social state is the manner in which they treat their slaves.

[175]   There does not perhaps exist, all things considered, a European colony in the New World where the physical condition of the blacks is less hard than in the United States. Nevertheless, the slaves there still experience horrible miseries and are constantly exposed to extremely cruel punishments.

It is easy to see that the lot of these unfortunates inspires little pity in their masters and that they see in slavery not only a state of affairs from which they profit, but also an evil that scarcely touches them. In this way, the same man who is full of humanity for his fellow men when they are at the same time his equals becomes insensitive to their sufferings the moment the equality ceases. It is therefore to this equality that one must attribute his mildness, even more than to civilization and enlightenment.

What I have just said about individuals applies to a certain extent to peoples.

When each nation has its own separate opinions, beliefs, laws, and customs, it considers itself as forming, by itself alone, humanity in its entirety and only feels touched by its own sufferings. If war breaks out between two peoples disposed in this way, it cannot fail to be conducted barbarically.

During the period of their greatest enlightenment, the Romans cut the throats of enemy generals after having dragged them in triumph behind a chariot and delivered their prisoners over to wild beasts for the amusement of the people. Cicero, who wailed so much at the idea of crucifying a citizen, found no fault with these atrocious abuses of victory. It is obvious that in his eyes a foreigner did not belong to the same human species as a Roman.

To the extent, on the contrary, that peoples become more like one another, they show themselves reciprocally more sympathetic to each other's misfortunes, and the law of nations becomes milder.

• • •

[200]   **CHAPTER 8**

INFLUENCE OF DEMOCRACY ON THE FAMILY

I have just examined how, among democratic peoples and in particular among the Americans, equality of conditions alters the relationships between citizens.

I wish to penetrate further into the matter and enter into the bosom of the family. My goal here is not to search for new truths, but to show how already known facts relate to my subject.

Everyone has noticed that, in our time, new relationships have been established between the different members of the family, that the distance that formerly separated the father and his son has diminished, and that paternal authority is, if not destroyed, at least altered.

Something analogous, but still more striking, is apparent in the United States.

In America, the family, taking this word in its Roman and aristocratic sense, does not exist. Some remnants of it are found during the first years that follow the birth of the children. Then, the father exercises, without opposition, the absolute domestic authority that the weakness of his sons makes necessary, and which their interest, as well as his indisputable superiority, justifies.

But from the moment that the young American approaches manhood, the ties of filial obedience are loosened daily. Master of his thoughts, he is soon afterward master of his conduct. In America, there is, in truth, no adolescence. At the end of childhood, the man appears and begins to mark out his path himself.

It would be wrong to believe that this occurs following an internal struggle in which the son obtained, by a sort of moral violence, the liberty that his father refused to him. The same habits, the same principles that drive the one to seize hold of independence, dispose the other to consider its exercise as an indisputable right.

Thus one does not see in the first any of those hateful and disordered [201] passions that still agitate men a long time after they have freed themselves from an established power. The second does not experience those regrets full of bitterness and anger that usually live on after the loss of power: the father has seen from a distance the term at which his authority must expire, and when time brings him near to this term, he abdicates easily. The son has foreseen in advance the precise moment when his own will would become his rule, and he takes possession of liberty without hurry and without effort, much as he would a good that is due to him and of which no one seeks to deprive him.[1]

---

1. The Americans, however, have not yet conceived, as we have done in France, of depriving the fathers of one of the principal elements of their power by taking away their liberty of disposing of their property after their death. In the United States, the right to dispose of property in a will is unlimited.

In this as in almost all the rest, it is easy to see that if the political legislation

It is perhaps useful to show how these changes that have taken place in the family are tightly linked to the social and political revolution whose accomplishment is being completed before our eyes.

There are certain great social principles that a people makes penetrate everywhere or does not permit to survive anywhere.

In aristocratically and hierarchically organized countries, power never directly addresses the whole body of the governed. Since men are dependent upon one another, one limits oneself to directing the first ones among them. The rest follow. This applies to the family as to all associations that have a head. Among aristocratic peoples, society only recognizes, in truth, the father. It has a hold on the sons only through the hands of the father; it governs him, and he governs them. The father thus has not only a natural right in that society. He is also granted a political right to command. He is the author and the support of the family; he is also its magistrate.

In democracies, where the arm of the government goes to seek out [202] each man in particular in the middle of the crowd in order to bend him individually to the common laws, there is no need for such an intermediary. In the eyes of the law, the father is merely a citizen who is older and richer than his sons.

When most conditions are very unequal, and the inequality of conditions is permanent, the idea of the superior individual increases in the imagination of men. Were the law not to grant him prerogatives, custom and opinion would concede them to him. When, on the contrary, men differ little from one another and do not remain different forever, the general notion of the superior individual becomes weaker and less clear. It is futile for the will of the legislator to endeavor to place the one who obeys much below the one who commands: mores bring these two men closer to one another and draw them every day toward the same level.

---

of the Americans is much more democratic than ours, our civil legislation is infinitely more democratic than theirs. This is easy to understand.

The author of our civil legislation was a man who saw his interest in satisfying the democratic passions of his contemporaries in everything that was not directly and immediately unfriendly to his power. He gladly permitted a few popular principles to regulate property and govern families, provided that there was no claim to introduce them into the management of the State. While the democratic torrent submerged the civil laws, he hoped to keep himself safely sheltered behind the political laws. This view is at once full of cunning and selfish; but such a compromise could not be lasting. For in the long run, the political society cannot fail to become the expression and the image of the civil society, and it is in this sense that it can be said that there is nothing more political among a people than its civil legislation.

If therefore I do not see, in the legislation of an aristocratic people, particular privileges accorded to the head of the family, I am nonetheless certain that his power in it is much respected and more extensive than in a democracy, for I know that, whatever the laws may be, the superior will always appear higher and the inferior lower in aristocracies than among democratic peoples.

When men live in the memory of what was, rather than in the preoccupation with what is, and when they worry much more about what their ancestors thought than they try to think themselves, the father is the natural and necessary connection between the past and the present, the link where these two chains end and join together. In aristocracies, the father is thus not only the political head of the family: he is the organ of tradition in it, the interpreter of custom, the arbiter of mores. He is listened to with deference, he is approached only with respect, and the love that is borne toward him is always tempered by fear.

When the social state becomes democratic, and men adopt for a general principle that it is good and legitimate to judge all things themselves by taking the old beliefs as a piece of information and not as a rule, the power of opinion exercised by the father over the sons, as well as his legal power, becomes less great.

The division of patrimonies that democracy brings about contributes perhaps more than all the rest to changing the relations between the father and the children.

When the father of the family has little property, his son and he live without interruption in the same place and do the same work together. Habit and need bring them closer and force them to communicate with [203] each other at every moment. Thus there cannot fail to become established between them a kind of familiar intimacy that makes authority less absolute and that accords poorly with the external forms of respect.

Now, among democratic peoples, the class that possesses these small fortunes is precisely that which gives power to ideas and an orientation to mores. It makes its opinions as well as its wishes prevail everywhere, and the very ones who are most inclined to resist its commandments end up allowing themselves to be carried off by its examples. I have seen fierce enemies of democracy who caused themselves to be addressed familiarly as "thou" by their children.*

---

* The word translated as "thou" is *tu*. The French have two forms for "you": *vous* is formal and respectful and is normally used when addressing those older than oneself or who are not close friends or relations; *tu* is familiar and is used by adults when they address children, close friends, or family members, and by children when they address other children. As Tocqueville indicates, prior to the democratic

In this way, at the same time that power slips from the aristocracy, the austere, conventional, and legal elements of paternal power disappear, and a kind of equality is established around the domestic hearth.

I do not know if, all things considered, society loses by this change, but I am led to believe that the individual gains by it. I think that as the mores and laws are more democratic, the relations between father and son become more intimate and milder; there is less rule and authority in them; confidence and affection are often greater, and it seems that the natural tie tightens while the social tie loosens.

In the democratic family, the father exercises scarcely any power other than that which one is pleased to accord to the affection and experience of an old man. His orders may perhaps be ignored, but his counsel is usually full of authority. If he is not surrounded by formal signs of respect, his sons at least approach him with confidence. There is no accepted form for speaking to him, but he is spoken to constantly, and his advice is willingly sought every day. The master and the magistrate have disappeared; the father remains.

It is enough, in order to judge the difference between the two social states on this point, to peruse the domestic correspondence that the aristocracies have left us. Their style is always correct, ceremonious, rigid, and so cold that the natural warmth of the heart can scarcely be sensed through the words.

Among democratic peoples, on the contrary, there prevails in all the words that a son addresses to his father something at once free, familiar, and tender, which reveals at the outset that new relations have been established within the family.

An analogous revolution modifies the mutual relations of the children.

In the aristocratic family, as well as in aristocratic society, all places [204] are marked out. Not only does the father occupy a separate rank and enjoy immense privileges. The children themselves are not equal to one another: age and sex fix irrevocably the rank of each one and assure them certain prerogatives. Democracy overturns or lowers the majority of these barriers.

In the aristocratic family, the eldest of the sons, by inheriting the greatest portion of the wealth and almost all the rights, becomes the

revolution children addressed their own parents formally and respectfully, using *vous*. Even today, this question of usage divides the French: some, especially members of the younger generation, will insist on using *tu* familiarly from the first encounter; others, even members of the younger generation, will refuse to use *tu* until a certain level of real familiarity and intimacy—and confidence—has been established. In this view, *tu* is an earned form of address; using it from the outset of a new acquaintanceship is too quick and facile.

head, and up to a certain point the master, of his brothers. To him belong grandeur and power, to them modest position and dependence. Nevertheless, it would be a mistake to believe that among aristocratic peoples the privileges of the elder are advantageous only to him and that they provoke only envy and hatred around him.

The elder usually makes every effort to procure wealth and power for his brothers because the general splendor of the house reflects on him who represents it, and the younger ones seek to help the elder in all his undertakings because the grandeur and strength of the head of the family puts him more and more in a position to lift up all its offspring.

The different members of the aristocratic family are thus very tightly bound to each other. Their interests are linked together, their minds are in agreement. But it is rare that their hearts are in accord.

Democracy also attaches the brothers to one another, but it goes about it in another manner.

Under democratic laws, the children are perfectly equal, and consequently independent. There is nothing that inevitably draws them closer, but also nothing that pulls them apart. And since they have a common origin, since they are raised under the same roof, since they are the object of the same cares, and since no particular prerogative either distinguishes them or separates them, the sweet and youthful intimacy of childhood arises easily among them. Once the tie is formed in this way at the beginning of life, scarcely any occasions for breaking it arise, for brotherhood brings them together every day without being a source of difficulty.

It is thus not by means of interests but by means of the community of memories and the free sympathy of opinions and tastes that democracy attaches brothers to one another. It divides their inheritance, but it allows their souls to unite.

The mildness of these democratic mores is so great that even the partisans of aristocracy allow themselves to adopt them, and after having savored them for some time, they are not tempted to return to the respectful and cold forms of the aristocratic family. They would gladly keep the domestic habits of democracy, provided that they were able to reject its social state and its laws. But these things are linked together, [205] and it is not possible to enjoy the ones without accepting the others.

What I have just said about filial love and fraternal affection must be understood for all the passions that originate spontaneously in nature itself.

When a certain manner of thinking and feeling is the product of a particular state of humanity, and this state changes, nothing remains. Thus, the law may attach two citizens to one another very closely; once the law is abolished, they separate. There is nothing tighter than the knot that unites the vassal with the lord in the feudal world. Now these two men no longer recognize one another. The fear, gratitude, and love that formerly linked them have disappeared. Not a trace of them is to be found.

But that is not the case for the sentiments natural to mankind. It is rare that the law, by endeavoring to bend them in a certain manner, does not weaken them, that by wanting to add to them, it does not remove something from them, and that they are not always stronger when left to themselves.

Democracy, which destroys or obscures almost all the old social conventions and which prevents men from easily settling on new ones, causes most of the sentiments that arise from those conventions to disappear entirely. But it only modifies the others, and it often gives them an energy and a mildness that they did not have.

I think that it is not impossible to comprehend in a single sentence the whole meaning of this chapter and of several others that precede it. Democracy loosens social ties, but it tightens natural ties. It brings kin closer together at the same time that it pulls citizens apart.

[206]   CHAPTER 9

THE EDUCATION OF YOUNG WOMEN IN THE UNITED STATES

There are no free societies without morals, and, as I said in the first part of this work, it is the woman who forms moral habits. Everything that has an influence on the condition of women, on their habits and their opinions, therefore has great political interest in my view.

In almost all Protestant nations, young women are in infinitely greater control of their actions than among Catholic peoples.

This independence is still greater in the Protestant countries that, like England, have conserved or acquired the right to govern themselves. Liberty then penetrates into the family by means of political habits and religious beliefs.

In the United States, the doctrines of Protestantism are combined with a very free constitution and a very democratic social state; and nowhere is the young woman more quickly or more completely delivered over to herself.

Long before the American girl has reached the age of consent, she begins to be freed gradually from maternal tutelage; she has still not entirely left childhood behind when she already thinks for herself, speaks freely, and acts on her own. The great spectacle of the world is constantly exposed before her; far from trying to conceal its sight from her, one discloses it to her view more and more every day, and she is taught to consider it with a firm and calm eye. In this way, the vices and the perils that society presents are not long in being revealed to her; she sees them clearly, judges them without illusion, and faces them without fear; for she is full of confidence in her own powers, and her confidence seems shared by all those who surround her.

One must therefore almost never expect to encounter in the young woman of America that virginal naivete in the midst of nascent desires or those naive and ingenuous charms that usually accompany the pas- [207] sage from childhood to youth in the young woman of Europe. It is rare for the American woman, whatever her age, to show a childish shyness and ignorance. Like the young woman of Europe, she wants to please, but she knows precisely at what price. If she does not abandon herself to evil, at least she knows about it; she has pure morals rather than a chaste mind.

I was often surprised and almost frightened to see the remarkable deftness and happy boldness with which these young women of America knew how to manage their thoughts and words amid the hazards of a playful conversation; a philosopher would have stumbled a hundred times on the narrow path that they traversed without mishaps and without difficulty.

It is easy, in fact, to recognize that in the very midst of the independence of her early youth, the American woman never entirely ceases to be mistress of herself; she enjoys all of the permitted pleasures without abandoning herself to any of them, and her reason does not relax the reins, although it often seems to allow them to hang loose.

In France, where we still mix up in such a strange manner, in our opinions and in our tastes, remnants of all the ages, it often happens that we give to women a timid education, secluded and almost cloistered, as in the time of aristocracy, and then we abandon them suddenly, without a guide and without help, in the midst of the disorders inseparable from a democratic society.

The Americans are in better accord with themselves.

They saw that in a democracy individual independence could not fail to be very great, youth rash, tastes poorly contained, custom fickle, public opinion often uncertain or impotent, paternal authority weak, and marital power questioned.

In this state of things, they judged that there was little chance of suppressing in woman the most tyrannical passions of the human heart and that it was more sure to teach her the art of combating them herself. Since they could not prevent her virtue from being often at risk, they wanted her to know how to protect it, and they counted more upon the free effort of her will than upon fences that were weakened or destroyed. Instead of making her distrust herself, they therefore seek constantly to increase her confidence in her own powers. Having neither the possibility nor the desire to keep the young woman in perpetual and complete ignorance, they hastened to give her a precocious knowledge of all things. Far from concealing the corruptions of the world from her, they wanted her to see them first and train herself to flee them on her own, and they [208] preferred to secure her decency than to overly respect her innocence.

Although the Americans are a very religious people, they do not rely upon religion alone to protect woman's virtue; they have sought to arm her reason. In this, as in many other circumstances, they followed the same method. They first made incredible efforts to get individual independence to govern itself on its own, and it is only when they arrived at the ultimate limits of human power that they finally called religion to their aid.

I know that such an education is not without risk; nor am I unaware that it tends to develop judgment at the expense of imagination and to make decent and cold women rather than loving wives and attractive companions of man. If society is more tranquil and better regulated, private life often has fewer charms. But those are secondary ills, which a greater interest should make us brave. Having reached the point we are at, we are no longer permitted to make a choice: a democratic education is necessary in order to protect woman from the dangers with which she is surrounded by the institutions and the mores of democracy.

[209]   CHAPTER 10

HOW THE YOUNG WOMAN REAPPEARS
IN THE FEATURES OF THE WIFE

In America, the independence of the woman comes to be lost irrevocably in the midst of the bonds of marriage. If the young woman is less constrained there than anywhere else, the wife submits to tighter obligations. The one makes of the paternal home a place of liberty and of pleasure, the other lives in the house of her husband as if in a cloister.

These two such different states are perhaps not so opposed as one supposes, and it is natural that the Americans pass through the one in order to arrive at the other.

Religious peoples and industrial nations form a particularly solemn idea of marriage. The first consider the regularity of the life of a woman as the best guarantee and the most certain sign of the purity of its morals. The second see in it the sure guarantee of the order and the prosperity of the house.[*]

The Americans are both a Puritan nation and a commercial people. Their religious beliefs as well as their industrial habits thus lead them to demand of the woman an abnegation of herself and a constant sacrifice of her pleasures and her affairs that is rarely demanded of her in Europe. In this way, there prevails in the United States an inexorable public opinion that carefully confines the woman within the small circle of domestic interests and duties and that prohibits her from going outside it.

Upon entering the world, the young American girl finds these notions firmly established; she sees the rules that follow from them; she is not long in persuading herself that she cannot for a moment evade the customary practices of her contemporaries without immediately putting her tranquility, her honor, and even her social existence at risk, and she finds, in the resoluteness of her reason and in the virile habits that her education has given her, the strength to submit to them.

One may say that it is from the exercise of independence that she has [210] drawn the courage to accept its sacrifice without struggle and without protest when the time comes to impose it upon herself.

Besides, the American woman never falls into the bonds of marriage as into a trap set for her simplicity and her ignorance. She has learned in advance what is expected of her, and she places herself under the yoke on her own and freely. She bears her new condition courageously because she has chosen it.

Since in America paternal discipline is very loose and the marriage bond very tight, a young woman contracts it only with circumspection and anxiety. One sees hardly any premature marriages there. Thus, American women only marry when their reason is practiced and matured, whereas elsewhere most women normally only begin to exercise and mature their reason within marriage.

I am, besides, very far from believing that this great change that occurs in all the habits of women in the United States, as soon as they are married, must be attributed only to the constraint of public opinion. Often they impose it upon themselves by the sole effort of their own will.

---

* The word translated as "house" is *maison,* which means "house" in the ordinary sense, but it also means "family" in a sense identified with place. This is a usage with roots in hereditary royalty and nobility, where it means the family as a hereditary line, as in the House of Tudor. An industrial or commercial company may also be called a *maison.*

When the time has come to choose a husband, the cold and austere reason that her unfettered view of the world has enlightened and strengthened indicates to the American woman that a frivolous* and independent spirit within the bonds of marriage is a cause of eternal trouble, not of pleasure; that the amusements of the young woman cannot become the diversions of the wife, and that for the woman the sources of happiness lie within the conjugal abode. Seeing in advance and with clarity the only path that can lead to domestic happiness, she enters it from her first steps and follows it to the end without seeking to go back.

This same strength of will that is shown by the young wives of America, in submitting suddenly and without complaint to the austere duties of their new state, reappears moreover in all the great trials of their lives.

There is no country in the world where particular fortunes are more unstable than in the United States. It is not unusual for the same man, in the course of his life, to go up and come back down all the grades that lead from opulence to poverty.

The women of America bear these upheavals with a calm and indomitable energy. One would think that their desires constrict with their fortune as easily as they expand.

Most of the adventurers who go every year to settle the solitary expanses of the West belong, as I said in my first volume, to the old Anglo-
[211] American stock of the North. Some of these men who rush toward riches with so much daring already enjoyed a comfortable existence in their own regions. They bring their wives with them and make them share in the innumerable dangers and hardships that are always the signposts of the beginnings of such undertakings. I often encountered even at the extreme limits of the wilderness young women who, after having been raised in the midst of all the refinements of the large cities of New England, had passed, almost without transition, from the rich abode of their parents into a poorly sealed cabin in the depths of a forest. Disease, solitude, and boredom had not broken the springs of their courage. Their features seemed drawn and weathered, but their gaze was firm. They appeared at once both sad and resolute.

I do not doubt that these young American women had amassed, in their early education, that interior strength which they then put to use.

It is thus still the young woman who in the United States reappears in the features of the wife; the role has changed, the habits are different, the spirit is the same.

---

* The word translated as "frivolous" is *léger* ("light"), which can also mean "capricious" and, morally speaking, "loose."

CHAPTER 11

HOW EQUALITY OF CONDITIONS CONTRIBUTES TO THE MAINTENANCE OF GOOD MORALS IN AMERICA

There are philosophers and historians who have said, or have given to understand, that women are more or less severe in their morals according to whether they live more or less far from the equator. That is getting oneself out of the difficulty on the cheap, and on this account a globe and a compass would suffice to resolve in an instant one of the most difficult problems that humanity presents.

I do not see that this materialist doctrine is proven by the facts.

The same nations have shown themselves, at different periods of their history, chaste or dissolute. The regularity or the disorder of their morals was thus due to some variable causes and not uniquely to the nature of the country, which did not change.

I will not deny that, in certain climates, the passions that arise from the reciprocal attraction of the sexes are particularly ardent; but I think that this natural ardor can always be inflamed or contained by the social state and the political institutions.

Although the travelers who have visited North America differ among themselves on several points, they all agree in remarking that the morals there are infinitely more severe than everywhere else.

It is obvious that, on this point, the Americans are very superior to their ancestors the English. A superficial glance at the two nations suffices to prove it.

In England, as in all the other countries of Europe, the public's malice is constantly brought to bear on the weaknesses of women. Philosophers and statesmen are often heard to complain there that morals are not sufficiently regular, and every day their literature makes one assume as much.

In America, all books, without excepting the novels, assume the women to be chaste, and no one there recounts stories of amorous liaisons. [213]

This great regularity of American morals no doubt results in part from the country, the stock, and the religion. But all these causes, which exist elsewhere, are still not sufficient to explain it. For that it is necessary to have recourse to some special reason.

This reason appears to me to be equality and the institutions that flow from it.

Equality of conditions does not of itself produce regularity of morals; but one cannot doubt that it facilitates and augments it.

Among aristocratic peoples, birth and wealth often make man and woman into beings so different that they can never succeed in uniting with one another. The passions draw them toward one another, but the social state and the ideas that it inspires prevent them from becoming united to one another in a permanent and open manner. From this arises necessarily a great number of fleeting and clandestine unions. Nature compensates itself in secret for the constraint imposed on it by the laws.

These things do not transpire in the same way when equality of conditions causes all the imaginary or real barriers that separate man from woman to fall. Then there is no young woman who does not believe that she can become the wife of the man who prefers her, which makes disorderliness of morals before marriage very difficult. For whatever the gullibility of the passions, there is hardly any way for a woman to persuade herself that a man loves her when he is perfectly free to marry her and he does not do it.

The same cause operates, although in a more indirect manner, within marriage.

Nothing serves better to render an illegitimate love legitimate in the eyes of those who feel it or of the crowd who contemplates it than marriages that are forced or entered into by chance.

[214]   In a country where the woman always freely exercises her choice and where her education has made her capable of choosing well, public opinion is pitiless regarding her transgressions.

The moral severity of the Americans arises in part from that. They consider marriage as a contract that is often onerous, but all of whose clauses they are nevertheless bound to execute rigorously because they could know all of them in advance and because they enjoyed complete liberty to not put themselves under any obligation at all.

What makes fidelity more obligatory also makes it easier.

In aristocratic countries marriage has as its aim to unite property rather than persons; and so it sometimes happens that the husband is gotten while still in school and the wife while still with a wet nurse. It is not surprising that the conjugal bond that keeps the fortunes of the two spouses united allows their hearts to stray haphazardly. That flows naturally from the spirit of the contract.

When, on the contrary, each man always chooses his wife himself, without any external hindrance or even guidance, it is normally only similarity of tastes and ideas that brings man and woman together; and this same similarity keeps and fixes them at each other's side.

. . .

CHAPTER 12

HOW THE AMERICANS UNDERSTAND THE EQUALITY
OF MAN AND WOMAN

I have shown how democracy destroys or modifies the different in-equalities that society brings into being. But is that all, and does it not finally succeed in acting upon this great inequality between man and woman, which has seemed up until our time to have eternal foundations in nature?

I think that the social movement that brings son and father, servant and master, and, in general, inferior and superior, nearer to the same level, will raise up woman and is bound to make her more and more the equal of man.

But it is here, more than ever, that I feel the need to be well understood; for there is no subject on which the crude and disordered imagination of our time has given itself a freer rein.

There are men in Europe who, confounding the different attributes of the sexes, claim to make of man and woman beings who are not only equal but alike. They give to both of them the same functions, impose on them the same duties, and grant them the same rights; they mix them together in all things—work, pleasure, public affairs. One can easily conceive that by endeavoring to make one sex equal to the other, both of them are lowered, and that this crude mixing of nature's works can never produce anything except weak men and indecent women.

It is not in this way that the Americans have understood the kind of democratic equality that can be established between woman and man. They have thought that since nature had established such a great difference between the physical and moral constitution of the man and that of the woman, its clearly indicated aim was to give a different use to their different faculties; and they have judged that progress did not consist in making beings that are dissimilar do more or less the same things, but in [220] arranging for each of them to perform their tasks as well as possible. The Americans have applied to the two sexes the great principle of political economy that rules industry in our day. They have carefully divided the functions of man and woman in order that the great work of society be better done.

America is the country in the world where the most constant care has been taken to mark out clearly separated lines of action for the two sexes and where they are obliged to march at the same pace, but always in different paths. You do not see American women govern the external affairs of the family, manage a business, or, finally, enter the political sphere;

but neither does one encounter any of them who are obliged to engage in the rough work of ploughing or in any hard work that demands the development of physical strength. There are no families so poor that they make exception to this rule.

If the American woman cannot escape from the peaceful circle of domestic occupations, she is not, on the other hand, ever constrained to go out of it.

From this it results that American women, who often display a masculine reason and a very virile energy, conserve in general a very delicate appearance and always remain feminine in their manners, even though they sometimes show themselves to be masculine in mind and in heart.

Nor have the Americans ever imagined that the consequence of democratic principles was to overturn marital authority and introduce a confusion of authorities into the family. They have thought that every association, in order to be effective, had to have a head and that the natural head of the conjugal association was man. They therefore do not refuse to the latter the right to govern his wife, and they believe that, in the small society of husband and wife just as in the larger political society, the object of democracy is to regulate and to make legitimate necessary powers and not to destroy all power.

This opinion is not peculiar to one sex and opposed by the other.

I have not noticed that American women considered conjugal authority as a happy usurpation of their rights nor that they believed that to submit to it was to abase themselves. It appeared to me, on the contrary, that they fashioned for themselves a kind of glory out of the voluntary renunciation of their will and that they placed their grandeur in bending themselves to the yoke and not in escaping it. That, at least, is the sentiment that the most virtuous ones express: the others keep quiet, and in [221] the United States one does not hear an adulterous wife noisily clamoring for woman's rights while trampling on her most sacred duties.

In Europe one often notices a certain contempt visible in the very midst of the flatteries that men lavish upon women: even though the European man often makes himself the slave of the woman, one sees that he never sincerely believes her to be his equal.

In the United States, women are hardly ever praised, but it is shown every day that they are respected.

American men constantly display a complete confidence in the reason of their wives, and a profound respect for their liberty. They consider that a woman's mind is as capable as man's of discovering the naked truth and her heart firm enough to follow it; and they have never sought to shield the virtue of the one any more than the other from prejudices, ignorance, or fear.

It seems that in Europe, where one submits so readily to the despotic empire of women, they are nevertheless denied some of the greatest attributes of mankind, and they are considered as seductive and incomplete beings; and, what is most astonishing, the women themselves end up seeing themselves in the same light, and they are not far from considering as a privilege the faculty they are left with of showing themselves frivolous, weak, and timid. American women do not clamor for such rights as these.

One might say, on the other hand, that with respect to moral habits, we Europeans have granted a kind of singular immunity to the man, so that it is as if there were one virtue for his use, and another for the use of his wife, and that, according to public opinion, the same act may be either a crime or merely a misdeed.

The Americans do not recognize this iniquitous division of duties and rights. Among them, the seducer is as dishonored as his victim.

It is true that American men rarely show women the attentive consideration with which we love to surround them in Europe; but they always show by their conduct that they assume them to be virtuous and refined, and they have such a great respect for their moral liberty that in their presence everyone watches his words with care, for fear that the women will be forced to hear language that offends them. In America, a young woman undertakes a long trip alone and without fear.

The legislators of the United States, who have made almost all the clauses of the penal code milder, punish rape with death, and there are no crimes that public opinion pursues with more inexorable ardor. That is understandable: since the Americans think nothing more precious [222] than the honor of woman, and nothing more deserving of respect than her independence, they consider that there is no punishment too severe for those who take them away from her against her will.

In France, where the same crime is punished with far milder sentences, it is often difficult to find a jury that will convict. Is this contempt for modesty or contempt for woman? I cannot prevent myself from thinking that it is both.

Thus, the Americans do not believe that man and woman have the duty or the right to do the same things, but they show the same respect for each of their roles, and they consider them as beings of equal worth, although their destiny is different. They do not give to woman's courage the same form or use as man's, but they never doubt her courage; and if they think that the man and his wife must not always employ their intellect and their reason in the same manner, they consider, at least, that her reason is as sure as his and her intellect as clear.

The Americans, who have allowed woman's inferiority to survive in the society, have thus raised her with all their power, in the intellectual and moral world, to the level of man; and in this they appear to me to have admirably understood the true notion of democratic progress.

For myself, I will not hesitate to say it: even though in the United States the woman scarcely leaves the domestic sphere, and she is, in certain respects, very dependent within it, nowhere does her position seem to me higher; and if, now that I am approaching the end of this book in which I have pointed out so many remarkable things accomplished by the Americans, I were asked to what I think must be principally attributed the remarkable prosperity and growing strength of this people, I would answer that it is to the superiority of their women.

. . .

[236]   **CHAPTER 17**

HOW THE ASPECT OF SOCIETY, IN THE UNITED STATES, IS AT ONCE AGITATED AND MONOTONOUS

Nothing seems to be more suited to exciting and nourishing curiosity than the aspect of the United States. Fortunes, ideas, and laws are constantly changing there. One would think that unchanging nature itself is changeable, it is transformed so much every day under the hand of man.

Eventually, however, the sight of this much agitated society appears monotonous, and after having contemplated this very changeable spectacle for some time, the observer becomes bored.

Among aristocratic peoples, each man is more or less fixed within his sphere, but the men are enormously dissimilar; they have fundamentally different passions, ideas, habits, and tastes. Nothing there moves; everything there differs.

In democracies, on the contrary, all the men are alike and do more or less similar things. They are subject, it is true, to great and continual vicissitudes, but since the same successes and the same reversals recur continually, only the names of the actors are different; the play is the same. The aspect of American society is agitated because men and things change constantly, and it is monotonous because all the changes are alike.

The men who live in democratic times have many passions, but the majority of their passions end in the love of wealth or emerge from it. That is not because their souls are smaller, but because the importance of money is in reality greater during those times.

When fellow citizens are all independent and indifferent, it is only by paying that the support of each of them can be obtained, which infinitely multiplies the use of wealth and increases its value.

Since the prestige that was attached to old things has disappeared, birth, rank, and profession no longer distinguish men or barely distinguish them. There remains scarcely anything but money that creates very visible differences between them and that is capable of placing some of [237] them above the others. The distinction that is produced by wealth is augmented by the disappearance and the diminution of all the others.

Among aristocratic peoples, money leads only to a few points on the vast circumference of the desires; in democracies, it seems that it leads to all.

Love of wealth, as the principal thing or as an accessory, is thus usually at the bottom of Americans' actions. This gives all their passions a family resemblance and is not long in making the spectacle of them tiring.

This perpetual recurrence of the same passion is monotonous. So also are the particular means that this passion uses to satisfy itself.

In an established and peaceful democracy like that of the United States, where one cannot become rich by means of war, public employments, or political confiscations, the love of wealth directs men chiefly toward industry. Now, industry, which often leads to such great disorders and such great disasters, nevertheless cannot flourish except by means of very regular habits and a long series of very uniform small actions. The stronger the passion, the more regular the habits and more uniform the actions. One may say that it is the very strength of their desires that makes the Americans so methodical. It disturbs their soul, but it orders their lives.

What I am saying about America applies, moreover, to almost all the men of our time. Variety is disappearing from mankind; the same ways of acting, thinking, and feeling are found in every corner of the world. This results not only from the fact that all the peoples frequent each other's countries and copy each other more exactly, but from the fact that in every country the men, distancing themselves more and more from the ideas and sentiments particular to a caste, a profession, or a family, simultaneously arrive at what stems more nearly from the constitution of man, which is everywhere the same. They thus become similar even though they did not imitate one another. They are like travelers dispersed in a great forest all of whose paths end up at a single point. If all perceive the central point at the same time and direct their steps that way, they all come closer together imperceptibly, without seeking to, without noticing, and without knowing it, and they will be surprised in the end to see each other assembled together in the same place. All peoples who take for the object of their study and their imitation not some particular man, but man himself, will end up by converging in the same mores like those travelers at the crossroads.

CHAPTER 18

ON HONOR IN THE UNITED STATES AND IN DEMOCRATIC SOCIETIES[1]

Men seem to make use of two very different methods in the public judgment that they bring to the actions of their fellow men: sometimes they judge them according to simple notions of just and unjust that are widespread throughout the world; sometimes they judge them by means of very particular notions that belong to one country and one epoch only. Often it happens that these two rules differ; sometimes they are opposed to each other, but they never completely merge with one another or destroy one another.

Honor, in the time of its greatest power, governed the will more than belief, and men, even if they submitted without hesitation and without a murmur to its commandments, still felt, by a sort of obscure but powerful instinct, that there existed a more general, more ancient, and more holy law, which they disobeyed sometimes without ceasing to recognize it. There are actions that were judged at the same time decent and dishonorable. The refusal of a duel was often an instance of this.

I believe that one can explain these phenomena other than by the caprice of certain individuals and certain peoples, as has been done up to now.

Mankind feels permanent and general needs, which have brought [239] into being moral laws to whose breach all men have naturally attached, in all places and in all times, the idea of blame and shame. They have called evading them *acting badly* and submitting to them *acting well*.

In addition, within the vast human association, more restricted associations develop that are called peoples and, in the midst of these last, other still smaller ones called classes or castes.

---

1. The word *honor* is not always used in the same sense in French.

1° It signifies first the esteem, the glory, the consideration that is obtained from one's fellow men: it is in this sense that one says *to win honor.*

2° Honor also signifies the body of rules by virtue of which one obtains this glory, this esteem, and this consideration. It is thus that one says *that a man has always conformed strictly to the laws of honor: that he was false to honor.* In writing the present chapter, I have always used the word *honor* in this last sense.

Each of these associations forms, as it were, a distinct species within the human genus, and even though they do not differ essentially from the mass of men, they hold themselves somewhat apart and feel needs that belong to them alone. These are special needs that modify in a certain way and within certain countries the manner in which one thinks about human actions and the judgment of worth that it is proper to make of them.

The general and permanent interest of mankind is that men not kill one another; but it may happen that it is the particular and momentary interest of a people or class to justify and even honor homicide.

Honor is nothing other than this particular rule founded upon a particular state by means of which a people or class distributes blame or praise.

There is nothing more sterile for the human mind than an abstract idea. I hasten therefore to recur to facts. One example will bring out my thought.

I will choose the most extraordinary species of honor that has ever appeared in the world, and which we know the best: the aristocratic honor born in the bosom of feudal society. I will explain it by means of the preceding thought, and I will explain the preceding thought by means of it.

I do not have to investigate here when and how the aristocracy of the Middle Ages had come into being, why it had separated itself so profoundly from the rest of the nation, and what had founded and consolidated its power. I find it already standing, and I seek to understand why it considered most human actions in such a particular light.

What strikes me first is that, in the feudal world, actions were not always praised or blamed on account of their intrinsic value, but it sometimes happened that their worth was judged exclusively in relation to the one who was their author or their object, which is repugnant to the general conscience of mankind. Certain acts which dishonored a nobleman were thus of no consequence when done by a commoner; others changed character depending upon whether the person who suffered them belonged to the aristocracy or existed outside of it.

When these different opinions originated, the nobility formed a body [240] apart, in the midst of the people, which it ruled from the inaccessible heights to which it had withdrawn itself. In order to maintain this particular position which constituted its power, it not only had need of political privileges: it needed virtues and vices for its own use.

That some particular virtue or some particular vice belonged to the nobility rather than the commonalty, that some particular action was of no consequence when its object was a commoner, or condemnable when it involved a noble, was often arbitrary; but that honor or shame were accorded to the actions of a man depending upon his condition resulted from the very constitution of an aristocratic society. This has been visible, in fact, in all countries that have had an aristocracy. To the extent that there remains a single vestige of it, these peculiarities reappear: to corrupt a girl of color hardly harms the reputation of an American man; to marry her dishonors him.

In some cases, feudal honor demanded vengeance and condemned forgiveness of insults; in others, it imperiously commanded men to conquer themselves; it ordered the forgetting of oneself. It did not make a law of humanity or of gentleness; it extolled generosity; it prized liberality more than charity; it allowed one to gain riches by gambling, by war, but not by work; it preferred great crimes to small profits. Greed revolted it less than miserliness, violence often pleased it, whereas trickery and betrayal always appeared contemptible to it.

These bizarre notions did not arise exclusively from the caprice of those who had conceived them.

A class that has succeeded in placing itself at the head of and above all the others and that makes constant efforts to maintain itself in this supreme rank must especially honor the virtues that possess grandeur and brilliance and that can be combined easily with pride and love of power. It does not fear upsetting the natural order of the conscience in order to place those virtues ahead of all the others. It is even understandable that it readily raises certain daring and brilliant vices above some peaceful and modest virtues. It is in a way constrained to do so by its condition.

Ahead of all the virtues, and in place of a great number of them, the nobles of the Middle Ages put military courage.

This again was a singular opinion which arose necessarily from the singularity of the social state.

[241]   The feudal aristocracy came into being by war and for war; it had discovered its power in arms, and it maintained it by arms; nothing was therefore more necessary to it than military courage, and it was natural for it to glorify it above all the rest. Everything that manifested this virtue to the outside world, even if at the expense of reason and humanity, was therefore approved and often commanded by it. The caprice of men only reappeared in the details.

Whether a man regarded a blow on the cheek as an enormous insult and was obliged to kill in single combat the one who had thus lightly struck him was something arbitrary; but that a noble could not peacefully receive an insult and was dishonored if he allowed himself to be struck without giving combat flowed from the very principles and needs of a military aristocracy.

It was thus true, up to a certain point, to say that honor had a capricious appearance; but the caprices of honor were always confined within certain necessary limits. This particular rule, called honor by our ancestors, is so far from appearing to me to be an arbitrary law that I would readily undertake to connect its most incoherent and most bizarre dictates to a small number of fixed and invariable needs of feudal societies.

If I followed honor into the political sphere, I would not have more difficulty explaining its movements there.

The social state and political institutions of the Middle Ages were such that the national power during that period never directly governed the citizens. This power did not, in a manner of speaking, exist in their eyes; each one only knew some one man to whom he was obliged to give obedience. It was through that man that, without knowing it, he was connected to all the others. In feudal societies, the whole public order thus rested on the sentiment of fidelity to the very person of the lord. Were that destroyed, one fell immediately into anarchy.

Fidelity to the political chief was in addition a sentiment whose value all the members of the aristocracy perceived every day, for each of them was at the same time lord and vassal, and had to command as well as obey.

To remain faithful to one's lord, to sacrifice oneself for him if necessary, to share his fortune whether good or bad, to help him in his undertakings no matter what they were, these were the first dictates of feudal honor as regards politics. The infidelity of the vassal was condemned by opinion with an extraordinary severity. A particularly heinous name was created for it: it was called *felony*.

On the contrary, one finds in the Middle Ages few traces of a passion that shaped the life of the societies of antiquity. I mean to speak of patri- [242] otism. The very name of patriotism is not old in our idiom.[2]

Feudal institutions concealed the fatherland from view; they made love of it less necessary. They made men forget the nation by attaching them powerfully to a single man. For this reason feudal honor never made it a strict law to remain faithful to one's country.

It is not that love of the fatherland did not exist in the hearts of our ancestors; but it only formed a sort of weak and obscure instinct there, which became clearer and stronger as classes were destroyed and power centralized.

This is well shown by the contrary judgments that the peoples of Europe make about the different deeds of their history depending upon the generation that judges them. What dishonored the constable of Bourbon most in the eyes of his contemporaries is that he bore arms against

---

2. The word *fatherland* itself is only found in French authors beginning in the 16th century.

his king; what dishonors him most in our eyes is that he made war on his country. We condemn those deeds as much as our ancestors but for other reasons.

I chose feudal honor in order to make my thought clear because the traits of feudal honor are more and better marked than any other; I might have chosen my example elsewhere, but I would have arrived at the same point by another path.

Although we know the Romans less well than our ancestors, we nevertheless know that there existed among them, with respect to glory and dishonor, particular opinions that did not follow exclusively from general notions of good and evil. Many human actions were considered in a different light then, depending upon whether it involved a citizen or a foreigner, a free man or a slave; certain vices were glorified, and certain virtues were elevated above all the others.

"Now, in that time," says Plutarch in the life of Coriolanus, "the heroic exploit was honored and prized in Rome above all other virtues. This is proven by the fact that it was called *virtus*, the name of virtue itself, by assigning the name of the common genus to one particular species. So much so that virtue in Latin was as much as to say valor." Who does not recognize here the particular need of that singular association which was formed for the conquest of the world?

Every nation will offer analogous observations; for just as I have said above, every time men are brought together in a particular society, an idea of honor is immediately established among them, that is to say a [243] whole body of opinions that is proper to them about what must be praised or blamed; and these particular rules always have their source in the particular habits and the particular interests of the association.

This is applicable, to a certain extent, to democratic societies just like the others. We will again find proof of this among the Americans.[3]

One still finds scattered among the opinions of the Americans some notions detached from the old European aristocratic conception of honor. These traditional opinions are very few in number; they have shallow roots and little power. This is a religion some of whose temples were allowed to survive but in which one no longer believes.

In the midst of these half-effaced notions of an exotic honor, some new opinions appear which constitute what might be called in our day the American idea of honor.

I have shown how the Americans were pushed unceasingly toward

3. I am speaking here of the Americans who inhabit the country where slavery does not exist. These are the only ones who are capable of offering the complete picture of a democratic society.

commerce and industry. Their origin, their social state, their political institutions, the very place they inhabit carries them irresistibly in this direction. They thus form, at present, an association almost exclusively industrial and commercial, placed in the midst of a new and immense country whose exploitation is its principal object. This is the characteristic trait that today most particularly distinguishes the American people from all others.

All the quiet virtues that tend to give a regular bearing to the social body and to promote business are therefore bound to be especially honored among this people and cannot be neglected without falling into public contempt.

All the unruly virtues that often throw out dazzling light but still more often disturbance into the society, on the contrary occupy in the opinion of this same people a secondary rank. They may be neglected without losing the esteem of one's fellow citizens, and one would perhaps run the risk of losing it by acquiring them.

The Americans do not make a less arbitrary ranking among the vices.

There are certain inclinations that are condemnable in the eyes of the general reason and common conscience of mankind, which turn out to be in accord with the particular and momentary needs of the American association; and it reproves them only weakly, and sometimes it praises them. I will cite particularly the love of wealth and the secondary inclinations that are attached to it. In order to clear, make fertile, and trans- [244] form this vast uninhabited continent that is his domain, the American must have the daily support of an energetic passion. This passion can only be the love of wealth. The passion for wealth is therefore not condemned in America, and provided that it does not go beyond the limits that public order assigns it, it is honored. The American calls a noble and estimable ambition what our ancestors in the Middle Ages called servile greed; just as he gives the name blind and barbaric furor to the passion for conquest and the warlike temper that sent them every day into new combats.

In the United States, fortunes are destroyed and recovered easily. The country is without limits and full of inexhaustible resources. The people has all the needs and appetites of a being that is growing, and no matter what efforts he makes, he is always surrounded by more goods than he can grasp. What is to be feared among such a people is not the ruin of some individuals, soon repaired: it is the inactivity and apathy* of all. Daring in industrial enterprises is the first cause of its rapid progress, its

---

* The word translated as "apathy" is *mollesse,* which derives from *mou (f. molle),* "soft" (also "limp," "flabby"), and can also be translated as "weakness" or "softness."

strength, its grandeur. Industry is for it like a vast lottery where a small number of men lose each day but where the State gains continually; such a people is therefore bound to view with favor and to honor daring as regards industry. Now, every daring enterprise puts at risk the fortune of the one who engages in it and of all those who trust in him. The Americans, who make a sort of virtue of commercial boldness, cannot, in any case, condemn those who are bold.

This is why in the United States such remarkable indulgence is shown for the merchant who goes bankrupt: the honor of the latter does not suffer from such a mishap. In this, the Americans differ not only from the European peoples but from all the commercial nations of our time; nor therefore do they resemble any of them in their position and their needs.

In America, all the vices that are liable to degrade the purity of morals and destroy marriage are treated with a severity unknown in the rest of the world. That contrasts oddly, at first sight, with the tolerance that is shown there in other matters. It is surprising to find in the same people a morality so relaxed and so austere.

These things are not as inconsistent as is supposed. Public opinion, in the United States, suppresses only feebly the love of wealth, which serves the industrial grandeur and prosperity of the nation; and it particularly condemns bad morals, which distract the human mind from the pursuit of well-being and disturb the internal order of the family, so necessary to the success of business affairs. In order to be esteemed by their [245] fellows, the Americans are thus constrained to submit themselves to regular habits. It is in this sense that one may say that they place their honor in being chaste.*

The American idea of honor is in agreement with the former idea of honor in Europe on one point: it places courage at the head of the virtues, and in fact as the greatest of moral necessities for man; but it does not envisage courage from the same point of view.

In the United States, martial valor is little prized; the courage that is best known and most esteemed is that which makes men brave the wrath of the ocean in order to arrive at port sooner, bear without complaint the miseries, and the solitude, more cruel than all the miseries, of the wilderness; the courage which renders men almost insensible to the reversal suffered by a fortune painfully acquired, and immediately suggests new efforts to build up a new one. Courage of this kind is principally necessary to the maintenance and the prosperity of the American

---

* The word translated as "chaste" is *chastes*. Someone who is *chaste* abstains from all pleasures judged illicit (not just sexual ones).

association, and it is particularly honored and glorified by it. One cannot show that one lacks it, without dishonor.

There is one last trait that will finish bringing out clearly the idea of this chapter.

In a democratic society like that of the United States, where fortunes are small and not very secure, everyone works, and work leads to everything. This has turned honor around and directed it against idleness.

In America I have sometimes met men who were rich, young, by temperament averse to any difficult effort, and who were forced to take up a trade. Their nature and their fortune permitted them to remain idle; public opinion absolutely forbid them to do so, and they had to obey it. I have often seen, on the contrary, in the European nations where aristocracy still struggles against the torrent that is sweeping it along, I have seen, I say, men continually goaded by their needs and desires, who remain in a state of idleness in order not to lose the esteem of their peers and who yield more easily to boredom and embarrassment than to work.

Who does not see in these two obligations, so opposed to one another, two different rules, both of which, however, emanate from the idea of honor?

What our ancestors called honor par excellence was, in truth, only one of its forms. They gave a generic name to what was only a particular species. Honor thus reappears in democratic times as in aristocratic times. But it will not be difficult to show that in those times it presents a different physiognomy.

Not only are its dictates different; we will see that they are fewer in [246] number and less clear and that its laws are followed more weakly.*

A caste is always in a much more peculiar situation than a people. There is nothing more exceptional in the world than a small society composed always of the same families, like the aristocracy of the Middle Ages, for example, and whose object is to concentrate and retain within itself, exclusively and hereditarily, enlightenment, wealth, and power.

Now, the more the position of a society is exceptional, the more numerous are its special needs and the more its notions of honor, which correspond to its needs, increase.

The dictates of honor will therefore be fewer in a people that is not divided into castes than in another. If nations are ever established in which it is even hard to find any classes, honor will be limited there to a small number of precepts, and these precepts will be less and less distant from the moral laws adopted by the generality of mankind.

---

* The words translated as "more weakly" are *plus mollement. Mollement*—"without vigor or energy"—is the adverbial form of *mou (f. molle)*. See the note at [244].

Thus the dictates of honor will be less bizzare and less numerous in a democratic nation than in an aristocracy.

They will also be more obscure; this necessarily results from the foregoing.

The characteristic traits of honor being fewer in number and less unusual, it is often bound to be difficult to discern them.

There are still other reasons.

In the aristocratic nations of the Middle Ages, generations succeeded one another without effect; each family was like an immortal and permanently immobile man; the ideas varied hardly more than the conditions.

Every man therefore always had the same objects before his eyes, which he considered from the same point of view; his sight gradually penetrated into the smallest details, and his perception could not fail, in the long run, to become clear and distinct. In this way, men in feudal times not only had very extraordinary opinions that constituted their idea of honor, but each of these opinions took shape in their mind within a clear and precise form.

It cannot ever be like this in a country like America where all the citizens are in restless motion; where the society, modifying itself every day, changes its opinions with its needs. In such a country, one catches a glimpse of the rule of honor, but one rarely has the leisure to consider it in a settled fashion.

Were the society immobile, it would still be difficult to settle the meaning that ought to be given to the word honor in it.

[247]   In the Middle Ages, since each class possessed its own idea of honor, the same opinion was never accepted at the same time by a very great number of men. This allowed it to be given a settled and precise form, all the more so because all those who accepted it, having a perfectly identical and very exceptional position, were naturally disposed to agree on the dictates of a law that had been made for them alone.

Honor thus became a complete and detailed code in which everything was anticipated and prescribed in advance and which offered a fixed and always visible rule for human actions. In a democratic nation like America, where the ranks are merged together and the entire society forms only a single mass, all of whose elements are analogous without being entirely alike, it is impossible ever to agree in advance on exactly what is permitted and forbidden by honor.

There indeed exist, in this people, certain national needs that give rise to common opinions as regards honor, but such opinions never present themselves to the minds of all the citizens at the same time, in the same manner and with equal force; the law of honor exists, but it often lacks interpreters.

The confusion is much greater still in a democratic country like ours, where the different classes that composed the old society, coming to be mixed up with one another without having been able yet to merge completely, every day introduce into each other's midst their different and often opposed notions of honor; where each man, following his whims, abandons one portion of the opinions of his ancestors and retains the other; so that in the midst of so many arbitrary measurements of value, a common rule can never be established. Then, it is almost impossible to say in advance which actions will be honored or condemned. These are miserable times, but they do not last.

In democratic nations, honor, since it is poorly defined, is necessarily less powerful, for it is difficult to apply with certainty and firmness a law that is imperfectly known. Since public opinion, which is the natural and supreme interpreter of the law of honor, does not see clearly in what direction it is advisable to make blame or praise incline, it only pronounces its judgment with hesitation. Sometimes it happens to contradict itself; often it sits still and lets matters take their course.

The relative weakness of honor in democracies also results from several other causes.

In aristocratic countries, the same idea of honor is always accepted only by a certain number of men, often limited in number and always separated from the rest of their fellow men. Honor is thus easily mixed [248] up and united, in their mind, with the idea of everything that sets them apart. It appears to them as the distinctive trait of their physiognomy; they apply its rules with all the ardor of personal interest, and they put, if I can express myself thus, passion into obeying it.

This truth is manifested very clearly when one reads the codes of customs of the Middle Ages, in the article on trial by combat. One sees there that the nobles were obligated, in their quarrels, to use the lance and the sword, whereas the commoners made use of the staff among themselves, "inasmuch," add the customs, *"as the commoners do not have honor."* This does not mean, as we imagine today, that these men were contemptible; it signifies only that their actions were not judged according to the same rules as those of the aristocracy.

What is surprising, at first sight, is that when honor reigns with this full power, its dictates are very strange, so that it seems to be obeyed better in proportion as it appears further removed from reason; from which the conclusion is sometimes drawn that honor was strong precisely because of its extravagance.

These two things have, in fact, the same origin; but they do not flow from one another.

Honor is bizarre to the degree that it represents needs that are more particular and felt by a smaller number of men; and it is because it represents needs of this kind that it is strong. Honor therefore is not powerful because it is bizarre; but it is bizarre and powerful due to the same cause.

I will make another observation.

Among aristocratic peoples, all ranks are different, but all ranks are fixed; everyone occupies within his sphere a place he cannot leave and where he lives in the midst of other men around him who are fixed in the same way. In these nations, therefore, no one can hope or fear not to be seen; there is no man placed so low who has not his stage, and who will escape blame or praise by virtue of his obscurity.

In democratic states, on the contrary, where all the citizens are merged together in the same crowd and are constantly moving about restlessly there, public opinion has no point to get hold of; its object disappears at each instant and eludes it. Honor will always be less imperious and exercise less pressure there, for honor is only effective in view of the public, unlike simple virtue, which subsists on itself and is content to be its own witness.

If the reader has grasped well all of the foregoing, he must have understood that there exists, between the inequality of conditions and what [249] we have called honor, a tight and necessary relation which, if I am not mistaken, had not hitherto been clearly pointed out. I must therefore make a final effort to shed light on it well.

A nation sets itself apart within mankind. Independently of certain general needs inherent in mankind, it has its particular interests and needs. Certain opinions regarding praise and blame that are proper to it and that its citizens call honor are immediately established within it.

Within this same nation, a caste comes to be established which, separating itself in its turn from all the other classes, acquires particular needs, and those, in their turn, give rise to particular opinions. The honor of this caste, a strange composite of the particular notions of the nation and of the still more particular notions of the caste, will be as far removed as it is possible to imagine from the simple and general opinions of men. Having reached the extreme point, let us go back down.

Ranks are mixed up together, privileges are abolished. The men who compose the nation having become once more alike and equal, their interests and needs merge, and all the singular notions that each caste called honor vanish one after another. Honor no longer flows from anything other than the particular needs of the nation itself; it represents the nation's individuality among peoples.

Finally, if one may suppose that all the races are merged together and that all the peoples in the world come to have at this point the same interests, the same needs, and to no longer distinguish themselves from one another by means of any characteristic trait, a conventional value would completely cease to be attributed to human actions; all would consider them in the same light; the general needs of humanity, which the conscience reveals to each man, would be the common measure. Then one would no longer encounter in this world anything except simple and general notions of good and evil, to which ideas of praise and blame would become attached by a natural and necessary connection.

Thus, to condense finally my whole thought into a single phrase: it is the differences and the inequalities of men that have created honor; it weakens as these differences are effaced, and it will disappear with them.

CHAPTER 19   [250]

WHY THERE ARE SO MANY AMBITIOUS MEN AND SO FEW GREAT AMBITIONS IN THE UNITED STATES

The first thing that strikes one in the United States is the countless multitude of those who seek to escape their original condition, and the second is the small number of great ambitions that reveal themselves in the midst of this universal motion of ambition. There are no Americans who do not show themselves to be consumed by the desire to rise; but one sees almost none who appear to nourish very vast hopes, nor to aim very high. All want constantly to acquire goods, reputation, power; few conceive of all these things on a grand scale. And at first glance that is surprising, since there is nothing noticeable either in the mores or in the laws of America that ought to limit desires and prevent them from taking flight in all directions.

It seems difficult to attribute this remarkable state of things to the equality of conditions, because when this same equality was established among us, it immediately caused a flowering of almost unlimited ambitions. I nevertheless believe that it is principally in the social state and the democratic mores of the Americans that one must seek its cause.

Every revolution increases the ambition of men. That is above all true of the revolution that overturns an aristocracy.

When the former barriers that separated the masses from fame and power are suddenly lowered, there occurs a movement of impetuous and universal ascent toward those long-envied splendors whose enjoyment is finally permitted. In this initial exhilaration of victory, nothing seems impossible to anyone. Not only are desires without limits, the power to satisfy them has almost none. In the midst of this general and sudden renovation of customs and laws, in this vast confusion of all men and all rules, citizens rise and fall with unprecedented rapidity, and power passes so quickly from hand to hand that no one need despair of getting hold of it in his turn.

[251]   One must also remember that the men who destroy an aristocracy have lived under its laws; they have seen its splendors, and they have allowed themselves to be penetrated, without knowing it, by the sentiments and ideas that it had conceived. Thus, at the moment that an aristocracy dissolves, its spirit still hangs over the mass of men, and its instincts are conserved for a long time after it has been vanquished.

Ambitions therefore always prove to be very great as long as the democratic revolution lasts. This will still be the case for some time after it has ended.

The recollection of the extraordinary events that they have witnessed is not erased from the memory of men in one day. The passions that the revolution has evoked do not disappear with it. The feeling of instability perpetuates itself in the midst of order. The idea of the ease of success survives the strange vicissitudes that had produced it. The desires remain vast even though the means of satisfying them diminish daily. The taste for great fortunes persists, even though great fortunes become rare, and everywhere disproportionate and thwarted ambitions are aroused that consume, secretly and fruitlessly, the hearts that contain them.

The last traces of struggle nonetheless gradually disappear. The remnants of aristocracy finally disappear. The great events that accompanied its fall are forgotten. Calm succeeds war, the sovereignty of convention is reborn within the bosom of the new world; desires proportion themselves to means; needs, ideas, and sentiments are linked together; men complete the process of becoming equal with one another: democratic society is finally established.

If we consider a democratic people arrived at this permanent and normal state, it will present us with a spectacle very different from the one we have just looked at, and we will easily conclude that if ambition becomes great while conditions are becoming equal, it loses this character when they are equal.

Since great fortunes are broken up, and knowledge is widespread, no one is completely deprived of enlightenment or property. Since the privileges and disqualifications of class are abolished, and men have broken forever the ties that kept them immobile, the idea of progress presents itself to the mind of each of them; the desire to rise is born in all hearts at once; every man wants to escape his place. Ambition is the universal sentiment.

But if the equality of conditions gives some resources to all citizens, it prevents any one of them from having very extensive resources, which necessarily confines desires within rather narrow limits. Among democratic peoples, ambition is thus ardent and constant, but it usually cannot [252] aim very high, and life there is ordinarily passed in coveting with ardor small objects that one sees within one's reach.

What especially turns men in democracies away from great ambition is not the meagerness of their wealth, but the fierce effort that they make every day to increase it. They force their soul to employ all its strength in order to accomplish mediocre things: something that cannot fail to soon limit their view and circumscribe their power. They might be much poorer and retain larger souls.

The small number of opulent citizens that are found in a democracy are not an exception to this rule. A man who rises by degrees toward wealth and power contracts, in this lengthy effort, habits of prudence and restraint that he is afterward unable to lose. One does not gradually enlarge one's soul as if it were one's house.

An analogous remark is applicable to the sons of this same man. They are born, it is true, into a high position, but their parents were humble. They have grown up in the midst of sentiments and ideas from which it is afterward difficult for them to escape; and one must believe that they will inherit their father's instincts along with his property.

It may happen, on the contrary, that the poorest offshoot of a powerful aristocracy displays a vast ambition because the traditional opinions of his stock and the general spirit of his caste keep him for some time yet above the level of his wealth.

What also prevents men in democratic times from easily abandoning themselves to the ambition for great things is the time that they foresee must pass before they are in a position to undertake them. "It is a great advantage," said Pascal, "that title puts a man, from the age of eighteen or twenty, in a position to succeed that another might be in at fifty; that is thirty years gained without effort." Those thirty years are ordinarily lacking to ambitions in democracies. Equality, which gives to everyone the capability of achieving everything, prevents them from doing so quickly.

In a democratic society, as elsewhere, there are only a certain number of great fortunes to be made; and since the careers that lead to them are open without distinction to every citizen, the progress of all is bound to be slowed. Since the candidates appear more or less alike, and since it is difficult to make a choice among them without violating the principle of equality, which is the supreme law of democratic societies, the first idea that presents itself is to make them all move forward at the same pace and put them all through trials.

[253]   To the degree, therefore, that men become more alike and that the principle of equality penetrates more peacefully and more profoundly into institutions and mores, the rules of advancement become more inflexible and advancement more slow. The difficulty of arriving quickly at a certain degree of grandeur increases.

Out of hatred of privilege and perplexity over choosing, all men, whatever their stature, are obliged to pass through the same channels, and they are all subjected without distinction to a multitude of petty preliminary exercises, in the midst of which their youth is spent and their imagination extinguished, so that they despair of ever being able to fully enjoy the goods that are proffered to them, and when they are finally in a position to accomplish extraordinary things, they have lost the desire for them.

In China, where the equality of conditions is very great and very ancient, a man passes from one public office to another only after having submitted to a competitive examination. He encounters this test at each step of his career, and the idea of it has so well entered into the mores that I remember having read a Chinese novel in which the hero, after many trials and tribulations, finally touches the heart of his mistress by passing an examination. Great ambitions do not breathe easily in such an atmosphere.

What I am saying about politics extends to all things: equality produces the same effects everywhere. Where the law does not take it upon itself to regulate and slow the progress of men, competition suffices to do so.

In a well-established democratic society, great and rapid rises are therefore rare; they are exceptions to the common rule. It is their exceptional character that makes one forget their small number.

Men in democracies end up glimpsing all these things. They at length perceive that the lawmaker opens an unlimited field before them, in which they may easily make a few strides but which no one may flatter himself to move through quickly. Between them and the vast and ultimate object of their desires, they see a multitude of small intermediate barriers that they must slowly get over; this perspective tires their ambition in advance and discourages it. They therefore give up these distant and dubious aspirations in order to seek near to themselves for less high and more accessible pleasures. The law does not limit their horizon, but they constrict it themselves.

I have said that great ambitions are rarer in democratic times than in aristocratic times. I will add that when, despite these natural obstacles, they succeed in coming into being, they have a different physiognomy.

[254]   In aristocracies, the path open to ambition is often wide, but its limits are fixed. In democratic countries, it ordinarily moves within a narrow field; but if it succeeds in going outside it, it appears as if there is no

longer anything to limit it. Since the men in it are weak, isolated, and changeable, and since precedents have little force and laws short duration, resistance to new things is weak, and the social body never appears very erect or firm on its foundation. So that when ambitious men once have power in their hands, they believe they can dare to do anything; and when it eludes them, they immediately think about overturning the State in order to take it back.

This gives great political ambition a violent and revolutionary character that it rarely has, to the same extent, in aristocratic societies.

A multitude of very sensible modest ambitions, in the midst of which a few great disorderly desires spring forth from time to time: such is the spectacle ordinarily presented by democratic nations. A proportionate, moderate, and vast ambition is scarcely ever encountered there.

I have shown elsewhere by what secret force equality makes predominate, in the human heart, the passion for material pleasures and the exclusive love of the present. These different instincts mix with the sentiment of ambition and tint it, so to speak, with their colors.

I think that ambitious men in democracies are less preoccupied than any others with the interests and judgments of the future. The present moment alone occupies and absorbs them. They complete many undertakings rapidly, rather than erecting a few very lasting monuments. They love success much more than glory. What they demand of men above all is obedience. What they want above all is power. Their moral habits almost always remain less high than their social rank, which very often causes them to bring very vulgar tastes to an extraordinary level of wealth and to seem to have risen to supreme power only in order to more easily obtain for themselves small and crude pleasures.

I believe that in our time it is necessary to purify, control, and make proportionate the sentiment of ambition but that it would be very dangerous to try to weaken and suppress it excessively. It is necessary to try to place some ultimate limits upon it in advance, which it will never be permitted to exceed. But one must guard against hindering its flight too much within the permitted limits.

I confess that, for democratic societies, I fear the audaciousness of desires much less than their mediocrity. What seems to me most to be feared is that, in the midst of the constant small occupations of private [255] life, ambition will lose its impetus and its grandeur, and that the human passions will become at the same time milder and lower, so that the bearing of the social body will become every day more tranquil and less high.

I think, therefore, that the leaders of these new societies would be wrong to want to lull their citizens to sleep in a too smooth and too calm contentment, and that it is good to sometimes give them some difficult and dangerous business in order to elevate ambition and open up a theater for it.

The moralists constantly complain that the preferred vice of our time is pride.

That is true in one sense: there is no one, in fact, who does not believe he is better than his neighbor and no one who consents to obey his superior. But it is very false in another: for this same man, who cannot tolerate either subordination or equality, nonetheless despises himself to the point of believing himself to be made only for enjoying vulgar pleasures. He willingly comes to a stop in mediocre desires without daring to embark on high undertakings: he scarcely imagines them.

Therefore, far from believing that humility must be recommended to our contemporaries, I would wish every effort to be made to give them a more ample idea of themselves and of their kind. Humility is not healthy for them. What they lack most, in my opinion, is pride. I would gladly trade several of our petty virtues for this vice.

· · ·

[258]

CHAPTER 21

WHY GREAT REVOLUTIONS WILL BECOME RARE

A people who lives for centuries under the regime of castes and classes attains a democratic social state only after a long succession of more or less painful transformations, by means of violent efforts, and after numerous vicissitudes during which wealth, opinions, and power change position rapidly.

Even when this great revolution is brought to a close, the revolutionary habits created by it still survive for a long time, and profound disturbances follow upon it.

Since all this occurs at the moment when conditions are becoming more equal, it is concluded from this that there exists a hidden relation and a secret connection between equality itself and revolutions, so that the first cannot exist without the latter occurring.

On this point, the reasoning seems to agree with experience.

Among a people where ranks are more or less equal, no apparent tie unites men and holds them firmly to their place. No one among them has either the permanent right or the power to command, and none are obligated to obey by virtue of their social rank; but each one, finding himself provided with some enlightenment and some resources, can choose his way and go forward apart from all his fellows.

The same causes that make the citizens independent of one another push them every day toward new and restless desires and constantly goad them on.

It thus seems natural to believe that, in a democratic society, ideas, things, and men must perpetually change form and place and that democratic times will be times of rapid and unceasing transformations.

Is that in fact the case? Does equality of conditions lead men in a habitual and permanent manner toward revolutions? Does it contain some principle of perturbation that prevents society from establishing itself on a solid base and disposes its citizens to constantly renovate their laws, [259] their doctrines, and their mores? I do not believe it. The subject is important; I beg the reader to follow me well.

Almost all the revolutions that have changed the face of peoples have been made in order to consecrate or to destroy inequality. Put aside the secondary causes that have produced great human unheavals, and you will almost always end up with inequality. It is the poor who have tried to take away the wealth of the rich, or the rich who have tried to enslave the poor. If, therefore, you can found a state of society in which everyone has something to conserve and little to take, you will have done much for the peace of the world.

I am not unaware that, among a great democratic people, there are always very poor and very rich citizens; but the poor, instead of composing the vast majority of the nation as always happens in aristocratic societies, are few in number, and the law has not attached them to one another through the bonds of an irremediable and hereditary poverty.

The rich, on their side, are sparse and powerless; they do not have privileges that attract attention; their very wealth, no longer bound up in the earth and represented by it, is intangible and, as it were, invisible. In the same way that there are no longer races of poor men, there are no longer races of rich men; the latter emerge every day from the depths of the crowd and constantly return to it. They therefore do not form a class apart that may be easily defined and despoiled; and since they are, in addition, attached to the mass of their fellow citizens by a thousand secret threads, the people can hardly strike them without harming itself. Between these two extremes of democratic societies there is a numberless multitude of men who are nearly alike, who, without being precisely either rich or poor, possess enough wealth to want order and not enough to provoke envy.

These latter are naturally averse to violent upheavals; their immobility keeps everything above and below them in a state of rest and steadies the social body on its foundation.

It is not that the latter are themselves satisfied by their present fortune nor that they feel natural horror for a revolution whose spoils they would share in without experiencing its evils. On the contrary, they desire, with an unequaled passion, to get rich, but the perplexity is to know whom to despoil. The same social state that constantly evokes desires in them contains these desires within unavoidable limits. It gives men more liberty to change and less interest in changing.

Not only do democratic men not naturally desire revolutions, but they fear them.

[260]   There is no revolution that does not more or less threaten acquired property. The majority of those who inhabit democratic countries are proprietors; they not only have properties, they live in the condition in which men attach the greatest value to their property.

If one considers carefully each of the classes that compose the society, it is easy to see that there are none in which the passions that property brings into being are more fierce and more tenacious than among the middle classes.

Often the poor do not worry much about what they possess because they suffer from what they lack much more than they enjoy the little they have. The rich have many other passions to satisfy than that of wealth, and, in addition, the long and tiring usage of a great fortune sometimes ends up making them almost insensible to its pleasures.

But the men who live in a state of prosperity equally far removed from opulence and poverty place an immense value upon their possessions. Since they are still very near to poverty, they see its rigors close up, and they dread them; between it and them, there is nothing but a small patrimony on which they immediately fix their fears and their hopes. At every moment, they take a greater interest in it because of the constant cares it gives them, and they are attached to it by the daily efforts they make to increase it. The idea of giving up the least portion of it is intolerable, and they consider its entire loss as the ultimate misfortune. Now, it is the number of these passionate and restless small proprietors that the equality of conditions constantly increases.

Thus, in democratic societies, the majority of citizens does not see clearly what they might gain from a revolution, and they feel at every moment, and in a thousand ways, what they might lose by it.

I have described, in another part of this work, how the equality of conditions naturally pushes men toward industrial and commercial careers and how it increases and diversifies property in land. I have shown, finally, how it inspires in each man an ardent and constant desire to increase his well-being. There is nothing more contrary to revolutionary passions than all these things.

It may happen that the final result of a revolution serves industry and commerce; but its first effect will almost always be to ruin the manufacturers and merchants because it cannot fail initially to change the general state of consumption and temporarily reverse the ratio that existed between production and needs.

Besides, I know of nothing more opposed to revolutionary moral habits than commercial moral habits. Commerce is naturally hostile to [261] all violent passions. It loves well-tempered expedients, takes pleasure in compromises, and takes great care to avoid anger. It is patient, flexible, ingratiating, and it does not recur to extreme measures except when the most absolute necessity obliges it to do so. Commerce makes men independent of one another; it gives them a lofty idea of their individual worth; it leads them to want to create their own businesses and teaches them to succeed in them; it thus disposes them to liberty, but it pushes them away from revolutions.

In a revolution, the possessors of personal property have more to fear than all the others; for, on the one hand, their property is often easy to seize, and, on the other hand, it can at any moment disappear completely, something which is less to be feared by landed proprietors, who, while losing the revenue from their lands, hope at least to keep, through the trials and tribulations, the land itself. Therefore we see that the former are far more frightened than the latter of the sight of revolutionary movements.

Peoples are thus less disposed to revolutions to the extent that, among them, personal property is multiplied and diversified and the number of those who possess it increases.

In addition, no matter what occupation men take up, and no matter what kind of property they possess, they all have one trait in common.

No one is fully satisfied with his present fortune, and all make great efforts every day, by a thousand different means, to increase it. Consider each one of them at any time in his life, and you will see him preoccupied with some new plans whose object is to increase his prosperity. Do not talk to him about the interests and rights of mankind; this small family enterprise absorbs for the moment all his thoughts and makes him wish to put off public agitations to another time.

This not only prevents men from making revolutions, but turns them away from wanting to make them. Violent political passions have little hold on men who have thus tied their whole soul to the pursuit of well-being. The ardor that they put into small affairs leaves them without any passion for great ones.

There arise, it is true, from time to time, in democratic societies, enterprising and ambitious citizens, whose immense desires cannot satisfy

themselves by following the common path. These men love revolutions
and call for them; but they have great difficulty in bringing them about
unless exceptional events come to their aid.

One does not struggle with advantage against the spirit of one's time
and one's country; and one man, however powerful he is assumed to be,
[262] has a hard time making his contemporaries share sentiments and ideas
that are repellent to the whole body of their desires and sentiments. It is
not plausible, therefore, that once equality of conditions, having become
a long-standing and uncontested fact, imparts its character to moral habits, men will easily allow themselves to rush into dangers by following a
rash leader or a daring innovator.

It is not that they resist him in an overt manner, with the help of skillful maneuvers or even by means of a premeditated intention to resist.
They do not oppose him with any energy, sometimes they even applaud
him, but they do not follow him. To his ardor, they secretly oppose their
inertia; to his revolutionary instincts, their conservative interests, their
stay-at-home tastes to his adventure-loving passions; their common
sense to the excesses of his genius; to his poetry, their prose. With great
effort he arouses them for a moment, but they soon slip from his grasp
and, as if dragged down by their own weight, they fall away again. He
exhausts himself trying to animate this indifferent and distracted crowd,
and he finally sees himself reduced to impotence, not because he is vanquished but because he is alone.

I do not claim that the men who live in democratic societies are naturally immobile; I think, on the contrary, that a perpetual movement prevails within such a society and that no one there knows any rest; but I
believe that men there move about restlessly within certain limits that
they hardly ever overstep. Every day they vary, modify, or change secondary things; they take great care not to touch the principal ones. They
love change, but they dread revolutions.

Although the Americans constantly modify or repeal some of their
laws, they are far from displaying revolutionary passions. It is easy to
see, in the promptness with which they stop and calm down when public
unrest begins to become threatening and at the very moment that passions seem most aroused, that they dread a revolution as the greatest of
misfortunes and that each of them is inwardly resolved to make great
sacrifices to avoid it. There is no country in the world where the feeling
for property is more active and more anxious than in the United States
and where the majority shows less propensity for doctrines that threaten
to alter in any way whatsoever the constitution of property.

I have often remarked that the theories that are by their nature revolutionary, in the sense that they cannot be realized except by a complete
and sometimes sudden change in the state of property and persons, are

infinitely less in favor in the United States that in the great monarchies [263] of Europe. If some men profess them, the mass rejects them with a kind of instinctive horror.

I do not fear to say that most of the maxims that we are accustomed to call democratic in France would be proscribed by the democracy of the United States. That is easy to understand. In America, one has democratic ideas and passions; in Europe, we still have revolutionary passions and ideas.

If America ever experiences great revolutions, they will be brought about by the presence of the blacks on the soil of the United States: that is to say that it will not be the equality of conditions, but on the contrary their inequality that will bring them about.

When conditions are equal, everyone readily shuts himself up within himself and forgets the public. If the legislators of the democratic peoples do not seek to correct this fatal tendency, or if they encourage it with the thought that it will divert the citizens from political passions and thus keep them away from revolutions, they may end up themselves producing the evil that they want to avoid, and a time may come when the disordered passions of some men, making use of the stupid egoism and cowardice of the majority, will end up obliging the social body to undergo unusual vicissitudes.

In democratic societies, there are scarcely any small minorities that want revolutions; but minorities may sometimes make them.

I do not say that democratic nations are shielded from revolutions; I say only that the social state of these nations does not lead them to them, but instead keeps them away from them. Democratic peoples, left to themselves, do not readily engage in great risky adventures. They are carried along toward revolutions only unwittingly. Sometimes they undergo them, but they do not make them. And I will add that when they are allowed to acquire enlightenment and experience, they do not allow themselves to make them.

I know well that in this regard public institutions themselves can do a lot; they encourage or constrain the instincts that originate in the social state. I do not thus claim, I repeat, that a people is shielded from revolutions by the sole fact that, within it, conditions are equal; but I believe that, whatever the institutions of such a people, great revolutions will always be infinitely less violent and rarer than one supposes; and I easily foresee the particular political state that, combined with equality, would render society more stable than it has ever been in our Western World.

What I have just said about events is applicable in part to ideas.

In the United States two things are astonishing: the great instability of [264] human actions and the remarkable fixedness of certain principles. The men are in constant motion, and the human mind seems almost immobile.

292   Volume Two

When an opinion has once spread out over American soil and taken root there, one would think that no power on earth could uproot it. In the United States, general doctrines as regards religion, philosophy, morality, and even politics do not change, or at least they are modified only after a hidden and often imperceptible process; the crudest prejudices are themselves effaced only with an inconceivable slowness in the midst of the frictions, repeated a thousand times, of things and of men.

I hear it said that it is in the nature and the habits of democracies to change sentiments and thoughts at any moment. That may be true of small democratic nations, like those of antiquity that were gathered together in their entirety in a public place and then stirred up at the will of an orator. I have never seen anything similar in the great democratic people that occupies the opposite banks of our ocean. What struck me in the United States is the difficulty that is experienced in disabusing the majority of an idea it has conceived and of detaching it from a man it adopts. Writings or speeches are hardly successful; only experience prevails; sometimes it is even necessary for it to be repeated.

That is surprising at first glance. A more attentive examination explains it.

I do not think that it is as easy as one imagines to uproot the prejudices of a democratic people; to change its beliefs; to substitute new religious, philosophic, political, and moral principles for those that have once been established there; in a word, to make great and frequent revolutions in their thought. It is not that the human mind is idle there; it is in constant restless motion. But it applies itself to varying infinitely the implications of known principles, and to discovering new implications, instead of seeking new principles. It turns round and round over itself with agility rather than rush forward by a rapid and direct effort. It extends its range little by little by means of continuous and hurried small movements; it does not move it all at once.

Men equal in rights, in education, in wealth, and, to say it all in one word, in a similar condition necessarily have needs, habits, and tastes that differ very little. Since they perceive objects in the same way, their mind naturally inclines toward similar ideas, and since each of them can [265] draw apart from his contemporaries and fashion his own beliefs, they end up all meeting again, unwittingly and without wishing to do so, in a certain number of common opinions.

The more I consider closely the effects of equality on the mind, the more I am persuaded that the intellectual anarchy that we are witnessing is not, as some suppose, the natural state of democratic peoples. I believe that it must instead be considered as a particular accident of their youth and that it only appears during that period of transition when men have already broken the old ties that attached them to one another and still differ enormously in their origin, education, and moral habits; so that, having retained very different ideas, instincts, and tastes, nothing any longer prevents them from making them known. The principal opinions of men become similar to the degree that conditions are similar. That appears to me to be the general and permanent fact; the rest is fortuitous and transient.

I believe that it will rarely happen that in a democratic society a man will come to conceive, all at once, a system of ideas very remote from that which his contemporaries have adopted; and if such an innovator were to appear, I think that he would at first have great difficulty in making himself listened to and even more in making himself believed.

When conditions are almost equal, one man does not easily allow himself to be persuaded by another. Since they all view each other from close up, because they have all learned together the same things and lead the same kind of life, they are not naturally disposed to take one among them for a guide and follow him blindly: someone like oneself or one's equal is hardly ever believed on his word.

It is not only the confidence in the enlightenment of some individuals that is weakened among democratic nations, as I have said elsewhere. The general idea of the intellectual superiority that any man whatsoever can acquire over all the others is not long in becoming obscured.

To the degree that men resemble each other more, the dogma of the equality of intellects insinuates itself little by little into their beliefs, and it becomes more difficult for an innovator, whoever he is, to acquire and exercise a great power over the mind of a people. In such societies, sudden intellectual revolutions are thus rare, for if one casts a glance at the history of the world, one sees that it is much less the strength of an argument than the authority of a name that has produced great and rapid changes in human opinions.

Notice also that since the men who live in democratic societies are not attached to one another by any ties, it is necessary to convince each one of them individually. Whereas in aristocratic societies it is enough [266] to be able to act on the minds of some; all the others follow. If Luther had lived in an age of equality and had not had lords and princes for an audience, he would perhaps have found it more difficult to change the face of Europe.

It is not that men in democracies are very convinced of the certainty of their opinions and very firm in their beliefs; they often have doubts that no one, in their eyes, is capable of resolving. It sometimes happens during such times that the human mind would willingly change position, but since nothing pushes it powerfully or directs it, it oscillates on itself and does not move.[1]

When one has acquired the confidence of a democratic people, it is still a difficult business to get its attention. It is very difficult to make oneself listened to by the men who live in democracies when one is not talking to them about themselves. They do not listen to the things they are told because they are always very preoccupied by the things they are doing.

There are, in fact, few idlers in democratic nations. Life there is passed in the midst of movement and commotion, and men there are so busy acting that little time is left to them for thinking. What I want above all to remark is that not only are they occupied, but their occupations interest them passionately. They are perpetually in action, and each one of their actions absorbs their soul; the fire that they put into business affairs prevents them from becoming inflamed over ideas.

[267]   I think that it is very difficult to excite the enthusiasm of a democratic people for any theory whatsoever that does not have a visible, direct, and immediate relation to the daily conduct of its life. Such a people therefore does not easily abandon its former beliefs. For it is enthusiasm that propels the human mind outside the beaten paths and that makes great intellectual revolutions as well as great political revolutions.

Thus, democratic peoples have neither the leisure nor the taste to go and seek out new opinions. Even when they come to doubt those they possess, they conserve them nonetheless because they would need too

---

1. If I look for what is the state of society most favorable to great revolutions of the mind, I find that it is somewhere betweeen the complete equality of all citizens and the absolute separation of classes.

Under the regime of castes, the generations succeed one another without the men changing position; the ones do not expect anything more, the others do not hope for anything better. The imagination goes to sleep in the midst of this silence and this univeral immobility, and the very idea of movement is no longer present to the human mind.

When classes have been abolished and conditions have become almost equal, all men are in constant restless motion, but each of them is isolated, independent, and weak. This last state differs enormously from the first. Nevertheless, it is similar in one respect. The great revolutions of the human mind are very rare there.

But between these two extremes in the history of peoples there is an intermediate age, a glorious and unsettled age, where conditions are not fixed enough for the mind to sleep and where they are unequal enough for men to exercise a very great power over the mind of one another and for some of them to be able to modify the beliefs of all. It is at this moment that powerful reformers arise and that new ideas suddenly change the face of the world.

much time and investigation in order to change them; they keep them, not as certain, but as established.

There are still other and more powerful reasons that form obstacles to any great change occurring in the doctrines of a democratic people. I have already pointed them out at the beginning of this book.

If, within such a people, individual influences are weak and almost nonexistent, the power exercised by the mass on the mind of each individual is very great. I have given the reasons for this elsewhere. What I want to say at this time is that it would be wrong to think that this depends only on the form of government and that the majority is bound to lose its intellectual influence along with its political power.

In aristocracies, men often have a greatness and a strength of their own. When they find themselves in opposition to the majority of their fellow men, they withdraw into themselves, sustain themselves and console themselves there. It is not like this among democratic peoples. Among them, public favor seems as necessary as the air that one breathes, and to be in conflict with the mass is, so to speak, to not live. The latter has no need of laws to force those who do not think like it to adapt. It is enough for it to disapprove of them. The sense of their isolation and impotence immediately overwhelms them and drives them to despair.

Whenever conditions are equal, general opinion bears down with an immense weight upon the mind of each individual; it envelops, directs, and oppresses him: that results from the very constitution of the society much more than from its political laws. To the extent that all men are more alike, each one of them feels increasingly weak in the face of all of them. Finding nothing that raises him much above them and that distinguishes him from them, he distrusts himself as soon as he conflicts with them; he not only doubts his strength, but he comes to doubt his right, and he is very close to accepting that he is wrong when the majority affirms it. The majority has no need to constrain him; it convinces him. [268]

In whatever way the powers of a democratic society are organized and balanced, it will thus be very difficult to believe what the mass of men rejects and to profess what it condemns.

This promotes wonderfully the stability of beliefs.

When an opinion takes hold in a democratic people and establishes itself in the mind of the majority, it then persists by itself and perpetuates itself without making any efforts, because no one attacks it. Those who had at first rejected it as false end up accepting it as general, and those who continue to oppose it in the depths of their hearts show nothing of what they feel; they take good care not to engage in a dangerous and useless struggle.

It is true that, when the majority of a democratic people changes opinion, it can effect strange and sudden revolutions in the intellectual world at will; but it is very difficult for its opinion to change and almost as difficult to verify that it has changed.

It sometimes happens that time, events, or the individual and solitary effort of men's minds ends up gradually weakening or destroying a belief, without anything being apparent on the outside. It is not opposed openly. One does not unite in order to make war on it. Its partisans silently abandon it one by one; but every day some of them abandon it, until finally it is no longer shared except by the minority.

In this state, it still reigns.

Since its enemies continue to keep quiet or only secretly communicate their thoughts to each other, they are themselves for a long time unable to be sure that a great revolution has been accomplished, and, in doubt, they remain immobile. They watch and keep quiet. The majority no longer believes, but it still looks like it believes, and this hollow ghost of a public opinion is enough to chill the innovators and hold them in silence and respect.

We are living in a time that has seen the most rapid changes take place in the minds of men. However, it may happen that soon the principal human opinions will be more stable than they have been in the preceding centuries of our history; this time has not arrived, but it may be approaching.

As I examine more closely the natural needs and instincts of democratic peoples, I am persuaded that, if equality is ever established in the world in a general and permanent manner, great intellectual and political revolutions will become very difficult and rarer than one supposes.

[269]   Because men in democracies always appear agitated, uncertain, out of breath, ready to change their purpose and their place, one imagines that they are going to abolish their laws, adopt new beliefs, and take up new mores. One does not consider that if equality leads men to changes, it gives them interests and tastes that have need of stability in order to be satisfied; it pushes them and at the same time stops them, it goads them on and attaches them to the earth; it inflames their desires and limits their powers.

This is not what comes to light first. The passions that separate citizens from one another in a democracy become manifest on their own. But the hidden force that retains them and brings them together is not noticed at first glance.

Will I dare say it in the midst of the destruction that surrounds me? What I fear most for the generations to come is not revolutions.

If citizens continue to confine themselves more and more within the narrow circle of small domestic interests and to move about there every which way without respite, one may fear that they will end up becoming all but inaccessible to the great and powerful public emotions that disturb peoples, but that make them develop and renew them. When I see property become so mobile, and the love of property so restless and so ardent, I cannot prevent myself from fearing that men will come to the point of regarding every new theory as a danger, every innovation as an irritating bother, every piece of social progress as a first step toward revolution, and that they will refuse completely to be moved for fear that they will be carried away. I tremble, I confess, that they will in the end allow themselves to be so much possessed by a cowardly love of present pleasures that their interest in their own future and in that of their descendents will disappear and that they will prefer to follow the course of their fate listlessly* rather than to make, if need be, a sudden and energetic effort to set it right.

It is believed that the new societies are going to change their face each day, and I myself fear that they will end up being too invariably fixed in the same institutions, the same prejudices, and the same mores; so that mankind will come to a stop and circumscribe itself, the mind will withdraw constantly further and further into itself without producing new ideas, man will exhaust himself in small solitary and sterile movements, and humanity, while being in constant motion, will no longer move forward.

• • •

VOLUME TWO, PART FOUR   [293]

ON THE INFLUENCE THAT DEMOCRATIC IDEAS AND
SENTIMENTS EXERT ON POLITICAL SOCIETY

• • •

CHAPTER 1   [295]

EQUALITY NATURALLY GIVES TO MEN THE
TASTE FOR FREE INSTITUTIONS

Equality, which makes men independent of each other, makes them acquire the habit and the taste for following, in their individual actions, only their own will. This complete independence, which they enjoy con-

---

* The word translated as "listlessly" is *mollement*. See the notes to [244] and [246].

tinually in relation to their equals and in the habitual conduct of their private life, disposes them to look upon all authority with a dissatisfied eye and soon inspires in them the idea and the love of political liberty. The men who live in these times thus move down a natural slope that directs them toward free institutions. Take one of them at random: go back, if possible, to his first instincts: you will discover that the one he conceives first and prizes most is the government whose chief he elects and whose acts he controls.

Of all the effects that the equality of conditions produces, it is this love of independence that strikes us first and that frightens timid minds most, and one cannot say that they are absolutely wrong in this, for anarchy has more frightening features in democratic countries than elsewhere. Since the citizens have no influence on each other, the instant the national power that keeps everyone in their place fails, it seems that disorder is bound to immediately be at its peak and that, since each citizen withdraws to his own side, the social body will suddenly find itself reduced to dust.

I am nonetheless convinced that anarchy is not the principal evil that democratic times should fear, but the least.

Equality produces, in fact, two tendencies: the one leads men directly to independence and is capable of pushing them suddenly into anarchy, the other leads them by a longer, more secret, but more sure path toward slavery.

[296]   Peoples easily see the first and resist it; they allow themselves to be drawn on by the other without noticing it; it is particularly important to point it out.

For myself, far from reproaching equality for the indocility that it inspires, I praise it chiefly for that. I admire it, seeing it deposit at the bottom of the mind and heart of each man this obscure notion of and instinctive penchant for political independence, thus preparing the remedy for the ill to which it gives rise. It is this side of it to which I am attached.

[297]   CHAPTER 2

THAT THE IDEAS OF DEMOCRATIC PEOPLES REGARDING GOVERNMENT ARE NATURALLY FAVORABLE TO THE CONCENTRATION OF POWERS

The idea of secondary powers, placed between the sovereign and the subjects, presented itself naturally to the imagination of aristocratic peoples, because these powers contained within them individuals or families who were elevated above all others by birth, enlightenment, and wealth and who seemed destined to command. This same idea is naturally absent from the minds of men in times of equality for opposite reasons; it can only be introduced there in an artificial way, and it is only retained there with difficulty, whereas they conceive, as it were without thinking about it, the idea of a unique and central power that leads all the citizens by itself.

In politics, in addition, as in philosophy and religion, the mind of democratic peoples takes in general and simple ideas with delight. Complicated systems repel it, and it takes pleasure in imagining a great nation all of whose citizens resemble a single model and are directed by a single power.

After the idea of a unique and central power, that which presents itself most spontaneously to the minds of men, in times of equality, is the idea of a uniform legislation. Since each of them sees himself to be little different from his neighbors, he does not understand very well why the rule that is applicable to one man would not be equally applicable to all the others. The slightest privileges are therefore repugnant to his reason. The slightest differences in the political institutions of the same people offend him, and legislative uniformity appears to him to be the first condition of good government.

I find, on the contrary, that this same notion of a uniform rule, imposed equally on all the members of the social body, is, as it were, foreign to the human mind in aristocratic times. It does not get it, or it rejects it.

These opposite penchants of the mind end up, on both sides, by be- [298] coming instincts so blind and habits so invincible that they still govern actions even in the face of the exceptional cases. There were sometimes, despite the enormous differences of the Middle Ages, individuals who were perfectly alike: which did not prevent the legislator from assigning to each of them different duties and different rights. And, on the contrary, in our day governments exhaust themselves in order to impose the same practices and the same laws on populations who are not yet alike.

To the extent that conditions become more equal among a people, individuals appear smaller and the society seems greater, or rather each citizen, becoming similar to all the others, is lost in the crowd, and one no longers sees anything other than the vast and magnificent image of the people itself.

This naturally gives to men in democratic times a very high opinion of the prerogatives of the society and a very humble idea of the rights of the individual. They readily admit that the interest of the first is everything and that of the second is nothing. They grant rather easily that the power that represents the society possesses much more enlightenment and wisdom than any of the men who compose it, and that its duty, as well as its right, is to take each citizen by the hand and lead him.

If one wishes to examine our contemporaries well and closely and penetrate to the root of their political opinions, one will find there some of the ideas I have just described, and perhaps be surprised to find so much agreement among men who are so often at war with one another.

The Americans believe that, in each State, the social power must emanate directly from the people; but once this power is constituted, they do not conceive of its having, so to speak, any limits; they readily acknowledge that it has the right to do everything.

As for special privileges granted to towns, families, or individuals, they have lost even the idea of it. Their mind has never anticipated that one might not apply the same law uniformly to all the parts of the same State and to all the men who inhabit it.

These same opinions are spreading more and more widely in Europe; they are entering into the very heart of the nations that reject most violently the dogma of the sovereignty of the people. These nations claim a different origin for power than the Americans, but they view power in the same way. In all of them, the notion of intermediate power is becoming obscured and effaced. The idea of a right inherent in certain individuals is disappearing rapidly from the minds of men; the idea of the all-powerful and virtually unique right of the society is coming to fill its place. These ideas take root and grow as conditions become more equal and men more alike; equality brings them into being, and they in their turn speed up the progress of equality.

[299]

In France, where the revolution I am talking about is more advanced than among any other people of Europe, these same opinions have entirely taken possession of men's minds. If one listens closely to the speech of our different parties, one will see that there are none that do not adopt them. Most judge that the government acts badly; but all think that the government must constantly act and put its hand to everything. Even those that fight most brutally with one another do not fail to agree on this point. The unity, ubiquity, omnipotence of the social power, the uniformity of its rules, forms the outstanding trait of all the political systems created in our day. They reappear at the bottom of the most bizarre utopias. The human mind still follows these images when it is dreaming.

If such ideas occur spontaneously to the minds of private individuals, they occur still more readily to the imagination of princes.

While the old social state of Europe is changing and dissolving, the sovereigns fashion themselves new beliefs concerning their powers and their duties; they understand for the first time that the central power that they represent can and must administer by itself, and on the basis of a uniform plan, all affairs and all men. This opinion, which, I dare say, had never been conceived before our time by the kings of Europe, is penetrating to the deepest part of the mind of these princes; it holds firm there in the midst of the agitation of all other opinions.

The men of our day are thus much less divided than one imagines; they dispute with each other constantly in order to see in which hands sovereignty will be placed, but they agree easily about the duties and the rights of sovereignty. All conceive of government in the image of a unique, simple, providential, and creative power.

All the secondary ideas regarding politics are changing. That one remains fixed, unalterable, selfsame. The jurists and the state adopt it, the crowd avidly takes hold of it. The governed and the governors agree to pursue it with the same ardor: it comes first; it seems innate.

It does not therefore emerge from a caprice of the human mind, but is a natural condition of the present state of men.

CHAPTER 3   [300]

THAT THE SENTIMENTS OF DEMOCRATIC PEOPLES ACCORD WITH THEIR IDEAS IN LEADING THEM TO CONCENTRATE POWER

If, in times of equality, men easily understand the idea of a great central power, it cannot be doubted, on the other hand, that their habits and sentiments predispose them to accept such a power and to lend it a hand. The proof of this can be stated in a few words, since most of the reasons have already been given elsewhere.

Since the men who inhabit democratic countries have neither superiors, nor inferiors, nor habitual and necessary associates, they readily fall back on themselves and think about themselves in an isolated manner. I have had occasion to demonstrate this at length with respect to individualism.

These men therefore never tear themselves away from their private affairs in order to take care of common affairs without an effort. Their natural inclination is to leave the care of common affairs to the only visible and permanent representative of the collective interests, which is the State.

Not only do they not naturally have the taste for attending to the public realm, but they often lack the time to do it. Private life is so busy in democratic times, so agitated, so full of desires and of work, that each man has almost no energy or leisure left for political life.

I am not the one to claim that such inclinations are invincible, since my principal purpose in writing this book has been to combat them. I claim only that, in our day, a secret force continually makes them grow in the human heart and that if they are not stopped, they will fill it completely.

I have also had occasion to show how the increasing love of well-being and the mobile nature of property make democratic peoples [301] dread material disorder. The love of public tranquility is often the sole public passion that these peoples retain, and it becomes more active and more powerful in them as all the others subside and die. This naturally disposes the citizens to constantly give new rights to the central power or to allow it to take them, for it alone seems to have the interest and the means to protect them from anarchy while protecting itself.

Since, in times of equality, no one is obliged to lend his strength to his fellow man, and no one has the right to expect great help from his fellow man, everyone is at the same time independent and weak. These two states, which must not be considered apart from one another or confounded with one another, give to the citizen in democracies very contrary instincts. His independence fills him with confidence and pride amid his equals, and his weakness makes him feel, from time to time, the need of outside help that he cannot expect from any of them, since they are all powerless and unfeeling. In this extremity, he naturally turns his eyes toward the immense being that rises up alone in the midst of the universal abasement. It is back toward it that his needs and, above all, his desires constantly lead him, and it is it that he ends up considering as the sole and necessary support for individual weakness.[1]

---

1. In democratic societies, only the central power has some stability in its base and some continuity in its undertakings. All the citizens are constantly in motion and changing. Now, it is in the nature of every government to want to continually increase its sphere. It is thus very unlikely that it will not succeed in doing so in the long run, since it acts with a fixed mind and an unbroken will upon men whose postion, ideas, and desires vary every day.

It often happens that the citizens work for it without wanting to.

Democratic times are times of experiments, innovation, and adventures. There are always a multitude of men who are engaged in a difficult or new enterprise that they pursue in isolation, without bothering themselves with their fellow men. These men admit indeed, as a general principle, that the public power should not intervene in private affairs; but, as an exception, each of them wants it to help them in the particular affair that concerns them and seeks to attract the intervention of the government to his side, while wanting to close it off to all the others.

Since a multitude of men have this point of view at the same time about a host of different objects, the sphere of the central power expands imperceptibly

This will make better understood what often happens among democratic peoples, where one sees men who tolerate superiors with such difficulty patiently accept a master and show themselves at once proud and servile. [302]

The hatred that men bear toward privilege increases as the privileges become rarer and less great, so that it is as if democratic passions become more inflamed at the very moment that they find less nourishment. I have already given the reason for this phenomenon. When all conditions are unequal there is no inequality so great that it offends the eyes; whereas the smallest difference appears shocking in the midst of general uniformity; its sight becomes more intolerable as the uniformity is more complete. It is thus natural for love of equality to grow constantly along with equality itself; by satisfying it, one makes it grow.

This immortal, and increasingly inflamed, hatred, which animates democratic peoples to oppose the slightest privileges, greatly promotes the gradual concentration of all political rights in the hands of the representative of the State alone. The sovereign, being necessarily and indisputably above all the citizens, does not excite the envy of any of them, and each believes he deprives his equals of all the prerogatives that he concedes to it.

Man in democratic times only obeys his neighbor, who is his equal, with an extreme repugnance; he refuses to acknowledge that the latter possesses enlightenment superior to his own; he distrusts his fairness and views his power with jealousy; he fears it and despises it; he likes to make him feel at every moment the common dependence in which they both have the same master.

Every central power that pays close attention to these natural instincts loves equality and promotes it, for equality greatly facilitates the influence of such a power, extends it, and secures it.

One can also say that every central government worships uniformity; uniformity spares it the examination of an infinity of details with which it would have to concern itself, if it had to fashion the rule for the men, instead of subjecting all men without distinction to the same rule. Thus, the government loves what the citizens love, and it hates naturally what they hate. This community of sentiments which, in democratic nations,

---

from all sides, even though each one of them wishes to restrain it. A democratic government thus expands its powers by virtue of the sole fact that it lasts. Time works for it; all mishaps work to its advantage; individual passions aid it even without their being aware of it, and one can say that as democratic society is older, its government becomes all the more centralized.

continually unites each individual and the sovereign in the same way of thinking, establishes a secret and permanent sympathy between them. One pardons the government's faults in favor of its tastes, public confidence abandons it only with difficulty in the midst of its excesses or its errors, and it comes back to it as soon as it calls it back. Democratic peoples often hate the agents of the central power; but they always love this power itself.

[303]   Thus, I have arrived by two different paths at the same point. I have shown that equality suggests to men the idea of a unitary, uniform, and strong government. I have now shown that it gives them the taste for it; it is therefore toward a government of this kind that the nations of our day are tending. The natural inclination of their minds and their hearts leads them to it, and it is sufficient that they not hold themselves back in order for them to arrive there.

I think that, in the democratic times that are going to unfold, individual independence and local liberties will always be a product of art. Centralization will be the natural government.

· · ·

[322]   **CHAPTER 6**

WHAT KIND OF DESPOTISM DEMOCRATIC NATIONS HAVE TO FEAR

I had noticed during my stay in the United States that a democratic social state similar to that of the Americans could offer unusual opportunities for the establishment of despotism, and I had seen upon my return to Europe how much the majority of our princes had already made use of the ideas, sentiments, and needs that this same social state gave rise to, in order to extend the sphere of their power.

That led me to believe that the Christian nations would perhaps end up by suffering some oppression similar to that which once weighed heavily upon several of the peoples of antiquity.

A more detailed examination of the subject and five years of further meditations have not diminished my fears, but they have changed their object.

In past times one never saw a sovereign so absolute and so powerful that it undertook to administer by itself, and without the aid of secondary powers, all parts of a great empire. None of them were tempted to subject all their subjects without distinction to the details of a uniform rule, or descended to the side of each of them in order to direct and to lead them.* The idea of such an enterprise never presented itself to the human mind, and, if any man had happened to conceive of it, insufficient enlightenment, the imperfection of administrative procedures, and above all the natural obstacles produced by the inequality of conditions would have soon halted such a vast plan in the midst of its execution.

One sees that during the period of the Caesars' greatest power, the different peoples that inhabited the Roman world had still preserved different customs and mores: although subject to a single monarch, the majority of the provinces were administered separately; they were filled with powerful and active municipalities, and although the whole government of the empire was concentrated in the hands of the emperor alone, and although he remained always, when necessary, the arbiter of all [323] things, the details of social life and of individual life normally escaped his control.

The emperors possessed, it is true, a power that was immense and without counterweight, which allowed them to abandon themselves freely to the capriciousness of their inclinations and to employ the entire force of the State to satisfy them. They often abused this power to arbitrarily deprive a citizen of his property or his life: their tyranny weighed very heavily upon some; but it did not extend over a great number; it was attached to a few great principal objects and ignored the rest; it was violent and limited.

It seems that, if despotism were to establish itself among the democratic nations of our time, it would have different characteristics: it would be more far-reaching and milder, and it would degrade men without ill-treating them.

I do not doubt that, in times of enlightenment and equality like ours, sovereigns will succeed more easily in gathering all public powers into their hands alone and in penetrating more normally and more deeply into the sphere of private interests than those of antiquity were ever able to do. But this same equality, which facilitates despotism, tempers it; we have seen how, to the extent that men are more alike and more equal, public mores become more humane and milder; when no citizen has great power or great wealth, tyranny lacks, as it were, opportunity and a theater for action. Since all fortunes are modest, passions are naturally contained, imagination limited, pleasures simple. This universal moderation moderates the sovereign himself and arrests within certain limits the disordered impetus of his desires.

Independently of these reasons drawn from the very nature of the

---

* The verb translated as "direct" is *régenter,* which has the sense of directing "with an excessive or unjustified authority."

social state, I could add many others drawn from outside my subject; but I want to stay within the limits I have set for myself.

Democratic governments may become violent and cruel in certain moments of great turmoil and great danger; but these crises will be rare and temporary.

When I think about the small passions of the men of our day, the soft-ness* of their mores, the extent of their enlightenment, the purity of their religion, the mildness of their morality, their industrious and ordered habits, the restraint that they almost all retain in vice as well as in virtue, I do not fear that they will have tyrants for leaders, but rather guardians.[†]

[324]   I think therefore that the kind of oppression with which democratic peoples are threatened will not resemble anything that has preceded it in the world. Our contemporaries will not be able to find its image in their memories. I myself search in vain for an expression that reproduces ex-actly the idea that I form of it and that comprehends it; the ancient words despotism and tyranny are not appropriate. The thing is new; one must therefore try to define it, since I cannot name it.

I want to imagine under what new traits despotism could occur in the world: I see an innumerable mass of similar and equal men who go round and round without respite in order to procure for themselves small and vulgar pleasures, with which they fill their souls. Each of them, withdrawn to the side, has virtually nothing to do with the fate of all the others: his children and his particular friends form for him all of man-kind; as for the rest of his fellow citizens, he is next to them, but he does not see them; he touches them and does not sense them; he exists only in himself and for himself alone, and if a family still remains to him, one can at least say that he no longer has a fatherland.

Above them rises an immense and tutelary power, which alone is re-sponsible for securing their pleasure and watching over their fate. It is absolute, detailed, regular, provident, and mild. It would resemble pa-ternal authority if, like it, its object was to prepare men for adulthood; but it seeks only, on the contrary, to keep them irrevocably in child-hood; it likes the citizens to enjoy themselves, provided that they think only about enjoying themselves. It works willingly for their happiness, but it wants to be the only agent and the sole judge of that happiness; it

---

*   The word translated as "softness" is *mollesse*. See the note at [244].

†   The word translated as "guardians" is *tuteurs*. *Tuteur* is not a "tutor" in the sense of a "schoolteacher" but in the sense of a "guardian" who is charged with looking after a minor or an incompetent adult, managing their property and acting as their legal representative. See [324] where Tocqueville describes state power as *tutélaire*, "tutelary."

provides for their security, anticipates and assures their needs, facilitates their pleasures, conducts their principal affairs, directs their industry, settles their successions, and divides their inheritances. Why may it not entirely spare them the trouble of thinking and the effort of living?

It is in this way that every day it makes the use of free will less necessary and rarer; that it confines the action of the will to a smaller space and gradually robs each citizen even of the use of himself. Equality has prepared men for all these things: it has disposed them to tolerate them and often even to regard them as a benefit.

After having thus taken each individual by turns into his powerful hands and having molded him as he pleases, the sovereign extends his arms over the whole society; he covers its surface with a web of small, complicated, detailed, and uniform rules, through which the most original minds and most vigorous souls are unable to emerge in order to rise above the crowd; it does not break wills, but it softens them, bends them, and directs them; it rarely forces men to act, but it constantly op- [325] poses itself to men's acting; it does not destroy, it prevents things from coming into being; it does not tyrannize, it hinders, it presses down upon men, it enervates, it extinguishes, it stupefies, and it finally reduces each nation to no longer being anything but a herd of timid and industrious animals, whose shepherd is the government.

I have always believed that this sort of regulated, mild, and peaceful servitude, whose picture I have just painted, could be combined better than one imagines with some of the exterior forms of liberty and that it would not be impossible for it to establish itself under the very protection of the sovereignty of the people.

Our contemporaries are continually beset by two opposite passions: they feel the need to be led and the desire to remain free. Unable to destroy either the one or the other of these contrary instincts, they try hard to satisfy both of them at the same time. They imagine a power that is unitary, tutelary, all-powerful, but elected by the citizens. They combine centralization and the sovereignty of the people. That gives them some respite. They console themselves for being under tutelage by thinking that they have themselves chosen their guardians. Each individual tolerates being enchained because he sees that it is neither one man nor one class but the people itself that holds the end of the chain.

In this system, the citizens come out of their dependence for a moment in order to indicate their master, and go back into it.

There are, in our day, many men who accommodate themselves very easily to this kind of compromise between administrative despotism and the sovereignty of the people and who think they have sufficiently guaranteed the liberty of individuals, when it is the national power to which they hand them over. That does not suffice for me. The nature of the master is much less important to me than the submission to it.

Nevertheless, I will not deny that such a constitution is infinitely preferable to one which, after having concentrated all powers, places them in the hands of one man or an unaccountable body of men. Of all the different forms that democratic despotism could take, that would assuredly be the worst.

When the sovereign is elective or watched over closely by a really elective and independent legislature, the oppression to which it subjects individuals is sometimes greater; but it is always less degrading because each citizen, although he is hindered and reduced to impotence, can still imagine that by obeying he is only submitting to himself and that it is to one of his wills that he is sacrificing all the others.

[326] I understand as well that when the sovereign represents the nation and depends on it, the powers and the rights that are taken away from each citizen not only serve the head of the State, but benefit the State itself, and that the individuals draw some benefit from the sacrifice of their independence that they have made to the public.

To create a national representation in a very centralized country is thus to diminish the evil that extreme centralization can produce, but not to destroy it.

I see well that, in this way, individual intervention in the most important affairs is retained; but it is not any less suppressed in small and private ones. One forgets that it is especially in the details that it is dangerous to enslave men. For my part, I would be inclined to think liberty less necessary in great things than in smaller ones, if I thought that one could ever be assured of the one without possessing the other.

Subjection in small affairs manifests itself every day and makes itself felt by all citizens without distinction. It does not drive them to despair, but it impedes them constantly and leads them to give up the exercise of their will. It gradually extinguishes their spirit and enervates their soul, whereas the obedience which is owing only in a small number of very grave, but very rare, circumstances, exhibits servitude only from time to time and makes it weigh heavily only upon some men. It will be futile for you to oblige these same citizens, whom you have made so dependent upon the central power, to choose from time to time the representatives of this power; this exercise of their free will, which is so important but so brief and so rare, will not prevent them from gradually losing the ability to think, to feel, and to act on their own, and from thus gradually falling below the level of humanity.

I will add that they will soon become incapable of exercising the great and sole privilege that is left to them. The democratic peoples who have introduced liberty into the political sphere, at the same time that they were increasing despotism in the administrative sphere, have been led into some very strange anomalies. If it is a question of managing small matters where simple good sense may suffice, they judge that the citizens are incompetent; if it is a question of the government of the whole State, they entrust its citizens with immense prerogatives; they make them alternately the playthings of the sovereign and its masters, more than kings and less than men. After having exhausted all the different systems of election without finding one that suits them, they are surprised and recommence their search, as if the ill that they notice were not due to the constitution of the country much more than to that of the electoral body.

It is, in fact, difficult to see how men who have entirely given up the [327] habit of finding their way on their own could succeed in choosing well those who are supposed to lead them; and it is not plausible that a liberal, energetic, and wise government could ever emerge from the votes of a population of servants.

A constitution republican in its head and ultramonarchic in all the other parts has always seemed to me to be an ephemeral monster. The vices of the governors and the stupidity of the governed would not be long in leading it into ruin; and the people, tired of its representatives and of itself, would create freer institutions or soon go back to lying down at the feet of a single master.

CHAPTER 7   [328]

CONTINUATION OF THE PRECEDING CHAPTERS

I believe that is is easier to establish an absolute and despotic government among a people where the conditions are equal than among any other, and I think that if such a government were once established among such a people, not only would it oppress men, but in the long run it would deprive each of them of several of the principal attributes of humanity.

Despotism thus appears to me especially to be feared in democratic times.

I would, I think, have loved liberty in any age; but I feel inclined to worship it in the age in which we find ourselves.

I am convinced, on the other hand, that all those who, in the age we are entering, try to base authority on privilege and aristocracy will fail. All those who want to capture and keep authority within the bosom of a single class will fail. In our time, there is no sovereign skillful enough and strong enough to found despotism by reestablishing permanent distinctions between his subjects; nor is there any legislator so wise and so powerful that he can maintain free institutions if he does not take equality for his first principle and credo. It is therefore necessary that all those of our contemporaries who want to create or secure the independence and dignity of their fellow men show themselves to be friends of equality; and the only means worthy of showing oneself to be such is in fact to be one: the success of their holy enterprise depends on it.

Thus, it is not a question of reconstructing an aristocratic society, but of making liberty emerge from the depths of the democratic society where God obliges us to live.

These two primary truths seem to me simple, clear, and fecund, and they lead me naturally to consider what kind of free government can be established among a people where the conditions are equal.

[329]   It follows from the very constitution of democratic nations and from their needs that, in them, the power of the sovereign must be more uniform, more centralized, more far-reaching, more penetrating, and more powerful than elsewhere. Society there is naturally more active and stronger, the individual more dependent and weaker: the one does more, the other less; that is inevitable.

It must therefore not be expected that, in democratic countries, the sphere of individual independence will ever be as large as in aristocratic countries. But that is not desirable, for in aristocratic nations, society is often sacrificed to the individual, and the prosperity of the greatest number to the grandeur of a few.

It is at once necessary and desirable that the central power that governs a democratic people be active and powerful. It is not a matter of making it weak or lethargic but only of preventing it from abusing its agility and its strength.

What contributed most to securing the independence of private individuals in aristocratic times was that the sovereign did not take care of governing and administering the citizens alone; he was obliged to leave a portion of this task to the members of the aristocracy, so that the social power, being always divided, never weighed entirely and in the same way upon each man.

Not only did the sovereign not do everything by himself, but the majority of the officials who acted in his stead, drawing their power from the fact of their birth and not from him, were not continually in his control. He could not create or destroy them at any moment, according to his whims, and bend them all equally to his slightest wishes. That again guaranteed the independence of private individuals.

I understand well that, in our day, one cannot have recourse to the same means, but I perceive some democratic procedures that can substitute for them.

Instead of giving to the sovereign alone all the administrative powers taken away from corporate bodies or from noblemen, one can entrust a portion of them to secondary bodies temporarily composed of simple citizens; in this way, the liberty of private individuals will be more secure without their being less equal.

The Americans, who are not as attached as we are to words, have kept the name of "county" for the largest of their administrative districts, but they have replaced the county in part with a provincial assembly.

I will readily agree that in an age of equality like ours, it would be unjust and unreasonable to institute hereditary offices; but there is nothing to prevent our replacing them, in a certain measure, with elective offices. Election is a democratic expedient that secures the independence [330] of the officer vis-à-vis the central power, as much as and more than heredity is capable of doing among aristocratic peoples.

Aristocratic countries are replete with rich and influential private individuals who know how to take care of themselves and who cannot be oppressed easily or in secret; and these men keep power within general habits of moderation and restraint.

I know well that democratic countries do not naturally possess such individuals; but one can artificially create something analogous in those countries.

I firmly believe that one cannot once again found an aristocracy in the world; but I think that simple citizens, by uniting together, can constitute very rich, very influential, very strong beings; in a word, aristocratic persons.

In this way one would obtain several of the greatest political advantages of aristocracy without its injustices or its dangers. A political, industrial, commercial or even scientific and literary association is an enlightened and powerful citizen that one cannot bend at will or secretly oppress and which, by defending its particular rights against the demands of power, saves the common liberties.

In aristocratic times, each man is always linked in a very close way to his fellow citizens, so that one cannot attack him without the others coming to his aid. In times of equality, each individual is naturally isolated; he has no hereditary friends whose aid he can lay claim to nor any class whose sympathies are assured to him; he is easily isolated, and he is crushed underfoot with impunity. In our day, an oppressed citizen thus has only one means of defending himself; that is to appeal to the entire nation and, if it is deaf, to mankind. There is only one means of doing that: the press. Liberty of the press is thus infinitely more precious in democratic nations than in all the others; it alone cures the majority of the ills that equality may produce. Equality isolates and weakens men; but the press places beside each of them a very powerful weapon, which the weakest and most isolated can use. Equality deprives each individual of the support of those close to him; but the press allows him to call all his fellow citizens and all his fellow men to his aid. The printing press has hastened the progress of equality, and it is one of its best correctives.

I think that the men who live in aristocracies can, if need be, do without the liberty of the press; but those who live in democratic countries cannot. In order to guarantee the personal independence of the latter, I [331] do not place my trust in great political assemblies, in parliamentary prerogatives, or in the proclamation of the sovereignty of the people.

All those things are reconcilable, up to a certain point, with individual servitude; but this servitude cannot be complete if the press is free. The press is the democratic instrument of liberty par excellence.

I will say something analogous about the judicial power.

It is of the essence of judicial power to deal with private interests and to readily fix its attention on the small objects that are exposed to its view; it is also of the essence of this power not to come on its own to the aid of those who are oppressed, but to be always at the disposal of the most humble among them. The latter, however weak he is assumed to be, can always oblige the judge to listen to his complaint and to respond to it: that results from the very constitution of the judicial power.

Such a power is thus especially relevant to the needs of liberty in a time when the eye and the hand of the sovereign continually penetrate into the smallest details of human actions and where private individuals, too weak to protect themselves on their own, are too isolated to be able to count on the help of their peers. The strength of the courts has been, in all times, the greatest guarantee that may be given to individual independence, but it is above all true in democratic times; in those times, private rights and interests are always at risk if the judicial power does not increase and expand as conditions become more equal.

Equality inspires in men several inclinations very dangerous for liberty and over which the legislator must always keep close watch. I will recall only the principal ones.

Men who live in democratic times do not easily understand the usefulness of forms; they feel an instinctive disdain for them. I have given the reasons for this elsewhere. Forms provoke their contempt and often their hatred. Since they normally aspire only to easy and present pleasures, they rush impetuously toward the object of each of their desires; the slightest delays discourage them. This temperament, which they carry into political life, disposes them to be annoyed by the forms that slow them down or stop them in one or another of their designs.

This inconvenience that democratic men find in forms, however, is what makes them so useful to liberty, their principal merit being to serve as a barrier between the strong and the weak, the government and the governed, to slow down the one and to give the other the time to get his bearings. Forms are more necessary to the degree that the sovereign is more active and more powerful and that private individuals become [332] more lethargic and more feeble. Democratic peoples thus naturally have more need of forms than other peoples, and they naturally respect them less. This merits very serious attention.

There is nothing more pitiful than the arrogant disdain of the majority of our contemporaries for questions of forms; for the smallest questions of forms have acquired in our time an importance that they have not had up until now. Some of the greatest interests of humanity are connected to them.

I think that if the statesmen who lived in aristocratic times were sometimes able to disdain forms without risk and often rise above them, those who lead peoples today must consider the smallest of them with respect and ignore them only when a compelling necessity obliges them to do so. In aristocracies, men had a superstitious belief in forms; it is necessary for us to have an enlightened and thoughtful worship of them.

Another very natural and very dangerous instinct in democratic peoples is that which leads them to have contempt for individual rights and to take little account of them.

Men are in general attached to a right and show respect for it due to its importance or to the long use that they have made of it. The individual rights that one finds among democratic peoples are normally of little importance, very recent, and very unstable; this causes them to be sacrificed easily and violated almost always without remorse.

Now, it happens that at the same time and in the same nations that men conceive a natural disdain for the rights of individuals, the rights of the society spread naturally and strengthen; that is to say that men become less attached to individual rights at the moment when it is most necessary to retain and protect the few of them that remain.

It is therefore especially in the democratic times in which we find ourselves that the true friends of liberty and of human grandeur must constantly be standing and ready to prevent the social power from lightly sacrificing the private rights of a few individuals to the general execution of its designs. In these times there is no citizen so obscure that it is not dangerous to allow him to be oppressed nor individual rights so unimportant that they can be abandoned to arbitrary power without risk.

The reason for this is simple: when the private right of an individual is violated during a time when the human mind is steeped in the impor- tance and sacredness of rights of this kind, one does harm only to the one who is despoiled; but to violate such a right, in our day, is to corrupt [333] profoundly the national mores and place the entire society at risk, be- cause among us the very idea of these kinds of rights constantly tends to be degraded and lost.

There are certain habits, certain ideas, certain vices that are proper to the state of revolution and that a long revolution cannot fail to bring into being and spread, whatever its character, its object, and its theater may be otherwise.

When any nation whatsoever has repeatedly, in a short space of time, changed leaders, opinions, and laws, the men who compose it end up acquiring the taste for change and becoming habituated to all changes taking place rapidly by means of force. They then naturally develop contempt for forms, whose impotence they see every day, and they only put up impatiently with the dominion of rules, which are so often evad- ed right before their eyes.

Since the ordinary notions of equity and morality are no longer suffi- cient to explain and justify all the new things to which revolution gives birth every day, one becomes attached to the principle of social utility, one creates the dogma of political necessity, and one readily becomes accustomed to sacrificing individual interests without scruple and to crushing underfoot individual rights in order to attain more quickly the general end upon which one has fixed.

These habits and ideas, which I will call revolutionary because all revolutions produce them, make their appearance in aristocracies as well as among democratic peoples; but in the first they are often less power- ful and always less durable, because they encounter habits, ideas, de- fects, and obstacles that are opposed to them. They therefore fade away on their own as soon as the revolution is completed, and the nation re- turns to its old political ways. It is not always like this in democratic countries, where it is always to be feared that revolutionary instincts, be- coming milder and more regular without being extinguished, will gradu- ally be transformed into governmental mores and administrative habits.

I know of no country, therefore, where revolutions are more danger- ous than in democratic countries because, independently of the acciden- tal and passing evils that they can never fail to create, they always risk creating permanent and, as it were, eternal ones.

I believe that there are honest resistances and legitimate rebellions. I am not therefore saying, in an absolute manner, that men in democratic [334] times must never make revolutions; but I think that they are right to hesitate more than all the others before undertaking them and that it would be better for them to put up with many inconveniences of their present state than to recur to so hazardous a remedy.

I will conclude by way of a general idea that contains within itself not only all the particular ideas that have been expressed in the present chapter, but also most of those which it is the aim of this book to set forth.

In the aristocratic ages that have preceded our own, there were very powerful individuals and a very feeble social authority. The very image of the society was obscure and was constantly lost in the midst of all the different powers that ruled over the citizens. The principal effort of the men of this time had to be devoted to enlarging and strengthening the social power, to increasing and securing its prerogatives, and, on the other hand, to containing individual independence within more narrow limits and subordinating individual interest to the general interest.

Other dangers and other tasks await the men of our age.

In the majority of modern nations, the sovereign, whatever its origin, constitution, and name, has become nearly all-powerful, and individuals fall, more and more, into the final stage of weakness and dependence.

Everything was different in the old societies. Unity and uniformity did not exist anywhere in them. Everything threatens to become so alike in ours that the particular shape of each individual will soon be entirely lost in the common physiognomy. Our ancestors were always ready to abuse this idea, that individual rights are respectable, and we are naturally led to exaggerate this other, that the interest of an individual must always bend before the interest of several.

The political world is changing; it is necessary henceforth to seek new remedies for new ills.

To set wide but visible and fixed limits to the social power; to give to individuals certain rights and guarantee them the uncontested use of these rights; to preserve for the individual the little independence, strength, and originality that is left to him; to raise him up beside the society and support him in the face of it: this appears to me to be the principal object of the legislator in the age we are entering.

One would think that the sovereigns of our time sought only to do great things with men. I wish that they thought a bit more about making great men, that they attached less value to the work and more to the worker, and that they always remembered that a nation cannot remain strong for long when each man in it is individually weak and that neither social [335] forms nor political amalgams have yet been discovered that can make a people energetic while composing it of spineless and soft citizens.

I see among our contemporaries two contrary but equally disastrous ideas.

Some see in equality only the anarchic tendencies to which it gives rise. They dread their own free will; they are afraid of themselves.

Others, fewer in number but better enlightened, have another point of view. Alongside the path that, beginning with equality, leads to anarchy, they have in the end discovered another path that seems to lead men irresistibly toward servitude. They bend their souls in advance to this inevitable servitude, and, despairing of remaining free, they are already worshipping at the bottom of their heart the master who must soon arrive.

The first desert liberty because they consider it dangerous; the second because they consider it impossible.

If I had had this last belief, I would not have written the work you have just read; I would have limited myself to lamenting in secret over the fate of my fellow men.

I wanted to expose in broad daylight the dangers to which equality subjects human independence because I firmly believe that these dangers are the most formidable as well as the least anticipated of all those that the future holds. But I do not believe them to be insurmountable.

The men who live in the democratic times we are entering naturally have the taste for independence. They naturally bear rules with impatience: the permanence of the very state that they prefer wearies them. They love power, but they are inclined to despise and to hate the one who exercises it, and they easily elude his grasp because of their smallness and their very changeableness.

These instincts will always exist because they arise out of the social state, which will not change. For a long time, they will prevent any despotism from being able to establish itself, and they will furnish new arms to each new generation that wants to struggle on behalf of the liberty of men.

Let us therefore have that salutary fear of the future that causes men to be vigilant and to fight, and not that sort of soft and passive terror that beats down the hearts of men and enervates them.

[336]

CHAPTER 8

GENERAL VIEW OF THE SUBJECT

Before quitting forever the ground that I have just covered, I would like to embrace with one last glance all the different traits that mark the face of the New World and finally to make a judgment regarding the general influence that equality is bound to exercise over the fate of men. But the difficulty of such an enterprise stops me. In the presence of so great an object, I feel my view become cloudy and my reason shaky.

This new society that I have sought to depict and that I wish to judge is only just being born. Time has not yet fixed its form; the great revolution that has created it still persists, and, in what is happening in our time, it is almost impossible to discern what must disappear with the revolution itself and what must remain after it.

The world that is arising is still half-lodged beneath the debris of the world that is falling, and in the midst of the immense confusion that human affairs present, no one can say which of the old institutions and the old mores will remain standing and which of them will completely disappear.

Although the revolution that is occurring in the social state, the laws, the ideas, and the sentiments of men is still very far from being finished, already one cannot compare its works with anything that has previously been seen in the world. I go back from century to century up to the remotest antiquity; I perceive nothing that resembles what is before my eyes. Since the past no longer sheds light on the future, the mind walks in darkness.

Nevertheless, in the midst of a spectacle so vast, so new, so confused, I already have a glimmer of some principal traits that are beginning to emerge, and I will point them out:

I see that goods and evils are apportioned rather equally in the world. Great riches are disappearing; the number of small fortunes is increasing; desires and pleasures are multiplying; there is no longer extraordinary [337] wealth or irremediable poverty. Ambition is a universal sentiment, but there are few vast ambitions. Each individual is isolated and weak; society is agile, provident, and strong; individuals accomplish small things, the State immense ones.

Souls are not energetic, but mores are mild and laws humane. If there are few great acts of self-sacrifice or very elevated, very brilliant, and very pure virtues, habits are well-ordered, violence is rare, cruelty almost unknown. Men's lives become longer and their property more secure. Life does not have much adornment, but it is very comfortable and very peaceful. There are few pleasures that are very refined and few that are very crude, little courteousness in manners and little brutality in tastes. There are scarcely any very learned men nor any very ignorant groups of them. Genius becomes rarer and enlightenment more common. The human mind progresses through the combined small efforts of all men and not by means of the powerful impetus given by a few of them. There is less perfection in men's works, but they bear more fruit. All the ties of race, of class, of fatherland are relaxed; the great tie of humanity tightens.

If among all these different traits, I look for the one that appears to me the most general and the most striking, I come to see that what is noticeable with respect to men's fortunes shows up again in a thousand other forms. Almost all the extremes are becoming attenuated and losing their edge; almost all the points of prominence are being effaced in order to make room for something average, which is at once less high and less low, less brilliant and less obscure than what has been seen in the world.

I scan my eyes over this numberless mass composed of similar beings, where nothing rises to a higher level or sinks to a lower one. The spectacle of this universal uniformity saddens and chills me, and I am tempted to long for the society that no longer exists.

When the world was filled with the very great and the very small, the very rich and the very poor, the very learned and the very ignorant, I used to turn my eyes away from the second ones in order to fix them upon the first, and these delighted my eyes. But I know that this pleasure arose out of my weakness: it is because I cannot take in everything around me at the same time that I was enabled to choose in this way and separate out, among so many objects, those it pleased me to contemplate. It is not the same for the omnipotent and eternal Being, whose eye necessarily takes in all things as a whole and who sees distinctly, even though all at once, all mankind and each individual man.

[338]   It is natural to believe that what is most satisfying to the eyes of this creator and preserver of men is not the exceptional prosperity of some of them, but the greatest well-being of all: what seems to me to be decadence is thus in His eyes progress; what offends me pleases Him. Equality is perhaps less elevated, but it is more just, and its justice makes its grandeur and its beauty.

I am making every effort to enter into this point of view of God, and it is from there that I am seeking to consider and judge human things.

No one on earth can yet say in an absolute and general way that the new state of societies is superior to the old; but it is already easy to see that it is different.

There are certain vices and certain virtues that were attached to the constitution of aristocratic nations and that are so contrary to the character of the new peoples that they cannot be introduced into them. There are good inclinations and bad instincts that were foreign to the first and that are natural to the second; ideas that naturally present themselves to the imagination of the ones and that the mind of the others rejects. They are like two distinct humanities, each of which has its particular advantages and disadvantages, its goods and its evils that are proper to it.

It is therefore necessary to be careful not to judge the societies that are being born with ideas that have been drawn from those that no longer exist. That would be unjust, for these societies, immensely different from one another, are not comparable.

It would scarcely be more reasonable to demand of the men of our time particular virtues that emanated from the social state of their ancestors, since this social state itself has collapsed and has dragged down with it in a confused manner all the good and all the bad that it carried with it.

But these things are still not well understood in our day.

I see a great number of my contemporaries who try to make a choice among the institutions, opinions, and ideas that arise from the aristocratic constitution of the former society; they would gladly abandon some of them, but they would like to retain the others and transport them with them into the new world.

I think that these men are wasting their time and their powers in an honest and sterile effort.

It is no longer a question of retaining the particular advantages that the inequality of conditions furnishes to men, but of securing the new goods that equality can offer them. We must not try to make ourselves like our ancestors, but must make every effort to attain the kind of grandeur and happiness that is proper to us.

For myself, having arrived at the final conclusion of my journey and [339] viewing from afar, but together, all the different objects that I have contemplated separately in its course, I feel full of fears and full of hopes. I see great dangers that it is possible to avert, great evils that can be avoided or limited, and I am more and more firmly of the belief that in order to be decent and prosperous, it suffices only that democratic nations wish to be so.

I am not unaware that some of my contemporaries have thought that peoples are never masters of themselves here below and that they necessarily obey who knows what insurmountable and unintelligent force that arises from prior circumstances, of race, of soil, or of climate.

These are false and cowardly doctrines, which can never produce anything other than weak men and spineless nations: Providence has not created mankind either completely independent or entirely enslaved. It traces around each man, it is true, a fateful circle from which he cannot escape, but within these vast limits man is powerful and free; so likewise are peoples.

The nations of our day cannot cause conditions within themselves to not be equal. But it depends upon them whether equality leads them to servitude or to liberty, to enlightenment or to barbarism, to prosperity or to wretchedness.

SELECT BIBLIOGRAPHY

Primary Sources

Tocqueville, Alexis de. *Democracy in America*. Ed. J.-P. Mayer. Trans. George Lawrence. New York: HarperCollins, 1988.

―――. *"The European Revolution" & Correspondence with Gobineau*. Ed. and trans. John Lukacs. Garden City, N.Y.: Anchor Doubleday, 1959.

―――. *Journey to America*. Ed. J.-P. Mayer. Trans. George Lawrence. New Haven: Yale University Press, 1960.

―――. *The Old Regime and the French Revolution*. Trans. Stuart Gilbert. Garden City, N.Y.: Anchor Doubleday, 1983.

―――. *Recollections*. Ed. J.-P. Mayer. Trans. A. P. Kerr. Garden City, N.Y.: Anchor Doubleday, 1971.

―――. *Selected Letters on Politics and Society*. Ed. and trans. Roger Boesche with James Taupin. Berkeley and Los Angeles: University of California Press, 1985.

Secondary Sources

Boesche, Roger. *The Strange Liberalism of Alexis de Tocqueville*. Ithaca: Cornell University Press, 1987.

Eisenstadt, Abraham S., ed. *Reconsidering Tocqueville's Democracy in America*. New Brunswick and London: Rutgers University Press, 1988.

Jardin, André. *Tocqueville: A Biography*. Trans. Lydia Davis with Robert Hemenway. New York: Farrar, Straus and Giroux, 1989.

Kessler, Sanford. *Tocqueville's Civil Religion: American Christianity and the Prospects for Freedom*. Albany, N.Y.: State University of New York Press, 1994.

Lamberti, Jean-Claude. *Tocqueville and the Two Democracies*. Trans. Arthur Goldhammer. Cambridge, Mass., and London, England: Harvard University Press, 1989.

Lawler, Peter A. *The Restless Mind: Alexis de Tocqueville on the Origin and Perpetuation of Human Liberty*. Lanham, Md.: Rowman and Littlefield, 1993.

―――, ed. *Tocqueville's Political Science: Classic Essays*. Garland, 1992.

Lawler, Peter A., and Joseph Alulis, ed. *Tocqueville's Defense of Human Liberty: Current Essays*. Garland, 1992.

Lively, Jack. *The Social and Political Thought of Alexis de Tocqueville*. Oxford: Clarendon Press, 1962.

Manent, Pierre. *Tocqueville and the Nature of Democracy*. Trans. John Waggoner. Lanham, Md.: Rowman and Littlefield, 1995.

Masugi, Ken, ed. *Interpreting Tocqueville's Democracy in America*. Savage, Md.: Rowman and Littlefield, 1991.

Mitchell, Joshua. *The Fragility of Freedom: Tocqueville on Religion, Democracy, and the American Future*. Chicago: University of Chicago Press, 1995.

Pierson, George Wilson. *Tocqueville and Beaumont in America*. Baltimore and London: Johns Hopkins University Press, 1996.

Schleifer, James T. *The Making of Tocqueville's Democracy in America*. Chapel Hill: University of North Carolina Press, 1980.

Zetterbaum, Marvin. *Tocqueville and the Problem of Democracy*. Stanford: Stanford University Press, 1967.

INDEX

Entries list the volume number (1 or 2) followed by the Gallimard page numbers that appear in brackets in the margins of the text. Foot-of-the-page notes, marked "n," are found on the Gallimard pages listed.